THE STRUCTURE OF PRODUCTION

THE STRUCTURE OF PRODUCTION

New Revised Edition

MARK SKOUSEN

NEW YORK UNIVERSITY PRESS
NEW YORK & LONDON

New York and London
www.nyupress.org

First published in paperback in 2007.
New revised edition published in 2015.

Library of Congress Cataloging-in-Publication Data
Skousen, Mark.
    The structure of production / Mark Skousen ; with a new introduction. — New revised edition.
        pages cm
    Includes bibliographical references and index.
    ISBN 978-1-4798-4852-2 (pb : alk. paper)
    1. Production (Economic theory) 2. Macroeconomics. I. Title.

HB241.S63   2015
338.5—dc23   2015006888

New York University Press books are printed on acid-free paper,
and their binding materials are chosen for strength and durability.

Book design by Ken Venezio

Manufactured in the United States of America

10 9 8 7 6 5 4 3 2

MIX
Paper | Supporting
responsible forestry
FSC
www.fsc.org   FSC® C013604

To the memory of Carl Menger,
who paved the way

It appears to me of preeminent importance to our science that we should become clear about the causal connections between goods.—Carl Menger, *Principles of Economics*

CONTENTS

PART 3

APPLICATIONS

INTRODUCTION TO THE NEW REVISED EDITION: GO BEYOND GDP

Gross output [GO] is the natural measure of the production sector, while net output [GDP] is appropriate as a measure of welfare. Both are required in a complete system of accounts.—Dale W. Jorgenson, J. Steven Landefeld, and William D. Nordhaus, *A New Architecture for the U.S. National Accounts*

Gross Output, long advocated by Mark Skousen, will have a profound and manifestly positive impact on economic policy and politics.—Steve Forbes, "New, Revolutionary Way to Measure the Economy Is Coming—Believe Me, This Is a Big Deal"

On April 25, 2014, the Bureau of Economic Analysis (BEA) at the U.S. Department of Commerce announced a new data series as part of the U.S. national income accounts, and the BEA began reporting "Gross Output by Industry."[1] It wouldn't be long before other countries followed suit. For example, in late 2014, the United Kingdom began publishing annual "Total Output" statistics in their input-output tables.

It took nearly a quarter of a century for the federal government to recognize the critical importance of Gross Output (GO). Starting with my work in this book in 1990 and in *Economics on Trial* in 1991, I introduced the concept of GO as a macroeconomic tool, not to replace Gross Domestic Product (GDP), but to supplement it as a broader measure of total economic activity (see chapter 6, this volume). In these works, and later in my own textbook, *Economic Logic* (first published in 2008), I made the case that we needed a statistic that went beyond GDP, a new statistic that would measure spending throughout the entire production process, not just final output, and that the statistic would need to be updated regularly. GO is a move in that direction.

I view the BEA's adoption of this measure as a personal triumph twenty-five years in the making, and it prompted the publication of this new revised edition of *The Structure of Production*.

What is Gross Output? It is an attempt to measure total sales volume at all stages of production, what we might call the "make" economy. Most importantly, it includes all business-to-business (B2B) transactions that GDP leaves out. In the third quarter of 2014, GO hit $31.3 trillion, almost twice the size of GDP, which was $17.6 trillion.

GDP is the standard yardstick for measuring the value of final goods and services purchased by consumers, businesses, and government in a year, what we call the "use" economy. While GDP measures the "use" economy, now with GO we have a way to measure the "make" economy every quarter too. Finally, we have a full picture of the economy. As Steven Landefeld, the BEA director who spearheaded the new "Gross Output by Industry" data series, declared at a press conference, GO offers a "unique perspective" and a "powerful new set of tools of analysis."

The BEA initiative prompted a serious reexamination of my thesis and a series of articles and interviews in the media and the academic community. In anticipation of the BEA's new series, *Forbes* magazine ran my article "Beyond GDP: Get Ready for a New Way to Measure the Economy" (Skousen 2013). Steve Forbes editorialized about GO in the April 14, 2014, edition of *Forbes* magazine, calling it a "big deal" and "a great leap forward" (Forbes 2014). I wrote the lead editorial, entitled "At Last, a Better Economic Measure," in the April 23, 2014, *Wall Street Journal*'s European and Asian editions (Skousen 2014a). Gene Epstein, economics editor at *Barron's*, ran a story on GO, "A New Way to Gauge the U.S. Economy," in the April 28, 2014, issue. Professor Steve Hanke of Johns Hopkins University also wrote a column on GO for *Global Asia* magazine (Hanke 2014). And David Colander of Middlebury College endorsed the benefits of GO in the *Eastern Economic Journal* (Colander 2014), followed by my rejoinder (Skousen 2015). Since then, I've been approached by foreign press about the possibility of GO's being reported in foreign countries, which, as mentioned above, has already begun in the UK. I'm also now working with several academic economists to analyze further the implications of GO as well as the creation of a new measure, the Skousen B2B Index, a measure of B2B or business spending every quarter. The textbooks are starting to include GO in their new editions. The first one to do so is the 18th edition of *Economics Today* by Roger LeRoy Miller (Miller 2015:180–81). I've also appeared regularly on CNBC, on the financial news program, with Rick Santelli, their bond expert, to discuss the latest quarterly GO and B2B data.

WHAT REALLY DRIVES THE ECONOMY: CONSUMER SPENDING, GOVERNMENT STIMULUS, OR BUSINESS INVESTMENT?

Based on my research, GO is a better indicator of the business cycle than other measures are, and it is the indicator that is most consistent with economic growth theory. Let's review these arguments.

While GDP is a decent measure of national economic performance, it has a major flaw: in ignoring most B2B sales, GDP downplays the size and importance of the "make" economy, that is, the supply chain and intermediate stages of production needed to produce all those finished goods and services. GDP is comprised of consumer spending, government spending, investment, and net exports, with the first two of these being the biggest contributors.

The narrow focus on GDP has created much mischief in the media, government policy, and boardroom decision making. For example, the media naively conclude that any slowdown in retail sales or government stimulus is necessarily bad for the economy. Journalists are constantly overemphasizing consumer and government spending as the driving force behind the economy, and they ignore the supply-side benefits of saving, business investment, and technological advances.

So, for example, the *Wall Street Journal* reported, "Household spending generates more than two-thirds of total economic output, so sturdy spending gains should translate into economic growth" (Heubsdorf 2014). Or take the *New York Times*: "Consumer spending makes up more than 70 percent of the economy, and it usually drives growth during economic recoveries" (Rampell 2010).

In short, by focusing only on final output (GDP), reporters underappreciate the significant role businesses and entrepreneurs play in raising capital and moving the intermediate products along the production process toward final use. If we look only at GDP, the manufacturers and shippers and designers aren't fully acknowledged in their contribution to overall growth or decline.

THE MANY BENEFITS OF GO

Gross Output exposes these misconceptions. In my own research, I've discovered many benefits of GO statistics. First, compared to GDP, GO provides a more accurate picture of what drives the economy. In the latest U.S. data on GDP, valued at $17.6 trillion, consumer spending accounts for $12 trillion, or 68 percent of GDP, followed by government spending at $3.2 trillion, or 18 percent. Private investment comes in third at $2.9 trillion, or 16 percent. (Net exports make up the difference at -2 percent.) But if you use GO as a more comprehensive indicator of economic activity, spending by consumers turns out to represent less than 40 percent of total yearly sales ($31.3 trillion), not 68 to 70 percent as is commonly reported. Spending by business (private investment plus business-to-business sales at the intermediate level) is substantially larger, hitting $16.6 trillion, or more than 50 percent of economic activity. That's more consistent with economic growth theory, which emphasizes productive saving and investment in technology on the producer side as the drivers of economic growth. *Consumer spending is largely the effect, not the cause, of prosperity.*

Drawing from the quarterly GO data, I estimate total business spending (B2B activity) to be over $23 trillion in 2014. Figure I demonstrates how business spending is substantially larger than consumer spending in the economy.

Second, GO and B2B activity are significantly more sensitive to the business cycle than GDP is. During the Great Recession of 2008–2009, nominal GDP fell only 2 percent (due largely to countercyclical increases in government), but GO fell by 6 percent and B2B spending collapsed by 10 percent. From 2009 to 2014, consumer spending increased less than 2 percent a year, but B2B activity advanced by more than 4 percent a year. (See figures I and II.)

Figure I. U.S. Business Spending (Skousen B2B Index) versus Consumer Spending, (2007–2014), Nominal Value in Billions of Dollars

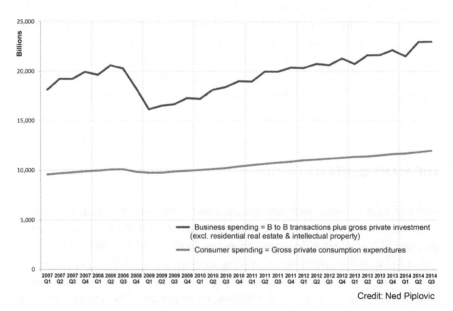

Credit: Ned Piplovic

Figure II. Quarterly Changes in U.S. Business Spending vs. Consumer Spending, 2007–2014

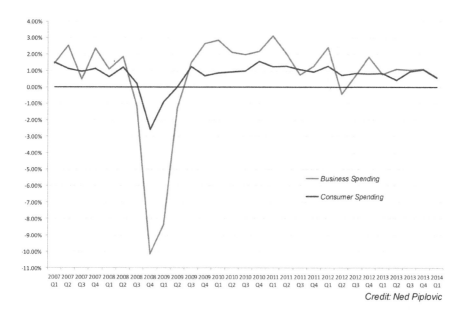

Credit: Ned Piplovic

I believe that Gross Output fills in a big piece of the macroeconomic puzzle. It establishes the proper balance between production and consumption, between the "make" and the "use" economies, between aggregate supply and aggregate demand. In fact, I would argue that Gross Output is a more comprehensive measure than GDP of what Keynes called "Aggregate Effective Demand." As Jeremy Siegel, professor of finance at the Wharton School, puts it, "Gross output is truly a measure of the aggregate demand for money."[2] Finally GO is more consistent with growth theory than GDP is.

SOME DEFECTS IN BEA'S DEFINITION OF GROSS OUTPUT

Since writing *The Structure of Production*, I discovered that the BEA's measure of GO does not include all sales at the wholesale and retail level. Wholesale and retail trade figures are included in GO only as "net" or value added. David Wasshausen, a BEA staff researcher, offers this rationale: since "there is no further transformation of these goods . . . to the production process, they are excluded from wholesale/retail trade output" (Wasshausen 2014).

This is a serious omission, in my judgment, amounting to more than $7 trillion dollars in business spending in 2014. To measure all economic activity, including the cost of distributing finished goods, we need to include gross wholesale and retail trade figures. They are legitimate B2B transactions that deserve to be counted.

Therefore, in the paperback edition of *The Structure of Production*, published in 2007, I created my own aggregate statistic, Gross Domestic Expenditures (GDE), which includes gross sales at the wholesale and retail level and is therefore significantly larger (more than double GDP). I estimate GDE in 2014 at over $37.5 trillion, 25 percent higher than GO and 120 percent more than GDP.

Using GDE as a measure of total new economic activity, we come to the startling conclusion that consumer spending actually represents only about 31 percent of the U.S. economy. This is consistent with leading economic indicator statistics and also employment data. As I demonstrated in chapter 9 of *this book* and in the Introduction to the Previous Edition, virtually all the leading economic indicators are measured in the earlier stages of production. Even the much publicized "Consumer Confidence Index" has recently been changed to "Average Consumer Expectations *for Business Conditions*" (emphasis added).[3] The structure of employment also fits better with GO data than with other measures. Only about 20 percent of the work force is involved in the retail and leisure industries. The vast majority of workers are employed in the mining, manufacturing, and professional services attached to the business community.[4]

AN ADVANCE IN SUPPLY-SIDE AND AUSTRIAN ECONOMICS

I consider the adoption of Gross Output on equal footing with GDP as perhaps the most significant advance in national income accounting since World War II. Steve Hanke says GO is a reflection of Say's law, a supply-side statistic, while GDP is a symbol of Keynes's law, a demand-side number (Hanke 2014). The difference is stark. If you use supply-side GO as the proper measure of economic activity, business investment is the most important sector. But if you rely on Keynesian GDP, consumer spending and government stimulus are the most important factors. (See figure III.) The rise of GO may also signify a second round of debates between Hayek and Keynes, with GO representing the Austrian perspective (the stages of production), and GDP representing the Keynesian perspective (final effective demand). My

Figure III. Relative Size of Consumer Spending, Business Investment, and Government Using Two Models (GDP and GDE), 2013

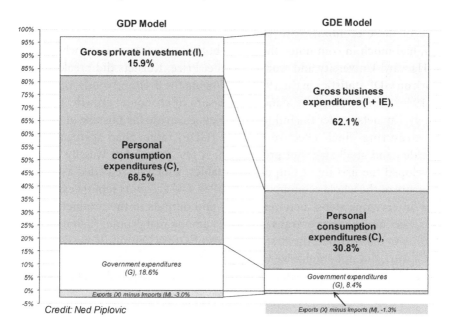

Credit: Ned Piplovic

Source: Bureau of Economic Analysis, author's data for GDE.

own preliminary work, with the assistance of Sean Flynn of Scripps College at Clermont, shows that industries in the earlier stages of production are more volatile in GO (using both the quantity and price indexes) than are industries involved in later stages of production. This confirms figure F in the Introduction to the Previous Edition.

In a sense the Keynesians, Austrians, and supply-siders can all claim victory, since both numbers are now being used by government to determine the direction of the economy. GO is a measure of the "make" economy, while GDP represents the "use" economy. Both are essential to understanding how the economy works. As Steve Landefeld, former director of the BEA, and co-editors Dale Jorgenson and William Nordhaus state in their work, *A New Architecture for the U. S. National Accounts* "Gross output [GO] is the natural measure of the production sector, while net output [GDP] is appropriate as a measure of welfare. Both are required in a complete system of accounts" (Jorgenson, Landefeld, and Nordhaus 2006: 5).

HISTORICAL BACKGROUND

The history of these two economic statistics goes back to several pioneers. Two of these economists in particular, Simon Kuznets and Wassily Leontief, had much in common—they were both Russian Americans who taught at Harvard University and won the Nobel Prize. Kuznets did breakthrough work on GDP statistics in the 1930s. Following the Bretton Woods Agreement in 1946, GDP became the standard measure of economic growth. Unfortunately, Kuznets, under the influence of Keynes, made the mistake of focusing on measuring "final" effective demand (GDP) rather than aggregate effective demand at all stages of production. A few years later, Wassily Leontief developed the first input-output (I-O) tables, which he regarded as a better measure of the whole economy than GDP is. I-O accounts require examining the "intervening steps" between inputs and outputs in the production process, "a complex series of transactions . . . among real people" (Leontief 1986: 4–5). I-O data created the first estimates of Gross Output. However, Leontief's work did not emphasize GO as an important macroeconomic tool. He focused on the inner workings between industries, not on the aggregate GO.

A GENERAL MODEL OF THE ECONOMY

In my own work, *The Structure of Production,* I created a universal four-stage model of the economy (see the upgraded diagram below) demonstrating the

Figure IV. A Universal Four-Stage Model of the Economy

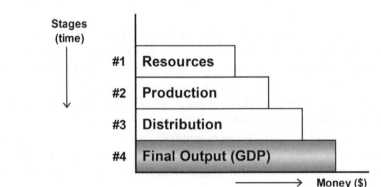

relationship between total spending in the economy and final output. (I also use it extensively in my textbook, *Economic Logic*, which is now in its fourth edition.) In chapter 6 of *The Structure of Production*, I made the point that GDP is not a complete picture of economic activity, and I compared it to GO for the first time, contending that GO is more comprehensive than GDP and that business investment is far bigger in the economy than consumption is. In 1990, I called the new measure Gross National Output (GNO).

CONTROVERSIES OVER THIS NEW STATISTIC

Over the years, several objections to the use of GO and GDE have been made. Economists are especially fixated over the perceived problem of "double counting" with GO and GDE. I am the first to acknowledge that GO and GDE involve double counting when a commodity is sold repeatedly as it goes through the resource, production, wholesale, and retail stages. Economists ask, Why not just measure the value added at each stage rather than double or triple count? This is what GDP does; it eliminates double counting and measures only the value added at each stage. But that does not mean double counting is somehow superfluous and can be dismissed as unessential to the economic system.

There are reasons why double or triple counting is actually a necessary feature in the production process. First, the raw commodity or resource usually changes its nature at each stage of production. Examples: iron ore becomes steel; raw coffee beans are roasted and ground; cowhide becomes leather and then shoes. Second, a business cannot operate or expand on the basis of value added or profits only. The business must raise the capital necessary to cover the gross expenses of the company—wages and salaries, rents, interest, capital tools and equipment, supplies, and goods-in-process. B2B transactions are the critical steps in moving the production process along the supply chain toward final use. GO and GDE reflect this vital business-decision-making process at each stage of production. Can publicly traded firms ignore the top line of sales/revenues and focus only on the bottom line of earnings when they release their quarterly reports? Wall Street would rightly object to such a narrow focus. Aggregate sales/revenues are important measures for an individual firm and cannot be ignored in national income accounting either. Earnings are the result of a company's productive activities, but sales create the earnings. In a real sense, GO (or, more accurately, GDE) is the top line of national accounting, and GDP is the bottom line. Now finally, in the twenty-first century, they are treated as equals.

GO data appear to better reflect the severity of the business cycle than GDP data do. In my own research, I find it significant that GO and GDE are far more volatile than GDP during the business cycle. As noted in figure II, sales/revenues rise faster than GDP during an expansion, and collapse more quickly during a contraction (for example, wholesale trade fell 20 percent in 2009; retail trade dropped over 7 percent). Economists need to explore the meaning of this cyclical behavior in order to make accurate forecasts and policy recommendations. In short, double counting matters.

Another objection involves outsourcing and merger/acquisitions. Companies that start outsourcing their products will cause an increase in GO or GDE, while companies that merge with another company will show a sudden decrease, even though there may be no change in final output, or GDP. But then again, perhaps there would be a change in the size and composition of final output if the outsourcing or merger/acquisitions activity caused a change in productivity. Clearly these dynamic changes in the economy should be factored into the data.

GO isn't the only macroeconomic data dealing with the dynamics of creative destruction. Similar issues occur with GDP. For example, when a homeowner marries his maid, the maid may no longer be paid and therefore her services may no longer be included in GDP. Black market activities also often fail to show up in GDP data. Certainly if a significant trend develops in outsourcing or merger/acquisition activity, it will be reflected in GO or GDE statistics, but not necessarily in GDP. This is bears further investigation to see how serious it is. No aggregate statistic is perfect, but GO and GDE offer forecasters an improved macro picture of the economy.

A GENERAL MODEL OF THE ECONOMY

In conclusion, GO or GDE should be the starting point for measuring aggregate spending in the economy, as these statistics measure both the "make" economy (intermediate production) and the "use" economy (final output). They complement GDP and can easily be incorporated in standard national income accounting and macroeconomic analysis. To see how, take a look at the fourth edition of my textbook, *Economic Logic* (Skousen 2014b). In chapter 3 of the textbook, I created the following diagram to describe the production ("make") and the consumption ("use") side of the economy, with GDP measuring final output. The "make" side adds value during the production process, and the "use" side involves the using up of the finished product or service.

Figure V. The Production Process, GDP, and Consumption in the Economy

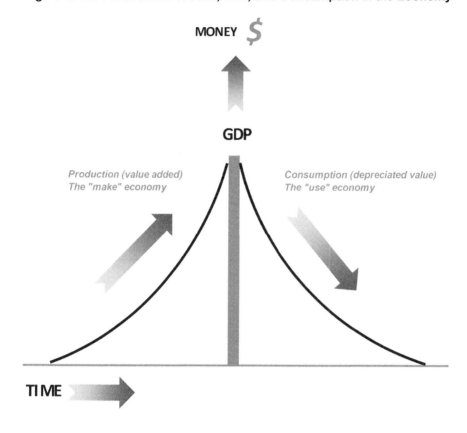

A NEW WAY TO LOOK AT THE ECONOMY

In many ways, the adoption of Gross Output is part of a whole new way of ana-lyzing the economy, a Weltanschauung developed throughout *The Structure of Production*.

- Instead of focusing solely on final output (GDP), economists and the media should analyze the whole production process (GO or GDE), from raw com-modities to finished retail products.
- We should count B2B transactions, not just B2C (business-to-consumer) or B2G (business-to-government) sales.
- Journalists should incorporate business expectations, not just consumer expectations, in their analysis of the economy.

- The consumer price index isn't the only price index worth noting, but analysts should take into account relative prices, which are the relationship between commodity, producer, and consumer prices.
- Reporters should look beyond "the" unemployment rate, and see what is happening to the structure and growth of employment and unemployment in various sectors.
- Good financial experts don't just take note of "the" interest rate (usually the ten-year Treasury rate), but also the yield curve, which is the difference between short-term and long-term rates.
- Security analysts should look at trends in various sectors of the stock market and not just at the Dow Jones Industrial Average.

In sum, the structure of the economy matters.

—January 2015

NOTES

1. To review the data, going back to 2005 on an annual basis and 2011 on a quarterly basis, go to www.bea.gov, click on "Quarterly GDP by Industry," then click on "Interactive Tables: GDP by Industry," begin using data, and click on "Gross Output by Industry."
2. Personal communication, 2014.
3. Terminology of the Bureau of Economic Analysis. For more information, go to www .conference-board.org.
4. For more information, go to http://www.bls.gov/emp/ep_table_201.htm.

REFERENCES

Bureau of Economic Analysis, U.S. Department of Commerce. 2014. "New Quarterly Statistics Detail Industries' Economic Performance" (April 25). News release. http://www.bea .gov/newsreleases/industry/gdpindustry/2014/gdpind413.htm.

Colander, David. 2014. "Gross Output." *Eastern Economic Journal* 40:451–55.

Epstein, Gene. 2014. "A New Way to Gauge the U.S. Economy," *Barron's* (April 28). http://online .barrons.com/news/articles/SB50001424053111903409104579515671290511580?mod= BOL_columnist_latest_col_art.

Forbes, Steve. 2014. "New, Revolutionary Way to Measure the Economy Is Coming—Believe Me, This Is a Big Deal," *Forbes* (April 14). http://www.forbes.com/sites/steveforbes/2014/ 03/26/this-may-save-the-economoy-from-keynesians-and-spend-happy-pols/.

Hanke, Steve. 2014. "GO: Keynes vs. Say." *Global Asia* (July). http://origin.library.constantcontact .com/download/get/file/1117426113940–15/GO+J.M.+Keynes+versus+J.-B.+Say,+July+2014. pdf.

Heubsdorf, Ben. 2014. "Consumer Spending Rises and Inflation Slow," *Wall Street Journal* (September 30).

Jorgenson, Dale W., J. Steven Landefeld, and William D. Nordhaus, eds. 2006. *A New Architecture for the U.S. National Accounts*. Chicago: University of Chicago Press.

Leontief, Wassily. 1986 [1966]. *Input-Output Economics*. 2nd ed. New York: Oxford University Press.

Miller, Roger LeRoy. 2015. *Economics Today*, 18th ed. (New York: Prentice-Hall).

Rampell, Catherine. 2010. "Consumers Give Boost to Economy," *New York Times* (May 1). http://query.nytimes.com/gst/fullpage.html?res=9C0CE6DC123DF932A35756C0A9669D8B63.

Skousen, Mark. 2013. "Beyond GDP: Get Ready for a New Way to Measure the Economy," *Forbes* (December 16). http://www.forbes.com/sites/realspin/2013/11/29/beyond-gdp-get-ready-for-a-new-way-to-measure-the-economy/.

Skousen, Mark. 2014a. "At Last, a Better Economic Measure," *Wall Street Journal* (April 23). http://on.wsj.com/PsdoLM.

Skousen, Mark. 2014b. *Economic Logic*. 4th ed. Washington: Capital Press.

Skousen, Mark. 2015. "On the Go: De-Mystifying Gross Output." *Eastern Economic Journal* 42.

Wasshausen, David. 2014. Private email to Mark Skousen.

INTRODUCTION
TO THE PREVIOUS EDITION

The Next Economics will have to be . . . centered on supply . . . [and] the factors of *production* rather than being functions of demand.—Peter E Drucker, Claremont Graduate University

The influence of *The Structure of Production* can be measured in several ways: as the underground bible for supply-side economics; a revival of Say's law; an Austrian advance over the Keynesian macroeconomic model and the monetarist disequilibrium model of the business cycle; and a new tool for financial analysis. Its most important function is to serve as a theoretical counterpoint to the standard Keynesian Weltanschauung. What drives the economy? According to Keynesians and Keynes's law, "demand creates supply." Consumption drives the production process; consumer spending is paramount. On the other hand, according to supply-siders and Say's law, "supply creates demand." Production drives consumption; saving and investment, technology and productivity, are paramount.

Which is correct? In national income accounting, gross domestic product (GDP) is a function of four elements:

$$GDP = C + I + G + NX,$$

where

C = Personal consumption expenditures,
I = Gross private domestic investment,
G = Government consumption expenditures and gross investment, and
NX = Exports minus imports, or net exports.

Since consumption represents over two-thirds of GDP in the United States and in most industrial countries, Keynesians are convinced that Keynes's law in vindicated and that the best way to maintain high aggregate demand is to encourage consumer spending. Moreover, under the simplified Keynesian system, investment (I) is a function of current consumption (C). If consumers spend more, it stimulates production and investment. If they spend less, investment falls. Finally, there are policy implications. If C and I fail to increase, Keynesians urge G to step in and make up the difference to keep aggregate demand high. And progressive taxation is good because it encourages a higher propensity to consume and therefore higher aggregate demand.

In this context, there is a clear bias against saving, and not just among Keynesian economists during a downturn. The media constantly promotes this antisaving mentality. During the most recent global recession, most reporters focused on consumer spending. In 2001, the French government, fearful that its citizens were not buying enough, increased government spending by 6 percent. Slowing retail sales in Europe "will spoil the party," warned the *Economist* magazine. In Japan, economic analysts contended that Japanese consumers were saving too much, and the only way to jump-start the giant Asian economy was to get Japanese consumers to stop saving and start spending.

"What the consumer does is the No. 1 issue for the economic outlook," stated Edward McKelvey, senior economist at Goldman Sachs (Skousen 2005b). In the United States, pundits on CNN and CNBC frequently warned after the Bush tax cuts became law in 2001, "If the Bush tax rebates are saved, and not spent, they will do nothing for the economic recovery" (Skousen 2005b).

What is the key to economic growth? According to Keynesian Hyman Minsky, "The policy emphasis should shift from the encouragement of growth through investment to the achievement of full employment through consumption production" (Minsky 1982:113). The *New York Times* (December 6, 2004) editorialized along these lines in reference to the Bush tax cuts and the 2000–2003 recession: "Tax cuts were misdirected at investment rather than consumption, resulting in an economic recovery weaker than it might have been."

Yet economists also solemnly declare that saving and investment are keys to long-term growth and issue warnings from time to time that the saving rate is too low in many countries. As Harvard economist N. Gregory Mankiw states in his popular textbook, *Macroeconomics*, "the saving rate is a key determinant of the steady-state capital stock. If the saving rate is high, the economy will have a large capital stock and a high level of output. If the saving rate is low, the economy will have a small capital stock and a low level of output" (Mankiw 1994:86).

But even as Keynesians accept the virtues of saving in the long run, the promotion of saving is roundabout. "The key to saving is growth, not thrift," declares Franco Modigliani (1987:24). Robert Eisner adds, "To raise the saving rate, try spending. . . . Private saving, to the extent people in a free society want to save, is best promoted by providing maximum employment and income" (1988). In other words, consumption must come first, before saving, and consumer spending habits should never be broken. Buying fewer consumer goods, paying off debts, and increasing the saving rate will have the misfortune of "reducing the level of aggregate demand and retard the growth of demand" unless investment picks up the slack, which is uncertain (Modigliani 1987:25).

In chapter 6 of this book, I resolve this thorny issue by demonstrating that consumer spending is not, in fact, the largest sector of the economy and thus is not the driving force behind economic growth. The consumer-spending myth comes from a misreading of GDP statistics. Estimated quarterly in the industrial world, GDP represents the value of all final goods and services produced in a country during the year. In every nation, personal consumption expenditures represent by far the largest sector of GDP. For example, in the United States, consumer spending now represents 70 percent of GDP, 65 percent in the United Kingdom, 58 percent in Germany, and 57 percent in Japan. Knowing this fact, reporters often follow retail spending patterns as the key to future economic behavior and the stock market because, they note in the United States, "consumer spending represents two-thirds of the economy."

GROSS OUTPUT: A NEW MEASURE OF TOTAL ECONOMIC ACTIVITY

However, GDP is not meant to be a complete measure of all activity or spending in the economy. GDP measures only *final* output of goods and services. It deliberately leaves out all intermediate production or goods-in-process, that is, all the sales of products in earlier stages of production, such as steel in car production. Why? Because GDP is meant to measure only finished goods and services-usable products in homes, businesses, and government. To include spending at every stage of production would be "double" and "triple" counting. For example, in bread making, it would count both the wheat and the flour in the value of the bread. Yet GDP is only interested in the final usable product—the bread that people consume at home.

At the same time, economists recognize the importance of intermediate production processes, the stages-of-production that lead to final output. This process begins in the earliest stages of raw commodity production and resource development, such as research and development, then continues in manufacturing and semimanufacturing production, wholesale and distribution channels, and ultimately to final sales at the retail level. Spending at the final stage of production (GDP) is important, but so is spending at each of the intermediate stages. It is at each point along the production process that entrepreneurs and capitalists make vital decisions about capital investment, technological change, and customer demand. Each firm seeks to maximize net income, but it must raise sufficient capital to finance *gross* expenditures to pay wages, rent, interest, and supplies.

To measure all transactions in the economy, we must add up all sales of goods and services at every stage of production, not just the final stage. There are literally millions of intermediate transactions occurring prior to the sale of finished goods and services to final users. Figure A in a more generalized version of my four-stage model introduced in chapter 5 (figure 5.16, p. 171).

In this book, my four-stage model is based on a manufacturing economy, the four stages being (1) raw commodities, (2) manufactured goods, (3) wholesale goods, and (4) final retail goods.[1] Since the original publication of the book, I have created a more general model that covers services and the knowledge economy as well as manufacturing. Figure A reflects a more universal model. The four stages are (1) resources, (2) production, (3) distribution, and (4) consumption and investment (final goods and services).

Figure A. Four-Stage General Model of the Economy

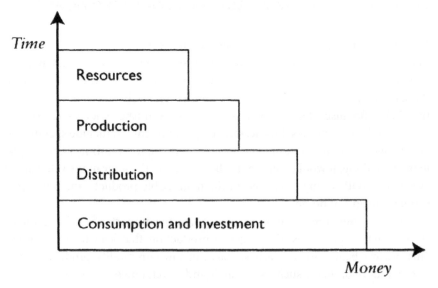

In figure A, GDP is equal to stage 4, the value of final consumption and investment goods and services. I define the value of output at all four stages of production equal to Gross Domestic Expenditures (GDE),[2] so that

$$GDE = IP + GDP,$$

where

GDE = Gross Domestic Expenditures
IP = Intermediate Production or Output
GDP = Gross Domestic Product

To measure Gross Domestic Expenditures (GDE) in this book, I had to depend on input-output statistics collected from census and IRS data, which came out every five years. In recent years, however, the Bureau of Economic Analysis (BEA) of the U.S. Commerce Department has recognized the need for an annual measure of total spending in the economy and has introduced a new national-income statistic called Gross Output (GO). It seeks to determine the value of output at all stages of production, including services, along the lines I originally proposed in chapter 6 of this hook. GO turns out to be almost twice the size of GDP. For example, in 2002,[3] Gross Output amounted to $18.7 trillion, while GDP equaled $10.6 trillion. (For more information on GO, go to www.bea.gov and look under "GDP by Industry," then "interactive tables.")

Using the new GO data, one sees an alternative picture of the components of the American economy. If you add up the spending at all stages of production (using GO as this figure), consumption represents 40 percent of the total spending in the U.S. economy, and business investment (gross fixed investment plus goods-in-process) accounts for 52 percent. Although GO statistics have yet to be compiled in Europe, Asia, and Latin America, I suspect the results would be strikingly similar-business investment is significantly larger than consumer spending in all major industrial nations. Gross Output in other countries should not be difficult to calculate, since many countries already do just that when they calculate the Value Added Tax (VAT).

However, it should be pointed out that GO is not a complete measure of "total spending" or economic activity. Both wholesale and retail numbers are net, rather than gross, figures, because the BEA seeks to measure only "output," not spending per se, so they net out transactions involving the same physical product at the wholesale and retail level. In addition, GO leaves out used goods manufactured in earlier years. If you add in gross wholesale and retail figures with the value of used goods sold during the year, I estimate that consumption expenditures represent only approximately 30 percent of total economic activity (Skousen 2007, chap. 15).

WHAT THE LEADING ECONOMIC INDICATORS ARE TELLING US

Now let us examine how important consumer spending and the investment sector are when it comes to the leading economic indicators. Here we see that both sectors influence economic performance, but the business sector appears to play a much larger role. Take a look at the Index of Leading Economic Indicators in major countries. The Conference Board (see www.conferenceboard.org) publishes indexes for nine countries. Here are the results:

- Of the nine leading indicators of Germany compiled by the Conference Board, two are linked to consumer spending: the consumer confidence index and the consumer price index for services. The rest are connected to earlier-stage production, such as inventory changes, new purchases of capital equipment, and new construction orders.
- Among France's ten leading indicators, two are consumer related, and the remainder are tied to commercial measures such as stock prices, productivity, building permits, the yield spread, and new industrial orders.
- The United Kingdom's leading indicators are linked to export volume, new orders in engineering industries, inventories, housing starts, and money supply. Consumer Confidence Index is the lone consumer indicator.
- None of Japan's leading indicators are consumer related: overtime worked in manufacturing, business conditions survey, labor productivity, real operating profits, and new orders for machinery and construction.
- Mexico's six indicators include a monthly survey of inventories, industrial construction, stock prices, interest rates, and the cost of crude oil. Retail sales is a coincident indicator in Mexico.
- In the United States, the Conference Board highlights the Consumer Confidence Index,[4] while the other nine indicators are only remotely related to final use, such as manufacturers' new orders for consumer goods and materials, building permits, average weekly manufacturing hours, stock prices, and new orders for nondefense capital goods.

I pointed out the relative unimportance of consumption data on the leading economic index in this book (chapter 9, pp. 307–12), but it is only now being noticed (Kates 2003:21).

KEYNES'S LAW AND DEMAND-DRIVEN ECONOMICS

Now let us return to the question we posed at the beginning: What is the catalyst of economic growth and performance? We see two factors at work, the demand side (consumption) and the supply side (investment) of the economy. In the short run, especially during a recession, most economists emphasize the important of the demand side, and the role consumers play in keeping the economy going during a downturn. This is known as Keynes's law, "demand creates its own supply."

SAY'S LAW AND SUPPLY-SIDE ECONOMICS

The supply side of the economy is the main determinant of economic growth in the long run, when the economy is near full employment. The breakdown of GO and leading economic indicators supports this thesis. A historical example may he helpful in explaining this point. Why did the West Coast of the United States (such as the cities of San Francisco, Portland, and Seattle) boom in the 1990s? New technology in telecommunications and the Internet created a whole new level of wealth and prosperity in the region. Intel, Cisco Systems, and Microsoft became household names. Note that only after the technology boom began did consumer spending in cars, housing, travel, jewelry, and entertainment move sharply higher. Thus, we learn that consumption is the effect, not the cause, of prosperity, in the long run. This phenomenon is known as Say's law, "supply creates its own demand," named after the French economist Jean-Baptiste Say (1767–1832). Say's law is making a comeback in economics (Kates 2003; Skousen 2001:54–57).

The key to the economic boom of the 1990s was increasing technology, productivity, and entrepreneurship, what economists call the "supply side" of the economy. An increase in aggregate demand did not cause the technology boom of the 1990s, but the other way around. Technological, productive, and entrepreneurial advances create new and better products for consumers at lower costs, which in turn opens up new markets, increases income, and benefits consumption. However, when the technology boom ended abruptly in 2000, business investment fell, unemployment rose, and consumer spending slowed. During the 2000–2003 recession, it was consumer spending that kept the economy from falling further (Keynes's law). But in general, production comes first, followed by consumption (Say's law).

Throughout the business cycle, investment spending tends to be more volatile than consumer spending, as I note in chapter 9 of this book (business cycles). Retail spending by consumers tends to be relatively steady throughout the ups and downs of the economy. In fact, consumer-spending data is relatively uninteresting. It tends to rise month after month, and when it falls it falls only slightly. Thus, it was not surprising that consumer spending held up well during the 2000–2003 global recession. The recession was primarily a business recession. And once the economy recovered in 2003, it was business spending that led the recovery.

Studies in business cycles and marketing demonstrate repeatedly that CEOs, entrepreneurs, capitalists, and other business decision-makers are the primary activators of the economy and determine when to start investing in capital again and turn the economy around. Government leaders cannot depend on consumers to lead the recovery. In marketing surveys, consumers tend to be passive, responding to rather than creating new products and services.

In normal times, increased savings expands the pool of capital investment, lowers interest rates, and allows firms to adopt new production processes and new technologies and to create new jobs. Thus, saving is just as much a form of spending as consumption, only a different form of spending, and in some cases, a better form of spending when it fulfills a need for more capital and investment. Yet this fact—productive savings—seems to be lost on journalists and media who are caught up in the old Keynesian mindset (see chapter 7 of this book).

The fundamental defect of the Keynesian model is the failure to recognize the demand for *future* consumption, which is what productive saving is all about. That is,

$$Y = f(C_e) + f(C_f),$$

where

$$C_r = \text{current consumption, and}$$
$$Cf = \text{future consumption.}$$

The fatal flaw of the Keynesian model is that it assumes that investment is a function of current demand only, as figures 7.12 and 7.13 demonstrate (pp. 249–50). Under this oversimplified model, if current consumption rises, so does investment; when consumption falls, investment falls.

But as figures 7.14 and 7.15 (pp. 251 and 254) demonstrate, the dynamic economy is more complex and involves multiple stages of production, wherein consumption and investment can move in opposite directions. Thus, a decline in interest rates alters the structure of production, so that when current consumption declines, the demand for capital and higher-order capital goods gradually increases and offsets the fall in final consumer demand. Aggregate demand remains relatively unchanged. This is what journalists are missing when they report on retail sales and consumer spending but ignore the beneficial effects of new savings on aggregate demand through lower interest rates and an increased investment structure.

In conclusion, let me respond to the Keynesian arguments:

Statement: Consumer spending represents two-thirds of economic activity.

Response: Consumer spending represents two-thirds of GDP (the value of final goods and services) but only between 30 and 40 percent of total economic activity. Business investment represents more than 50 percent of total spending, making it more significant than consumption in every advanced economy.

Statement: If a tax rebate is saved rather than spent (on consumer goods), it will do nothing to stimulate the economic recovery.

Response: An increase in savings will increase the supply of capital, reduce interest rates, and encourage more business investment. A reduction in consumption expenditures will therefore be offset by an increase in business spending. If the new savings are invested in the stock market, it will increase demand for investment capital and future IPOs.

Statement: If millions of consumers decide to save money and refrain from buying new cars, the higher savings rate will cut the production of cars, lay off workers, slash profits of the automobile companies, and hurt the economy.

Response: The new savings will increase the pool of investment capital, causing banks and other intermediaries to cut interest rates. This in turn will allow businesses to upgrade their facilities, replace old equipment (such as old computers), and invest in research and development. It may even allow automobile companies to create new, better facilities to build more and cheaper cars for the future. A fall in consumer spending will be offset by a rise in business spending. The reduction in interest rates may also reduce the cost of consumer spending on credit.

SAVING VS. CONSUMPTION: A TALE OF TWO DIAGRAMS

Since the original publication of this book, I have come across two diagrams that reflect the clash of these two models, the Keynesian demand model and the Austrian supply model. The Keynesian "paradox of thrift" comes from a diagram produced in early editions of Paul Samuelson's popular textbook (see figure B).

Figure B. Saving Leaks Out of the System While the Hydraulic Investment Press Pumps Up the Economy

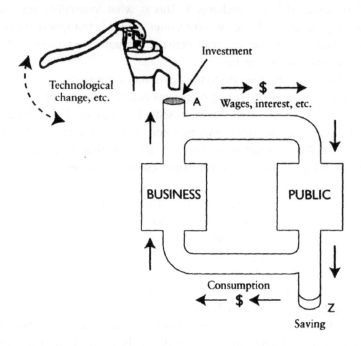

Technological change, population growth, and other dynamic factors keep the investment pump handle going. Income rises and falls with changes in investment, its equilibrium level, at any time, being realized only when intended saving at Z matches intended investment at A.

Source: Samuelson 1948:264. Reprinted by permission of McGraw-Hill.

In this circular-flow diagram, Samuelson separates saving from investment, and consumption spending drives the economy: consumers buy goods and services from business, and business pays workers with income to buy goods. Saving leaks out of the system, unconnected to the investment hydraulic handle above.

But I also uncovered another diagram (published in a book by Paul Ekins and Manfred Max-Neef in 1992) that takes an alternative approach. In figure C, the economy is portrayed such that consumption is used up as "utility/welfare" while saving (nonconsumption) is invested back into the system in the form of capital improvements, education, training, and machinery. In other words, in figure C, saving/investment drives the economy, not consumption. The ultimate goal of the saving/investment mechanism and the production process is to provide increasing utility/welfare from better and cheaper consumer goods

Figure C. How Savings Is Invested into the Economic System

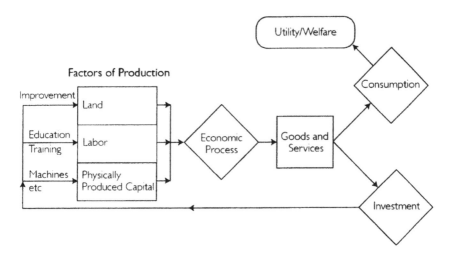

Source: Ekins and Max-Neef 1992:148. Reprinted by permission of Routledge.

and services. But if agents artificially increase the consumer demand, it may stimulate production of current final goods and services, but it will do nothing to encourage the creation of new products and processes.

Which diagram more accurately describes the dynamic global economy of the twenty-first century? I sent copies of both diagrams to Paul Samuelson. He admitted that the diagram in figure C was a more accurate model of today, although he said that Japan might be a good example of a place where excessive saving was leaking out of the system and that the Japanese needed to consume more to reignite their economy. In response, I pointed out that the problem in Japan was not excessive saving but unproductive saving; that is, most of the postal savings were invested in unproductive public works and government securities. (Interestingly, Samuelson no longer uses the diagram of the hydraulic model in his textbook.)

RESPONSE TO THIS BOOK

It continues to be an uphill battle to change the mindset of the media when it comes to the importance of consumer spending, saving, and productivity in the economy. Most reporters, with the exception of the Associated Press, have discontinued use of the blatantly inaccurate statement that "consumer spending represents two-thirds of economic activity." On a positive note, CNBC commentator Larry Kudlow, taking a leaf from this book, reported recently, "Though not one in a thousand recognizes it, it is business, not consumers, that is the heart of the economy. When businesses produce profitably, they create income-paying jobs and thus consumers spend. Profitable firms also purchase new equipment because they need to modernize and update all their tools, structures, and software. Capital formation is the key to worker productivity and consumer prosperity. Visionary entrepreneurs, those who discover new technologies or innovate those that exist, must be financed with capital. In the longer term, capital-induced productivity increases lead to greater wage gains and enhanced consumer spending power" (Kudlow 2006). Kudlow understands that Say's law must be fulfilled before Keynes's law kicks in.

THE BUSINESS CYCLE AND ASSET BUBBLES

The establishment media has also expressed interest in applying the Austrian theory of the business cycle to the global economy, especially with regard to the global boom-bust cycle of 1995–2003. Austrian cycle theory was developed by Ludwig von Mises and Friedrich Hayek during the early twentieth century and was advanced by this book and by Roger Garrison (2001). Essentially, Austrian cycle theory relies on three parts:

1. *Capital theory:* As founders of the Austrian school, Carl Menger and Eugen Böhm-Bawerk noted, the production process involves lengthy "roundabout" stages and capital goods limited to specific uses. In general, an inflationary boom sends false signals that artificially inflate this heterogeneous capital/ production structure, leading to a real estate boom, high-tech bubble, bull market in stocks, intensified research and development, and increased mining. When the demand for these overproduced markets falls short, the malinvested capital industries cannot easily recover and adjust to the new downsized conditions.
2. *Natural rate of interest hypothesis:* Swedish economist Knut Wicksell distinguished between the social rate of time preference, or natural saving rates of the community, which he called the "natural" rate of interest, and the actual market rate of interest for loanable funds to business. Normally, the two are matched through the dynamics of supply and demand for loanable funds. However, a government-controlled monetary authority can intervene and

temporarily reduce the market rate below the "natural" rate through an easy-money policy (see figure D). If the market rate is less than the natural rate, a "cumulative process" of price inflation occurs. Eventually the economy overheats, forcing interest rates to go back up and even rise above the natural rate. The high real interest rates choke off the boom, resulting in a depression (see chapter 9).

Austrians emphasize that excessive credit expansion beyond gold reserves does more than increase prices; it also distorts the production process and the value of investment assets. It creates a "cluster of business errors" in the capital markets that is almost impossible to avoid (Rothbard 1983:16). By expanding the higher-order capital goods more than the lower-order consumer goods, an easy-money policy creates an unsustainable boom that will inevitably collapse when the government stops expanding credit, or when interest rates rise and cut off the boom, returning the consumption/investment ratio to previous levels.

Essentially, the model demonstrates that monetary inflation and easy-money policies by central banks cause unsustainable structural imbalances in the economy, including asset bubbles in real estate and the stock market. As explained in chapter 9, Austrian macroeconomics goes beyond the simplified monetarist

Figure D. The "Natural" Rate of Interest (i_n) vs. the "Market" Rate (i_m)

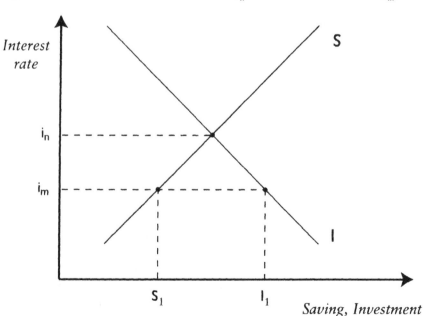

theory. Monetary inflation does more than cause the general price level to rise; it temporarily distorts the spending and employment patterns of consumers, workers, and businesses. When interest rates are held artificially low, below the "natural" rate of interest, an economic boom develops in capital-intensive markets (higher-order goods, as Carl Menger calls them). But the boom is artificial and unsustainable, and eventually it must collapse as interest rates inevitably return to their natural rate.

AGGREGATE SUPPLY AND DEMAND VECTORS (ASV AND ADV)

In order to explain the coordination problem in the economy and the business cycle created by an easy-money policy, I developed a new concept in this book called the Aggregate Supply Vector (ASV) and Aggregate Demand Vector (ADV) (see figure E).

ASV is a downward-sloping vector representing the production process (from resources to final output) and is therefore a function of the "market" rate of interest. ADV is an upward-sloping vector representing the public's time preference and is therefore a function of the "natural" rate of interest. If the market

Figure E. Aggregate Supply Vector (ASV) and Aggregate Demand Vector (ADV)

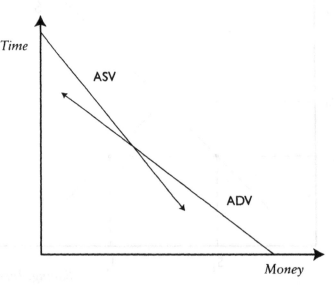

rate is equal to the natural rate-that is, the public's time preference matches up with the demands of businesses and consumers for loanable funds-then the ASV and the ADV move along a parallel path, and macroeconomic equilibrium is achieved (what Mises calls the "evenly rotating economy"). But if the central bank engages in an easy-money policy that pushes market rates below the natural rate, ASV and ADV separate and there is macroeconomic disequilibrium, that is, the development of a business cycle. But it is a separation, not a divorce, and eventually the two must come back together. (For an explanation of ASV and ADV, see chapter 6, pp. 200–204, and chapter 9, pp. 296–99.)

AN AUSTRIAN INTERPRETATION OF THE BOOM-BUST CYCLE

Many historical examples confirm the Mises-Hayek theory of the business cycle. For example, in the United States monetary inflation was relatively modest throughout the 1950s and early 1960s, and so was the business cycle. But when monetary inflation picked up its pace and grew much more rapidly in the late 1960s and 1970s, the result was a much more volatile economy. The expansions were greater and the contractions were more severe, just as Mises-Hayek would predict.

A look at Japan in the 1980s and 1990s reveals some Austrian insights as well. If the Bank of Japan had adopted the Friedman monetarist rule, increasing the money supply steadily at 3–4 percent a year, the Austrians would have predicted only a mild inflationary buildup and subsequent recession. But the Bank of Japan engaged in an extremely liberal money policy in the 1980s, expanding the monetary base by 11 percent for four straight years and keeping interest rates artificially low. The result was (1) dramatic economic growth in the late 1980s, followed by (2) a crash and prolonged depression in the 1990s. The data support the Mises-Hayek thesis. In fact, Japanese economist Yoshio Suzuki accepts the Austrian interpretation of his nation's boom-bust cycle: "As Hayek teaches us, easy money does not always raise the price of goods and services, but always creates an imbalance in the structure of the economy, particularly in the capital markets. . . . This is exactly what happened in Japan [in the 1980s]" (Suzuki 1994). Suzuki also adds an important footnote: "In my 40 years' experience as a monetary economist, I have never felt as strongly as I do today the need to bring back to life the essence of Hayek's trade cycle theory."[5]

A third example is the boom-bust cycle of the late 1990s and early 2000s. What fueled the "irrational exuberance" of the high-tech boom and stock bubble of the late 1990s, beyond the genuine technological advances in telecommunications and computers? The Austrians point to the Federal Reserve, which deliberately cut interest rates and injected large amounts of liquidity into the banking system between 1995 and 2000, prompted by the Asian financial crisis in 1997, the Russian economic collapse in 1998, and the Y2K fears of 1999. When the Y2K disaster was averted, the Fed sopped up liquidity by squeezing the money supply and raising short-term interest rates sharply in 2000. Consequently, the economy came unglued, and Wall Street, especially the high-tech-dominated Nasdaq, suffered its worst bear market since the Great Depression, lasting three years. The *Economist* (September 28, 2002, issue) was one of the first to acknowledge that the Austrian business-cycle theory, long out of fashion, seems a plausible explanation of the 1995–2003 boom-bust cycle. Prior cycles had been explained by an exogenous oil-price shock, policy mistakes, or productivity changes, but "this cycle was different. . . . It was an investment-led boom that carried the seeds of its own destruction. The recent business cycles in both America and Japan displayed many 'Austrian' features" (Woodhall 2002:9; cf. Callahan and Garrison 2003).

Following the *Economist's* cover story, Barry Eichengreen (Berkeley) and Kris Mitchener (Santa Clara) collaborated in writing a working paper, "The Great Depression as a Credit Boom Gone Wrong." The authors adopt a remarkable Austrian interpretation of the 1920s and 1990s, describing both episodes as an unsustainable asset inflation in securities, property, technology, and consumer durables, caused by easy-credit policies during a period of low consumer/commodity price inflation. "The development of excesses . . . threaten[s] economic stability even if there is no sign of inflationary pressure [and in the case of the 1920s and the 1990s] the credit boom thus contained the seeds of the subsequent crisis" (Eichengreen and Mitchener 2003:1, 8). However, the authors do not go so far as to say that the credit-boom interpretation of the business cycle is superior to the standard explanations of the Great Depression—the role of the international gold standard, the monetary blunders, and perverse fiscal policies. To them it is a "useful supplement to these more conventional interpretations" (2003:53). What is most surprising about their paper is that it is written by Keynesians. Discussant Michael D. Bordo, a monetarist at Rutgers, said he was "skeptical" of the Eichengreen-Mitchener paper. It appears that Keynesians may approve of the Austrian structural model before the monetarists do![6]

THE INFLATIONARY TRANSMISSION MECHANISM

Over the years, the Austrians (led by Mises and Hayek) and Chicagoans (led by Milton Friedman) have argued over the role of money and the business cycle

(Skousen 2005a:161–93). Basically the debate comes down to a question of whether the transmission of inflation causes structural imbalances in the economy, particularly in the "higher order" capital markets and industries. If it does, the Austrians are right. If it does not, or if the structural imbalances are relatively minor, then the Chicagoans are right. Friedman and the Chicago school take a cue from the Keynesians by adopting a highly aggregate "cash balance" approach. The Chicago business-cycle theory bases its approach on the work of Irving Fisher and his quantity theory of money, as well as on the stock-flow "perpetual fund" capital theories of John Bates Clark and Frank Knight (see chapter 2, pp. 28–33, and chapter 3, pp. 68–70). Under these aggregate macro conditions, there is no significant capital structure and no stages of production, and time plays no explicit role.

According to the "cash balance" approach, the increase in the money supply, whether it takes place through the credit markets or output markets, creates no significant distortions in the economy. The new money is distributed evenly (or "as if" evenly) throughout the economy. Monetary expansion may raise interest rates, but it does not systematically alter various production processes; it may raise general but not relative prices; it may stimulate general output but not relative output.

In 1974, in the middle of an oil crisis and inflationary recession, Friedman was asked a very "Austrian" question: "What is the possibility that a process of inflation, by producing a misallocation of resources and malinvestment, will raise the natural rate of unemployment?" Friedman responded, "If the inflation is open—if there are no restrictions—there is no reason why it should produce malinvestment" (Friedman 1991:81).

Friedman uses the make-believe helicopter analogy to make his point: "Let us suppose now that one day a helicopter flies over this community and drops an additional $1,000 in bills from the sky," doubling the amount of money each individual enjoys (Friedman 1969:4; cf. Patinkin 1965:44–59). He then describes how this additional money affects the community through the "real cash balance" effect, raising prices without ultimately increasing real output. "The additional pieces of paper do not alter the basic conditions of the community," he explains (Friedman 1969:6).

In discussing the transition toward the "final position" (long run), Friedman surprisingly entertains the possibility of Austrian-type distortions: "There might be overshooting and, as a result, a cyclical adjustment pattern" (1969:6). In a seminal paper, "The Lag in Effect of Monetary Policy," Friedman identifies "first-round effects" of monetary expansion through variations in interest rates, which may affect various asset classes differently. "The increased demand will spread sooner or later affecting equities, houses, durable producer goods, durable consumer goods, and so on, though not necessarily in that order"

(1969:255). Following this discussion, Roger Garrison concludes tentatively, "If the misallocation of capital sets the pace, as Friedman's discussion of the lag suggests it well may, then the Monetary theory of boom and bust becomes one with the Austrian theory" (Garrison 2001:218).

But, alas, in the final analysis Friedman is unsure: "We have little confidence in our knowledge of the transmission mechanism, except in such broad and vague terms as to constitute little more than an impressionistic representation rather than an engineering blueprint" (1969:222). Axel Leijonhufvud (a monetarist at UCLA) adds,

> The first thing to say, surely, is that we know very little about how inflations work their way through the economy. Our empirical evidence is scant, which becomes less surprising once one notices that the theoretical work needed to lend it analytical structure has been neglected, too. The neoclassical monetary general equilibrium growth model has inflation as 'near neutral' as if it made no difference. The Austrian tradition has inflation associated with systematic and serious distortions of the price system and hence of resource allocation. My own 'hunch' with regard to present-day conditions would be that the price distortions are apt to be less systematic than in the Austrian view but none the less serious. There is no good evidence for this view either. (1977:287)

Leijonhufvud must not have looked very closely at the evidence. Austrian-type asset bubbles and unsustainable industrial booms are clearly demonstrated in the business cycles over the years. Capital-intensive goods and industries, including real estate, manufacturing, and mining, are far more cyclical than consumer goods and government-oriented industries. Austrian capital theory predicts that the further removed the production process is from final consumption, the more volatile are prices, employment, inventories, and output, due to the time value of money (interest rates). Indeed, the data support this Austrian insight: earlier-stage prices, employment, inventories, and output are more volatile over the business cycle than later-stage markets. Research on a variety of U.S. prices from 1952 to 1984 reveals that "raw industrial materials prices proved to be the most volatile, consumer prices the most stable, and producer prices somewhere in between" (see chapter 9, p. 293). Empirical work and time-series evidence by Frederick C. Mills at National Bureau of Economic Research (NBER) in the 1930s and 1940s and Charles Wainhouse's doctoral dissertation at NYU confirm significant malinvestment, structural imbalances, and intertemporal volatility in the real economy throughout the business cycle. The 1995–2003 experience in the high-tech economy supports the relevance of the Austrian model, which can no longer be so easily dismissed. The evidence appears to support the model depicted in figure F.

Figure F. Variations in Stages of Production during Expansion and Contraction

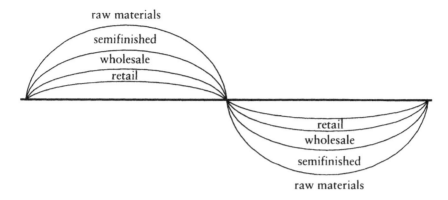

raw materials
semifinished
wholesale
retail

retail
wholesale
semifinished
raw materials

Mises and the Austrians reject as unrealistic the helicopter analogy by Friedman. New money is not distributed equally but usually through open-market operations in the banking system. "Who gets the money first?" is the overwhelming question the Austrians want answered. Mises suggests that an increase in the quantity of money can affect either consumer goods or producer goods, or both, depending on "whether those first receiving the new quantities of money use this new wealth for consumption or production" (Mises 1978:124–25). Hayek adds, "Everything depends on the point where the additional money is injected into circulation (or where the money is withdrawn from circulation), and the effects may be quite opposite according as the additional money comes first into the hands of traders and manufacturers or directly into the hands of salaried people employed by the State" (Hayek 1931:11). Lately the answer has been the banks, the mortgage companies, and Wall Street.

Why are the Chicago economists so blind to the Austrian evidence, when they are normally willing to change their minds in the face of empirical evidence? Three reasons are suggested: first, the overwhelming influence of Knight (and to some extent Marshall and Fisher) against the Austrian capital theory; second, the philosophical underpinnings of Friedman and other New Classical economists, the notion that "markets work" and a freely competitive environment will quickly erase distortions in the economy, so that any Austrian-style malinvestments are of secondary importance; and third, a lack of familiarity with the empirical evidence on intertemporal business-cycle data. Robert Lucas, Jr., reiterates this view, dismissing Austrian capital theory, malinvestments, and behavioral economics all in one as "too small" in their effects and importance. Gary Becker, however, was more open-minded on the issue. In a conversation with me, Becker acknowledged that "malinvestments do occur and are important in the economy." As Fritz Machlup concluded in an interview, "I don't know why a man as intelligent as Milton Friedman doesn't see that point. It is quite true that his ideas on price level and expectations of rising price levels explain much—but not everything. There are many things that are very important but cannot be explained by that approach alone. I don't understand why he doesn't give more emphasis to relative prices, relative costs, even in an inflationary period" (Machlup 1980).

FINANCIAL IMPLICATIONS

In chapter 11 of this book, I suggest the idea that an intertemporal structural model might be useful to investment analysis and portfolio management (pp. 374–77). Essentially, I found that monetary inflation had different effects on various financial assets, depending on how far removed their industries are from final use. For example, stock prices of capital-intensive and early-stage producers tend to be more volatile than consumer-goods companies. In a subsequent article, I suggested an "intertemporal pricing model" (IPM) that compartmentalizes stocks into sectors according to their place along the time-structural process. The model predicts that stock prices will tend to be more volatile (hence inherently more risky) in industries in the earlier stages of processing and less volatile in industries concentrated in the final stages of consumption. For example, a portfolio of gold-mining companies and manufacturers would be much more volatile than a portfolio of retail supermarkets and utilities.

Moreover, when central banks artificially lower interest rates and create an inflationary boom, earlier-stage and capital-intensive stocks will tend to rise more rapidly than later-stage consumer stocks. Equally, when the inflationary boom ends in a recession, stock prices of higher-capital-goods companies will fall more rapidly than stock prices of consumer-oriented companies (Skousen 1994:236–38). Figure G illustrates the effect of the boom-bust cycle on various companies/industries along the intertemporal path.

Figure G demonstrates what happens to the economy and markets during the business cycle. Throughout the cycle, the early stages (capital-goods industries) tend to expand and contract on a magnitude much greater than that experienced by the later stages (consumer-goods industries). Thus, note that BC/AC is substantially smaller than EF/DE Output, prices, employment, inventories, and stock prices in capital-goods industries tend to be more volatile than those in consumer-goods industries.

Figure G. Variations in the Aggregate Production Structure during the Boom-Bust Cycle

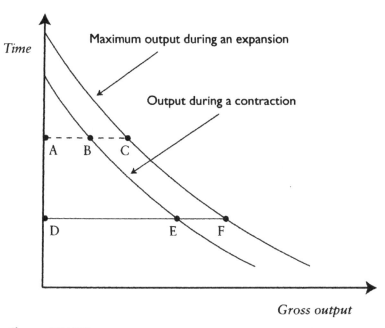

Source: Skousen 1994:237.

This book has become a sourcebook in the mining industry and securities business to help analysts and investors understand why mining stocks, especially in the developmental and early production stage, are inherently volatile in both earnings and stock performance. Because they are so distant from final consumer use, extreme volatility is the norm. During an easy-money inflationary era, natural-resource stocks can skyrocket in price, sometimes by 500 percent or more, but when the boom turns into a deflationary bust, these stocks can quickly lose 70 percent of their value on the exchange. In short, junior resource companies are not for the faint-of-heart investor and certainly should not be viewed as a "buy and hold" investment without recognizing their inherent high risks.

IMPROVEMENTS IN ECONOMICS TEXTBOOKS

If there is one area where this book has the most to offer, it is in the textbook arena. Neither my general four-stage model of the economy (figure A) nor Paul

Ekins's dynamic-growth diagram (figure C) have yet to appear in the most popular course works. But there have been some important changes that suggest a movement in the right direction. For example, John Taylor (Stanford) introduces a four-stage micro model in his textbook's chapter on GDP to demonstrate value added in the production process. Figure H reproduces this diagram.

Here Taylor uses the example of how a cup of espresso is produced through four stages: the coffee grower, the roaster, the shipper and wholesaler, and finally the coffee maker at Caribou Coffee in Minneapolis. Although he uses this example to explain the "value added" approach to GDP, it would not be difficult to expand this example to the macro sphere and introduce students to Gross Domestic Expenditures (GDE). In my macroeconomics course at Columbia University, students found it easy to follow this transition.

Since writing this book, I have incorporated most of my macro model and conclusions in my other works: *Economics on Trial* (1991), a review of the top-ten textbooks in economics; *The Making of Modern Economics* (2001), a history of economic thought; *The Power of Economic Thinking* (2002), a series

Figure H. Value Added in Coffee: From Beans to Espresso

Value added by espresso machine and service at a cafe

Value added by shipping and wholesale services

Value added by roasting and packaging

Value of shipped, roasted, and packaged beans purchased by Caribou Coffee

Value of roasted and packaged beans

Value added by growing and picking beans

Value of beans

Value of a cup of espresso ($1.50)

| Coffee grower | Coffee roaster | Coffee shipper and wholesaler | Caribou Coffee in Minneapolis |

Source: Taylor 2004:147.

of essays; and my own college textbook, *Economic Logic,* now in its second edition (Skousen 2007).

In *Economic Logic,* I created a micro version of my general macro model. Time and money again are the two variables, but instead of four stages of production, the micro model has only two, a firm's fiscal year of expenditures and revenues. Figure I reproduces this two-stage micro model.

Figure I shows annual expenses, revenues, and profit and loss of a firm. Economists call this a "point input, point output" model, and with it, students can visualize the dynamics of the economy better than standard supply-and-demand analysis: downsizing, upsizing, and the introduction of new products and services. The two-stage micro model is a perfect way to demonstrate Schumpeter's "creative destruction" process. It also illustrates disequilibrium in the economy, that firms will constantly test new products, vary prices and the quality of goods, and alter the production process in an effort to maximize their position in the global marketplace. Standard supply and demand curves have a hard time showing this dynamic aspect of markets. Students react the same way Robert Solow's students reacted to a similar Austrian "input-output" model at MIT "A time-structured model looks so different on the surface, tells so different a story, that one is first surprised and then enlightened" (Solow 1974:189–92).

Standard supply-and-demand analysis is derived from the two-stage micro model. From the revenue side comes the demand and supply schedule, and from the expenditure side comes the factors of production (land, labor, and capital).

Judging from my experience teaching economics at both the graduate and undergraduate level at Rollins College and Columbia University, I am convinced that my new micro and macro models can improve the way economics is

Figure I. Income Statement as Micro Model of the Economy

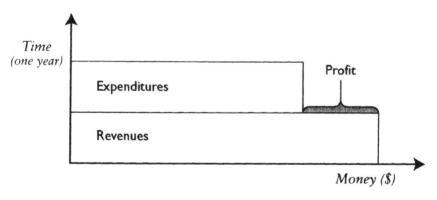

Source: Skousen 2007.

taught in the classroom. Students have an easier time understanding microeconomics starting with the P&L income statement (micro model) before they are introduced to supply and demand. And my disaggregate four-stage model does a better job of analyzing the dynamics of the global economy than the standard aggregate-output and price-level models (AS and AD).

Although textbooks have not yet adopted my methodology, they are making improvements in macroeconomic pedagogy. Instead of beginning the macro sections with the Keynesian model of stabilizing the economy, most are now focusing on the classical model of economic growth. N. Gregory Mankiw (Harvard) began this trend in the early 1990s with his *Macroeconomics* textbook: "In the aftermath of the Keynesian revolution, too many economists forgot that classical economics provides the right answers to many fundamental questions" (Mankiw 1994:i). Mankiw begins his textbook with the classical prosaving model of economic growth. Accordingly, "the saving rate is the key determinant of the steady-state capital stock. If the saving rate is high, the economy will have a large capital stock and a high level of output. If the saving rate is low, the economy will have a small capital stock and a low level of output" (Mankiw 1994:62). Mankiw does not discuss Say's law per se, but his approach is gaining appeal.

What is the future of this book? The epigraph to this introduction is a quotation on the future of economics from Peter Drucker, the great Austrian management guru, who read my book with approval before he died. Here is the full quotation from which the epigraph was taken: "That there is both a productivity crisis and a capital-formation crisis makes certain that the Next Economics will have to be again micro-economic and centered on supply. Both productivity and capital formation are events of the micro-economy. Both also deal with the factors of *production* rather than being functions of demand" (Drucker 1981:13, emphasis in original). It is my hope that *The Structure of Production* will go a long way toward fulfilling Drucker's prophetic vision of the next generation.

NOTES

1. When I wrote the historical overview of the four-stage time-structural model of the economy (the first three chapters of this book), I failed to recognize Adam Smith's contribution to the structure of production, other than a short reference to his pin factory and the making of a woolen coat. Somehow I overlooked a paragraph in Adam Smith's *Wealth of Nations* that identified the four stages of production: "A capital may be employed in four different ways: . . . in the first way are employed the capitals of all those who undertake the improvement or cultivation of lands, mines, or fisheries; in the second, those of all master manufacturers; in the third, those of all wholesale

merchants; and in the fourth, those of all retailers" (Smith 1965 [1776]:341). It's all in Adam Smith after all!

2. I refer to GDE as GNO in this book. See chapter 6, pp. 191–92. I now feel that Gross Domestic Expenditures is a better measure of total spending in the economy during the year.

3. The latest GO data is for 2002; unfortunately, GO is not figured as quickly as GDP data, which is updated every quarter.

4. The media also highlights the Consumer Confidence Index while ignoring the other nine indicators. Interestingly, the Consumer Confidence Index is not as consumer oriented as the name suggests. In the survey, consumers are asked a series of questions that are more related to business conditions than consumer spending habits, such as: Are current business conditions good, bad, or normal, or what will they be over the next six months? Do you expect jobs to be more plentiful over the next six months? Do you expect to buy a new car/home/appliance in the next six months? Are you going on a vacation soon? In other words, the survey of consumer confidence is more about business prospects than about current consumer spending. See http://www.conference-board.org/economics/consumerPubCCS.cfm.

5. For a discussion of Japan's long recession from an Austrian perspective, see Powell 2002.

6. I asked Milton Friedman to read the Eichengreen-Mitchener paper. His response was, "Eichengreen's paper is excellent: clear, well written, thoughtful. There is little in it that I disagree with. At the same time, I share the views expressed by his discussants, Bordo and Goodhart, that it does not contribute much to the key issue in question. That issue is whether the depth and seriousness of the depression is attributable to what took place during the twenties or to what took place during the thirties. The only item that has any bearing on that is his correlation of his measures of the credit boom with the depths of the subsequent recession (figure 6). Here he gets a positive correlation of 0.43 for the component which measures the height of the stock boom. That is pretty low. Moreover a glance at the chart shows that it is produced primarily by Canada and the United States. Neither of the other components, in particular not M2/GDP, has any correlation at all. Thus the bulk of his evidence is that what happened in the thirties explains the thirties, not what happened in the twenties" (personal correspondence, March 29, 2004).

REFERENCES

Callahan, Gene, and Roger W Garrison. 2003. "Does Austrian Business Cycle Theory Help Explain the Dot-Com Boom and Bust?" *Quarterly Journal of Austrian Economics* 6, no. 2 (Summer): 67–98.

Drucker, Peter F. 1981. *Toward the Next Economics, and Other Essays.* New York: Harper and Row.

Eichengreen, Barry, and Kris Mitchener. 2003. "The Great Depression as a Credit Boom Gone Wrong." BIS Working Papers No. 137 (September). Basel: Bank for International Settlements.

Eisner, Robert. 1988. "To Raise the Saving Rate, Try Spending." *New York Times*. (August 29): A19.

Ekins, Paul, and Manfred Max-Neef. 1992. *Real-Life Economics: Understanding Wealth Creation*. London: Routledge.

Garrison, Roger W. 2001. *Time and Money: The Macroeconomics of Capital Structure*. London: Routledge.

Friedman, Milton. 1969. *The Optimum Quantity of Money and Other Essays*. London: Macmillan.

———. 1991. *Monetarist Economics*. Oxford: Basil Blackwell.

Hayek, Friedrich A. 1931. *Prices and Production*. London: George Rutledge.

Kates, Steven, ed. 2003. *Two Hundred Years of Say's Law*. Cheltenham, UK: Edward Elgar.

Kudlow, Larry. 2006. "On Jobs, Tax Cuts, and the Democrats." *National Review Online* (September 5).

Leijonhufred, Alex. 1977. "Costs and Consequences of Inflation." *Microeconomic Foundations of Macroeconomics*, edited by G.C. Harcourt. New York: Stockton Press.

Machlup, Fritz. 1980. "An Interview with Fritz Machlup." *Austrian Economics Newsletter* (Summer), 3:1.

Mankiw, N. Gregory. 1994. *Macroeconomics*. 2d ed. New York: Worth.

Minsky, Hyman P. 1982. *Can "It" Happen Again? Essays on Instability and Finance*. New York: M. E. Sharpe.

Mises, Ludwig von. 1978. *On the Manipulation of Money and Credit*. New York: Free Market Books.

Modigliani, Franco. 1987. "The Key to Saving Is Growth, Not Thrift." *Challenge* (May–June): 24–29.

Patinkin, Don. 1965. *Money, Interest and Prices*. 2d ed. New York: Harper and Row.

Powell, Benjamin. 2002. "Explaining Japan's Recession." *Quarterly Journal of Austrian Economics* 5, no. 2 (Summer): 35–50.

Rothbard, Murray N. 1983. *America's Great Depression*. 4th ed. New York: Richardson and Snyder.

Samuelson, Paul A. 1948. *Economics*. New York: McGraw-Hill.

Skousen, Mark. 1990. *The Structure of Production*. New York: New York University Press.

Skousen, Mark. 1994. "Financial Economics." In *The Elgar Companion to Austrian Economics*, edited by Peter J. Boettke. Hants, UK: Edward Elgar.

———. 2001. *The Making of Modern Economics*. New York: M. E. Sharpe.

———. 2002. *The Power of Economic Thinking*. New York: Foundation for Economic Education.

———. 2005a. *Vienna and Chicago, Friends or Foes?* Washington, DC: Capital Press.

———. 2005b. "Which Drives the Economy, Consumer Spending or Saving/Investment?" Initiative for Policy Dialogue. Available online at http://www2.gsb.columbia.edu/ipd/j-gdp.html.

———. 2007. *Economic Logic*. 2d ed. Washington, DC: Capital Press.

Smith, Adam. 1965 [1776]. *The Wealth of Nations*. New York: Modern Library.

Solow, Robert. 1974. "Review of Hicks's *Capital and Time*." *Economic Journal* 84:189–92.

Suzuki, Yoshio. 1994. "Comments on Papers by Benegas Lynch and Skousen." Mount Pelerin Society Meetings, September 27, Cannes, France.

Taylor, John. 2004. *Economics.* Boston: Houghton Mifflin.

Woodhall, Pam. 2002. "The Unfinished Recession: A Survey of the World Economy." *Economist* (September 28): 3–28.

PREFACE

In the summer of 1988, 1 had the opportunity to meet 84-year-old Sir John Hicks, the Nobel laureate who transformed Keynesian economics into the grand neoclassical synthesis with his 1937 article in *Econometrica*, "Mr Keynes and the 'Classics.'" Despite his age and physical ailments, his mind was alert and, during our meeting, he recounted how he had gradually become disenchanted with many aspects of the modern economic theory he helped to develop. In particular, he seemed greatly displeased by the failure of orthodox economists to teach the importance of time and the stages-of-production concept in macro-economics, a subject he emphasized in his own textbook, *The Social Framework*, and more recently in his treatise, *Capital and Time*. He called it a great mistake that most economists had abandoned this essential doctrine.

Several years earlier, I had met with another Nobel-prize-winning econo-mist, Friedrich von Hayek, at his summer home in the Austrian Alps. Like Hicks, Hayek reflected on his long career, and expressed dismay and disappointment that so few economists had attempted to extend his work on the time theory of capital, which he regarded as a critical link to understanding macroeconomic phenomena.

It is my intention to fulfill this ambitious role. My efforts to bring together the essentials of capital, production, and time into a coherent macroeconomic theory have not been easy. But the thesis is starting to show tangible results. This work culminates ten years of research, writing, and theorizing; efforts aimed toward a practical alternative to the standard neoclassical model of macroeconomics. Like Hicks and Hayek, I have serious misgivings about the way economics is taught. As a young economics student, I concluded that the two main forces in eco-nomics today, Keynesianism and monetarism, were both technical and ethically flawed. I sensed that there was something inherently wrong with the Keynesian *paradox of thrift* as well as with the monetarist's rigid quantity theory of money. But like the mathematician Karl Friedrich Gauss, "I have been sure of my results for some time; what I don't know is how I shall arrive at them."

I was led to the intertemporal structural approach developed in this treatise upon reading Ludwig von Mises's *Theory of Money and Credit* many years ago. In the development of my thesis, I have relied most heavily on Mises's followers, F. A. Hayek, Murray Rothbard, and Roger Garrison, who have developed the most rigorous theoretical foundation for a macroeconomic model based on time and capital. In this treatise, I have attempted to broaden the Austrian concepts of time and production into a full-scale macroeconomic model that, as the reader will see, is especially useful in analyzing the aggregate effects of a wide variety of market and government actions, including such variables as an increase in savings, the adoption of technological improvements, an expansion of the money supply under a gold standard as well as a fiat-money standard, an increase or reduction of taxes, and the adoption of anti-recession policies.

During my research, I have come across several books that I found particularly insightful, many of which are now out of print, but which deserve a wider audience, including but not limited to: *Common Sense Economics,* by German economist L. Albert Hahn; *The Economics of Knut Wicksell,* by Carl G. Uhr; *Market Theory and the Price System,* by Israel M. Kirzner; *Prices in Recession and Recovery,* by Frederick C. Mills, a professor of statistics at Columbia University who pioneered the relative price studies at the National Bureau of Economic Research; and *Business Cycles,* by James Estey. There were also several noteworthy textbooks published prior to 1960, which preserved the Böhm-Bawerkian vision: *Economics: Principles and Problems,* by Paul F. Gemmill and Ralph H. Blodgett; *The Economic Process,* by Raymond T. Bye and William H. Hewett; and *Introduction to Economics,* by John V. Van Sickle and Benjamin A. Rogge.

THIS WORK AS A "ROUNDABOUT" PROCESS

The writing and publishing of this book is itself, in many ways, an example of my central thesis: *a time-oriented process of production* aimed at achieving an economic end. My book went through a myriad of stages before the final work was completed and ready for use by the reader. My method was very roundabout, to use Böhm-Bawerk's favorite expression. At first it was merely an idea. The early, raw-production stage included researching and reading literally hundreds of books and journal articles on the structure of production and related macroeconomic topics. The research time was lengthened (or delayed) by the necessity of going through card catalogs and book stacks at over twenty university libraries in the United States and England, since no single university, no matter how large, possesses everything needed. The works of former economists served as the *"fixed"* capital necessary to help me transform my *"working"* capital into a finished good.

After researching, reading, and making notes on a wide variety of books and journals, I formulated an outline and summary of my thesis, the next stage of production. I spent many hours thinking through a maze of often contradictory theories, trying to make sense out of a complex subject. Sometimes it was necessary to create a whole new apparatus or original technique as a tool to explain an economic phenomenon. For example, my diagrams on time preference and technology in chapter 7, my use of the Hayekian triangles to explain inflationary recession in chapter 9, and contrasting supply-credit inflation with demand-credit inflation in chapter 10 were all created to illustrate certain economic conditions. Most significantly, I have been able to demonstrate in chapter 7 the fallacy of the paradox of thrift by recasting the Keynesian mold onto the Hayekian framework. I have also created a new economic statistic, Gross National Output, as a more accurate and complete description of economic activity than GNP.

Just as a manufacturer will experiment with his product to refine and perfect it, several drafts were made of this manuscript as new material came to light and mistakes were corrected. Copies of the completed draft were sent to several economists of varying backgrounds and schools of thought, not necessarily in agreement with my own theories or policy recommendations. They suggested many additions and changes. In particular, I would like to thank the following for their assistance: Israel Kirzner at New York University, G. C. Harcourt at Cambridge University, Michio Morishima at the London School of Economics, Mark Blaug at the University of London, Larry Wimmer at Brigham Young University, Murray N. Rothbard at the University of Nevada at Las Vegas, Roger Garrison at Auburn University, Gary North of the American Bureau of Economic Research, Richard Band of *Personal Finance,* Kenna Taylor at Rollins College, Malte Faber at University of Heidelberg, Richard Ebeling at Hillsdale College, and Joe Salerno at Pace University. I would also like to thank my editor, Colin Jones, at New York University Press, for his support and efforts in publishing this work, and to Charts & Graphs Unlimited for doing an excellent job on the graphs.

A great deal of crucial work was provided by Royal Skousen at Brigham Young University, who helped immensely in developing the mathematics, diagrams, and statistical studies herein.

I would also like to thank my wife, Jo Ann, for reading the manuscript carefully for stylistic improvement. I was lucky enough to marry an English major with an uncanny eye for accuracy and a felicity of literary expression. She has been a tremendous support in this seemingly never-ending project, and without her steady encouragement and farsightedness, I suspect the whole production process would never have ripened into a fruitful work.

Once the manuscript is edited, printed, and marketed by the publisher—an intricate process in and of itself—the book reaches the point of final consumer use, to be bought, read, and referred to by teachers, students, businessmen, and readers in general. Is a book a final consumer good or an intermediate capital good? I suppose it depends on the audience. A paperback novel read by consumers at home or on vacation may only be read once, and then discarded, never to be opened again. As such, it is consumed as soon as the last page is read. But a classic novel or philosophical book may be read over and over again, especially if it is available at a library, thus making it a durable consumer good. Books of a technical nature used in college classes or on-the-job training must be regarded as intermediate capital goods, in furtherance of a degree or a job.

Needless to say, I am hopeful that this work will serve well as a durable capital good that will not depreciate too rapidly in the minds of its readers.

THE PHILOSOPHICAL DEBATE OVER MACROECONOMICS

My time-oriented approach to macroeconomics is far more significant than a simple entry in the debate over which model best describes the inner workings of the economy. It is a continuation of the great philosophical debate that began in earnest in the 1930s. During that decade, John Maynard Keynes turned the world on its head by developing a "general theory" aimed at overturning classical economics. Over the centuries, the classical economists had created a body of economic theory which supported the traditional virtues of thrift, the gold standard, and balanced budgets. The Great Depression of the 1930s provided fertile ground for Keynes's attack on these old-fashioned values. By developing a theory which justified unconventional policies whenever there were unemployed resources, he was able gradually to convince the economics profession that savings may be counterproductive and deficit financing beneficial whenever the economy was at "less than full employment."

Keynes's principal theoretical opponent in the 1930s was the Austrian economist, Friedrich A. Hayek, who argued strenuously that Keynes's new theories were defective because, among other criticisms, they failed to take into account the critical role of time. According to Hayek, Keynesianism was purely a short-term theory, and its policy recommendations would be disastrous in the long run.

Keynes won the battle of men's minds in the depression years. But his anti-savings, anti-gold, and pro-inflationary theories endured beyond the 1930s. We are now living in the Keynesian long run that Hayek warned about. Despite the development of monetarism, rational expectations, and other new theories, many Keynesian concepts are still being taught today, including the paradox of thrift and the necessity of running a government deficit during an economic downturn.

It is not enough to dismiss a theory simply because it may be morally bankrupt or financially ruinous. An unsound theory must be shown to be defective on purely theoretical grounds as well. The goal of this work is to create a model which answers the excesses of Keynesianism and other forms of macroeconomic interventionism on their own theoretical grounds. I believe that the time structural approach, as developed by Hayek and other economists over the years, forms the basis for this counterattack.

I am hopeful that economists and students of all persuasions will give an impartial and fair hearing to this reconstructed theme in macroeconomics. Far too often, academicians too quickly label this or that theory as representing one particular school of thought, and reject it out of hand without much analysis. The fact that many neoclassical economists, including Michio Morishima, Kenneth Boulding, G. L. S. Shackle, and John Hicks, have been attracted to this method should be grounds for a dispassionate review.

When Keynes introduced his revolutionary new approach to economic theory in the 1930s, he warned about the "struggle of escape from habitual modes of thought and expression."[1] After having been indoctrinated by Keynesian themes for many decades, economists face this same challenge today to give a fair hearing to alternative ideas. In the early 1930s, Lionel Robbins introduced a new translation of Hayek's work with a caution that applies just as much today as when he wrote it: "The criteria of scientific validity take no account of origins, and the economist who refuses to avail himself of a particular set of propositions because they were foreign would be acting no less unscientifically than the chemist or physician who acted on similar principles. It has been well said that there are only two kinds of economics-good economics and bad economics. All other classifications are misleading."[2]

It is in this spirit that I make a case for a new macroeconomics.

NOTES

1. Keynes, *The General Theory*, xxiii.
2. Robbins, Foreword to Hayek, *Monetary Theory and the Trade Cycle*, 5–6.

ONE

INTRODUCTION: THE CASE FOR A NEW MACROECONOMICS

> If we are witnessing the dissolution of an intellectual establishment, and its fragmentation into conflicting schools, what this eventually leads to—if one reads the history of any intellectual discipline—is the development of a new, comprehensive framework.—Daniel Bell and Irving Kristol, *The Crisis in Economic Theory*

Macroeconomics needs a new approach. The corpus of contemporary macroeconomic modeling is excessively aggregative, too abstract, and ultimately deficient as a way of analyzing the inner workings of a constantly changing economic landscape. The conventional "neoclassical" models seem almost helpless in rescuing the economy from fundamental *structural* defects (defects that their macro models are unable to uncover) which have built up over the past fifty years, created by ruinous and vacillating fiscal and monetary policies.[1]

Orthodox economists have been chipping away at the foundation of these macro models for decades, but have been unable to salvage them. A growing number of economists, recognizing this dilemma, are searching for a workable alternative. With this in mind, I propose an entirely different edifice with which to describe and analyze the production process for the whole economy, a new *tableau économique*. My method could be called a Mengerian "vertical" framework, which is strictly the opposite of the conventional Clark-Walrasian "horizontal" method, the basis of standard macroeconomics today. I am not suggesting that my task of reconstruction is entirely new or original—it is not—but I have attempted to extend my analysis of the whole economy beyond what has been done in the past in an effort to show how this alternative method is a better and more useful macroeconomic tool for economists than the currently orthodox perspective.

A SHORT CRITIQUE OF CONVENTIONAL MACRO THEORY

Let me be more specific in my criticism of conventional macro theory, and why I think it should be replaced with a new model. Essentially, neoclassical macroeconomics, which forms the foundation of Keynesian, monetarist, and other modern theories, envisions the economy as a collection of large aggregates in a timeless dimension of simultaneous production and consumption. Although its roots can be traced back as far as Adam Smith and the "classical" economists, the modern formula goes back primarily to John Bates Clark, who envisioned the economy as a large reservoir, where the production of goods and services are seen as a permanent, malleable, flowing fund, and to Leon Walras, who saw the economy in a horizontal, timeless fashion where the factors of production were converted instantly into final consumer products.

This Clark-Walras confluence is apparent throughout modern macroeconomic models—in the *circular flow* diagram, the neoclassical production function, capital theory, the Keynesian consumption function, the monetary "cash balance" effect, and aggregate supply and demand curves.

The standard circular flow diagram, which is used in introductory economics textbooks to describe the interdependence of production, consumption, and exchange, is an abstraction that completely ignores the time element. "It assumes everything is happening *at the same time*, a false and misleading assumption," says L. Albert Hahn.[2] Moreover, there are no savings, no financial institutions, and no intermediate capital goods of any kind. The circular flow diagram offers no explanation for dynamic changes in the economy—shifts in employment, prices, production, the business cycle, and economic growth, for example.

The neoclassical production function, commonly used in intermediate economics textbooks to analyze changes in output and economic growth, is just as obtuse and barren as the circular flow diagram. The conventional production function envisions the volume of output as a function of inputs, expressed in the form of isoquants, where labor and capital are substituted at varying levels of production.

Michio Morishima is one of many economists who are highly critical of the neoclassical production function, which assumes "that all capital goods are made of putty" that can be combined in any fashion "instantly" and "costlessly." The concept "is like trying to build a tower on a large anthill."[3] Because the "immobility of capital goods" makes "aggregation" virtually impossible, Morishima rejects the neoclassical model and opts for a "de-centralized" microeconomic approach involving a "vertical genealogy" of product transformation, similar to mine.

Neoclassical capital theory follows the same lines as the production function and the circular-flow diagram. Capital, as characterized by J. B. Clark and Frank

Knight, is represented as a permanent homogeneous fund or stock, rather than as distinct commodities of varying age distributions. As such, notes B. S. Keirstead, their theory "not only does not answer the question of what determines the structure of real capital at any time, it does not even permit the question to be asked."[4]

Robert M. Solow refers to the permanent fund concept as a "homogeneous jelly," where capital goods are nonspecific and "instantaneously substitutable" for labor and other inputs. Solow, a principal proponent of the neoclassical position, admits that such an oversimplified view is wrong, especially in the short run.[5] Solow is also critical of an attempt by Clark-Knight followers to represent capital models in terms of a single number instead of a variety of heterogeneous goods. "For there is no reason to suppose that any single object called `capital' can be defined to sum up in one number a whole range of facts about time lags, gestation periods, inventories of materials, goods in process, and finished commodities, old and new machines and buildings of varying durability, and more or less permanent improvements to land."[6]

According to F. H. Hahn, the neoclassical models of capital involve numerous unrealistic assumptions, such as: capital lasts forever, there are no intermediate goods, nor is there a time factor, workers do not save, and capitalists do not consume.[7]

EXCESSIVE AGGREGATION IN MAINSTREAM ECONOMICS

Mainstream economists, still under the influence of Keynes, think in terms of gross national product, the inflation rate, the interest rate, total investment, the unemployment rate, and other singular figures.

For Keynesians, national income is expressed in terms of broad aggregates, as indicated in the well-known consumption function. As Benjamin M. Anderson states, "Throughout Keynes's analysis he is working with aggregate, block concepts. He has an aggregate supply function and an aggregate demand function. But nowhere is there any discussion of the interrelationships of the elements of these vast aggregates, or of elements in one aggregate with elements in another."[8]

Monetarists, with their attention to the real balance effect and the quantity theory of money, are not so distinct from Keynesians in terms of their methodological approach. They also analyze the economy in terms of such broad aggregates as the money supply, the price level, and national output.[9] Indeed, the quantity theory of money is expressed mathematically in aggregate form, with single numbers for the money stock, velocity, output, and the price level. According to proponents of the quantity theory of money, velocity is relatively stable, and under full employment the national product is held constant. Hence, the consumer price index is directly correlated to the change in the quantity of money.

Aggregate supply and aggregate demand curves, now a standard method of introducing macroeconomics to students, are only two-dimensional in nature. The economy is neatly fit into an apparatus that links the *price level* on the vertical axis and *real output* on the horizontal axis.

Each of these quantities represents large aggregates or averages which completely obscure changes in relative prices, the allocation of resources among various sectors of the economy, and the progressive nature of the production process.[10]

Kenneth E. Boulding is highly skeptical of macroeconomic models, which he calls an "unworkable fallacy." According to Boulding, it is essential to realize the "composition" or "structure" of the economy or national income. "It is clearly not merely the aggregate total of production, consumption, and accumulation that matters; it matters *what* is produced, consumed, and accumulated, i.e., of what goods these aggregates are composed."[11]

INPUT-OUTPUT ANALYSIS: A STEP IN THE RIGHT DIRECTION?

In response to these criticisms, economists have been in search of new directions in macroeconomics. One alternative for describing and analyzing the economy has been input-output analysis.

Wassily Leontief suggests the use of input-output analysis as a valuable way of looking at the whole economy, and has written extensively on the subject. According to Leontief, economists should not rely solely on GNP, the interest rate, and price levels, but on the "intervening steps" between inputs and outputs, steps which involve "a complex series of transactions . . . among real people."[12]

Input-output analysis appears to be the only major alternative presented by mainstream economists to describe the *micro* foundations of the economy. Don Lavoie comments, "What is compelling about this approach is that it is, in principle, microscopic rather than macroscopic. That is, it directs attention to the complex details of interdependence of the structure of production rather than to some single-dimensional measure of the size of the nation's wealth or capital stock."[13]

In an input-output table, the horizontal rows show how the output of each sector or industry (agriculture, apparel, vehicles, and so on) is used by the other sectors, while the vertical columns show how each sector obtains from the other sectors its needed inputs of goods and services. For example, the vertical column for the automobile industry shows such inputs as ferrous metals, rubber, electrical equipment, and textiles. These are the basic materials which go into the making of vehicles. The horizontal rows indicate who are the final users of automobiles, trucks, and other vehicles: construction, manufacturing, other industries, and individual consumers.

However, while input-output analysis is a move in the right direction—i.e., as a microfoundation for macroeconomics—it has limitations. The input-output table is essentially only two-dimensional in nature. It links various industrial sectors with their direct factors of production and direct users, but not the indirect, more distant factors. It may demonstrate how shoes come primarily from leather products, but obscures the whole series of processes shoe production goes through, from cowhides to footwear. In short, the input-output (I-O) table does not delineate the entire genealogy of a particular product or industrial sector. It only lists the sector's close relatives.[14]

Input-output analysis becomes hardly useful as a macroeconomic tool if one concludes from the I-O table that "everything depends on everything else," a common interpretation in economics textbooks. In the end, such a holistic notion amounts to nothing more than a homogeneous Clark-Walrasian version of neoclassical macroeconomics.

There has been an effort to rearrange the input-output table according to the natural stages of economic production, "the hierarchy of interindustrial dependence," as Leontief calls it. This method is termed "triangulation."[15] Sectors are arranged in the upper rows of the table which deliver most of their output to final demand and little to other industrial sectors more distant from consumption. At the same time, the outputs of the sectors toward the bottom of the table are distributed primarily as inputs to the other sectors. In general, sectors above any row are *customers* of that industrial sector, and industries below any row are their *suppliers*. At best, however, triangulation amounts to a two-dimensional division of the industrial sector, the consumer-goods industry and the capital-goods industry. While this technique provides greater detail and reflects a more natural relationship between goods, it does not provide the whole picture that we seek in order to analyze the full effects of changing economic events. Our objective is to develop an economic model that represents an *array* of capital and consumer goods, not just a two-sector economy.

THE STAGES OF PRODUCTION: AN ALTERNATIVE APPROACH TO MACROECONOMICS

Morishima suggests that neoclassical economists turn to a vertical approach to production economics instead of the more popular horizontal method. He says that looking at the economy from the point of view of what he terms a "vertical genealogy of production" is very recent and generally ignored by mainstream economists.[16]

What is this vertical method of analyzing macroeconomics? Basically, it is a conceptual framework which visualizes the whole economy in terms of stages of production passing through time. Economics, in fact, may be defined as a process of transforming raw materials into intermediate goods and eventually into final consumer goods. Initially, every product starts with the crudest of raw materials and then, through a long string of intermediate steps, is gradually changed into a finished product ready for use by consumers or business. In a modern economy, this process involves a long and complex chain of economic stages running over varying periods of time.

AN INTERDISCIPLINARY APPROACH

In researching this subject, I have found that a number of associated disciplines use this natural concept of economic hierarchy, including the theories of industrial organization, marketing and retailing, statistical data gathering, and investment analysis. These disciplines are what economists have generally referred to as *applied economics.*

In the field of industrial organization, a common subject is *vertical integration.* Oliver E. Williamson notes that vertical integration involves three elements: "backward into materials, laterally into components, and forward into distribution."[17] F. M. Scherer discusses the stream or flow of production in relation to vertical integration, and a firm's decision to incorporate either "downstream" or "upstream" to minimize costs. He points out that such decisions are made frequently in the steel, auto, and other major industries. Scherer notes that "Most goods pass through numerous intermediate transactions before reaching the consumers' hands. Consumers buy from retailers, who may obtain their supplies from wholesalers, who buy from consumer goods manufacturers, who secure raw materials, equipment, and parts from other manufacturing and mining firms, who in turn purchase from still other companies, etc."[18]

In the area of marketing and retailing, distribution channels have become a subject of intense interest since the late 1960s. Marketing analysts have developed extensive techniques to improve the distribution of goods and services through these *marketing channels,* whether it is between manufacturers and dealers or between wholesalers and retailers. Marketing specialists are not particularly interested in the production or construction of the product itself, but in its distribution to the final user once it's manufactured. Lusch and Lusch define a *marketing channel* as "the set of institutions or people that participate in moving goods and services from point of initial source or production to point of final consumption or use."[19] According to Lusch and Lusch, the study of marketing channels serves in part to improve customer services, reduce costs of distribution, control inventories, and reduce negotiation time.

In statistical research and data gathering, government and private research organizations extend their resources far beyond the preparation of national income, the consumer price index, consumer expenditures, and other macroeconomic figures. Detailed microeconomic data are also a main area of research. Standard classifications include price, employment, and output figures for specific industrial groups classified according to their distance from final use. Price, inventory, and output indices are put together for raw commodities, agricultural products, producers' goods, manufactured products, wholesale goods, and final consumers' goods, among others. Frederick C. Mills, who pioneered this method at the National Bureau of Economic Research, refers to the these price and output relationships as "of central importance in the working of the economic system."[20] As I will demonstrate, such micro data will prove extremely valuable in analyzing the economy and the financial markets according to the time structure of production and the associated theoretical framework.

THE CHALLENGE OF A NEW CONCEPT

My use of the stages-of-production viewpoint may seem somewhat unfamiliar to students of conventional economic analysis. Today most introductory college textbooks ignore this basic process inherent in all economies, except as it may apply to a discussion of the *value added* tax, or *cost push* inflation. The value added tax is imposed on businesses at each stage of production. In the case of cost push inflation, researchers try to determine to what extent changes in wholesale costs affect retail prices. For example, during an energy crisis, if the price of crude oil doubles, how much will gasoline prices go up? Or, if the price of agricultural commodities declines, how will this affect food prices in the grocery store?

But other than these two examples, the time structural view is not discussed. Nor is it a familiar subject in intermediate macro or micro textbooks. Anne P. Carter notes that this alternative theory that "converts inputs into final output" is very much an "economic black box."[21] The only place the structure-of-production concept may be introduced is in conjunction with input-output analysis, business cycle theory, and the history of economic thought.

The vertical production methodology has a long history in economics and was a major theme of conventional economists in the late nineteenth and early twentieth centuries, and can even be found in a number of economics textbooks through the 1950s. I have devoted the next three chapters to an extensive review of this approach in the history of economic thought in order to put it into proper perspective.

While the Clark-Walras system of macroeconomics became the pervasive orthodoxy by the 1930s, it is appropriate that we resurrect the notion of a "natural" market process and structure of production. The structure-of-production concept can be an extremely valuable tool for economists in analyzing aggregate supply and demand and the effect of government policy on the economy. I would even venture to suggest that viewing the economy in this manner can serve as an essential link between micro and macro theory. Moreover, such an approach is a more realistic method of analyzing aggregate economics than the Keynesian consumption function, the monetarist cash balance effect, or aggregate supply and demand.

NOTES

1. The crisis in conventional macroeconomic orthodoxy is discussed intelligibly in D. Bell and I. Kristol, eds., *The Crisis in Economic Theory,* as well as in Wiles and Routh, eds., *Economics in Disarray.*
2. L. A. Hahn, *Common Sense Economics,* 116.
3. Morishima, *The Economic Theory of Modern Society,* 50.
4. Keirstead, *Capital, Interest and Profits,* 47.
5. Solow, *Capital Theory and the Rate of Return,* 26–27.
6. Ibid., 13–14. See also Solow, Review of J. Hicks's *Capital and Time,* 191. Paul Samuelson adds, "Repeatedly in writings and lectures I have insisted that capital theory can be rigorously developed without using any Clark-like concepts of aggregate 'capital,' instead relying on a complete analysis of a great variety of heterogeneous physical capital goods and processes through time." Samuelson, "Parable and Realism in Capital Theory," 193. Unfortunately, in this same article, Samuelson develops a homogeneous capital concept based on a single "surrogate" production function!
7. Hahn, "Equilibrium Dynamics," 634.
8. B. Anderson, *Economics and the Public Welfare,* 393. Roger Garrison adds, "Keynes's propensity to aggregate conceals critical market processes." "The Austrian-Neoclassical Relation," 155.
9. Milton Friedman rejects many of the Keynesian policy recommendations and economic theories, but uses many of the methodological aggregates such as consumption, investment, and income. "We all use the Keynesian language and apparatus; none of us any

longer accepts the initial Keynesian conclusions." Friedman, *Dollars and Deficits*, 15. The emphasis on aggregate analyses is apparent in all Friedman's works. For example, see Friedman and Schwartz, *Monetary Trends*, 16–72.

10. Don Patinkin's monetary theory is a prime example of the high degree of aggregation in neoclassical macroeconomics. See D. Patinkin, *Money, Interest and Prices*. On Patinkin's methodology, Roger Garrison comments, "Patinkin equals, actually outdoes, Keynes in his willingness to use broad economy-wide aggregates and hence to suppress capital-theoretical considerations . . . and, like Wicksell, he elevates the real-cash-balance effect to the status of the sole equilibrating force in the economy. . . . Real cash balances are one-dimensional and homogeneous. Disequilibrium in the Patinkin model is reduced to a comparison of the actual quantity of money in existence to the quantity demanded." See Garrison, "The Austrian-Neoclassical Relation," 117, 128.

11. Boulding, *A Reconstruction of Economics*, 202. See also 175, 187–188.

12. Leontief, *Input-Output Economics*, 14–15.

13. D. Lavoie, *National Economic Planning: What Is Left?*, 105.

14. G. L. S. Shackle comments, "Leontief was concerned with the technical structure, but within this technical structure there is latent a *temporal* structure, residing in the fact that what exists today as yam, and what exists today as cloth, and what exists today as finished garments, do not and never will belong in the same physical object, yet today's finished garment was at an earlier time cloth, and that cloth at any earlier time still was yarn. Leontief was not immediately concerned with the temporal structure, but if changes are made in the `bill of goods for final use' these changes will require time spans in order to have their full effects, and those time spans will reflect the technical capital structure of production. They are the reality of the time-structure of production." Shackle, "New Tracts for Economic Theory, 1926–1939," 34.

15. Leontief, *Input-Output Economics*, 162.

16. Morishima, *The Economic Theory of Modern Society*, 35–36. Carl G. Uhr agrees that a "revitalized analysis" of a time-structure of production concept "may be of great service." Uhr, *Economic Doctrines of Knut Wicksell*, 146.

17. Williamson, *The Economic Institutions of Capitalism*, 86.

18. Scherer, *Industrial Market Structure*, 239. See also 69–71, 85–86.

19. R. F. Lusch and V. N. Lusch, *Principles of Marketing*, 302. Also, see B. Rosenbloom, *Marketing Channels: A Management View*, and Stern and El-Ansary, *Marketing Channels*.

20. Mills, *Prices in Recession and Recovery*, 26. Referring to price and production indices of individual sectors, Carl Uhr adds, "The 'standard' classifications still in use were developed several decades ago, long before analyses of national income, employment, and economic growth came to demand so much attention of economists, leaders of the business community, and elected and appointed public officials in charge of developing economic policy." Uhr, *Economics in Brief*, 120.

21. Carter, *Structural Change in the American Economy*, 3–4. Referring to her alternative approach to production theory—which generally resembles mine—she writes in the preface, "This book is a mere drop in an enormous—and barely damp—intellectual bucket." (vii).

THE STRUCTURE OF PRODUCTION: A HISTORICAL SURVEY

A study of the history of opinion is a necessary preliminary to the emancipation of the mind.—Lord Keynes

PART 1

THE STRUCTURE OF PRODUCTION:
A HISTORICAL SURVEY

TWO

THE THEORY OF PRODUCTION IN CLASSICAL ECONOMICS

The whole of the organon of pure economics thus finds itself unified in the light of a single principle—in a sense in which it never had been before.—Schumpeter on Carl Menger, *History of Economic Analysis*.

The idea that production takes time and passes through a series of stages before reaching consumption was not seriously developed as an important economic principle until the Austrian economist, Carl Menger, wrote about it in the 1870s. Earlier economic thinkers referred to the manufacturing process through time, but did not dwell on it or develop it into a complete macroeconomic concept.

EARLY FRENCH VIEWS OF THE ECONOMY

In the early eighteenth century, the French physiocrat François Quesnay (1694–1774) attempted to describe the production process in his famous work *Tableau Economique*. His complex diagrams tried to show, in a zigzag fashion, the successive rounds of annual expenditures by the major sectors of the economy. Although Quesnay incorporated capital (*avances*) in his model, he focused primarily on the relationship between the "productive" agricultural sector and the "unproductive" manufacturing and landlord sectors rather than on the time-consuming transformation process of individual goods.[1]

The French financial magistrate, A. R. J. Turgot (1727–81), worked out a proto-"Austrian" theory of production in his short work, "Reflections on the Formation and Distribution of Wealth," published in 1766. "The products of the earth require long and difficult preparations in order to make them suitable for the wants of man," he wrote.[2] Using the examples of shoes and leather, Turgot discussed how labor, combined with land and "capitals," is used to transform goods through intermediate "operations." He stated: "A vast number of Crafts, and even those Crafts engaged in by the poorest members of Society, require that the same materials should pass through a multitude of different hands, and undergo, for a very long time, exceedingly difficult and varied operations."[3]

ADAM SMITH AND THE CLASSICAL VIEW

Ten years later, in his monumental work, *The Wealth of Nations,* Adam Smith (1723–90) examined the industrial process using his well-known example of pins. Smith referred to eighteen distinct operations, some occurring simultaneously, in the pinmaking trade. Although he used the manufacturing of the pin to demonstrate the principle of division of labor, it also demonstrated the sequential "assembly line" nature of the pin factory. "One man draws out the wire, another straights it, a third cuts it, a fourth points it, a fifth grinds it at the top for receiving the head; to make the head requires two or three distinct operations."[4]

Beyond this brief outline, however, Smith moved on to an extended discussion of "productive" and "unproductive" labor, which could be loosely defined as a distinction between *capital goods* and *consumer goods.*[5] Smith favored the accumulation of capital over consumption, but did not develop a general theory based on the causal nexus between capital goods and consumer goods. His theory of production was more *cross-sectional* in nature, analyzing the economy in terms of the factors of production—land, labor, and capital—in contrast to Turgot's *longitudinal* approach of analyzing the intertemporal transformation of raw materials and intermediate goods into final consumer products. He used the terms, *fixed capital,* referring to machinery and durable producer goods, and *circulating capital,* referring to unfinished products that are transformed by manufacturing firms, but did not extend his analysis any further.[6]

Smith's theory of production became known as the "classical" position. His emphasis on the factors of production (land, labor, and capital) and their costs, irrespective of their place in the industrial hierarchy, became the traditional framework for Ricardo, Malthus, Mill and other classical economists. In this sense, they were the forerunners of the Clark-Walrasian formula of the neoclassical production function and macroeconomic analysis (hence, the appropriate term, *neoclassical*). Like the classical economists, the neoclassical economists see the economy in a "cross-sectional" or "horizontal" fashion, in a timeless, homogeneous realm, as opposed to the "longitudinal" or "vertical" view of a time-oriented structure of economic processes.

Schumpeter argued that David Ricardo (1771–1823), despite his emphasis on the costs of production and the labor theory of value, was a forerunner of Jevons and Böhm-Bawerk because he analyzed capital and machinery from the point of view of the time it took to bring commodities to market. Thus, Ricardo wrote,

> On account then of the different degrees of durability of their capitals, or, which is the same thing, on account of the time which must elapse before one set of commodities can be brought to market, they will be valuable, not exactly in proportion to the quantity of labour bestowed on them, . . . but something more, to compensate for the greater length of time which must elapse before the most valuable can be brought to market.[7]

By the same token, classical economists J. B. Say (1767–1832) and J. S. Mill (1806–73) developed embryonic notions of Menger's forthcoming theory of imputation. Mill, for instance, dealt with the value of indirect factors of labor in lengthy processes of production, as in the case of breadmaking: "All these persons ultimately derive the remuneration of their labour from the bread, or its price: the ploughmaker as much as the rest."[8] However, Mill was more concerned with the distinction between the production of "necessities" and "luxuries" and how such luxuries constituted a "fund" available for "pleasures and for all higher uses."[9]

Fortunately, a more complete picture was developed by a few lesser known nineteenth-century writers, such as Mountifort Longfield (1802–84) and John Rae (1796–1872). Longfield used the example of a cotton gown, referring to the labor and materials that went into it—raw materials, freight, nails in building the freight ship, and so on. "Carry on this analysis in your mind, as far as your imagination dares to wonder, and you will find in the most distant ages, certain employments of labour, and accumulation of capital, indirectly contributing to the production of this cotton gown."[10]

John Rae's theory of production was much more elaborate than Longfield's. He used the example of bread and discussed its gradual transformation, from the farmer's wheat seed to the consumer's loaf of bread. Rae proposed that "the steps of these various processes depends on a knowledge of the course of natural events" and referred to capital instruments as the "supply of future wants." In his description of capital, he noted that (1) instruments are made by labor and other instruments; (2) capital is consumed, slowly or quickly (thus forming the important distinction between durable and nondurable goods); and (3) there is a time element in production and consumption. "Between the formation and exhaustion of instruments a space of time intervenes." Sometimes it could be months, sometimes years.[11]

Despite these occasional forays into a time-oriented, capital-using description of the economy, the idea that capital goods were unfinished products which ripened into consumption goods over a period of time was an uncommon approach in the early nineteenth century. It was only briefly and occasionally referred to by the principal classical economists. The most one can generally expect to find in that era was a highly simplified distinction between capital goods and consumer goods, or more generally, between production and consumption.[12]

THE MARXIAN NATURE OF CAPITALISTIC PRODUCTION

Karl Marx (1818–83), the most influential theorist in socialist economic thought, was heavily affected by Ricardian economics and adopted a labor factor-of-production approach to explain his peculiar theory of capitalist exploitation. Accordingly, Marx viewed capital and labor as essentially homogeneous in value, with no concept of a time structure of production in the Mengerian sense. Capital was heterogeneous in physical things and in exchange, but homogeneous in terms of labor value, when converted to monetary terms. Marx, like Adam Smith, also divided his economic model into two departments only: "commodity capital and commodity consumption."[13]

Granted, Marx made frequent reference to what he called the "process of capitalist production," but his formulation is quite distinct from the one presented here. When he analyzed the transformation of commodities over time, he stressed almost exclusively the monetary or exchange aspect of the industrial process. Marx used the term *metamorphosis of capital,* as if to liken the production process to the successive stages of larva, chrysalis, and moth; but not at all in the sense of the physical transformation of raw commodities into final consumer goods. Rather, he meant the production of goods for the marketplace, for money instead of self-consumption, and the separation of money from labor.

Marx's three stages of "circuit capital," mathematically represented as M—C—M, meant (1) the capitalist as buyer of commodities and labor, called *money capital;* (2) the transformation of capital into commodities of greater value, known as *productive capital;* and (3) the capitalist as seller to another capitalist or the consumer, termed *commodity capital.*[14] Only the second stage approaches the concept of a vertical production schedule, but even here Marx's emphasis is on the rate of profit for individual firms, irrespective of the position of the capitalist and his employees in the production process. Time and the durability of capital are also crucially important in Marx's methodology, but only insofar as they affect the "turnover of capital," and the necessity for capitalists to expand their market to avoid the "inevitable" decline in the rate of profit.[15]

Friedrich Engels (1820–95), in his preface to volume 3 of Karl Marx's *Capital,* made a short reference to the technical stages of production in an effort to expose the injustice of the capitalistic system. But while capitalists are categorized according to their distance from final consumption, Marxists see no reason why workers should be.

The capitalistic sellers, i.e., the raw material producer, the manufacturer, the wholesale trader and the retailer, make a profit in their businesses by each selling dearer than he buys, i.e., by increasing the price that his commodities cost him by a certain percentage. Only the worker is unable to obtain an additional value of this kind, for his unfortunate position vis-à-vis the capitalist compels him to sell his labour for the same price that it costs him himself, i.e., for the means of subsistence that he needs.[16]

MENGER: THE CAUSAL CONNECTION BETWEEN GOODS

The publication of Carl Menger's *Grundsätze der Volkswirtschaftslehre* (later translated into English as *Principles of Economics*) in 1871 was a landmark in the history of economic theory for two reasons. First, Carl Menger (1840–1921) established himself as one of the principal architects of microeconomics by formulating the principle of marginal utility, along with William Stanley Jevons (1835–82) and Léon Walras (1834–1910). (In contrast to Jevons and Walras, Menger's approach to marginal utility was strictly individualistic and subjective.) Second, he was the first economist to develop more fully a time structure of production and thus formulate the basis for a theory of macroeconomics. These two monumental contributions to the science of economics places the founder of the Austrian school among the great economic thinkers of our age.

Schumpeter recognized the universal applicability of Menger's marginal utility principle, which "covers the cost phenomenon and in consequence also the logic of the allocation of resources." Moreover, Menger's insights meant that the theory of distribution "really ceases to be a distinct topic," wrote Schumpeter, concluding, "The whole of the organon of pure economics thus finds itself unified in the light of a single principle—in a sense in which it never had been before."[17] Thus, there is little dispute over who was the primary mentor of the Austrian school: "Its fundamental ideas belong fully and wholly to Carl Menger," Hayek stated unequivocally.[18]

Menger's first chapter, "The General Theory of the Good," developed the principle of the "causal connection between goods." Menger rejected the simple two-good model (production goods and consumption goods) of the classical school. Instead of focusing on goods as if they were homogeneous, he envisioned consumer and capital goods as an *array* of goods—of the first order, the second order, the third order, and so forth.

Consumer goods are defined as "goods of first order," because they "serve our needs directly."[19] Goods of a second order are used in the production of goods of a first order. Goods of a third order are used in the production of second-order goods. And so forth. There is a vertical hierarchy in Menger's ordering of goods—from lower-order goods (close to consumption) to higher-order goods (furthest from consumption).

Production is defined as the process of transforming higher-order goods into successively lower-order goods. Menger viewed economic production as "[t]he process by which goods of higher order are progressively transformed into goods of lower order and by which these are directed finally to the satisfaction of human needs."[20] Like so many others, he used the simple example of making bread, a consumer good. Starting at the beginning of production, seed grain is planted in the ground by machines and labor. This stage represents "goods of a fourth order." The "goods of a third order" consist of grain mills, wheat, rye, and labor services, all used to produce flour. "Goods of a second order" include flour, baking utensils, and the journeyman baker and other workers to produce bread. The bread is a "good of first order," consumed by individuals.

Menger also emphasized the critical factors of time and uncertainty in the production process: "Time is an essential feature of our observations." The period of time it takes for higher-order goods to be transformed into lower-order goods may be long or short. An oak tree may take one hundred years before it can be cut, while the serving of food or beverages may take only a few moments, Menger commented.[21] Menger stressed the subjective nature of goods and the mutual interdependence of value between goods. Specifically, he developed the principle of imputation of value, how the value of higher-order capital goods depends on the value of lower-order consumer goods. As Menger put it, "The goods-character of goods of higher order is derived from that of the corresponding goods of lower order."[22]

Moreover, if the demand falls for a particular lower-order consumer good, the higher-order capital good used to produce the consumer good would not necessarily lose its value, but would fall to its next best *marginal* use. Menger used as his example tobacco consumption. If people stopped smoking, the price of all final tobacco products would fall to zero. But what about the value of higher-order goods used in the production of tobacco, such as raw tobacco leaves, tools used in making tobacco, tobacco seeds, tobacco farms, and accompanying labor services? Menger points out that those of *exclusive* or specialized use, such as tobacco seeds, would lose their entire value. But because farms and machinery have other uses, they do not lose their value completely. Their value falls to the next best *marginal* use. "Goods of higher order thus do not lose their goods-character," said Menger, "if but one, or if, in general, but a part of these needs ceases to be present."[23] In this manner Menger developed the principle of marginal utility.

Roger Garrison makes the critical point that Menger's value theory (as well as Turgot's) was a "sharp break from the Ricardian cost-of-production theories. . . . [T]he direction of causation was reversed by Menger. A consumption good is not valued *because* of the labor and other means of production that were used to produce it. Rather, the means of production are valued because of the prospective value of the consumption goods."[24]

JEVONS'S INVESTMENT FIGURES

William Stanley Jevons (1835–1882) pursued the same line as Menger, in both the principle of marginal utility and the theory of production. This was evidenced in his seminal work, *The Theory of Political Economy*, published in 1871. Jevons emphasized the importance of time and the period of production. He stated, "The single and all-important function of capital is to allow the laborer to await the result of any long-lasting work—to put an interval between the beginning and the end of enterprise."[25] Jevons also used his triangular "investment" figures to show the marginal increase in values as production moved from higher stages to lower stages toward consumption (see figure 2.1).

Figure 2.1. Jevons's Investment Figures

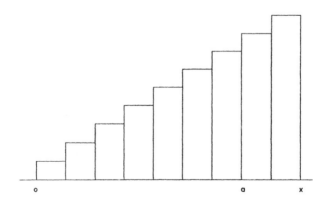

"The length along the line ox indicates the duration of investment, and the height attained at any point, a, is the amount of capital invested." Jevons, *The Theory of Political Economy*, 250.

Later in his *Principles of Economics,* he developed the concept of a period of production. He wrote extensively about "the orders of industry" and "the classification of trades," according to the stages of industrial production. He divided various occupations and trades into six general levels of industry, according to their distance from consumption: (1) sources of raw materials (e.g., landowners), (2) producers of raw materials (farmers), (3) dealers in raw materials (cotton traders), (4) manufacturers (bakers), (5) wholesalers (shippers), and (6) retailers (shopkeepers).[26]

However, Jevons ultimately rejected the concept of goods in varying lengths from consumption because the manufacture of products is often complex, involving many other intermediate goods of varying stages. "But, though the principal material of a trade, such as wheat, cotton, or wool, often pursues a simple linear course from the field to the household, there is often a very complicated pedigree when we take into account the series of minor materials and implements required at the several stages of production."[27] He reached the conclusion that "it is hopeless to attempt to draw out any written or printed scheme of classification which could in the least degree cope with the complexities of industrial relations."[28]

Fellow British economist Alfred Marshall (1842–1924) concurred with Jevons's conclusions. "Of course a good may belong to several orders at the same time," Marshall stated in the third edition of his popular textbook.[29] In a later edition, he stated that Carl Menger "says bread belongs to the first order, flour to the second, a flour mill to the third order and so on. It appears that if a railway train carries people on a pleasure excursion, also some tins of biscuits, and milling machinery and some machinery that is used for making milling machinery; then the train is at one and the same time a good of the first, second, third and fourth orders." The Mengerian distinction between consumers' goods and producers' goods seemed "vague and perhaps not of much practical value."[30]

MENGER'S STUDENTS: WIESER AND BÖHM-BAWERK

Menger's followers continued to amplify and refine his theory of sequential processes. Friedrich von Wieser (1851–1926) defined Menger's structure of production as a "stratification" and "complete genealogy" of the economy, elucidating the "vertical and horizontal relationship of all productive goods and all products."[31] Wieser developed a theory of economic growth based on this framework. "As production becomes more highly developed, it extends through a greater number of stages. It operates with the aid of many more capital goods and much more labor."[32] In essence, the length of the capital process increases, and "capital in its simultaneous increase and improvement is applied to more and more remote stages of production."[33]

Eugen von Böhm-Bawerk (1851–1914), who was one of Austria's foremost economists and statesmen at the turn of the century, made a systematic critique of the theories of capital and interest, and engaged in a broadside attack on Marx. His principal theoretical work, *The Positive Theory of Capital*, was first published in 1889, and was based on Menger's premises, although at critical junctures he departed from Menger. The work received considerable acclaim and criticism, especially after it was translated into English in 1890. Böhm-Bawerk's period of production model is still a principal point of debate in capital theory, and in the words of one sympathetic critic, his concept is "a ghost that haunts the structure of economic theory."[34]

Böhm-Bawerk was also the principal architect and defender of the time preference theory of interest. It is based on the "cardinal principle . . . that present goods have a higher value than future goods of like kind and quantity."[35] He defended this approach against Clark's productivity theory of interest and other competing theories, although he adopted some elements of the productivity arguments in his concept of "roundaboutness."

Böhm-Bawerk began by defining capital: "Capital is nothing but the complex of intermediate products which appear on the several stages of the roundabout journey."[36] His definition of capital excluded lands, durable consumer goods, and "all goods that serve for immediate satisfaction of wants."[37] Following Menger's path, he stated that capital goods lie at varying distances from consumption, which he illustrated with "concentric annual circles," similar to tree rings (see figure 2.2). As Böhm-Bawerk stated:

Many an intermediate product has just entered on a very lengthy roundabout road, as, for instance, a boring machine, whose life-work it will be to drive a gallery in a mine. Some are midway. Others, again, like clothing stuffs ready for making into coats and mantles, are near the end of the journey their particular production process has to take.[38]

Thus, Böhm-Bawerk's "Austrian" approach envisioned capital "longitudinally through time rather than cross-sectionally, as a succession of intermediate products moving through the production process, changing at every stage as they absorbed primary factor services, and ultimately destroying themselves in a harvest of consumption goods."[39] According to Kuenne, Böhm-Bawerk's view of capital is "organic," like a seed that is planted, absorbs primary services, and over a period of time, is harvested as a consumption good.[40] This sets the stage for two contrasting views of capital theory—the Austrian view of circulating capital moving through stages versus the neoclassical view of fixed capital yielding a return. Frank H. Knight made the comparison succinctly: "What Jevons

Figure 2.2. Böhm-Bawerk's "Concentric Annual Circles"

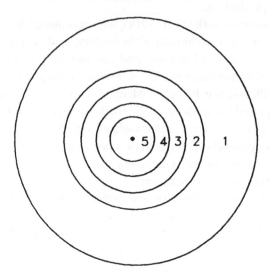

"The outmost circle embraces those goods which will be transformed into goods ready for consumption within the coming year; the second circle represents those goods which will ripen into consumption goods in the year after; the third circle, those which will be ready in the year after that, and so on." Eugen von Böhm-Bawerk, *Capital and Interest*, trans. George D. Huncke, Hans F. Sennholz, 3 vols. (Spring Mills, Penn.: Libertarian Press, 1959) vol. 2, *The Positive Theory of Capital*, 106–7.

and Böhm-Bawerk do to the Ricardo-Mill theory of distribution and of capital is essentially to drop the assumption of a natural annual cycle in production and the corresponding fixity of proportions between labour and capital, and to make the quantity of capital (for a given quantity of labour and land) a linear function of a variable production period."[41]

ROUNDABOUT METHODS AND THE "AVERAGE" PERIOD OF PRODUCTION

Böhm-Bawerk made extensive use of the term *roundabout* in describing the capitalistic process as the basis for his theory of economic expansion. By roundabout, he meant the indirect use of capital goods in order to make consumption goods. Roundabout methods are used, according to Böhm-Bawerk, to increase output. He used several examples, one of which is as follows:

I require stone for building a house. There is a rich vein of excellent sandstone in a neighbouring hill. How is it to get out? First, I may work the loose stones back and forward with my bare fingers, and break off what can be broken off. This is the most direct, but also the least productive way. Second, I may take a piece of iron, make a hammer and chisel out of it, and use them on the hard stone—a roundabout way, which, of course, leads to a very much better result than the former. Third method—having a hammer and chisel I use them to drill a hole in the rock; next I turn my attention to procuring charcoal, sulphur, and nitre, and mixing them in a powder, then I pour the powder into the hole, and the explosion that follows splits the stone into convenient pieces—still more of a roundabout way, but one which, as experience shows, is as much superior to the second way in result as the second was to the first.[42]

The lesson is: "A greater result is obtained by producing goods in roundabout ways than by producing them directly." Böhm-Bawerk concluded, "That roundabout methods lead to greater results than direct methods is one of the most important and fundamental propositions in the whole theory of production."[43]

But the formation of capital takes time. "The roundabout ways of capital are fruitful but long," said Böhm-Bawerk. "They procure us more and better consumption goods, but only at a later period of time."[44] He continued, "And again, the higher the degree of capitalism is, the more remote will be the period at which these intermediate products mature."[45]

Böhm-Bawerk then tried to measure the period of production—the total number of stages it takes to produce a good, from the time "that lies between the expenditure of the first atom of labour and the last" in producing a good. Böhm-Bawerk was well aware of the historic fact that the number of stages might be infinite—"cracking of nuts with a hammer which might chance to be made of iron brought from a mine opened by the Romans would perhaps be the most 'capitalistic' kind of production."[46] He therefore opted for an "average" period-of-production concept, since indirect work done a good many centuries earlier would be so small that it would "scarcely influence the average, and may in most cases be simply neglected."[47]

Böhm-Bawerk's idea of an average period of production came under heavy criticism by opponents and supporters alike. Garrison states that Böhm-Bawerk "tried to capture this important insight into the relationship between the maturity classes with a single number, the average period of production. The attempt to stipulate just how such an average period could be calculated led Böhm-Bawerk away from the Mengerian vision in which all values are subjective."[48] It was in part because of this average formulation that Menger referred to Böhm-Bawerk's theory as "one of the greatest errors ever committed."[49] And Streissler opined that "Böhm's analysis was much *too one-dimensional* for Menger. . . .

Menger would describe the accumulation of capital as an increase in the range of capital goods and an ever-increasing complexity of the web of complementarities, while Böhm unified capital by the concept of the period of production."[50]

THE AUSTRIAN INFLUENCE ON
WICKSELL AND THE SWEDISH SCHOOL

Knut Wicksell (1851–1926) and other Swedish economists favored the Austrian concept of a time-consuming, capital-using process of production, but did not apply it consistently. No doubt this was due to the fact that Wicksell was greatly influenced by two works, Böhm-Bawerk's *Positive Theory of Capital,* and Leon Walras's *Elements of Pure Economics. As* Lachmann aptly put it, "Wicksell's major claim to fame was to have linked the Böhm-Bawerkian theory of capital to the Walrasian equilibrium system."[51]

Wicksell referred to the Austrian view of the economy as "the stratification of capital through time."[52] Capital was not treated as a lump sum, but as something having "technical dimensions and composition," with an emphasis on the future.[53] Wicksell's particular emphasis was on capital as a way of maturing or seasoning resources toward their ultimate consumption.

Wicksell used a general diagram (see figure 2.3) to describe the output of consumer and producer goods over a four-year period. (Note the similarity to Jevons's investment figures, figure 2.1.)

Figure 2.3. Wicksell's Production Diagram

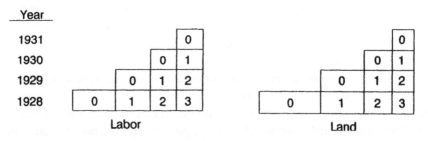

The figures 1, 2, and 3 indicate capital groups which are 1, 2, and 3 years old, respectively, i.e., originated in 1927, 1926, and 1925. 0 represents current resources of labor and land. Total consumption goods for 1928 are 0, 1, 2, and 3 combined. Total capital production for 1929 represents 0, 1, and 2 combined, and so on. Note how each section increases—in 1928, 0 is larger than 1, 1 larger than 2, and 2 larger than 3. The total group increases each year as new land and labor are added. Wicksell, *Lectures on Political Economy,* vol. 1, 152, 159. Reprinted by permission of Routledge.

The Swedish economist favored Böhm-Bawerk's roundabout concept of capital accumulation and economic growth. One of his prime examples was the case of wine maturing over time, in which he showed that an increase in the savings/capital ratio could make an older (more roundabout) year of wine more profitable.[54] As Carl G. Uhr noted, "Wicksell's discovery that as capital formation proceeds, other factors constant, investment in capital goods of long-maturation terms becomes relatively more profitable than in goods of short term, and that therefore investment will progressively be shifted to goods of long term, with the result that wages and rents rise and interest declines less than they would otherwise do, constitutes an important hypothesis." According to Uhr, this means that there is a direct link between the time dimension of real capital and interest rates.[55] Erik Lindahl said that this hypothesis was Wicksell's most important contribution to capital theory.[56]

Perhaps as a result of Walras's influence, Wicksell did not use the variable capital structure concept in analyzing his "cumulative process" of credit expansion and the development of business cycle theory. In *Interest and Prices,* Wicksell made a number of oversimplified assumptions which glossed over the multi-stage concept of production. For example: "We neglect the fact that capital changes hands before it has completed the full circle."[57] According to Garrison, "Not only is the concept of capital simplified and sterilized in Wicksell's exposition, but the time dimension of the production process, which was so emphasized by Böhm-Bawerk, is also put in a straitjacket. The multi-stage process of production becomes in effect a single stage."[58]

Wicksell foresaw a credit boom first occurring in capital goods, but felt it would quickly spread to consumer goods as well. He therefore assumed a Walrasian-type closed economy where there is no variable production structure, based on unrealistic assumptions (economy only producing consumer goods, capitalists do not own any capital, and so on).[59] Hicks also noted that Wicksell's monetary theory only suggested price changes in response to an artificial decline in the interest rate below the natural rate. "Nothing is said about the movement of quantities (inputs and outputs)."[60]

Gustav Cassel (1866–1944) discussed the concept of "waiting for production" in his work, *The Nature and Necessity of Interest,* published in 1903. In addressing the question of how much time is required to produce a good, he stressed the fact that historically business and technology have sought to "shorten the periods of production," and concluded that time is not a significant factor of production.[61]

Moreover, Cassel rejected the stages-of-production approach of Menger and the Austrians, at least in theory. Writing in Clark-Walrasian fashion, he exclaimed, "In actual life, production is always a continuous process, whose partial processes are continually being concluded and commenced again, and which, after a certain lapse of time, will show the same features as the present, provided its scale has not increased and methods of production have remained unchanged."[62]

Rejecting the Mengerian stage concept as "completely futile," he concluded: "In other words, the productive process as a whole does not share the characteristic movement of the material it transforms, which, in production, ascends to higher and higher stages of transformation, until it emerges from the process as a finished article. The productive process has no beginning and no end."[63]

However, according to Howard Ellis, Cassel was the first economist to statistically demonstrate that "booms are characterized by an increase in the production of fixed capital, depressions by a slackening of that production" while the prices of consumer goods vary slightly. Cassel also pointed out that the greatest variability in employment was in the capital-goods industries.[64] Such an approach to the business cycle suggests that Cassel did not reject all the tenets of Austrian economic theory.

Gustav Åkerman (1888–1959) was the first Swedish economist to introduce durable capital goods in his highly mathematical treatise *Real Kapital and Kapitalzins,* published in the early 1920s.[65] By contrast to Böhm-Bawerk, his model does not refer to circulating capital. Åkerman also rejected Böhm-Bawerk's concept of the average period of production, and tried to determine the optimum length of life of a machine, given its market price and wage rate (cost). But Åkerman's model is flawed by the very fact that he tried to measure the optimum life of a machine without using the interest rate. As Lutz states, "The correct way to calculate the value of durable goods is that of discounting the flow of their future returns."[66]

It should also be noted at this time that a French economist, Albert Aftalion (1874–1956), developed a theory of business cycles based on the imputation theory of Menger and the theory of roundabout, capitalistic production by Böhm-Bawerk. In his two-volume work, *Les crises periodiques de surproduction,* published in Paris in 1913, Aftalion argued that changes in the demand for consumer goods caused accelerated changes in the demand for investment goods, thus anticipating the "acceleration principle" developed by J. M. Clark. "There are products, notably raw materials, sold in highly centralized markets, the prices of which are very sensitive and vary with much greater rapidity than do those of the semimanufactured and finished goods in the manufacture of which they are used."[67] Aftalion, however, did not realize how the overissue of bank credit could cause the same effect through lower interest rates, as Mises and Hayek argued elsewhere.

THE DEBATE BETWEEN CLARK AND BÖHM-BAWERK

The first major attack on the Austrian theory of capital and production came in the late 1890s from John Bates Clark (1847–1938), a professor at Columbia University, in response to the publication of the 1890 English translation of Böhm-Bawerk's *Positive Theory of Capital.*

Strange as it may seem, Clark initially developed an economic model based on Menger's view of stages of output. In his principles text, *The Distribution of Wealth,* published in 1899, he used several examples of products going through a process of transformation. In the following table (figure 2.4), Clark marked groups A, B, and C, followed by subgroups:

Figure 2.4. Clark's Table of Commodity Groups and Subgroups

A'''	B'''	C'''	H'''
A''	B''	C''	H''
A'	B'	C'	H'
A'	B'	C'	H'

Source: Clark, The Distribution of Wealth, 268.

In the above example, A represents the production of bread; B the production of clothing; and C the production of houses. Each case was highly simplified. ("We are putting a myriad of facts for the moment out of sight, in order that we may isolate and clearly understand certain other facts.") A is standing wheat, A' threshed and winnowed wheat stored in the granary, A'' is flour and A''' is bread. B is wool on the sheep's backs, B' is wool stored in the warehouse, B'' is cloth, B''' is clothing. C is forest trees, C' is saw-logs, C'' is lumber, and C''' is housing. Clark also created an H category to represent the production of tools and machinery used in the production of A, B, and C output.[68] The H's "go everywhere through the system, replacing instruments that are worn out."[69]

However, Clark argued that once the production system is complete (where, for example, all stages A through A''' are being produced), there is a "synchronised process of production and consumption."[70] Production and consumption are occurring simultaneously. In a critique of Böhm-Bawerk's capital theory in the November 1893 issue of *Yale Review,* he stated that there is, ipso facto, no waiting involved in the production process. (He preferred the term *abstinence*.) "Today we work, and today we eat; and the eating is the effect of working."[71] In further explanation, Clark stated several years later, "I have claimed that no one has to wait for his income through the so-called periods of production, so that, in connection with them, this comparison of present and future does not need to be made at all. It is made only in connection with the creation of new capital."[72]

Clark denied the existence of a period of production, the lengthening of production, or time sacrifice. "Production might go on forever, either by long periods or by short ones; and, if there is no new capital created, there is no time sacrifice incurred. This is equivalent to saying that interest can be earned under perfectly static conditions, and that in such conditions there is no incurring of time sacrifice."[73]

Clark did not treat "true capital" as "concrete capital goods," as did the Austrians, but rather as a "permanent fund" that continually yields services and interest. Clark used several mechanical examples to demonstrate his theory. In the case of a reservoir, the river of water flows in (production) and out (consumption), while the reservoir itself remains a permanent quantity. "Pumping water in at one end will cause an outflow at the other. And this is a sufficiently accurate picture of what takes place in industry."[74]

In another well-used example, he compared the economy to a forest of trees, with firewood as the ultimate consumption good.

> The fact . . . is that, if we have once secured the permanent forest, we have no waiting to do for fuel. The identity of the tree that we burn is of no consequence. To plant one and burn another that is at once made available in consequence of the planting of the one is to annihilate the interval that would have existed if it had been necessary to depend on one particular tree. Moreover, the rate at which the trees grow is of no consequence, except as it fixes the size of the forest that we have to maintain. If one row of trees has to be cut each year, and if the trees mature in twenty years, then the forest must contain twenty rows in order to supply the demand that is made on it and to continue undiminished in size. If it takes forty years for the trees to grow to the point at which we cut them, the forest will have to contain forty rows. It will be twice as large as in the former case. If, however, the larger forest has once been secured, there is no waiting to be done in order to get those that had forty years of growth. We continue the planting and the simultaneous cutting, as in the former case.[75]

In general, Clark argued, "All products are gradually matured; and it is necessary to maintain in constant existence a series of them in various stages of competition. We must have growing cattle, hides, tanned leather, partly made shoes and finished shoes, all maintained in a constant quantity, in order that a certain number of shoes may each day be taken for use; but, *if this series of capital goods is so maintained*, the ranchman, the tanner, and the shoemaker may all get finished shoes today in consequence of the work of today."[76]

In the end, ultimately, Clark adopted a "productivity" theory of interest, instead of Böhm-Bawerk's time preference theory of interest. Clark denied any meaning for the lengthening or roundaboutness of capital output. "What is clear," he concluded, "is that the periods of production marked by the ripening time of particular capital goods may be lengthened or shortened without affecting the productivity of industry."[77] On the other hand, Clark's own view on capital and interest was: "As the capital, and not the time required for creating and using it, is the cause of the product that takes the form of interest, so changes in the amount of capital itself, and not a lengthening or shortening of productive periods, are the causes that affect the rate of interest. Make the social fund larger, and you make the rate of interest smaller."[78]

BÖHM-BAWERK'S RESPONSE

Böhm-Bawerk responded to Clark's attack in a series of articles in the *Quarterly Journal of Economics* during 1895–96. Both Clark and Böhm-Bawerk wrote additional responses to each other, as well as other critics, in the economics journals during this time as well as 1906–1907.

Böhm-Bawerk rejected Clark's definition of capital as well as his "timeless, permanent fund" idea. Labeling Clark's theory "a mystical concept," he added, "Everything accomplished by the so-called capital in the world of mechanics and commerce is accomplished solely by the concrete, useful capital goods—or it is not accomplished at all."[79] Responding to Clark's idea that individuals can produce and consume simultaneously, Böhm-Bawerk stated that "a laborer who in the year 1894 dresses a hide, out of which in the year 1895 a pair of shoes is made, can in the year 1894 in immediate exchange for his raw product, leather, obtain a pair of shoes ready-made, *if* and *because* there was on hand in society in the year 1894 a separate stock of concrete capital goods in more advanced stages of production, out of which to create in the year 1894 a pair of finished shoes."[80]

A decade later, Böhm-Bawerk continued the counterattack in a review of Clark's text, *The Distribution of Wealth*. In the book, Clark argued that a completed coat is the product of *today's* labor.[81] But Böhm-Bawerk disagreed: "The undeniable fact is that my coat has been fashioned with the co-operation of the shepherd of a past period. He alone supplies the wool for *my* coat; so of the spinner, the weaver, and the like. Society does not enjoy, in the shape of completed coats, the product of the laborer who is now tending sheep. Society must wait as many days, months or years as are inevitable in the process of production which transform the raw material, wool, into the completed coat."[82]

In the same article, he labeled Clark's productivity theory of capital as a "value jelly" which is a "fiction" and a "fatal notion." He noted similarities between Clark and Marx—both teach that "production brings enjoyable results without an interval of time."[83]

CLARK'S REJOINDER

Clark offered a rejoinder regarding the completed coat. He stated, "If we want the coat that will at some time have been made out of the wool that is now on the sheep's back, we shall have to wait for it; but, if we merely want a coat, we shall not. . . . The securing of the coat made of wool taken out of the existing stock is by the co-operation of the man who is raising other wool to take the place of it."[84] In the same article, Clark made another comparison to illustrate his macro concept of the economy: "As the Hudson River, which flows by my door, is regarded as the same river that the Dutch explorer discovered in 1609, so the capital, some portion of which may have been handed down from a father to his descendants for as long a period, is regarded as having a like continuance." But: "The present Hudson is the original one, and so is the present Danube."[85]

In a final rejoinder, Böhm-Bawerk concluded, "The capital of today is not identical with the capital goods of yesterday. . . . I do not deny that the desired commodities are in fact obtained, under the conditions described by Professor Clark, without waiting; but they are obtained not in consequence of today's labor, not in consequence of present pumping, but because they have been made ready by a chain of operations extending through the past."[86]

OTHER COMMENTS ON THE DEBATE
BETWEEN CLARK AND BÖHM-BAWERK

T. N. Carver (1865–1961) was also critical of Clark's timeless capital theory. In response to Clark's example of tree forests to show that there is no waiting in the economy, Carver stated: "It was the planting of a tree twenty years ago, and that alone, which enables the family to have a fire today. Here, as before, the only way in which the family can realize at once on the labor of planting trees is by finding some one who is willing to advance the present value of the trees and himself wait for them to mature." Exchange shifts the burden of waiting to another, but does not eliminate it. The tree-planter "can reap a virtual reward at once by selling the trees just planted to some one who is willing to do the waiting. What he will normally be able to get will be the expected future value of the trees, minus the cost of waiting for them to mature. . . . What really happens here is that one member of the community has undertaken to do the waiting for another."[87]

Thus, waiting is always present in the economy—it can never be eliminated. In response to Clark's example of the cowboy who gets his shoes today by his own efforts, Carver stated, "The laborer does not wait for the product of today's labor because others do the waiting for him."[88]

Harvard Professor Frank W. Taussig (1859–1940) also took issue with Clark's view of synchronized production and consumption. He developed a diagram similar to Clark's (figure 2.5), as follows:

Figure 2.5. Taussig's Stages of Production

In 1907	A	A'	A''	A'''
In 1908	A	A'	A''	A'''
In 1909	A	A'	A''	A'''
In 1910	A	A'	A''	A'''

Source: Taussig, "Capital, Interest, and Diminishing Returns," 338. Reprinted by permission of John Wiley and Sons, Inc.

A through A''' represent successive stages of production, with A being the earliest capital good and A''' being the final end product. Note that each stage is being produced simultaneously in each year. The horizontal line represents current production. The diagonal line represents the transformation of A to A''' over a four-year period of time. Figure 2.5 assumes that each stage takes only one year to complete, a distortion that Taussig readily admitted. "Any scheme, or diagram, or classification of the stages of production must have a rigid and arbitrary character, and can not conform to the endless complexities of the living industrial world."[89] In responding to Clark's view of this diagram, Taussig stated, "It is not the horizontal line running through 1907 that represents the course of production, but the oblique [diagonal] line that runs through all four periods." Clark argued that once the full process is working (A to A'''), it makes no difference which order is considered. But Taussig made a profound observation—Clark had made a fundamental error in equating the horizontal production function with the diagonal function! As Taussig concluded: "There is not, in fact, any 'synchronization' of production or any 'instantaneous' clothing of the people."[90]

THE DEBATE OVER CAPITAL IN THE UNITED STATES

Taussig appears to be one of the few major American economists who adopted a pro-Austrian view of the economy in the early twentieth century. According to Schumpeter, Taussig considered Böhm-Bawerk the second greatest economist of all time (next to Ricardo).[91] In *Wages and Capital,* he surveyed the economy in terms of various stages of production. "Some laborers are at work in mines digging out ore and coal. Others are at work conveying coal and ore, which had been brought out days or weeks before, to the spot where they are to be used. Others, again, at that spot are engaged in converting materials of still earlier extraction into pig iron. Elsewhere, men are at work fashioning tools and machinery for spinning or weaving; or making up cloth into garments wherewith to protect us from cold and wet, and to satisfy our vanity or caprice."[92]

Taussig adopted Böhm-Bawerk's roundabout thesis of economic growth. He referred to several historical examples of how production techniques and machines have replaced older, less productive methods. In each case, it involved more time and capital to build. "The spinning wheel and the hand loom, easily and simply made, have given way to . . . the power loom, fixed in a great building, and moved by complicated machinery; all involving a longer stage of preparatory effort, and yielding the enjoyable commodity in the end on easier terms."[93] However, Taussig rejected Böhm-Bawerk's average period of production concept, because "[i]f we would be mathematically accurate, we should need to carry it [production] back, to the time when the first tool was made."[94]

Later, in his textbook, *Principles of Economics,* Taussig devoted a chapter to the "organization of production," which he divided according to where the worker or producer is located on the intertemporal transformation process,

One producer—that is, a capitalist hiring and directing a group of workmen—carried on ore mining, and disposed of his ore to other producers engaged in smelting it into pig iron. Still another producer similarly cut the wood and converted it into charcoal—this in earlier days when wood supplied the fuel for iron making; or, after coke supplanted charcoal, mined the coal and made it into coke. The pig-iron maker, who had bought the ore and the fuel, sold his product to the puddler or steel maker, who in turn sold his bar iron or steel to the machinist, the builder, the wire maker.[95]

On the other hand, Yale's Irving Fisher (1867–1947), America's foremost quantity theorist, pursued a theoretical angle more compatible with Clark's capital theme. "Capital is a fund and income a flow," stated Fisher in his work, *The Nature of Capital and Income*.[96] Fisher focused on a heavily macroeconomic approach, emphasizing general price levels and an aggregate quantity of capital.[97]

Frank A. Fetter (1863–1949), professor of economics at Cornell and Princeton, has been called "the leader in the United States of the early Austrian school of economics," particularly for his explanation of interest rates solely on the basis of time preference.[98] In a series of articles in the early 1900s, Fetter objected to some of the views of both Clark and Böhm-Bawerk.[99] He questioned Clark's capital concept of a timeless, permanent fund.

Fetter also pointed out that while Böhm-Bawerk adopted a time preference theory of interest, Böhm-Bawerk contradicted himself by claiming that interest is accounted for by the productivity of roundabout processes. Fetter stated, "And yet this is out of harmony, first, with the author's own strong negative criticism of productivity theories as affording only incomplete answers to the interest problem and, secondly, with his formal statement of the theory of interest as due to the difference between the value of present and that of future goods."[100]

In his textbook, *The Principles of Economics,* Fetter devoted a section to the "genealogy of value," which traces "various intermediate products to consumption goods." Figure 2.6 reproduces his diagram showing the "complex relations

Figure 2.6. Fetter's Genealogy of Value

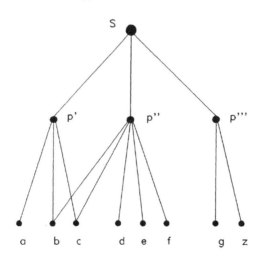

Source: Fetter, *Principles of Economics*, 280.

through intermediate products."[101] S represents the primary source of the inter-mediate circulating capital goods, p. Note how one of the intermediate goods, p″, is used as an input in the manufacture of more than one consumer good (b and c).

However, Fetter may have weakened in his support of the Austrian view of economics near the end of his career. In 1927, he gave a glowing tribute to John Bates Clark at the celebration of his eightieth birthday. At the symposium, he surprisingly stated, "Böhm-Bawerk's conclusions on the capital concept were surprisingly old-fashioned." He quoted approvingly of Fisher's view of the stock/flow dichotomy and concluded that Clark "advanced in the right direc-tion, showing the way to us."[102]

SCHUMPETER AND MISES: EXTENDING THE AUSTRIAN ANALYSIS

While the Clark-Fisher treatment of capital as a homogeneous fund gained sup-port in the United States, the Austrian view of capital as an array of hetero-geneous capital goods continued to flourish in Europe (with the exception of Cassel, who favored Clark's view of capital).

The early writings of Joseph Schumpeter (1883–1950) were partly influ-enced by Menger and Böhm-Bawerk. In *The Theory of Economic Development*, he utilized Menger's concept of the "orders" of goods.[103] However, in due time Schumpeter, under heavy influence from Walras, favored the Clark-Fisher fund-and-flow approach. Like Clark, he envisioned the economy as a "river-bed" with water ("stream") flowing through it.[104] Still, Schumpeter included three Austrian economists—Menger, Böhm-Bawerk, and Wieser—in his biographical work, *Ten Great Economists*.[105] In addition, in his work on business cycles, Schumpeter granted Hayek's trade-cycle theory as a correct interpretation of the 1929–33 economic debacle.[106]

Ludwig von Mises (1881–1973) was a more consistent follower of Menger and Böhm-Bawerk. However, Mises appears to have devoted little attention in his published writings to capital and interest theory until his magnum opus, *Human Action*, was published in 1949.[107]

In his *Theory of Money and Credit*, the first edition of which was published in German in 1912, Mises developed a business-cycle theory based on Wicksell's natural interest rate hypothesis, Menger's hierarchy of production, and Böhm-Bawerk's roundaboutness. An artificially lower rate of interest will lengthen the period of production, according to Mises, but the expansion of capital goods cannot last, precipitating a crisis and economic depression. "A time must nec-essarily come when the means of subsistence available for consumption are all used up although the capital goods employed in production have not yet been transformed into consumption goods . . . [A] counter-movement sets in: the prices of consumption goods rise, those of production goods fall."[108]

In *Human Action,* Mises defined capital goods as "intermediary products which in the further course of production activities are transformed into consumers' goods."[109] Mises was highly critical of economists who defined capital as an aggregate of all physical goods. "Capital, it is said, reproduces itself and thus provides for its own maintenance. Capital, says the Marxian, hatches out profit. All this is nonsense."[110] Instead, Mises adopted Menger's structural order of goods. "It is possible to think of the producers' goods as arranged in orders according to their proximity to the consumers' good for whose production they can be used."[111]

Mises challenged Böhm-Bawerk's view of time and the average period of production. The role that time "plays in action consists entirely in the choices acting man makes between periods of production of different length. The length of time expended in the past for the production of capital goods available today does not count at all. . . . The 'average period of production' is an empty concept."[112]

The stage was thus set for Mises' most famous student, Friedrich A. Hayek, to usher in a brand-new vision of macroeconomics, capturing the imagination of some of the brightest young economists in the Anglo-American world for a few brief years.

NOTES

1. Quesnay, *Tableau Economique.* See also Hollander, *Classical Economics,* 49–59.
2. Turgot, "Reflections on the Formation and the Distribution of Wealth (1766)," 44.
3. Ibid., 70.
4. Smith, *The Wealth of Nations,* 8.
5. "The classical economists considered as productive labour only that which was embodied in the production of material goods. All services which were intended for the immediate satisfaction of wants, and served the consumer without the intervention of material goods, were regarded as unproductive." Cassel, *The Theory of Social Economy,* 20. Cassel rejected this dichotomy. "All personal services . . . must be regarded as productive."
6. Smith, *The Wealth of Nations,* 294–301. Smith may have adopted a one-stage production concept: "The value of the goods circulated between the different dealers never can exceed the value of those circulated between dealers and consumers; whatever is bought by the dealer being ultimately destined to be sold to the consumer." (342).
7. Ricardo, *On the Principles of Political Economy and Taxation,* 34. According to Schumpeter, Ricardo viewed capital as immature consumer goods, like Taussig's "inchoate

wealth." Schumpeter, *History of Economic Analysis,* 636–37. Knut Wicksell also discerned in Ricardo a conception of the greater productivity of longer "construction periods" *à la* Böhm-Bawerk. See Stigler, *Production and Distribution Theories,* 284. Nevertheless, it is clear that Ricardo's cost-of-production approach was quite the opposite of the marginal subjectivists *à la* Menger and Jevons: "The prices of commodities, too, are regulated by their cost of production." Ricardo, "On Machinery," in *On the Principles of Political Economy and Taxation,* 397.

8. Mill, *Collected Works,* book 2, 31. Similarly, J. B. Say developed a theory of imputation, but he did not have any marginal analysis available. See Bowley, *Studies in the History of Economic Theory,* 127.

9. See S. Hollander, *The Economics of John Stuart Mill,* 259.

10. *The Economic Writings of Mountifort Longfield,* 163. Cf. Schumpeter, *History of Economic Analysis,* 465.

11. J. Rae, *New Principles of Political Economy* (1834), reprinted as *The Sociological Theory of Capital,* 19–24. Cf. Schumpeter, *History of Economic Analysis,* 468–69. Mixter argued strenuously that Rae was "A Forerunner of Böhm-Bawerk" (*Quarterly Journal of Economics,* January 1897), and "By reason of the lack of a theory of invention, Böhm-Bawerk's doctrine of capital, although coming much later, is in essentials the less complete of the two." *The Sociological Theory of Capital,* xvi.

12. Thus, Sismondi considered "the balance of consumption and production" to be "the fundamental question in political economy." J. C. I. Simonde de Sismondi, *Etudes sur l'économie politique,* vol. 1 (Chez Treuttel et Wurtz, Libraries, 1887), 96–97.

13. Desai, *Marxian Economics,* 29, 40–41. Jeremy Bray notes, "In seeking a socialist theory of production, we are concerned not with the actual chemistry or mechanics—the technology—of physical processes, but with the human actions and more particularly the human decisions which bring the physical processes about." Bray, *Production, Purpose and Structure,* 8.

14. Karl Marx, *Capital,* vol. 2, 109. The only direct reference I could find by Marx on the technical stages of production is in his lengthy comment, "The Chapter on Capital," in *Grundrisse,* 361. Referring to the "simple production process," Marx stated, "When cotton becomes yarn, yarn becomes fabric, fabric becomes printed etc. or dyed etc. fabric, and this becomes, say, a garment, then (1) the substance of cotton has preserved itself in all these forms. . . . (2) in each of these subsequent processes, the material has obtained a more useful form, a form making it more appropriate to consumption."

15. Marx, *Capital,* vol. 2, 200–236, 316–68.

16. Engels, Preface to Marx, *Capital,* vol. 3, 99. Engels failed to take into account the fact that the capitalist at each stage has as his cost the price of the previous stage; there is no profit gained from the previous stage's profit; his profit is the marginal compensation for taking the risk of transforming the product into the next stage, while the laborer is paid his marginal product, discounted according to the distance from final consumption of the product he helps produce.

17. Schumpeter, *History of Economic Analysis,* 913. Knut Wicksell added that by 1921, "No book since Ricardo's *Principles* has had such a great influence as Menger's *Grundsätze,*

not even the work of Jevons, nor that of Walras." Quoted in Uhr, "Wicksell and the Austrians," 200. See Wicksell, "Carl Menger [1921]," *Selected Papers on Economic Theory*, 186–92.

18. Hayek, quoted in E. Streissler, "To What Extent Was the Austrian School Marginalist?" 162n.
19. Menger, *The Principles of Economics*, 56.
20. Ibid., 67. Menger's choice of terminology ("higher" and "lower" orders) has been criticized as confusing. Higher order goods may be confused with, e.g., highly finished goods. Perhaps "early" and "later" stages are more appropriate, but I have stayed with the original Menger usage, particularly in developing the graphic representation of the production process.
21. Ibid., 67–68. Streissler added, "One might, perhaps, condense the contrast between Menger and Walras thus: Walras's tâtonnement takes a minute; Menger's tâtonnement takes a century!" Streissler, "To What Extent Was the Austrian School Marginalist?" 174.
22. Menger, *The Principles of Economics*, 63.
23. Ibid., 65–66.
24. Garrison, "The Austrian-Neoclassical Relation," 19. Streissler summarized Menger's philosophy: "Menger's *Grundsätze* was an attempt to sketch a theory of economic development. . . . The central thesis of the book [is]: It is not so much the division of labor, that is to say, a feature of the productive process, that increases welfare, but the constant widening of the range of goods and the improvement of their quality, i.e., changes in the productive output." (Streissler, "To What Extent Was the Austrian School Marginalist?" 164). Streissler noted that even the division of labor is enhanced by this technical progress, which involves three dimensions of dynamic change: quantity, quality, and variety (164–65).
25. Jevons, *The Theory of Political Economy*, 226.
26. Jevons, *The Principles of Economics*, 108–13.
27. Ibid., 117.
28. Ibid., 115.
29. Marshall, *Principles of Economics*, 64–65.
30. Marshall, *Principles of Economics*, 64.
31. Wieser, *Social Economics*, 47–48.
32. Ibid., 72.
33. Ibid., 71–72.
34. Kuenne, *Eugen von Böhm-Bawerk*, 73.
35. Eugen von Böhm-Bawerk, "The Positive Theory of Capital and Its Critics, I," 115. Also see Böhm-Bawerk, *History and Critique of Interest Theory*, vol. 1 of *Capital and Interest*.
36. Böhm-Bawerk, *The Positive Theory of Capital*, 22.
37. Ibid., 31.
38. Ibid., 107–8.
39. Kuenne, *Eugen von Böhm-Bawerk*, 11–12.
40. Ibid., 20.
41. F. H. Knight, "Capitalistic Production, Time and the Rate of Return," 328.

42. Böhm-Bawerk, *Positive Theory of Capital*, 18–19.

43. Ibid., 20.

44. Ibid., 82.

45. Ibid., 91.

46. Ibid., 90.

47. Ibid., 89.

48. Garrison, "The Austrian-Neoclassical Relation," 25. Garrison also added, "Examples of production processes which allowed for the calculation of an average period of production required the assumption of a steady state and hence made the production period seem economically meaningless. Böhm-Bawerk opened the door to criticisms of the type made by Clark (and later by Knight)" (25).

49. Menger's statement to Schumpeter, *History of Economic Analysis*, 847n. Menger's remark still seems baffling—no one knows for sure what it meant. It may have been an off-the-cuff verbal statement to Schumpeter.

50. Streissler, "To What Extent Was the Austrian School Marginalist?" 169. According to Streissler, Menger also objected to Böhm-Bawerk's emphasis on "the" rate of interest. For Menger, "interest was not a homogeneous quantity" (169).

51. Lachmann, "A Reconsideration of the Austrian Theory of Fluctuations," in *Capital, Expectations, and the Market Process*, 268.

52. Wicksell, *Lectures on Political Economy, Volume 1: General Theory*, 151. Schumpeter commented, "no student of economics has completed his training who has not read the whole of this volume." *History of Economic Analysis*, 863.

53. Ibid., 202.

54. Ibid., 172–84. In Wicksell's wine example, the price of wine increases with the age of wine, as follows:

Age of Wine	Price	Yield
3 yrs.	905	—
4 yrs.	100s	11%
5 yrs.	110s	10%
6 yrs.	120s	9%

Wicksell assumed the most profitable wine is the 4-year-old wine. But if the interest rates decline, due to an increase in the rate of savings, it makes the six-year-old wine the most profitable (176).

55. C. Uhr, *Economic Doctrines of Knut Wicksell*, 114.

56. Lindahl, *Studies in the Theory of Money and Capital*, 310n.

57. Wicksell, *Interest and Prices*, 128.

58. Garrison, "The Austrian-Neoclassical Relation," 64.

59. Uhr, *Economic Doctrines of Knut Wicksell*, 241–46. Wicksell recognized that a credit boom (caused by an interest rate below the natural market level) involved a substantial rise in prices for raw materials and higher rate of profit for processes involving "a long period of production" (*Interest and Prices*, 92, 133). Unfortunately, Wicksell eventually abandoned this micro method of analysis. In a later article, he adopted a "monetarist" prospective: "[T]he demand for all commodities increases . . . and this must result in

an increase in prices, which cannot cease until cash holdings have, as a result of the higher prices, again attained a normal relation to turnover." "The Influence of the Rate of Interest on Commodity Prices," in Wicksell, *Selected Papers on Economic Theory*, 74.

60. Hicks, "The Hayek Story," 205.

61. Cassel, *The Nature and Necessity of Interest*, 123–31. But Cassel fails to note that the shortening of production processes can only be accomplished by investing initially in more capital.

62. Cassel, *The Theory of Social Economy*, 25.

63. Ibid.

64. Ellis, *German Monetary Theory 1905–1933*, 308. See Cassel, *The Theory of Social Economy*, 543–82.

65. Gustav Akerman, *Real Kapital and Kapitalzins*. Lutz calls it "one of the most laborious in economic literature," which may be one reason it has not been translated into English. Lutz, *The Theory of Interest*, 35.

66. Lutz, *The Theory of Interest*, 53.

67. Aftalion, "The Theory of Economic Cycles," 165.

68. Clark, *The Distribution of Wealth*, 268–69.

69. Clark, "Concerning the Nature of Capital," 359.

70. Clark, *The Distribution of Wealth*, 308.

71. Clark, "The Genesis of Capital," 310.

72. Clark, "The Origin of Interest," 261.

73. Ibid., 269.

74. Clark, "Concerning the Nature of Capital," 367.

75. Clark, "The Origin of Interest," 267. Note that all of Clark's examples—the reservoir, the forest of trees, and so forth—are mechanical examples that assume no human action between beginning and end.

76. Ibid., 268.

77. Ibid., 275. Böhm-Bawerk's point, however, is that industry would not voluntarily take on a longer, more expensive capital expenditure unless it was ex ante more profitable to do so.

78. Ibid., 277. If Clark's productivity theory were correct, we should expect interest rates to be lower in countries which have the largest quantity of capital. But this is not always the case. For example, the United States has much more capital than Switzerland, yet Switzerland has consistently lower interest rates. Interest rates depend more on the ratio between capital and consumption, than an absolute quantity of capital, as well as inflationary expectations and other factors.

79. Böhm-Bawerk, "The Positive Theory of Capital and Its Critics, I," 121.

80. Ibid., 124.

81. Clark, *The Distribution of Wealth*, 315–18, especially 317.

82. Böhm-Bawerk, "Capital and Interest Once More: II," 269.

83. Ibid., 269, 277, 280–82.

84. Clark, "Concerning the Nature of Capital," 367–68. Interestingly, Clark adopted language closely connected with Austrian business cycle theory in an introduction he

wrote for Rodbertus's *Overproduction and Crises*, 1–18. He used such phrases as, "Overproduction is practically misdirected production" (3) or "unbalanced production" (5).

85. Ibid., 356.

86. Böhm-Bawerk, "The Nature of Capital: A Rejoinder," 29, 46.

87. Carver, "Clark's Distribution of Wealth," 596.

88. Ibid., 598.

89. Taussig, *Wages and Capital*, 25.

90. Taussig, "Capital, Interest, and Diminishing Returns," 338–39.

91. Schumpeter, *History of Economic Analysis*, 847n.

92. Taussig, *Wages and Capital*, 2.

93. Ibid., 9.

94. Ibid., 11.

95. Taussig, *Principles of Economics*, 60.

96. I. Fisher, *The Nature of Capital and Income*, 52.

97. I. Fisher, *The Purchasing Power of Money*, 59–60. Occasionally, Fisher used Austrian terminology such as "maladjustments in the rate of interest" and "overinvestments" in reference to short-run fluctuations in the economy, but Thomas M. Humphrey's argument that Fisher adopted a nonneutral monetary theory is farfetched. Fisher clearly emphasized long-run neutrality in the inflationary process. See Humphrey, "On Nonneutral Relative Price Effects in Monetary Thought," 13–19.

98. Rothbard, Introduction to F. Fetter, *Capital, Interest, and Rent*, 1, 4.

99. Fetter, "Recent Discussion of the Capital Concept," *Quarterly Journal of Economics* (November 1900); Fetter, "The 'Roundabout Process' in the Interest Theory," *Quarterly Journal of Economics* (November 1902).

100. Fetter, "Review of Böhm-Bawerk," *Political Science Quarterly* 17 (March 1902), reprinted in *Capital, Interest, and Rent*, 90.

101. Fetter, *Principles of Economics*, 279–280.

102. Fetter, "Clark's Reformation of the Capital Concept," 145, 156.

103. Schumpeter, *The Theory of Economic Development*, 16–17.

104. Ibid., 46.

105. Schumpeter, *Ten Great Economists*.

106. Schumpeter, *Business Cycles*, vol. 1, 296n.

107. Kirzner, "Ludwig von Mises and the Theory of Capital and Interest," 51.

108. Mises, *The Theory of Money and Credit*, 362–63.

109. Mises, *Human Action*, 514.

110. Ibid., 515.

111. Ibid., 94.

112. Ibid., 488–89. For an overview of Mises' theories of time, money, capital, and business cycles, see Butler, *Ludwig von Mises*, 231–88.

THREE

HAYEK AND THE 1930s:
A NEW VISION OF MACROECONOMICS

Here is a school of thought which can only be neglected at the cost of losing contact with what may prove to be the most fruitful scientific development of our age.—Lionel Robbins, "Foreword," Hayek's *Prices and Production*

Between the great wars there was a battle for men's minds, waged between two great warriors, Keynes and Hayek. Ultimately, the outcome of this battle was as significant as the outcome of the two World Wars.

Friedrich A. Hayek (1899–) was a student of Mises and Wieser in early twentieth century Vienna, but did not have an impact on macroeconomic thought until he lectured at the London School of Economics in February 1931. At the invitation of Lionel Robbins, he delivered a series of lectures that were later published as a book, *Prices and Production.* This little volume, his first to be published in English, introduced a coherent "Austrian" conception of the whole economy in terms of stages of production, and their application to current economic problems. It was, as Howard S. Ellis called it, a "thorough recasting of the whole productive apparatus."[1] The severe depression of the 1930s demanded a new paradigm, and young British economists such as J. R. Hicks, Abba P. Lerner, Nicholas Kaldor, Lionel Robbins, and G. L. S. Shackle quickly absorbed Hayek's theories.

Prices and Production was a popular book, reprinted three times, translated into German and Japanese and followed by a second English edition in 1935. Schumpeter reported that Hayek's work "met with a sweeping success that has never been equaled by any strictly theoretical book," including Keynes's *General Theory.*[2] Shackle referred to Hayek's book as an enigma.[3] It "fascinated many minds, not only at LSE [London School of Economics], partly, I believe, because of its arcane and obscure suggestion of a radical telescoping together of ideas into some new incisive simplicity."[4] And Robbins, writing in the foreword to the 1931 edition of *Prices and Production,* said that Hayek's theory offered "profound theoretical insight and power to open up total new horizons."[5] Kaldor added that the Austrian economist "had a tremendous impact on minds in the early nineteen-thirties, far outside strictly academic circles." Kaldor pointed out that most contemporary statesmen and government officials supported the view that more thrift and retrenchment were the cure for a depression, which had been caused by excessive spending. "When therefore Professor Hayek's famous *Prices and Production* appeared in 1931, it fell on ready ears—it provided, seemingly, scientific justification for views already strongly held."[6]

Finally, Hicks wrote of the times,

> When the definitive history of economic analysis during the nineteen-thirties comes to be written, a leading character in the drama (it was quite a drama) will be Professor Hayek. Hayek's economic writings . . . are almost unknown to the modern student, it is hardly remembered that there was a time when the new theories of Hayek were the principal rival to the new theories of Keynes.[7]

Hayek's *Prices and Production* became the catalyst of controversy with the Keynesian circle at Cambridge. His book established a new approach which rivaled Keynes's blossoming theory of aggregate demand and countered demands for big government during the great depression. What made Hayek's analysis so appealing was his ability to change the direction of Austrian economics from micro theory to macro theory. This shift was essential if free-market economists were going to justify a laissez faire anti-depression policy. Hayek employed the Mengerian stages-of-production approach to develop a new way to analyze the whole economy, monetary policy and the business cycle, quite apart from the contemporary economic orthodoxy. This novel method was essential since standard classical economics seemed to be unable to cope with the growing economic abyss in the 1930s.

As O'Driscoll summarized Hayek's efforts:

> Hayek called for an entire restructuring of economic theory. In part, he was attempting to counter the revived interest in the general equilibrium theories-the neo-Walrasian and neo-Paretian theories of the 1930s as found, for example, in John R. Hicks' writings.
>
> [H]is work is viewed as providing a basis for a radical alternative to the "neo-classical" paradigm of efficient allocation with timeless production, perfect anticipation, costless exchanges, (almost) instantaneous attainment of equilibrium, and a world of no institutions . . .[8]

HAYEK'S THEORETICAL FRAMEWORK

An early chapter of *Prices and Production* set up Hayek's theoretical foundation. He used a simplified heuristic method to describe the macro economy:

a triangular diagram of the "structure of production" in a stationary state where "[t]he area of the triangle thus shows the totality of the successive stages through which the several units of original means of production pass before they become ripe for consumption."[9] Figure 3.1 reproduces this diagram, which Hayek created on his own, later discovering its similarity to the triangular figures used by Jevons (see figure 2.1) and Wicksell (see figure 2.3). Several points should be made about Hayek's triangles.

First, it shows the "total amount of intermediate products which must exist at any moment of time in order to secure a continuous output of consumers' goods."[10] Second, the figure represents money values and not physical production.

Figure 3.1. Hayek's Triangle

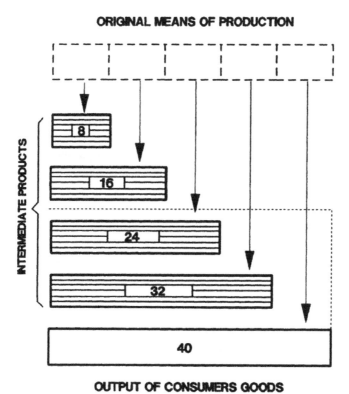

Hayek's Triangle represents the economy's structure of production. In his model, there are four intermediate stages, valued at 8, 16, 24, and 32, respectively. Total value of producers' goods equals 80, while value of consumers' goods totals 40, i.e., a 2:1 ratio. Hayek, *Prices and Production*, 44.

Third, it makes the simplified assumption that all intermediate products are unfinished (nondurable) producers' goods. And fourth, Hayek neglected interest. These simplified assumptions were later dropped. According to Hayek, equilibrium between producers' goods and consumers' goods is achieved if the rate of profit is the same at each stage of production.

After establishing the basic theoretical framework, Hayek analyzed the effect of various changes in the economy. First, he examined the effect of a voluntary increase in savings. Such an increase, according to Hayek, results in an expansion or lengthening of the production process (becoming more "capitalistic") through additional stages even further remote from consumption, and a temporary reduction in consumption expenditures. "The amount of money spent in each of the later stages of production has also decreased, while the amount used in the earlier stages has increased, and the total spent on intermediate products has increased also because of the addition of a new stage of production."[11] Since the act of saving is voluntary, Hayek argued that the change in the structure of production is permanent, and "there would accordingly exist no inherent cause for a return to the old proportions."[12]

Then Hayek investigated the effects of an increase in the money supply, in the form of government credits to producers. The injection of new money will, as in the case of increased savings, cause an expansion in the producers' goods industries and create new stages remote from consumption. Furthermore, such an economic expansion is characterized by what Hayek called "forced savings," i.e., an artificial increase in investment and capital output induced by the government and not savers.[13]

But, according to Hayek, this boom cannot persist. For, once workers in the higher-order industries receive income in the form of wages and salaries, "they would immediately attempt to expand consumption to the usual proportions."[14] This sudden surge in consumption demand undercuts the demand for the still incomplete projects involving higher-order producer goods far removed from consumption, resulting in a slump in the capital-goods industries. In short, the trend reverses itself, and the "structure of production . . . will have to return to the old proportion," that is, to a less capitalistic economy.[15] There is an "economic crisis," as the boom turns into a bust. Thus, Hayek used the time structure of production to develop a business cycle theory, one that he intended to use to explain the Great Depression that Britain and the rest of the world were entering in 1931.[16]

Hayek discussed the critical role that prices play in the dynamics of the economy, particularly how price changes create profits and losses between stages of production. Like all Austrian economists, he was skeptical of the "general price level" and price averages, and preferred looking at "relative" prices, such as the prices of consumers' goods compared to the prices of producers' goods, or even comparing an array of prices for each stage of production.[17]

Hayek argued that government mismanagement of monetary policy was the primary cause of the depression, and, in a pessimistic tone, suggested that the best cure is to adopt a *laissez faire* policy—"not to use artificial stimulants . . . but to leave it to time to effect a permanent cure by the slow process of adapting the structure of production to the means available for capital purposes."[18] Hayek strongly opposed the Keynesian prescription of granting new credits to consumers (via government deficit spending), which he said "would in fact have quite the contrary effect: a relative increase of the demand for consumers' goods could only make matters worse."[19]

Finally, Hayek opposed the idea of an "elastic" currency or even a deliberate policy to stabilize prices because such actions would only cause unstable misdirections in the economy. His solution was: "the supply of money should be invariable."[20]

THE KEYNES-HAYEK CONFLICT

Hayek and Keynes (1883–1946) seemed to represent opposite ends of the philosophical spectrum, and the theoretical conflict between them came to a head in the early 1930s with Keynes in Cambridge and Hayek in London. The antagonism between the two schools lasted for some time. In economic theory, Keynes emphasized homogeneous aggregates while Hayek stressed a heterogeneous structure of production. But the dispute went much deeper than differences in pure economic hypotheses. Keynes was a debunker of the puritan ethic—as embodied in classical economics—while Hayek was a defender. Keynes held his unorthodox views prior to the 1930s, but he used the Great Depression years to proclaim his heretical views to a ready audience. During the depression, Keynes advocated "money management" by the state; Hayek believed deeply in a noninterventionist policy by government. Keynes advocated inflation during a depression; Hayek favored a neutral monetary policy and a reliance on market flexibility in prices and wages. Keynes said hoarding and increased savings were bad during a depression; Hayek debunked the "paradox of saving" and favored the traditional value of thrift.

The disagreement became apparent when Hayek reviewed Keynes's *Treatise on Money* in a 1931 issue of *Economica*. He objected to Keynes's excessive macro approach in explaining entrepreneur profit and investment, writing that Keynes "treats the process of current output of consumption goods as an integral whole in which only the prices obtained at the end for the final products and the prices at the beginning for the factors of production have any bearing on its profitableness."[21]

Hayek was critical of Keynes for not developing an adequate theory explaining the violent fluctuation in the value of capital during 1929–30. According to Hayek, Keynes did not recognize the existence of a structure of production, but only a generalized division between consumption and investment. Nor did Keynes visualize a hierarchy of producers' goods in his macro model.[22] Finally, Hayek criticized Keynes for looking only at the nominal price level rather than at relative prices. He believed Keynes was following Wicksell's false relationship between the price level and the divergence of savings and investment, or as Wicksell notes, the divergence between the price level and the natural and money rate of interest.[23]

In the next issue of *Economica*, Keynes denied Hayek's view that voluntary savings "always finds its way into investment." Rather, he argued that there is "no automatic mechanism" for keeping savings and investment equal—they can "get out of gear."[24] He did, however, grant Hayek's criticism that he lacked a capital theory.[25] He took the opportunity to attack Hayek's *Prices and Production*, which "seems to me to be one of the most frightful muddles I have ever read, with scarcely a sound proposition in it beginning with page 45." While "his Khubla Khan is not without inspiration . . . it is an extraordinary example of how, starting with a mistake, a remorseless logician can end up in Bedlam."[26] Keynes characterized Hayek's approach as a "thick bank of fog."[27]

Keynes maintained that his own approach was a new one, and not representative of any past economist. "Thus those who are sufficiently steeped in the old point of view simply cannot bring themselves to believe that I am asking them to step into a new pair of trousers, and will insist on regarding it as nothing but an embroidered version of the old pair which I have been wearing for years."[28]

Hayek responded to Keynes's *ad hominem* attack in the same issue, adding: "Mr. Keynes's assertion that there is no automatic mechanism in the economic system to keep the rate of saving and the rate of investing equal . . . might with equal justification be extended to the more general contention that there is no automatic mechanism in the economic system to adapt production to any other shift in demand."[29] Hayek accused Keynes of not comprehending the function of interest.

Hayek continued his counterattack the following year. According to him, Keynes believed that a change in the rate of interest would have no effect on fixed capital. But Hayek countered: "Any change in the rate of interest will, obviously, materially alter the relative profitableness of the employment of circulating capital in the different stages of production."[30] Hayek was highly critical of the "purchasing power" theorists who, like Keynes, were opposed to savings during a depression and favored "direct inflation for consumption purposes." Keynes overlooked "the all-important fact that an increase in the demand for consumers' goods will not only tend to stop new investment, but may make a complete reorganisation of the existing structure of production inevitable— which would involve considerable disturbances and would render it impossible, temporarily, to employ all labour."[31]

THE SRAFFA-HAYEK DEBATE

Keynes's disciples at Cambridge rejected Hayek's critique of their master. As one historian notes regarding Hayek's attack, "But if the Young Turks of LSE [London School of Economics] were enthusiastic, those of Cambridge were unmistakably hostile."[32] A response was soon forthcoming.

Piero Sraffa (1898–1983), a younger colleague of Keynes's at Cambridge, reviewed Hayek's *Prices and Production* in a 1932 issue of the *Economic Journal,* when Keynes was editor. According to Ludwig M. Lachmann, Sraffa's review was highly significant.

> Mr. Sraffa's review of Hayek's book was his only [English] publication in 25 years. . . . With the benefit of hindsight we are now able to understand that Sraffa's critique of Hayek's book marked the start of the neo-Ricardian counterrevolution. . . . The aim of the neo-Ricardian counterrevolution is to undo the subjectivist revolution in economic thought which took place in the 1870s, led by Jevons, Menger, and Walras, in which it was shown that the value of economic goods depends on the (subjective) utility they have to different individuals, and not on their (objective) cost of production.[33]

Sraffa, like Keynes, attacked Hayek for "unintelligibility" and creating confusion. He described the discussion of Hayek's triangles as "a maze of contradictions" making "the reader completely dizzy, [so] that when he reaches the discussion of money he may out of despair be prepared to believe anything."[34]

Sraffa criticized Hayek for unrealistic assumptions: "There are no debts, no money-contracts, no wage-agreements, no sticky prices in his suppositions. Thus he is able to neglect altogether the most obvious effects of a general fall, or rise, of prices."[35]

Sraffa denied the possibility of a divergence between the equilibrium rate of interest and the actual rate in a money economy, and goes into some detail showing that in a barter economy "there might, at any moment, be as many 'natural' rates of interest as there are commodities, though they would not be 'equilibrium' rates."[36] "In Sraffa's opinion, any composite commodity for which there is a forward market can have an 'own rate' which is out of equilibrium with the 'own rates' on other commodities."[37] Consequently, he denied the "self-reversing" nature of credit inflation. "Sraffa's criticism implies that, far from being dissipated, the new capital will represent a new equilibrium position which will show no tendency to be reversed. . . . Sraffa treats inflation as a problem of distribution of income rather than the allocation of resources. Yet consumers' *incomes* have not changed; all that has happened is that producers have a larger share of *output* than before."[38]

Sraffa argued that the capital-goods boom does not result in higher consumption by wage-earners, suggesting that producers and workers save all of their money incomes.

> If they are wage-earners, who have all the time consumed every penny of their income, they have no wherewithal to expand consumption. And if they are capitalists, who have not shared in the plunder, they may indeed be induced to consume now a part of their capital by the fall in the rate of interest; but not more so than if the rate had been lowered by the "voluntary savings" of other people.[39]

Sraffa also repeated Keynes's fears that an increase in savings may "prove to a large extent 'abortive.' . . . When the saved goods flow out of the consumers' hands, they do not reach investment unimpaired."[40]

Hayek replied a few months later. He recognized that during the 1930s depression, "monetary policy is in a state of violent fermentation," and "it was not an easy, and perhaps not even a pleasant, task" to review *Prices and Production*. Sraffa's attitude, according to Hayek, was one of "extreme theoretical nihilism."[41] Hayek then summarized his approach to monetary theory, arguing that new credits to producers do indeed create disequilibrium. According to McCloughry, "For Hayek the recession is characterized by 'capital consumption' caused by wages being too high relative to the structure of production, elongated by an increase in the money supply. If wages are too high relative to their marginal product, then they claim a larger share of output, profits fall in the higher stages of production, and eventually producers discontinue the maintenance of their capital, operating it at prices below costs."[42]

Hayek granted Sraffa's point that there may be no single interest rate, but by doing so, "he was making a fatal concession to his opponent," according to Lachmann. "If there is a multitude of commodity rates, it is evidently possible for the money rate of interest to be lower than some but higher than others. What, then, becomes of monetary equilibrium?"[43]

Lachmann also added, "One thing is clear: when Hayek and Sraffa use the word 'equilibrium' they use it to denote quite different things. For Hayek it means market-clearing demand-and-supply equilibrium, for Sraffa long-run cost-of-production equilibrium."[44] He concludes with this significant historical point:

> The duel we have described did the reputation of Austrian economics a good deal of harm. Hayek's authority as an economic thinker of the first rank had been challenged with some vehemence in the august pages of the *Economic Journal*. Nobody knew what to make of it. Some of Hayek's recently gained supporters began to hesitate. When, four years later, the Keynesian revolution broke out, its assault forces encountered not a phalanx, but divided ranks.[45]

THE HAWTREY ATTACK ON HAYEK

While the Cambridge school attacked Hayek in *Economic Journal,* monetarist R. G. Hawtrey (1879–1975) criticized him in *Economica.* Hawtrey reviewed *Prices and Production* in 1932, which he said is "so difficult and obscure that it is impossible to understand."[46] He suggested that there is no change in the structure of production when new credit is created as long as there are unemployed resources. "But if industry is underemployed, it will take effect mainly in increased output."[47]

By contrast, Hayek's review of Hawtrey's book, *Trade Depression and the Way Out,* began on the next page following Hawtrey's review. According to Hayek, Hawtrey neglected monetary effects on production and only emphasized the general price effects.[48] He accused Hawtrey of a bad interpretation of the statistical evidence in business cycle data. "Against all empirical evidence, he insists that 'the first symptom of contracting demand is a decline in sales to the consumer or final purchaser.' . . . In fact, of course, depression has always begun in the demand, not for consumers' goods but for capital goods, and the one marked phenomenon of the present depression was that the demand for consumers' goods was very well maintained for a long while after the crisis occurred."[49]

Hawtrey continued his assault with a stinging review of Hayek's newly translated book, *Monetary Theory and the Trade Cycle,* in Cambridge's prestigious *Economic Journal* in late 1933. He denied any "price margins" between classes of capital goods. "Practically every commodity would belong to several groups, and the same commodity would of course command the same price whenever it occurred."[50] Hawtrey disagreed with Hayek's view that new credit goes toward capital creation. "In practice the greater part of the credit granted by banks is not for the construction of fixed capital but for working capital and for holding stocks of goods."[51]

Hawtrey followed with a broader indictment of Hayek in chapter 8 of his 1937 book, *Capital and Employment*. Defending his own monetarist position, Hawtrey argued that new credits granted to producers will create "excess demand" for "*all* goods" to "an exactly equal extent."[52] Hayek's fear of disturbing the structural balance of the economy is "baseless," said Hawtrey. "The measures by which the banking system modifies the flow of money take effect in the first instance through working capital, the effect upon long-term investment and instrument goods being relatively remote." A far more "potent cause of disturbance," he felt, is the fluctuation in consumers' incomes. Hawtrey favored stabilizing consumer income as the primary monetary goal, with a price stabilization policy as a second-best alternative.[53]

THE INFLUENCE OF HAYEK'S MACRO THEORY

Despite these criticisms by the establishment economists, and before the Keynesian revolution took hold in the late 1930s, Hayek's monetary approach gained widespread adherence, particularly among young economists. Nicholas Kaldor (1908–86) translated from the German Hayek's *Monetary Theory and the Trade Cycle,* which was published in English in 1933, for which Lionel Robbins (1889–1984) wrote the introduction. Ludwig von Mises's seminal work, *The Theory of Money and Credit,* was translated by H. E. Batson in 1934, with Robbins writing the introduction for that too, stating: "In continental circles it has long been regarded as the standard textbook on the subject. It is hoped that it will fill a similar role in English-speaking countries. I know few works which convey a more profound impression of the logical unity and the power of modern economic analysis."[54]

Robbins relied on Hayek's business cycle theory and Mises's critique of socialist planning in writing *The Great Depression,* which was published in 1934. Robbins placed the blame for the depression squarely on the governments' easy-money policies of the 1920s. Thus, the depression was not caused by capitalism, but by the "negation" of capitalism. "It was due to monetary mismanagement and State intervention operating in a *milieu* in which the essential strength of capitalism had already been sapped by war and by policy."[55]

Robbins discussed the basic cause of business cycles. Technically "a business cycle is generated by movements of interest rates which affect *relative* prices in such a way as to cause false expectation."[56] In his explanation, he made a distinction between consumers' goods and producers' goods. Interest rates are pushed lower.

This means that the profitability of all forms of production which involve making things which only yield services at a later date, or over a long period of time, is increased. . . . The longer-lived the capital instrument, or the greater its distance from consumption, the more its value is affected by the change in the rate of interest. The shorter-lived it is, or the less its distance from consumption, the less it is affected. The value of flour in the baker's shop is hardly affected by a cheapening of the cost of borrowing. The value of mines, forest, houses and heavy factory equipment is enormously affected.[57]

Robbins' plan for recovery included the reestablishment of an international gold standard, stable exchange rates, removal of trade barriers, and greater flexibility in prices and wage rates. He opposed the interventionist policies of maintaining wages and consumer demand, propping up business bankruptcies, and limiting farm output.[58]

Years later, Robbins changed his mind and switched to favoring deficit spending during a depression. Repudiating his laissez faire philosophy, Robbins called his siding with Hayek and his dispute with Keynes in the 1930s as the "greatest mistake of my professional career. . . . But it will always be a matter of deep regret to me that, although I was acting in good faith and with a strong sense of social obligation, I should have so opposed policies which might have mitigated the economic distress of those days."[59]

Nevertheless, Robbins did not disavow entirely the Hayekian theoretical framework.

I do not think nowadays that the analytical constructions which excited us so which in the lectures on *Prices and Production* had all the width or appropriateness of assumption which some of us—including conspicuously the present writer—were disposed to claim for them. . . . But at least it must be admitted that they drew attention to some of the profoundest problems of capital theory and were pioneers in a discussion which has continued ever since.[60]

Moreover, according to Robbins, "I still think there is much in this theory as an explanation of a *possible* generation of boom and crisis." He suggested the 1907 financial panic in the United States as an example. But it was "misleading," he believed, for the 1930s depression, which was "swamped by vast deflationary forces."[61]

Several other young economists in the 1930s were enamored with Hayek's monetary views but later became pro-Keynesian. Abba P. Lerner (190582), initially open to Hayek's views, spent a weekend in the mid-1930s in Cambridge and became a thorough-going Keynesian. The meeting with Keynes, Joan Robinson, and others resulted in "changing the Hayekian Saul into the Keynesian Paul."[62] Arthur Smithies (1907–81), another latter-day Keynesian, wrote briefly and favorably of the "Austrian" theory of capital and Böhm-Bawerk's period of production in the mid-1930s.[63] J. C. Gilbert confessed that he was "under the influence of Hayek" at the London School of Economics in 1930–31, but somehow "escaped."[64] Decades later, he felt it important to create a macroeconomic "Austrian-Keynesian synthesis." He wrote:

> It seems clear that a synthesis of Austrian and Keynesian theory would be a step in the right direction. The neglect of Hayek's work is unfortunate as in some ways it was nearer to dynamic economics than that of Keynes. Further, Hayek's particular emphasis on the immobility of labour and the heterogeneity of capital goods is of vital importance in certain contexts. There is a danger in thinking too much in terms of aggregates.[65]

Gottfried Haberler (1900–) endorsed an Austrian view of the business cycle in an article in 1932. To analyze an economic system, he referred to "the vertical structure of production," as opposed to a "horizontal cross-section" of different branches of industry. "Every good has to pass through many successive stages of preparation before the finishing touches are applied and it eventually reaches the final consumer."[66] New credits by government reduce interest rates, and stimulate an "excessive lengthening of the process of production." But the "processes are too long . . . and it becomes impossible to finish the new roundabout ways of production." A depression results.[67]

Commenting on the Russian five-year plan, Haberler stated, "What the Russians are doing now, or trying to do . . . is nothing else but an attempt to increase by a desperate effort the roundaboutness of production and, by means of this, to increase in the future the production of consumer's goods."[68]

Haberler opposed stimulating consumer demand during a depression. "The worst thing we could do is a one-sided strengthening of the purchasing power of the consumer, because it was precisely this disproportional increase of demand for consumer's goods which precipitated the crisis."[69]

Haberler warned the reader, however, that the Austrian theory of the business cycle is "so much more complicated than the traditional monetary explanation," as espoused by Hawtrey, Cassel and other monetarists.[70] By 1937, Haberler had rejected the main tenets of the Austrian theory and was critical of it in his well-received work on business cycles, *Prosperity and Depression*. He labeled the Austrian view the "monetary over-investment theories," which included such advocates as Hayek, Machlup, Mises, Robbins, Röpke and Strigl. Haberler's opinion concerning government was that, "If there are unemployed resources, evidently the expansion of credit may go on much longer than when all resources are employed. There need, then, be no shift of factors from the lower to the higher stages, but only the absorption of unused resources."[71] Moreover, if a "secondary deflation" hits, as it did in 1930–32, Haberler maintained that the Austrians might have a difficult time explaining "why the depression spreads to *all* stages and branches of industry."[72] In a severe depression, like the one in the 1930s when the money supply dropped by 30 percent, Haberler concluded that deficit spending by the government is good (despite his earlier assertion that stimulating consumer demand was bad during a depression).[73]

Alvin H. Hansen (1887–1975) who later became a principal proponent of Keynesianism in the United States, coauthored a "sympathetic criticism" (Hayek's words) in *Econometrica*. Hansen, along with Herbert Tout, offered ten theses describing Hayek's trade cycle theory. They expressed skepticism of public works projects: "[I]f the capital market is weak, the moment certain fields are stimulated by public works, a damper may be placed upon private enterprise by a vast issue of public bonds, and so operations elsewhere may be curtailed."[74]

But they disagreed with Hayek on a number of his claims, such as the thesis that the depression results in a shrinkage of the structure of production. They suggested that "there could be a violent fall in the rate of investment before any shrinkage in the structure of production occurred."[75] They also questioned the thesis that new savings lengthens the structure permanently at a higher level based on a quasi "acceleration principle." Hansen and Tout argued that there is no reason why bank credit cannot continue to rise indefinitely, thus averting the crisis, although they were concerned about the possibility that new money might cause high inflation and people might hoard rather than invest.[76] To them, the disturbing thing was the "fluctuations" in the quantity of bank credit.

Reflecting a pre-Keynesian view, Hansen and Tout disagreed with another one of Hayek's theses. They wrote that "a rise in the prices of consumers' goods occasioned by putting more money into consumers' hands will not cause [the prices of] producers' goods to fall, for entrepreneurs, enticed by the wider margin of profit in all the lower stages of production, will anticipate higher profits in all the various stages and will therefore apply for bank credit and seek to expand operations."[77]

Finally, Hansen and Tout labeled Hayek's no-money-growth policy "disastrous." Instead, they favored a "gently rising price level," or possibly a "gently falling price level," as Alfred Marshall suggested.[78]

Hayek responded to their criticisms in the second edition of *Prices and Production,* which was published in 1935. Hayek strongly objected to the "underconsumptionist fallacy" that the economy is solely dependent on aggregate consumer demand: "It is certainly not true to say that the demand for capital goods in general is directly determined by the magnitude of the demand for consumers' goods."[79] Hayek was also critical of Hansen and

Tout's monetarist "steady rate of credit expansion" thesis, which, according to Hayek, would still be destabilizing.[80]

M. A. Abrams wrote a thorough-going Hayekian study of the monetary system in his book, *Money,* published in 1934. Using Böhm-Bawerk's theory of roundaboutness and Hayek's triangles, Abrams blamed the banking system for creating an inflationary boom-bust cycle through an artificially low interest rate. He described the Austrian theory of the business cycle:

> Sooner or later the bulk of this money is paid out as net incomes to consumers—to wage-earners, etc.—and these people use their higher money-incomes to recover their old standards of consumption.
>
> Consequently there will be a sharp relative rise in the price per unit of consumption goods, and in their turn the producers of these goods will increase their offers of remuneration to the factors of production; those productive resources that are unspecialized will then move from the higher stages of production to the lower stages. The specialized ones—factories, machines, etc.—will be left high and dry since their owners will be unable to pay the higher rates necessary to obtain the services of the complementary factors needed to keep the specialised factors operating. . . . This stage of affairs is what we know as a depression.[81]

Abrams criticized a stable price-index policy, and joined Hayek in recommending an extreme policy of "no increase" in the money supply. After a depression strikes, Abrams echoed Hayek's warning against reinflating, which serves "merely to postpone and magnify the inevitable breakdown."[82] His work concluded: "Money, the progenitor of capitalism and the engine of its greatest victories, is also its destroyer."[83]

Franz Wien-Claudi wrote a sympathetic review of Hayek's theories in 1936, entitled *Austrian Theories of Capital, Interest, and the Trade Cycle.* His aim was to make the Austrian views better known in England. "No serious student of English economic theory can afford to ignore contemporary continental research."[84] According to Wien-Claudi, the outstanding achievements of Hayek, Mises and the other Austrians were the significance of the "movement in relative prices," the theory of "forced savings," and the refutation of the old quantity theory.[85]

However, Wien-Claudi's book was not entirely favorable, especially with regard to Hayek's analysis of an increase in the savings rate. According to Hayek, credit expansion was the primary cause of the boom-bust cycle, while a change in the rate of savings caused minimum dislocations and resulted in a permanent stability. Wien-Claudi disputed this claim, saying that there will be grave alterations in the structure of the economy as a result of an increased savings rate. "Hayek, therefore, does not prove that savings will not create serious disturbances in a money-economy. He overlooks that producers of consumption-goods will suffer great losses and that, due to this fact, the demand for capital-goods (on the market) must temporarily decrease."[86]

Several titles applying the Austrian business cycle theory to the 1930s depression were published in the late 1930s, after the Robbins book. German economist Wilhelm Röpke (1899–1966) wrote *Crises and Cycles,* which was translated into English in 1936 by Vera C. Smith. The book presented a strong Austrian perspective, lauded Robbins' *Great Depression* and called Austrian economist Richard Strigl's recently published work, *Kapital und Produktion,* the "most advanced" book on Austrian capital theory and "of special importance."[87] Röpke relied on a Hayekian "monetary over-capitalization theory," suggesting that the depression reflected a top-heavy structure due to previous inflation, especially in credits to producers. In a more recent book, Röpke suggested that one "must picture the entire process of production as a series of descending levels. At the highest level, raw materials are procured; at a lower level, capital goods are manufactured; and at the lowest level, consumption goods are produced."[88]

In 1937, *Banking and the Business Cycle,* a book written by C. A. Phillips, T. F. McManus, and R. W. Nelson, adopted a Hayekian structure of production viewpoint of cycle analysis. In the upswing of the cycle, the authors argued that "capital creation runs ahead of savings, which is to say that there results an increase in the rate of production of producers' goods disproportionate to the rate of production of consumption goods."[89] They concluded that the depression hits when "the production of producers' goods declines more rapidly than does the production of consumers' goods."[90]

They decided that the solution is "to direct all possible effects toward a revival of activity in the capital goods industries," particularly by lowering wage rates to reduce losses or increase profits.[91]

HISTORICAL PRICE STUDIES: MILLS'S WORK AT NBER

During the mid-1930s, Frederick C. Mills at the National Bureau of Economic Research (NBER) undertook a systematic study of the price structure of the U.S. and world economies which paralleled the theoretical work of Menger, Böhm-Bawerk, and Hayek. While Mills does not refer directly to the theoretical work of Menger, Böhm-Bawerk, or Hayek, it is clear that Mills adopted a proto-Austrian approach in many areas of study. For example, he relied heavily on a Mengerian "stages of production" concept, discussed a Hayekian time-structure of production, and made an indirect reference to Böhm-Bawerk's idea of roundaboutness.[92] But the fact that Mills was not an Austrian economist *per se* demonstrates that the stages-of-production theory of macroeconomics is a natural common-sense approach, not just an idiosyncratic dogma. Apparently his technique was developed before the Keynesian aggregative approach took over in statistical data-collecting.

Mills stressed the critical importance of *relative* price changes in the economy, a well-known Austrian concept. Moreover, his emphasis on relative price changes was quite distinct from the conventional aggregate approach used by Simon Kuznets, Geoffrey Moore, and George Stigler at the National Bureau of Economic Research. Their studies were devoted almost exclusively to monetary aggregates and changes in *general* price indices with little or no discussion of changes in price margins between raw commodities, producers' goods, and wholesale and retail markets.[93]

In a sense, Mills's *modus operandi* was a breakthrough in statistical research in economics. The U.S. Department of Labor had begun to gather data on individual commodity and wholesale prices as early as 1902, but it was not until Mills's study that relative price indices were used in any systemic way at NBER. *Prices in Recession and Recovery* is a broad discussion of general and relative price changes from 1920 until 1936, a time when there were "extreme inequalities of the changes occuring in different parts of the price system."[94] The entire work deals with the price structure during this critical boom-bust phase of the United States and the world. Mills analyzed price indices of raw materials, agricultural products, manufactured goods, producers' goods, wholesale goods and consumer products. Throughout the book, Mills compared one price index with another, which he regarded "of central importance in the working of the economic system."[95]

> The margins, or differentials, between the prices of goods of the same type at successive stages of the route from primary producer to ultimate consumer are a factor of major importance in the movement of goods in use. In a sense, goods move uphill from primary markets to final consumers. Labor must be expended upon them at each stage of their progress. The immediate stimulus to the activities of fabrication and transportation necessary to transform raw materials into ultimate finished goods is provided by a series of price differentials, which are appraised by the business man with reference to the number of units of goods that may be moved.[96]

Mills examined the price relationships between stages of production in both recession and recovery, and noted that the price differential between stages is a significant factor in a firm's ability to make a profit or loss. Mills referred to the dramatic changes in the price structure during the 1929–33 debacle as "badly twisted," stating, "Raw materials dropped precipitously; manufactured goods, customarily sluggish in their response to a downward pressure of values, lagged behind."[97] But consumer goods "fell less than did the average of all commodity prices."[98] In the 1933–36 recovery, "Low prices of industrial raw materials, together with relatively high prices for finished goods, put manufacturers in an advantageous position on the operating side. This price advantage, of course, failed to yield a corresponding reward in the form of real income as long as the volume of production and sales remained unusually low, but it offered attractive potential profits."[99]

Prices in Recession and Recovery followed a logical course of presentation, starting with a discussion of price changes of primary industries, followed by manufacturing, capital goods, and ultimately consumer goods.

Mills used the same method of analysis in a study of the inflationary war period, 1939–47. In *The Structure of Postwar Prices,* he emphasized how inflation was not felt equally, warning economists not to ignore the "unequal movements of prices, wages, and profits, affecting producing and consuming groups unequally. . . . Some traders gain in relative position, some lose."[100]

Mills compared average price changes for producers, wholesalers, and consumers as well as price indices for construction costs and food prices. He also looked at prices, costs of production, and wages and profits in various industries between 1939 and 1947, discovering that, as a result of worldwide shortages during the war and high purchasing power of consumers after the war, "The over-all price advance of 1939–47 was most pronounced in the consumption sector of the economy."[101]

HAYEK, DURBIN, AND THE CRITIQUE OF THE UNDERCONSUMPTIONISTS

Hayek's monetary approach had a significant impact on the underconsumptionist and anti-saving controversies which were prevalent during the 1920s and 1930s. An anti-savings bias has existed over the centuries among some economists, including Malthus (briefly), Veblen, and Hobson. The case against savings usually ended up as a justification for government inflation. Two underconsumptionist theories became popular in the twenties, one by Major Clifford High Douglas (1879–1952) and the other by William T. Foster and Waddill Catchings.

Foster and Catchings had written a series of books on an anti-savings theme in the 1920s, arguing that if corporations and individuals increased their savings, consumer buying could not keep pace with production, resulting in a crisis and depression. In discussing the "dilemma of thrift" in their book, *Business Without a Buyer*, they stated,

Individuals as well as corporations *must* save; yet savings tend to thwart the social object of thrift. For the individual as well as the corporation, a penny saved is a penny earned; but for society, a penny saved is a penny lost if it results in curtailed production. And often it does. For every dollar which is *saved and invested,* instead of *spent,* causes one dollar of deficiency in consumer buying unless that deficiency is made up in some way.[102]

The solution, according to Foster and Catchings, was to issue new credits to consumers on a regular basis to make up for consumer buying deficiency. "Progress requires a constant flow of new money to consumers."[103]

Hayek dissected the fallacy of Foster and Catchings' thesis in a 1931 issue of *Economica.* According to Hayek, they made "a number of fictitious assumptions" and had "a complete misunderstanding of the function of capital."[104] The two writers made the fatal assumption that the economy consisted of one single enterprise, the ultimate socialist state, where all production takes place under one roof. In essence, Foster and Catchings adopted a single-stage timeless production function, so that the supply of capital depends entirely and immediately on consumer demand. Under such restrictive assumptions, "there would be no inducement for that undertaking to save money," noted Hayek.[105] Hayek therefore rejected this assumption upon which Foster and Catchings built their model—and when that assumption is withdrawn, the anti-savings edifice collapses. Instead, using capital-using, time-oriented period of production, Hayek demonstrated that increased savings lengthens the production process, increases productivity and therefore enlarges profits, wages, and income sufficiently for consumers to buy the final product.[106]

E. F. M. Durbin (1906–48) was a young economist at Oxford who, under the influence of Lionel Robbins, used the Austrian view of the economy to critique a variety of under-consumptionist theories, especially that of Major C. H. Douglas. Durbin wrote a book on the subject, *Purchasing Power and Trade Depression,* which was published in 1933. Underconsumptionists such as Major Douglas argued that the depression was caused by excessive saving, which "increases the supply of and diminishes the demand for products of the industry system to the point at which production cannot be continued any longer with profit and at that point crisis and depression begins."[107]

Major Douglas, a professional engineer and leader of the social credit movement in the 1920s, wrote several books championing his position, including *Economic Democracy* and *Credit-Power and Democracy.* He maintained that there was a permanent deficiency of purchasing power in the economy. Summarizing his views, H. T. N. Gaitskell writes:

This "deficiency" arises from the fact that, of the costs incurred in the production of commodities for sale, only a part have involved the distribution of purchasing power to potential consumers. It follows that, when the commodities are ready for sale, consumers cannot buy them at prices which cover their costs of production, because the necessary purchasing power is not available.[108]

Major Douglas advocated the injection of increased purchasing power to consumers, not by increasing government credits, but by the forced reduction of prices to consumers.[109]

Durbin used Hayekian stages of production to show the fallacy of Major Douglas's thinking. If there is only one producer in the whole economy, then "every element in a producer's costs is an element in someone's income."[110] But with many stages and many producers, the cost of producers are not all payments for wages, rents, and interest (consumer income) but costs for goods, instruments, and so on. In fact:

The consumer's income becomes a smaller and smaller fraction of total costs as the complexity of the industrial structure grows greater. . . . The baker, for example, will only pay a *fraction* of his money costs to workmen and landowners who are consumers, because a large part of his costs must be paid for flour and ovens which are the products of previous stages of production and whose price therefore cannot enter immediately into consumer's income. . . . Hence at every stage only a fraction of the costs of that stage accrue to final consumers.[111]

The underconsumptionists, such as Major Douglas, argued that consumer income must cover *all* the costs of production, or else consumers will not have enough income to buy everything that is produced; hence, a depression. But Durbin pointed out the fallacy: "It is not the least necessary that consumer's income should cover the total current costs in the industrial system as a whole, but only the current costs of producing consumption goods."[112]

Durbin illustrated his point using a form of Hayek's diagram (see figure 3.2). He made use of four stages of production, with the same amount spent on labor and machinery at each stage. As the diagram demonstrates, the total costs of production are £150, and the amount accrued to consumers is £60. But total cost to produce bread, the final consumer product, is also £60. Therefore consumers do have enough to buy the product.

In another article, Durbin readily agreed that his diagram represented a static model, and that it did not allow for saving by individuals and businesses: "The actual system of production is not a static system—instead it is continually saving part of its money income, building up real physical capital and increasing the potential physical productivity of industry."[113]

Figure 3.2. Durbin's Production-Consumption Diagram

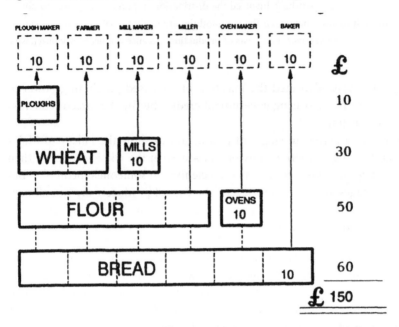

Source: Durbin, *Purchasing Power and Trade Depression,* 54. Reprinted by permission of Jonathan Cape, Ltd.

Durbin was not a disciple of Hayek, by any means. He rejected Hayek's extreme position that the money supply should be kept constant, and he accepted the Keynesian view that in a deep depression, consumer demand and investment are directly related. Acknowledging the difficulty of getting the economy moving again in a depression, Durbin wrote, "Only if a Government threatened to shoot anyone who refused to accept 1,000 notes free of charge on condition they were spent on capital construction could anything much be done."[114] He opined that most people would want to use the money to pay debts or for consumption. Long term, Durbin favored a policy "which looks to the stabilisation of money income rather than to the stabilisation of any other element in the system."[115]

Durbin followed up with another book, *The Problem of Credit Policy,* in 1935. He questioned Hayek's central assumption in his theory of the business cycle, i.e., that the new money in an inflationary credit boom would be spent according to the old consumption/savings pattern.[116] Then he urged the establishment of a centralized, planned monetary system through a central financial authority charged with stabilizing the economy. Instead of issuing industrial credits, which he regarded as "inherently unstable," Durbin suggested that the government should consider issuing "consumers' credits" or "free money" to the public— "money that is issued to persons in their private capacity upon which no interest is charged and which need not be repaid."[117]

ROBERTSON, FORCED SAVINGS, AND THE BUSINESS CYCLE

Dennis H. Robertson (1890–1963), along with his contemporaries Keynes and Pigou at Cambridge, was one of the most important British economists in the first half of the twentieth century. His overinvestment theory of the business cycle, about which he wrote extensively in the 1920s, had many remarkable similarities and conclusions akin to the Austrian theory as later espoused by Hayek. Robertson's theory of industrial fluctuations appeared in his principal works, *A Study of Industrial Fluctuation* (1915), *Money* (1922), and *Banking Policy and the Price Level* (1926), where he discussed occasionally the importance of the time-consuming production process, the length of the "gestation" period of investment and the concept of forced savings.[118] For example, he wrote that "the longer therefore this period of gestation, the longer will the period of high prices continue, the greater will be the overinvestment and the more severe the subsequent depression."[119]

Robertson considered the process of forced savings to be an important factor in his overinvestment theory of the boom-bust cycle. The expansion of bank credit involves an alteration in the structure of production with resources being shifted from the consumer-goods industry to the capital-goods industry.[120] According to Robertson, rising prices eventually reduce the real income of certain individuals, which in turn forces them to go without consumption. An economic contraction occurs because there is insufficient demand for the capital goods when they are finished.

But, for the most part, it does not appear that Robertson showed much interest toward changes in the structure of production, as Hayek did in *Prices and Production*. His method was too aggregative in nature. Indeed, Bridel Pascal comments:

At first sight one may be genuinely surprised by the lack of interest displayed by Robertson towards changes in the structure of production, a question forming the core of Hayek's trade-cycle theory. . . . In Robertson's theory of industrial fluctuations, of which *Banking Policy* examines only the strictly monetary aspects, "forced saving" and the ensuing changes in the structure of production are brought into the picture at two different stages only, each of them being of secondary importance if compared with the overwhelming influence of *real* forces.[121]

Hayek's rejuvenation of the Austrian structure of production in the 1930s encouraged young Swedish economists to develop their own version of macroeconomic theory, which turned out to be a mixture of Austrian and Swedish formulations. It was noted in chapter 2 that Wicksell had initially adopted a time-structural view of the economy, although he later discarded it in favor of a macro-monetarist framework.

One of Wicksell's most important students, Erik Lindahl (1891–1960), took up the importance of time in capital formation. In his work on money and capital in the 1930s, he spent considerable time on the concept of roundabout processes and referred to the fact that it takes time for intermediate producer goods to mature into consumption goods.[122] Lindahl also developed an algebraic description and diagram of the "maturing" of goods over time, as reproduced in figure 3.3. Note the similarity to Hayek's triangles (see figure 3.1).

Figure 3.3. Lindahl's Algebraic Expression of the Time Structure of Production

Time Structure of Production

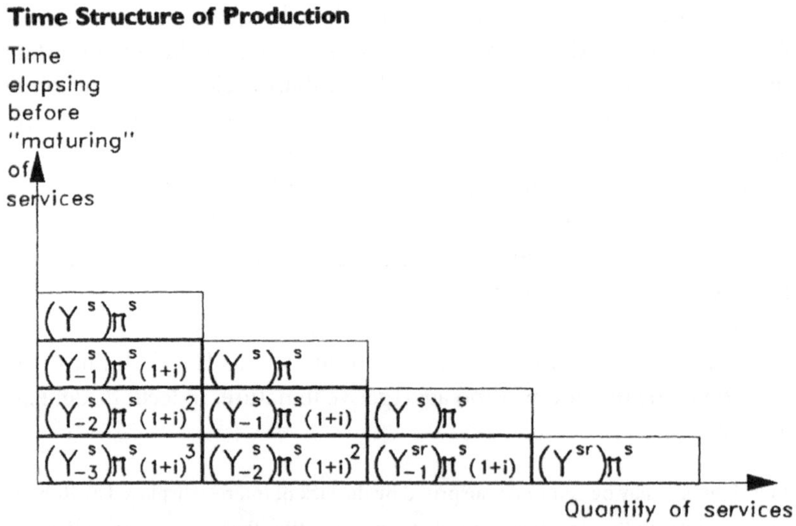

Y^s = original services of land and labor.
$Y^s_?$ = supply of circulating capital goods, i.e., "saved up" services.
Y^{sr} = whole quantity of Y^s used in manufacturing of goods.
i = the rate of interest.
π = prices of Y^s services.

Source: Erik Lindahl, *Studies in the Theory of Money and Capital* (London: Allen and Unwin, 1939).

However, he rejected Böhm-Bawerk's average period of production idea because it obscures the time factor. Defining this average production period as an "unweighted arithmetical mean of the lengths of time elapsing before all original services delivered in a given period mature in consumption goods," Lindahl said it is not appropriate as a measure of the quantity of capital. Instead, Lindahl measured capital as a "weighted average of the investment periods of all original services," based on compounded interest.[123]

Lindahl also divided economic phenomena into definite time periods, known as "sequence analysis" in Swedish economics. He discussed the effects that various government policies, such as credit expansion, lowering of interest rates, and control of the price level, would have on the structure of production.[124]

Gunnar Myrdal (1898–1987), in his classic work, *Monetary Equilibrium*, based his analysis of business cycles on Wicksell's natural interest rate hypothesis and Böhm-Bawerk's roundabout technical structure. The effect of a government-caused lowering of the money rate of interest (below the "natural" rate) would have a greater effect on capital goods than consumer goods:

The greater the remaining life of the capital goods, the more the capital value increases, since they then represent receipts in the more distant future, discounted at the now lower money rate. The increase of capital values is only an expression of the greater profit possibilities of longer, more roundabout processes of production, which follow immediately from the relatively low money rate of interest.

These special profit opportunities are greater, the longer the roundabout processes of production. The entrepreneurs will exploit these profit opportunities by shifting, to some extent, their activity from the production of consumption goods to the production of real capital goods, which is now more profitable. Furthermore, in every kind of production they will employ more capitalistic methods.[125]

Despite the influence of Böhm-Bawerk's law of roundaboutness and Wicksell's natural interest rate hypothesis, Myrdal rejected Hayek's policy recommendations during a depression.

Another Swedish economist, Alf Johansson, developed a model of the economy using four stages of production, from raw materials to consumer goods, to show the effects of higher wages and credit expansion. However, Johansson appeared to ignore the time factor between stages: "Demand between the stages is thus not bound in time to the payments, but occurs (as in reality) by anticipation in the form of advance orders."[126] As a result, Johansson reached the traditional long-run quantity-theory conclusion that production, prices and income would rise uniformly as a result of credit expansion (or in Johansson's example, wage increases) without any ill-effects in the distribution of income.

Erik Lundberg was highly critical of Johansson's analysis of the effect of wage increases and credit expansion, which he labeled Keynesian. He rejected Johansson's purchasing-power thesis that an autonomous increase in wages would stimulate aggregate income across the board. It is important to show the "interval between payment of costs and regeneration of income."[127] Macroeconomic models cause problems, according to Lundberg, "primarily because of time discrepancies between costs and purchasing power. . . . Attention must also be paid, however, to the fact that a time interval lies between the productive input and its payment, on the one hand, and between this payment of cost-income and its use for the purchase of consumption goods on the other."[128] In his analysis of varying "unit-periods," Lundberg referred frequently to Hayekian-type triangles and other more complex graphs.

Seligman concluded that Lundberg's models could possibly tie Hayek and Keynes together. "Two types of crises were involved in Lundberg's models: in one, the break in consumer outlays could be attributed to excessive saving and a lack of sufficient purchasing power; in the other, there was not enough saving to match new investment. At last, Keynes and Hayek were met on common ground."[129]

FRANK KNIGHT REKINDLES THE CLARK DEBATE

One of the most significant assaults on Hayek's capital theory came from University of Chicago's Frank H. Knight (1885–1962). Knight's own view of capital and production was along the lines of John Bates Clark. Just as Clark was on opposite sides with Böhm-Bawerk, so Knight appeared diametrically opposed to Hayek. The Knight-Hayek philosophical duel appeared to be a replay of the debate between Clark and Böhm-Bawerk.[130]

Knight's first foray into the battle over Hayek was in an essay written in honor of Gustav Cassel in 1933. According to Knight, the time-oriented structure of production concept was "originated by Jevons, popularized in a crude form by Böhm-Bawerk, and refined by Wicksell . . . and promulgated by Professor Hayek" on the business cycle. But, for Knight, the theory involves "a number of fatal confusions" and therefore cannot be employed "fruitfully as a tool of analysis."[131] Knight then repeated the view held by Clark: "In a stationary economy there is no interval between production and consumption."[132]

However, Knight granted some of the Austrians' arguments in a growth economy:

> There is no doubt some empirical correspondence between growth of capital and its embodiment in more durable forms and also the splitting up of production into more

"stages." Such changes may carry with them a more inflexible specialization of capital on the whole, making redirection of production a slower process, but this is more likely to be the result of technical advance than of capital accumulation as such.[133]

This was quite an admission for one of the foremost critics of Hayek and the Austrians. Knight admitted that he "completely accepted it [the time-production process] for years, taught it in class lectures and expounded it in text materials" before he abandoned it.[134] Knight continued his relentless attack on the Austrian theory of capital, while promoting his own version in various academic journals in 1934–35. In a 1934 issue of *Economica,* he expounded his own version of capital and interest as a stock-flow concept, where capital is a permanent asset which yields future income, and criticized the fallacies he saw in the time-structural view of a period of production. For Knight, "all capital is inherently perpetual."[135]

A year later, he responded specifically to Hayek's theory of investment (particularly in regard to the production of durable goods) which had been published in the *Economic Journal* in 1934.[136] Knight emphatically stated that a production period cannot be defined. "The sum of the construction period and service life averaged for individual capital instruments is neither determinate in itself nor significant for theory."[137] While granting the Austrian dictum that "in production particular materials go through technical processes and exist in the form of particular named things for intervals which can be *more or less* dated as to beginning and end," Knight rejected the notion that such materials can be identified by a specific stage.[138] It was better to visualize production and consumption in terms of "services," not "concrete things," he wrote.[139]

An increase in capital does not involve a lengthening of the production period, Knight asserted. Using an agricultural example, he wrote:

Taking population as given, raising *more* plants of the *same* growth period will also require more "stock," but *will not* affect the length of the cycle, while the *addition* to total production of new varieties of *shorter* growth, say yielding two harvests per year instead of one, will involve an increase in the capital, while *shortening* the average cycle.[140]

Before Hayek replied to Knight, Fritz Machlup (1902–83) wrote a rebuttal in the *Journal of Political Economy.* Machlup was a former student of Wieser and Mises. The contrasting opinions in this debate were wide-ranging; while Knight called Hayek's theory "worthless," Machlup called it an "indispensible" tool of economic analysis.[141] Contradicting the Knight-Clark view of capital as a "perpetual fund," Machlup affirmed, "There was and is always the choice between maintaining, increasing, or consuming capital."[142] Machlup had recently witnessed firsthand the "consumption of capital" in his homeland, Austria, and had written about it in another academic journal. His studies indicated that Austria had lost 79 percent of its capital base since the First World War, not to war or natural catastrophes, but to inflation, high taxes, and socialistic reforms. He concluded satirically: "Austria had most impressive records in five lines: she increased public expenditures, she increased wages, she increased social benefits, she increased bank credits, she increased consumption. After all these achievements she was on the verge of ruin."[143]

Machlup granted Knight's criticism of Böhm-Bawerk's average length of production, and Machlup also concluded that Hayek's use of a stage of production where there are only "original" factors of production (land and labor) without tools or instruments was "entirely unrealistic."[144] Nor did Hayek make clear enough in *Prices and Production* that "services employed for the making of a machine are, as to their consumption distances, distributed over a great range of time."[145] Nevertheless, Machlup supported Hayek's general thesis, the existence of a "time distance from consumption."

Knight had only a short comment to Machlup's article. Regarding the consumption of capital, he said, "Disinvestment is not in question unless society is decadent."[146] He reiterated that the period of investment lacks "practical significance or even determinate meaning. . . . The only sense in which there is finite time lag of consumption behind production is that it takes time to *change* production, to increase it or decrease it, or shift from one field to another."[147]

Hayek regarded Knight's "perpetual fund" view of capital as a "pseudo-concept" in a 1936 rebuttal, "The Mythology of Capital."[148] Hayek admitted that he saw no reason to measure the total period of production, but that the "period of investment" was relevant.[149] Moreover, referring to Knight's agricultural plant example, Hayek replied that Knight failed to take into account the time it takes to make the capital goods to raise more plants: "The amount of time that will elapse between the making of the instrument and the maturing of the crop will clearly be longer than the period which elapses between the direct application of labor in raising the crop and its maturity."[150]

According to Hayek, Knight assumed "perfect foresight," eliminated time entirely from the capitalistic process, and adopted a capital concept which "leaves us with the impression that there is a sort of substance, some fluid of definite magnitude which flows from one capital good into another."[151]

SUMMARY OF CLARK-KNIGHT CHALLENGE

Uhr summarizes the Clark-Knight theory of capital thusly:

1. "Capital is a permanent fund of wealth embodied in perishable capital goods." There is no relation between a period of production and the interest rate.
2. Production or investment periods have neither beginning nor end. They are infinite.
3. "Capital in the sense of a permanently maintained fund synchronizes consumption and production." In a stationary state, there is no waiting involved, only abstinence of consumption. Uhr suggests that the Clark-Knight analysis is close to Walras's.[152]

THE KALDOR ATTACK ON HAYEK'S NEW THEORY

Nicholas Kaldor's critical appraisal represents the final case of another young economist who eventually became disenchanted with Hayek's theory of capital and business cycles. As noted earlier, Kaldor attended Hayek's classes and, among other things, translated Hayek's *Monetary Theory and the Trade Cycle*. "However, by the mid-thirties," he noted, "faith in the curative powers of deflation had well-nigh vanished."[153] And so had Kaldor's sympathies for Hayek's theories. His fascination with Hayek gradually wore off as more and more "new and unsuspected gaps" appeared in the theory, "until one was driven to the conclusion that the basic hypothesis of the theory, that scarcity of capital causes crises, must be wrong."[154]

By 1939, Kaldor was writing articles opposing Hayek. In one article, he argued against Hayek's view that monetary inflation causes the period of production to lengthen. Kaldor argued instead that *less* capitalistic methods result. "Since real wages tend to fall and interest rates to rise during the upward phase of the business cycle, the probability is that investments undertaken during this period will be of *less capital intensity* than those undertaken during the depression."[155]

In 1942, Kaldor reviewed Hayek's new book, *Profits, Interest and Investment*, which had come out in 1939. In the first article, Hayek attempted to address his Austrian macroeconomic theory to a depression scenario and to respond to previous criticisms. He assumed a virtual Keynesian situation: "We shall start here from an initial situation where considerable unemployment of material resources and labor exists, and we shall take account of the existing rigidity of money wages . . . no mobility of labour . . . and, finally, that the money rate of interest is kept constant."[156] He introduced his concept of the "Ricardo effect," which involves a trade-off between capital and labor. Hayek argued that, in the later stages of a boom, rising consumer prices reduce real wages, causing businessmen to use more labor and less capital. This decline in demand for capital precipitates a crisis and eventually a depression. [157] Therefore, the Keynesian prescription of increasing aggregate demand during a depression would increase prices, cut real wages, reduce capital output (due to the Ricardo effect) and cause another collapse in the capital-goods market.[158]

But Kaldor claims that Hayek changed his mind in 1939:

[H]e put forward a completely new version of his theory in the following year [1939], which accepted the view that the expansion of credit tends to encourage the adoption of less (and not more) capitalistic methods of production, and relied instead on the supposed reduction in investment activity to explain the 'inevitable sequel' of depression and unemployment. Hence, whilst the mechanism was inverted, the moral remained: unemployment was the reflection of too much consumption and too little saving, and any attempted cure by way of expanding demand (through monetary or fiscal measures) would mean injecting more of the same poison which caused the disease.[159]

Kaldor called the lengthening or shortening of production periods the "concertina-effect." He dismissed this phenomenon as "non-existent or insignificant." Kaldor challenged Hayek's new thesis, stating the Keynesian position that *"under no circumstances* can total investment demand become smaller in consequence of a rise in the rate of profit."[160] (Presumedly the rate of profit would increase as a result of increased government spending.) According to statistical evidence provided by Kaldor, "there is no evidence whatever of a rise in margins leading to a fall in investment, or *vice versa.*"[161]

Hayek made a final attempt to explain capital theory in his work, *The Pure Theory of Capital,* published in 1941. It was, according to Shackle, "as it were a final report on Böhm-Bawerk's proposal."[162] Friedrich A. Lutz called it "an exceptionally difficult book," and Hayek himself may not have disagreed with such a characterization.[163] Hayek described capital theory as "the most difficult part of economic theory." He proceeded to develop an extremely intricate apparatus, involving at several points three-dimensional diagrams, in an effort to counter the arguments of critics and include the complex problems of durability and non-specificity of goods.[164] It proved to be an almost impossible task. Hayek himself admitted decades later that to refute Keynes would still require "an elaboration of the still inadequately developed theory of capital" and that World War II and the difficulties of capital theory precluded him from doing it.[165]

The reviews of *The Pure Theory of Capital* were generally unfavorable. R. G. Hawtrey considered Hayek's latest work incomplete and disappointing, proving the great "difficulties" in measuring aggregate capital.[166] And even pro-Austrian Fritz Machlup wrote, "Hayek's *Pure Theory* appeared at a time when writers and teachers of economics were concerned with problems of unemployment, war finance, rationing, industrial organization, and government control of business; they had no time and no inclination to concentrate on some of the most complex and difficult abstractions regarding a subject that did not seem to have any direct relevance to the 'real' problems of the day."[167]

However, G. L. S. Shackle is one of the few sympathetic critics to have something good to say about *Pure Theory*. Calling it "nothing short of heroic" and a "masterpiece," Shackle went on to describe in some detail the Hayekian skein. He adds: "*The Pure Theory of Capital* emerged in its published form from several manuscript versions which I had the privilege of reading during its composition. . . . In his prodigious effort at final vindication of the Jevons–Böhm–Bawerk–Wicksell idea, Hayek had disdained the principle of benign imprecision without which so much of economic theory cannot breathe."[168]

THE ECLIPSE OF HAYEK AND THE AUSTRIANS: A SUMMING UP

The debates in the 1930s over capital theory and its application to macroeconomic issues were a major turning point in the structure of economic theory. Looking back at this period, it is clear that the Clark-Knight and Keynesian schools gained the upper hand in the sense that it is their "stock-flow" aggregate approach that is taught today in nearly every university and textbook.

But the great intellectual war in the 1930s was not just over pure theory. New converts to the Keynesian doctrine, who thought that Keynes had somehow saved capitalism, lost more ground than they thought by accepting the new paradigm of aggregate demand. Once economists accepted the idea that Keynesian policies should be adopted whenever there was "less than full employment," the cancer spread quickly throughout the body politic. It destroyed everything in its path—the virtue of thrift, the gold standard, laissez faire, and other traditional Western values. In its place was created a new monument—inflation, big government, the welfare state, and the consumer society. The Keynesian victory on the theoretical battlefield granted new powerful weapons to the state. By adopting the Keynesian apparatus, the prevailing view among economists is that we can spend our way to prosperity. Government spending can increase aggregate demand, and thus pull a nation out of recession or depression. Consumer and business debt should be encouraged. Private citizens who hoard their savings to protect themselves from unsafe banks or in expectation of lower prices are treated as social outcasts. Unemployment should be avoided at all costs.

In today's macroeconomics, the prominent theories are Keynesian and monetarist, which may differ somewhat in policy recommendations but are not that far apart in methodology. Both schools emphasize the necessity of government intervention in monetary affairs. No doubt one of the principal reasons why Hayek and the Austrians were rejected was because of the 1930s depression and the consequent Keynesian revolution.[169] The depression was viewed as a universal phenomenon, where *all* prices declined in every sector of the economy. It was not just a case of changing *relative* prices between consumer goods and producer goods, as the Austrians had emphasized. It was the case of a devastating and lengthy deflation at every level of the economy. Moreover, Hayek's solution was one of nonintervention by government, which was considered a nonsolution by a growing number of economists and government officials as the depression wore on year after year with stubbornly high levels of unemployment. Norman P. Barry adds, "A theory that characterized the crisis in terms of over-consumption could have little appeal in the circumstances of the fall in effective demand in the early years of the 1930s."[170] Rejected by the Keynesians, the monetarists, and the Marxists, the Austrian school lay dormant for many decades.

NOTES

1. Ellis, *German Monetary Theory,* 345.
2. Schumpeter, *History of Economic Thought,* 1120. Keynes's *General Theory* proved far more influential in the forthcoming decades primarily for political reasons, according to Schumpeter. Although Hayek's view was in keeping with the conservative tone of government leaders in the early 1930s (anti-deficit spending, for example), by the mid-1930s the attitude was quite different, especially among professional economists. "Politically, Hayek's [views] swam against the stream." (1121n)
3. Shackle, *Epistemics and Economics,* preface.
4. Shackle, "F. A. Hayek," 235.
5. Robbins, Foreword to Hayek, *Prices and Production,* xi. Initially, Robbins was extremely exuberant about Hayek's new theories. For example, he remarked, "Good wine needs no bush, and Dr. Hayek provides a vintage over which all true economists will linger long." (xi) He compared *Prices and Production* to D. H. Robertson's classic work, *Banking Policy and the Price Level.* It was Robbins, as department chairman, who hired Hayek at the London School of Economics. Robbins later regretted his excessive enthusiasm, and the foreword was dropped in the 1935 edition even while Hayek lauded Robbins who "has most generously given me his help with all my English publications, including the present second edition of this book." *Prices and Production,* xiv.
6. Kaldor, *Essays on Economic Stability and Growth,* 10.
7. Hicks, "The Hayek Story," 203. Arthur Brown, a contemporary student at Oxford, also recalled the "struggle of our minds" between Hayek and Keynes in the early 1930s.

But unlike Hicks and others who were enamored with Hayek at first, Brown said he considered Hayek's thesis "nonsense" from the very beginning. See Arthur Brown, "A Worm's Eye View of the Keynesian Revolution," 24–25.

8. O'Driscoll, *Economics as a Coordination Problem*, xvii, xx.

9. Hayek, *Prices and Production*, 40.

10. Ibid.

11. Ibid., 53.

12. Ibid., 57.

13. Ibid., 18–20, 24, 133–35. See also Hayek, "A Note on the Development of the Doctrine of 'Forced Saving,'" *Profits, Interest and Investment*, 183–97.

14. Hayek, *Prices and Production*, 57.

15. Ibid., 58. Regarding Hayek's claim that a business slump is precipitated by the noncompletion of long-term capital projects, Erich Streissler maintained that such a situation applies "only in the case of speculative housing booms," and that Hayek's cycle theory is essentially a provincial description of Viennese housing investment cycles in the early twentieth century. ("What Kind of Microeconomic Foundations of Macroeconomics Are Necessary?" 106, 107.) However, Hayek confirmed that "it was in the studies of my descriptive work on American monetary policy that I was led to develop my theories of monetary fluctuations." Hayek, Introduction to *Money, Capital, and Fluctuations*, 2.

16. Hayek had written several articles in German on Austrian business-cycle theory prior to the Great Depression while he was director of the Austrian Institute for Trade Cycle Research. See, in particular, "Monetary Policy of the United States after the Recovery from the 1920 Crisis," in *Money, Capital, and Fluctuations*, 5–32. This essay was originally published in 1925. Note especially footnote 4 (27–28) which outlines for the first time Hayek's version of the Austrian theory of the trade cycle. In the introduction to this collection of early essays, Hayek stated unequivocally that Ludwig von Mises was his mentor and was the source of his theory of monetary fluctuations (1–3).

17. Hayek, *Prices and Production*, 53, 74–79, 89. Garrison compared the "Austrian" approach to the monetary concept with regard to the transmission mechanism of inflation: "The market process identified by Mises and developed by Hayek ignores almost completely the liquidity aspect of money and the corresponding real–cash-balance effect, and it ignores policy-induced changes in the general level of prices. Mises and Hayek focus instead on the effects that a fall of the rate of interest has on relative prices and hence on resource allocation. The theory is not intelligible if the real forces and the monetary factors are treated separately, as they are in Wicksell's writings and in the writings of most neoclassical theorists." "The Austrian-Neoclassical Relation," 98.

18. Hayek, *Prices and Production*, 99.

19. Ibid., 97. In the pages of the London *Times*, Hayek and Keynes debated the role of government during the depression in Britain. A letter to the editor on 17 October 1932, was signed by Keynes, Pigou, and other economists, opposing thrift in a depression. It was followed by a letter on 19 October, signed by Hayek, Robbins, and others, criticizing government spending. This debate is another indication of the broad philosophical battle that went on between the pro-government and pro-market forces during the 1930s.

20. Hayek, *Prices and Production,* 108. Hayek's goal was to stabilize MV (money times velocity), not just M, "so as to make the area of his triangle constant." Durbin, *The Problem of Credit Policy,* 121.

21. Hayek, "Reflections on the Pure Theory of Money," 274.

22. Ibid., 278. "Keynes, who had no appreciation for Böhm-Bawerk's theory, appeared to be confident that a macroeconomic theory could be constructed virtually in the absence of any theory of capital." Garrison, "The Austrian-Neoclassical Relation," 114.

23. Hayek, "Reflections on the Pure Theory of Money," 294.

24. Keynes, "The Pure Theory of Money," 391, 393. It is clear that by 1931 Keynes had already formulated many of his views that were incorporated into *The General Theory* in 1936.

25. Ibid., 394. Keynes downplayed intertemporal relationships and characterized Böhm-Bawerk's roundaboutness as "useless" in *The General Theory,* 21, 210–17. Garrison pinpoints the meaning of Keynes's concept of the marginal efficiency of capital: "Significantly, Keynes used a single variable, the marginal efficiency of capital, to gauge the value of capital goods. The Austrian theorists, by comparison, distinguished between the different stages of production and associated a demand price with each stage. It is precisely at this point in *The General Theory* that Keynes's propensity to aggregate conceals market processes." Roger Garrison, "Intertemporal Coordination and the Invisible Hand," 317.

26. Keynes, "The Pure Theory of Money," 394.

27. Ibid., 397.

28. Ibid., 390. Arthur W. Marget responded to Keynes's new pair of trousers comparison, stating that Keynes "insisted that we shall jump at once into his new, and in many respects looser, pair of trousers without being able to feel that the old ones are at hand to protect us when the weather is such as to make us long for a pair that will fit more snugly." Marget, "Review of Hayek's *Prices and Production,*" 263.

29. Hayek, "A Rejoinder to Mr. Keynes," 401.

30. Hayek, "Reflections on the Pure Theory of Money (continued)," 26. According to Shackle, Keynes did not think new credits affected the structure of production. See Shackle, "Some Notes on Monetary Theories of the Trade Cycle," 27.

31. Hayek, "Reflections on the Pure Theory of Money (continued)," 43.

32. Desai, "The Task of Monetary Theory," 158. Fritz Machlup commented that Hayek's critique of Keynes's *Treatise* initially angered the Keynesian followers at Cambridge. But today the attitude might be different: "I suspect, indeed I confidently believe, that the most loyal followers of Keynesian views, if they now re-read Hayek's criticisms, would accept many of them partly or fully." Machlup, "Friedrich von Hayek's Contributions to Economics," 506.

33. Lachmann, "Austrian Economics Under Fire," 227. The neo-Ricardian counterrevolution finally began in earnest with the publication of Sraffa's small but influential work, *Production of Commodities by Means of Commodities,* whose title gives the impression that Sraffa is going to discuss stages of production. Yet titles can be as deceptive as book covers. The title itself sounds almost mechanical in tone, with no reference

to prices or human action. Sraffa's method of analysis involves one of homogeneous labor, single-commodity, single-technique model in the Walrasian tradition. "Sraffa's book is after all a perfect example of what some economists have come to believe is wrong with economics: there is hardly a sentence in the book which refers to the real world." Blaug, *The Cambridge Revolution*, 28. Sraffa's work is discussed in further detail in chapter 4.

34. Sraffa, "Dr. Hayek on Money and Capital," 41, 45. In reviewing the debate, Ellis, while critical of Hayek's triangles as an "oversimplified scheme," said that Sraffa's review involved "astonishing misinterpretations." *German Monetary Policy,* 353–56, 356n.
35. Sraffa, "Dr. Hayek on Money and Capital," 44.
36. Ibid., 49.
37. McCloughry, "Neutrality and Monetary Equilibrium," 172. Under normal circumstances, commodity futures contracts bear a premium for interest, insurance, and so on. The interest rate is treated by commodity traders as a single rate for all commodities.
38. Ibid., 171, 173.
39. Sraffa, "Dr. Hayek on Money and Capital," 48. Sraffa's view that somehow consumption is fixed during an economic boom, so that little or nothing of new income is consumed, is an extreme position that goes contrary to all historical evidence. Clearly, consumption rises with income.
40. Ibid., 52.
41. Hayek, "Money and Capital: A Reply," 237, 238.
42. McCloughry, "Neutrality and Monetary Equilibrium," 173–74.
43. Lachmann, "Austrian Economics Under Fire," 237.
44. Ibid.
45. Ibid., 240.
46. Hawtrey, Review of Hayek's *Prices and Production,* 125. Hawtrey's review was a serious political blow to Hayek, considering that *Economica* is an official journal of the London School of Economics, where Hayek taught. Although he did not have an academic post, Hawtrey was a Treasury economist and a monetarist who rivaled Keynes in reputation and influence on government policy during the 1930s.
47. Ibid., 121–22.
48. As Robbins noted in the foreword to the first edition of *Prices and Production,* pure monetarists like Hawtrey cannot explain changes in the economy's structure. "In short, the monetary theories have been too monetary." (ix)
49. Hayek, Review of Hawtrey's *Trade Depression and the Way Out,* 126.
50. Hawtrey, Review of Hayek's *Monetary Theory and the Trade Cycle,* 670.
51. Ibid., 671.
52. Hawtrey, *Capital and Employment,* 250.
53. Ibid., 264–65.
54. Lionel Robbins, Introduction to Mises, *The Theory of Money and Credit,* 12. Robbins called Mises's work a "monumental treatise" in the foreword to Hayek's *Prices and Production,* 1st ed.
55. Robbins, *The Great Depression,* 194.

56. Ibid., 174–75.

57. Ibid., 36–37.

58. Ibid., 160–94.

59. Robbins, *Autobiography of an Economist,* 154, 155. Despite his confession, Robbins was quite prophetic in his book, *The Great Depression,* warning in 1934 of the dangers of war and the Nazis, "men to whom the kindly virtues of peace are contemptible and for whom the destruction of life is a better thing than its preservation." (196) He also suggested that government policies are getting worse, not better. "Governments today are actively engaged, on a scale unprecedented in history, in restricting trade and enterprise and undermining the basis of capitalism." (197) Jack Wiseman, former student of Robbins, disagrees with his teacher that the book should not have been written. See Wiseman, "Lionel Robbins, the Austrian School, and the LSE Tradition," 156.

60. Robbins, *Autobiography,* 128.

61. Ibid., 154.

62. Samuelson, "A. P. Lerner at Sixty," 176. Joan Robinson characterized the Hayekian encounter during the 1930s as a "pitiful state of confusion." Robinson, "The Second Crisis in Economic Theory," 2.

63. Smithies, "The Austrian Theory of Capital," 117–50.

64. Gilbert, *Keynes's Impact on Monetary Economics,* 90. Roger Garrison has also attempted to compare Austrian economics to Keynesian economics in diagrammatical form. See "Austrian Macroeconomics: A Diagrammatical Exposition," 167–204. Garrison's monograph has been published separately by the Mises Institute (Auburn, Ala., 1986).

65. Gilbert, "Professor Hayek's Contribution to Trade Cycle Theory," 52. Also cited in Gilbert, *Keynes's Impact on Monetary Economics,* 92.

66. Haberler, "Money and the Business Cycle." Reprinted in *The Austrian Theory of the Trade Cycle and Other Essays,* 13–14.

67. Ibid., 15.

68. Ibid.

69. Ibid., 19.

70. Ibid., 20.

71. Haberler, *Prosperity and Depression,* 63–64.

72. Ibid., 58.

73. Haberler, "Reflections on Hayek's Business Cycle Theory," 423.

74. Tout and Hansen, "Annual Survey of Business Cycle Theory," 131–32.

75. Ibid., 135.

76. Ibid., 139.

77. Ibid., 141. This paragraph demonstrates Hansen's failure to recognize that interest rates affect stages of production differently.

78. Ibid., 147. Incidentally, another review of business cycle theory appeared in *Econometrica* in 1935, this one by J. Tinbergen. The Dutch economist discussed Hayek's *Prices and Production,* and Keynes's *Treatise on Money.* He questioned the notion of changing lengths of roundaboutness in the Hayekian business cycle. "For a number of industries the period of production does, indeed, decrease during the boom period." Moreover,

an inflationary boom can last indefinitely because "[a]s soon as the producers of consumers' goods have higher receipts, they invest more." See Tinbergen, "Annual Survey," 264–66.

79. Hayek, *Prices and Production,* 143.
80. Ibid., 148–50.
81. Abrams, *Money,* 33.
82. Ibid., 114.
83. Ibid., 119. Another contemporary work which summarized Hayek's trade cycle theory and capital structure is Macfie, *Theory of the Trade Cycle,* 45–87. Macfie denied that the "elasticity" of technical stages of production vary during the business cycle; only the value of capital fluctuated.
84. Wien-Claudi, *Austrian Theories of Capital, Interest, and the Trade Cycle,* 11.
85. Ibid., 10.
86. Ibid., 152.
87. Röpke, *Crises and Cycles,* 109n, 110, 134. Strigl's book was not translated into English until 1988. *Capital and Production,* translated by Margaret Rudelich Hoppe and Hans-Hermann Hoppe, is highly theoretical and Austrian in tone. Although Strigi made virtually no reference to other economists, it is clear that his capital theory was built upon the pioneering work of Böhm-Bawerk and Mises, among others. Strigl's model depended greatly on such classical unidimensional concepts as the subsistence fund and wage fund. He defended the superiority of roundaboutness in production processes, the necessity of continual savings to maintain the capital structure, and the inability of government to stabilize an inflationary expansion.
88. Röpke, *Economics of a Free Society,* 43–44.
89. C. A. Phillips, T. F. McManus, and R. W. Nelson, *Banking and the Business Cycle,* 135, 132–39.
90. Ibid., 125.
91. Ibid., 164.
92. A discussion of Mengerian-style stages of production can be found in Mills, *Prices in Recession and Recovery,* 25–26. For a discussion of changes in the time-structure of production in the Hayekian tradition, see 384–85. For a mention of something akin to Böhm-Bawerk's productivity of more roundabout processes, see 385: "Every industrial order is geared to activity involving a certain average time interval between effort and consumption. In general, with economic growth and steady technical improvement, this interval is subject to slow expansion."
93. Contrast Mills's work on relative prices to Stigler and Kindahl, *The Behavior of Industrial Prices,* which contains none of the Mills-type analysis of price comparisons between stages of production.
94. Mills, *Prices in Recession and Recovery,* 4.
95. Ibid., 26.
96. Ibid., 25–26.
97. Ibid., 96–97, 222.
98. Ibid., 151.

99. Ibid., 157–58.

100. Mills, *The Structure of Postwar Prices*, 2.

101. Ibid., 47. Cf. also Mills, *Price-Quantity Interactions in Business Cycles*.

102. Foster and Catchings, *Business Without a Buyer*, 48.

103. Foster and Catchings, *The Road to Plenty* (Boston: Houghton Mifflin, 1928), 193.

104. Hayek, "The 'Paradox' of Savings," *Economica (May* 1921), reprinted with additions in Hayek, *Profits, Interest, and Investment*, 205, 221.

105. Ibid., 247.

106. This is a summary of Hayek's views in ibid., 225–33.

107. Durbin, *Purchasing Power and Trade Depression*, 22.

108. Gaitskell, "Four Monetary Heretics," 348.

109. Ibid., 370.

110. Durbin, *Purchasing Power and Trade Depression*, 47.

111. Ibid., 50–52.

112. Ibid., 52.

113. Durbin, "Money and Prices," 321. Moreover, Durbin's example indicates an unrealistic decline in the profit rate as final consumption approaches. Hayek makes the same simplistic assumption, but was corrected by Rothbard, *Man, Economy and State*, 314–15.

114. Durbin, *Purchasing Power and Trade Depression*, 161.

115. Durbin, "Money and Prices," 339. Despite Durbin's extensive use of Hayekian analysis, he did not endorse Hayek's *laissez faire* policies. Believing that capitalism caused business cycles, he favored socialism and state planning and was a leader in the British Labour Party in the 1940s. See Durbin, "Economic Calculus in a Planned Economy," *Economic Journal* 46 (December 1936): 676–90.

116. Durbin, *The Problem of Credit Policy*, 72–76.

117. Ibid., 129, 129–44, 203–5, 216–41. I analyze the policy of consumer-oriented credit expansion in chapter 10.

118. For an excellent study of Robertson's theories, see Presley, *Robertsonian Economics*.

119. Robertson, *A Study of Industrial Fluctuations*, 15.

120. Robertson, *Banking Policy and the Price Level*, 71–74, 88–91.

121. Bridel, *Cambridge Monetary Thought*, 121–22.

122. Lindahl, *Studies in the Theory of Money and Capital*, 182, 213, 296–313.

123. Ibid., 314.

124. Ibid., 42, 59, 162, 169–70, 180–83.

125. Myrdal, *Monetary Equilibrium*, 25–26.

126. Johansson, *Löneutvecklingen och Arbetslösheten*, 119. For a summary and critique of Johansson's model, see Lundberg, *Studies in the Theory of Economic Expansion*, 68–77.

127. Lundberg, *Studies in the Theory of Economic Expansion*, 76.

128. Ibid., 89, 91.

129. B. Seligman, *Main Currents in Modern Economics*, 602. Cf. Lundberg, *Studies in the Theory of Economic Expansion*, 225. Obviously, Hayek and Keynes came to vastly different conclusions, whatever similarities Seligman could find.

130. For a summary of the Knight-Hayek debate, see Kaldor, "Annual Survey of Economic Theory," 201–33.

131. Knight, "Capitalistic Production, Time and the Rate of Return," 327. Knight said he based his 1921 book, *Risk, Uncertainty and Profit*, on the view that "the 'entrepreneur' buys productive services at a given time, and converts them into a product which he sells at a subsequent time." But, then, he later became convinced that this "Austrian" view of production was "fallacious." See Knight, *Risk, Uncertainty, and Profit*, xl.

132. Ibid., 339.

133. Ibid., 341.

134. Knight, "Professor Hayek and the Theory of Investment," 79.

135. Knight, "Capital, Time, and the Interest Rates," 264.

136. Hayek, "On the Relationship between Investment and Output," 207–31.

137. Knight, "Professor Hayek and the Theory of Investment," 82.

138. Ibid., 88. Knight continued his broadside assault on the Austrian version of macroeconomics in his article, "Professor Mises and the Theory of Capital," 409–27. Knight was apparently determined to rid economics of any time dimensional approach, saying, "For my part, I am as sure as I am of anything whatever that the literature of economic thought hardly contains an error more egregious or palpable than the time-preference theory of interest" (411).

139. Knight, "Professor Hayek and the Theory of Investment," 85n. Knight, in an introduction to Menger's newly translated *Principles of Economics*, attacked Menger's position that factors of production are higher-order goods. "Perhaps the most serious defect in Menger's economic system . . . is his view of production as a process of converting goods of higher order into goods of lower order." Knight, Introduction to Merger, *Principles of Economics*, 25. Kirzner, commenting on this quotation, states: "Because the Knightian view of the productive process emphasizes the repetitive 'circular flow' of economic activity while denying the paramount importance of a *structural order* linked to final consumer demand, it is possible to simply ignore the Austrian critique of the productivity theory of interest. In essence, this is what Knight did." Kirzner, "Ludwig von Mises and the Theory of Capital and Interest," 62.

140. Ibid., 81.

141. Machlup, "Professor Knight and the 'Period of Production,'" 578.

142. Ibid., 580.

143. Machlup, "The Consumption of Capital in Austria," 13–19.

144. Machlup, "Professor Hayek and the 'Period of Production,'" 585–87.

145. Ibid., 609.

146. Knight, "Comment," 626. Knight stated that Kenneth Boulding repudiated the Austrian theory of production, but my reading of Boulding's article suggests that he was quite sympathetic with the Austrians.

147. Ibid., 625, 626.

148. Hayek, "The Mythology of Capital," 199–228.

149. Ibid., 361.

150. Ibid., 367. On Knight's agricultural "crusonia" plant example, see his "Diminishing Returns for Investment."

151. Ibid., 373, 377–81.

152. Uhr, *Economic Doctrines of Knut Wicksell*, 109–10.

153. Kaldor, "Introduction (1960)," in *Essays on Economic Stability and Growth*, 10–11.

154. Kaldor, "Capital Intensity and the Trade Cycle," in *ibid*, 148. Originally published in *Economica* (February 1939).

155. Ibid., 146–47.

156. Hayek, *Profits, Interest and Investment*, 5.

157. Ibid., 8–15. On the Ricardo effect, see also Hayek, "'The Ricardo Effect," 127–52; Hayek, "Three Elucidations of the Ricardo Effect"; and Moss and Vaughn, "Hayek's Ricardo Effect," 545–65.

158. Hayek, *Profits, Interest and Investment*, 27–28.

159. Kaldor, *Essays on Economic Stability and Growth*, 11.

160. Kaldor, "Professor Hayek and the Concertina-Effect," 153. Originally appeared in *Economica* (November 1942). In a letter to Kaldor, Keynes thought that his critique of Hayek was like "using a sledgehammer to crack a nut." Ibid., 11. In another review of Hayek's book, Hugh Townshend suggested that the book was "the record of a mind struggling to be clear." Townshend, Review of Hayek's *Profits, Interest and Investment*, 103.

161. Kaldor, "Professor Hayek and the Concertina-Effect," 175. In response, Hayek admitted that the Ricardo effect may encounter "considerable difficulties" in statistical data. See Hayek, "The Ricardo Effect," 150.

162. Shackle, "Hayek," 242.

163. Lutz, *The Theory of Interest*, 56n. In reviewing Hayek's final book on capital, Lutz concluded that his case was unclear and unproven.

164. Hayek, *Pure Theory of Capital*, of viii, ix. Despite numerous criticisms lodged against Hayek and the Austrian theories, Ludwig von Mises made the bold claim, "In the thirty-one years which have passed since the first edition of my *Theory of Money and Credit* was published, no tenable argument has been raised against the validity of what is commonly called the 'Austrian' theory of the credit cycle." Mises, "'Elastic Expectations' and the Austrian Theory of the Trade Cycle," 251.

165. Hayek, "The Keynes Centenary: The Austrian Critique," 48.

166. Hawtrey, "Professor Hayek's *Pure Theory of Capital*," 281–90.

167. Machlup, "Money, Credit, Capital and Cycles—Machlup on Hayek," *262*. Still, Machlup regarded *The Pure Theory of Capital* Hayek's "finest work," adding that it "contains some of the most penetrating thoughts on the subject that have ever been published." See Machlup, "Friedrich von Hayek's Contribution to Economics," 509.

168. Shackle, "Hayek," 248, 250.

169. "By supposing that aggregate consumption is a function of current (national) income and that savings and investment together determine the level of national income, the world suddenly was made intelligible in very simple terms. Such issues as 'forced savings,' the difference between money and natural rates of interest, and the investment period became irrelevant." O'Driscoll, *Economics as a Coordination Problem*, xv.

170. Barry, *Hayek's Social and Economic Philosophy*, 164.

FOUR

TIME AND PRODUCTION IN
THE POST-KEYNESIAN ERA

The concept of production as a process in time . . . is not specifically 'Austrian.' It is just the same concept as underlines the work of the British classical economists, and it is indeed older still—older by far than Adam Smith. It is the typical business man's viewpoint, nowadays the accountant's viewpoint, in the old days the merchant's viewpoint.—John Hicks, *Capital & Time*

Many economists of varying schools of thought have expressed dismay over the outcome of the debate between the Austrians and mainstream economists on capital theory and macroeconomics in the 1930s. To them, it seemed that the Austrians provided a great deal more information and theoretical analysis of the microeconomics of the economy, which the neoclassical school (including monetarists and Keynesians) sought deliberately to bury. Carl Uhr, for instance, believed that the Austrians won the theoretical battle, even though they lost the political war. He further stated:

Böhm-Bawerk and his followers, Wicksell, Åkerman and von Hayek with their "structural" analyses of real capital have succeeded in pointing out that society's real capital is permeated with complementarity. Production or capital structures consist of many parts interrelated with one another in complex ways or in several "dimensions." These structures are capable of harmonious change, only if the change occurs slowly and in ways which do not introduce increasing imbalances between component parts. Most of the time, they grow via the process of net investment. But the rate of net investment is capable of rapid change, independently of the structure's requirements, as income recipients change their allocation of income between consumption spending and saving. This often produces deep-seated maladjustments, to which is traceable much of the uncertainty and lack of foresight which would prevent Clark-Knight's rational investors from maintaining capital as a permanent fund of value.[1]

Uhr believed that an aggregate homogeneous capital fund loses sight of this relationship.

Kenneth E. Boulding made similar comments: "The attacks on the [Austrian] theory, made especially by J. B. Clark, F. H. Knight, and their followers, have not been particularly fruitful and are based on a view of capital which seems to be even less realistic than the one criticized."[2] While the application of Austrian capital theory was "disappointing," according to Boulding, he rejected the Clark-Knight concept of capital as a "homogeneous fund of values"—"in fact capital is a heterogeneous collection of physical objects *which are valued, and are revalued continuously.*"[3]

Boulding's basic concept of capital has always coincided with the Austrians'. In 1934, he rejected the "lake and stream" approach used by Clark and Knight. Instead he likened capital to changes in the population, having a birth (input), a death (output or consumption), and an age structure.[4] In a 1936 article commenting on the Knight-Hayek debate, he agreed that there were "many difficulties" with the period of production theory, but he still rejected the Knight alternative:

> All experienced flows are in fact heterogeneous: if only for the fact that it would not be possible to observe a perfectly smooth, homogeneous flow at all. Certainly all economic flows are heterogeneous: an income of one hundred dollars a week, for instance, is not a continuous drip of fractions of a cent per second but is a series of discrete payments of one hundred dollars with seven days interval between.[5]

Boulding continued his Böhm-Bawerkian methodology in his textbook, *Economic Analysis,* although the work is largely Keynesian in tone.[6]

Two pro-Austrian economists whose careers extended through the 1930s debates and beyond were Benjamin M. Anderson and L. Albert Hahn. Anderson, as early as 1922, wrote favorably of Menger's ranking of commodities. "It is the one great contribution of the Austrian economists to have shown that the causation in value runs, primarily, from consumption goods to the goods of higher 'orders' which are concerned with their production."[7] In the late 1940s, he emphasized the importance of capital formation in economic growth. "Capital," according to Anderson, "consists of producers' goods, of instruments to be used in further production, instead of commodities destined for immediate consumption." In his "Digression on Keynes," Anderson attacked Keynes for being anti-savings and anti-capital.[8]

HAHN'S "COMMON SENSE" ECONOMICS

L. Albert Hahn, a German economist, wrote as early as 1921 about the effects of bank credit on the structure of production. Initially, he appeared to be quasi-Keynesian and argued that new government bank credit would support an economic expansion indefinitely, creating a "permanent boom," as workers voluntarily increased their savings.[9] However, by the late 1940s, he appeared to have changed his mind and opposed Keynesian "pyramid building."[10] Finally, in 1956 he wrote a book, *Common Sense Economics,* which was highly favorable toward an Austrian time-oriented capitalistic system. Hahn, in fact, called the intertemporal hierarchy of the production process "common sense economics," and analyzes the macro economy in terms of this tool. He wrote:

As production takes time, and we cannot live from hand to mouth, a certain amount of goods in various stages of production must always be simultaneously present in the economy. Goods ready for consumption are, in the first place, essential for production by enabling the workers to survive during the production period; the other goods . . . are essential by enabling the workers to be more productive.[11]

Using Böhm-Bawerk's principle of roundabout methods of production, or what Hahn calls "detours," he discussed the relationship between production, consumption, and durable goods. He described the economy in the illustration shown in figure 4.1.

Figure 4.1. Hahn's View of Production

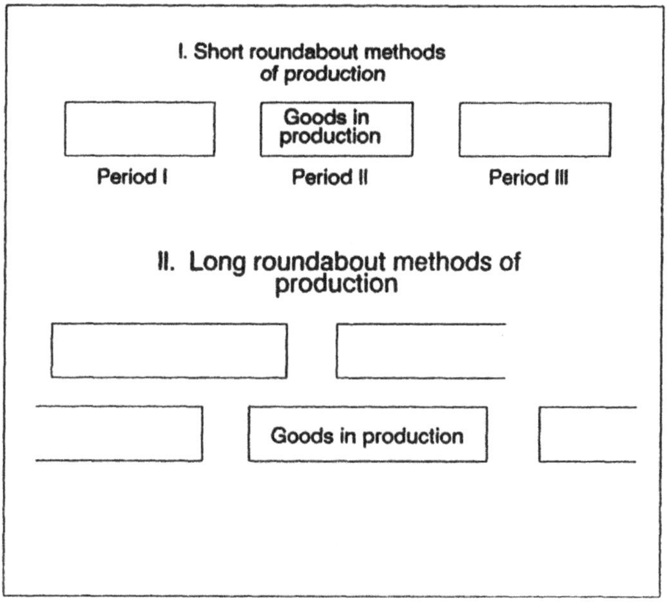

Source: Hahn, *Common Sense Economics,* 30.

As figure 4.1 demonstrates, there are varying degrees of production schedules. "Needless to say, different goods require production detours of entirely different lengths. . . . The production detours of domestic help is very short. For the building of houses and skyscrapers the production detour is very long. But if the capital structure is deepened, every production detour lengthens, although not in the same proportion."[12]

Hahn rejected the standard circular flow diagram to represent the economy, and instead opted for "sequence or chain analysis." Using this period analysis, he investigated the effects of inflation. He divided the effects into three periods:

Period I—the recent past (start of inflation)
Period II—the current production period (inflation taking place)
Period III—the future (effects of inflation)

Hahn argued that the boom following monetary inflation cannot last because the factors of production will inevitably raise their supply prices in a subsequent period.[13]

The German economist criticized the Keynesian multiplier and accelerator principles, and the purchasing power hypothesis. He also objected to modern growth theory because it assumes wage rigidity, fixed relationships between capital and labor, and other "mechanistic" assumptions. "Growth theories may turn out to be just as devoid of practical significance as the stagnational theories."[14]

Hahn blamed the length of the depression not on deficient aggregate demand, but on relatively high real wages: "The fact that the United States, at the peak of the boom in 1936, still had several million unemployed can be explained only by excessive real wages."[15]

THE AUSTRIAN SCHOOL IN THE HISTORY OF ECONOMICS

The neglect of the intertemporal structural theory of capital and macroeconomics is apparent in today s economics textbooks, and is a reflection of the neoclassical victory over the Austrian school of thought in the 1930s. But while this form of free-market economics fell out of favor with mainstream economists, it was not entirely abandoned in the post-1930s world of Keynesian domination. It continued to be the subject of debate and refinement in a variety of textbooks, history of economics, and business cycle theory. The following is a detailed review of the time-structural thesis in the last half of the twentieth century.

The Austrian theories of capital, inflation, and business cycles were the subject of intense debate in books dealing with the history of economic thought.

Works by such economists as George Stigler and Ben Seligman indicate the intense and sometimes acrimonious conflict over Menger and his intellectual descendants.

George J. Stigler, under the influence of Knight at the University of Chicago, is a striking example of the neoclassical assault on the Austrian intertemporal structural theory of economics. He ardently attacked Menger, Jevons, and Böhm-Bawerk. In his review of production and distribution theories prior to the 1940s, he objected to the Jevons-Menger "period of production" school. Jevons erred, according to Stigler, because he "implicitly assumes that every capital good is completely liquidated, once it is completed."[16] Menger's classification of goods into ranks was "of dubious value." Echoing the views of Alfred Marshall, Stigler stated: "The same good, say coal, might be used as a good of first order (in domestic heating) and perhaps a good of ninth order (in smelting ore) in even a simple economy. . . . And to attempt to trace in detail the stages in the production of even a simple commodity—a common pin, for instance—in a highly complex modern economy would amount to nothing less than a detailed description of economic life and its history."[17]

Institutionalist Ben B. Seligman tersely assailed Böhm-Bawerk and Hayek. On Böhm-Bawerk's lengthening of the economic process, Seligman was critical: "Entirely new goods were excluded, as was the possibility of maintaining output or even increasing it with a shorter period of production. Yet nothing in the logic of technology really eliminated such contingencies. The fact was that both shorter and longer processes existed in a dynamic system. . . . Böhm-Bawerk's argument that the period always had to be lengthened was simply not convincing."[18]

Seligman was also critical of Hayek's *Prices and Production* and took a Keynesian view of Hayek's pro-savings outlook:

Of course, Hayek did not take into account the patent fact that such voluntary saving might not have desirable effects, that it could lessen demand, enforce a cutback in sales, and actually reduce investment. The inducement to invest was dependent in large part on a lower rate of interest which could be interpreted as Keynes did, as a function of money and liquidity preference rather than saving. Thus in seeking to postulate a concept of neutral money, Hayek ignored its basic characteristics as both a medium of exchange and a store of value. Since these played little or no role in his theory, the relationships which were altered by shifts in relative prices seemed utterly obscured: contract prices and debts were virtually eliminated.[19]

Seligman called Hayek's triangles "curiously abstruse."[20] He objected to the Hayekian idea that inflation stimulates capital-goods industries more than consumer-goods industries, asking, "Why should not consumer income expand together with the producers' goods industries?" Contrary to Hayek's assertion that interest rates will have an effect on the output of higher-order goods, Seligman asserted that "recent investigations have suggested that investments which are previously committed are unlikely to be influenced by monetary restrictions."[21]

Seligman also did not agree with the so-called Ricardo effect. According to Hayek, the Ricardo effect occurs in the business cycle when the price of capital goods rises so high that labor is substituted for capital, resulting in a shortening of the production period, and thus ending the boom.[22] But according to studies quoted by Seligman, the Ricardo effect does not occur in the way Hayek envisioned it.[23] In the end, Seligman opted for a Keynesian prescription in depression times: "The injection of purchasing power would seemingly have had the effect of stimulating rather than dampening investment, for if consumer goods prices would have risen relative to producer goods prices it would appear that the marginal efficiency of capital would be heightened. And in a condition of unemployed resources, the notion of capital shortage seems highly questionable."[24]

Mark Blaug, in his popular work, *Economic Theory in Retrospect*, made a critical appraisal of the Austrian theory of capital and interest, highlighting the views of Böhm-Bawerk and Hayek. Blaug referred to Hayek as "Böhm-Bawerk's last and greatest pupil."[25] Nevertheless, Blaug raised strong reservations about the "period of production" concept.

> Given the level of investment, a reduction in the rate of interest does encourage the adoption of longer processes insofar as it reduces the opportunity cost of waiting for returns that accrue later in time, but it also renders hitherto unprofitable projects feasible by reducing initial capital costs; these projects may well require less time to complete than the range of previously adopted methods.[26]

Blaug also raised doubts about Hayek's Ricardo effect—an individual firm's own capital (through retained profits) will "usually render the Ricardo effect inoperative in the boom phase of the business cycle unless we introduce additional factors like restrictive monetary policy."[27]

Howard J. Sherman and Gary R. Evans, in their comparative study of macroeconomic schools, commented briefly on Hayek's structure of production. As a "disaggregated sector model," it can be used to explain the fact that "in most contractions, prices of consumer goods fell least, plant and equipment prices fell more, and raw materials prices fell most of all. This supports Hayek's argument that declining costs help stabilize profit margins at some point in the contraction, and this sets the stage for economic recovery."[28]

Sherman, a Marxist economist who specializes in business-cycle theory, wrote earlier that Hayek's stages-of-production schema is the only theory that explains the cyclical changes in various price indices. "In the purely aggregate approach, fashionable since Keynes, the full significance of the fluctuation in the cost-price ratio is not readily apparent." To understand the cyclical fluctuation in relative prices, "it is necessary to use Hayek's approach in terms of 'stages of production,' which consider intermediate transactions between firms as well as aggregate production."[29] Sherman's use of Hayek's stages fits well in the Marxist framework. Marxists often like to use disproportionality in various industrial stages, not to prove the ill effects of government-induced monetary inflation, but to demonstrate the alleged instability of capitalism.

Sherman and Evans sought to explain why Hayek's schema has not been well-received since the 1930s. "Hayek's model is not easy to formalize because it disaggregates the economic process into several stages of production. A complete model would require output, prices, costs, and profit margins for each stage of production. This type of model has been neglected by economists because of the Keynesian focus on the components of aggregate demand in the national income accounts."[30]

In the latest and most important contribution to the study of macroeconomic methodologies, Sheila C. Dow gives equal space to the Austrian viewpoint in conjunction with other major schools of thought (mainstream, post-Keynesian, and Marxian). "The increasing disarray in macroeconomics has encouraged a search for roots," she writes in the preface.[31] In the section on monetary theory, Dow indicates that "Hayek developed his monetary theory specifically to address the problem of explaining the business cycle." In explaining the Hayekian trade-cycle theory, she notes that "monetary factors within the private sector cannot cause cycles, since by definition they maintain the rate of interest at its natural rate. The problem lies with public sector influence on financial institutions. It is thus not surprising that Hayek (1978) should argue in favour of privatizing the entire banking system in order to remove that influence."[32]

BUSINESS CYCLE THEORY: IS FULL EMPLOYMENT NECESSARY?

Several works on business-cycle theory also reviewed the Austrian theory of capital and its relationship to the business cycle. The main thrust of these textbooks was to justify the prevailing Keynesian theory of aggregate demand and pro-government policy recommendations, and to reject the Austrian version of free-market economics unless full employment were achieved. For example, in a popular business-cycle text in the 1950s, Elmer Clark Bratt has a small chapter on "Austrian Investment Theory," and suggested that Hayek's theory of forced savings is not important unless the economy is close to full employment.[33] In short, full employment was the critical missing link that kept mainstream economists from adopting the *laissez faire* approach of the Austrians.

Alvin Hansen, who had previously written a critical evaluation of the Hayekian business cycle, included additional comments in his work on business cycles in 1951. In particular, Hansen rejected Hayek's notion that Keynesian spending on consumption during a depression necessarily reduced capital formation, arguing that "this need not be the case in a society that has unused resources."[34] Furthermore, assuming unemployed resources, "the increase in consumer demand can *induce* an increase in investment; and this increase in investment, via the multiplier process, can raise income until voluntary savings equals the new high level of investment."[35] Hansen also questioned the validity of the Ricardo effect.[36]

D. Hamberg, on the other hand, wrote a sympathetic review of Austrian business-cycle theory. According to Hamberg, business-cycle data confirms Hayek's theory that the capital-goods industry fluctuates more significantly than the consumer-goods industry. However, once again, Hamberg mimicked other economists in claiming that the Austrian view depends on full employment conditions. With unemployment, both capital and consumer goods production could occur simultaneously. "Forced savings" does not occur with unemployment, said Hamberg.[37]

Purdue economist James A. Estey stressed the nonuniformity of prices and costs in the business cycle. "In contraction, as in expansion, the rate of change in prices is quite unequal. Some goods fall but little; others suffer a veritable collapse."[38] However, Estey blamed these structural changes on custom, regulation, and contracts rather than supply and demand based on distance from final consumption. Some prices are "flexible," others "inflexible." Estey emphasized a macro view, not relative prices. In a contraction, prices fall, output is reduced, profits are cut, unemployment rises, and so on.

But then, in his section on the "monetary overinvestment theory," Estey suddenly argued that "no explanation of the business cycle can be regarded as adequate that does not account for the fact that the production of capital goods fluctuates so much more violently than the production of consumption goods." He called the monetarist version, the "monetary disequilibrium model," a "defect." Although it was "adequate to account for the ebb and flow of production in general," it cannot explain the capital-consumption dichotomy. "Indeed, there is nothing in the purely monetary theory to indicate that this extraordinary variation has any particular importance."[39]

Estey described in detail how the shape of the economy's structure of production is distorted by monetary inflation, creating initially a rapid expansion in the capital-goods industry. To keep the boom going, the banks and the central banks would have to advance further credits. "This further increase, however, would have to be greater than the initial one, for the general price level and the general level of incomes have now risen. . . . It is only a question of time until the changed structure becomes impossible and the former one must be restored."[40] Estey believed that the expansion of bank credit to finance World War II was a classic example of Hayek's thesis, if one considers war goods as capital.[41]

Why did the 1930s depression last so long? Estey gave his explanation in strictly Austrian terms:

> Theoretically, there should be a steady transfer of workers and nonspecific capital from the abandoned higher stages to these lower ones. In fact, this process is slow. Shorter processes still have to be started from the beginning. Goods still have to pass through the necessary steps. In addition, it is possible only gradually, as successive stages are reached in the passage of goods to the consumer, to absorb the labor and nonspecific capital released from longer and more roundabout processes. Moreover, this delay is increased by the uncertainty of producers in respect to appropriate methods in the shortened process where a relatively smaller amount of capital and a relatively larger amount of labor are needed.
>
> In brief, workers and mobile resources are released from the longer processes faster than they can be absorbed in the shorter, and the consequence is a growing volume of unemployment. . . . The attempt to restore the normal levels of consumption sets up a further disturbing factor—that is, deflation and a fall in prices—which lengthens the depression and adds to the obstacles facing recovery.[42]

Estey's coverage of Hayek's theory is extensive. He characterized the Hayekian model as "ingenious."[43] The only objection he raised was the one stressed by other orthodox economists, that full employment was somehow a necessary condition for competition to exist between intertemporal stages. Nevertheless, Estey finally admitted, unused resources may delay but cannot avert the consequences of monetary expansionism. "But sooner or later all effective resources will be at work, and if the credit expansion continues, there will be a flow of resources to the higher at the expense of the lower stages, and the full effects on the structure of production will set in."[44]

Another favorable analysis of the "monetary overinvestment theory" of the business cycle came from Lloyd M. Valentine's popular text, *Business Cycles & Forecasting*. Valentine compared the Hayekian theory of fluctuations with the "nonmonetary overinvestment theory" of Marxist Michel Tugan-Baranovsky, German cycle theorist Arthur Spiethoff, and Joseph Schumpeter, because of the many similarities between the two theories. According to the "nonmonetary" school, the economy is divided into four areas:

—Nondurable consumer goods.
—Durable and semidurable consumer goods.
—Durable capital goods.
—Materials used to produce durable goods.

In the upswing of the cycle, new types of durable capital goods are developed to reduce the costs of production (via Schumpeterian innovations), so that an excessively large proportion of resources is allocated to capital goods instead of consumption. Moreover, the demand for more durable capital goods may attract factors of production away from nondurable and semidurable consumer goods.[45]

The downturn occurs because either (1) a shortage of loanable funds forces investment down, or (2) the long-term projects are completed and the industry is depressed, with wages and income falling off just at the time the new plants and equipment are ready to produce more consumer goods. The result is over-investment and imbalance.[46]

Valentine showed that Hayek and the Austrians took a different approach, claiming that the structure of production is not accidental or arbitrary, but deliberate in establishing the proper balance between production and consumption, based on the interest rate. The producer-consumer division must correspond to the proper savings-consumption ratio, or else "vertical maladjustments" occur. An artificial credit expansion would make the structure of the economy "top-heavy." Thus, the downturn occurs because "[i]t is not merely a shortage of investment funds but a real shortage of capital in the lower stages of production, which is needed to achieve a new balanced pattern of production in line with the additional investment in the higher stages."[47]

Valentine concluded that the only major shortcoming of Hayek's thesis is the full-employment assumption. With unemployed labor and resources, *both* producer and consumer industries can increase at the same time.[48]

Meanwhile, Valentine was highly critical of the Keynesian "acceleration principle." The acceleration principle argues that a change in the demand for finished goods causes a more pronounced change in the demand for producer goods. But Valentine questioned the statistical evidence for the acceleration principle. "In the case of producers' durable equipment, for example, it is very unlikely in any economy that experiences marked fluctuations in demand that there will be any regularity in the replacement of equipment." Moreover, according to data from the National Bureau of Economic Research, "The most rapid rate of increase in the production of capital goods occurs early in the cycle, but the most rapid rate of increase in [finished goods] price does not occur until the last segment of expansion."[49]

Asher Achinstein's study of business cycles was also quite favorable toward Hayek's overinvestment theory, even as he ultimately seemed to adopt a Keynesian perspective. Achinstein called "negligible" Hayek's claim that the economy shifts to shorter processes at the end of the boom phase, and criticized Hayek for ignoring "the fact that during the period of expansion new technical processes and labor-saving devices are introduced."[50] Achinstein also chided Hayek for not submitting statistical evidence to support his fundamental proposition, i.e., that capital-goods industries become relatively more profitable during the boom. Nevertheless, Achinstein did not regard these criticisms as sufficient to dismiss Hayek's central theme.

> In contrast to writers who think along the lines of Kaldor, Hayek opens the door to the possibility that prosperity may terminate because of maladjustments arising from the relative profitability of various sectors of the economy. In other words, he is not content with analyses in which aggregate demand is the only mechanism for ascertaining the forces which produce cyclical movements. The factors emphasized by Hayek—the relative changes in different segments of aggregate demand and the shifts in production, costs, and prices that they necessitate—are usually ignored by adherents of the theory of effective demand. Unfortunately, Hayek relies upon artificial constructions and simplifications, arising from his particular type of speculative excursions, which prevent an appreciation of the issues that may be highly relevant to an understanding of cyclical phenomena.[51]

TIME AND PRODUCTION IN ECONOMICS TEXTBOOKS

Despite the preponderance of an excessively macroeconomic view among latter-day economists, there were quite a surprising number of basic economics textbooks published after 1940 that incorporated a supply-chain theory of production. This was a transition period for college textbooks, when many economics professors included the traditional theories of multistage production in the microeconomics section of the textbook while at the same time developing the new theories of Keynesian aggregate demand in the macroeconomics section. It made for strange bedfellows and led to a giant gap between micro and macro theory that is a major source of discontent among academic economists today.

A number of principles textbooks were mentioned in chapter 2 which discuss the stages of production, including Menger, Jevons, Clark, Taussig, and Fetter. Marshall's *Principles,* which hardly mentioned the multi-stage concept, was the primary economics text prior to the 1930s, but other basic economics texts included it as an integral part of their works. Of particular note are the principles textbooks by T. N. Carver, Fred M. Taylor, O. Fred Boucke, Raymond Bye, H. G. Brown, and John D. Black.[52] In this regard, Harry G. Johnson wrote:

> For a period in the 1920s and 1930s, a number of textbook and other writers took great care always to describe marginal products as "(discounted) marginal products"; but that fashion seems to have died out. The approach is in any case clumsy to use, as it is simpler to think of production as a flow process using inputs and producing outputs simultaneously, rather than to keep remembering that if the process were started up from scratch there would necessarily be an interval of time between the initiation of inputs and the delivery of finished outputs.[53]

Nevertheless, a number of textbooks continued the structural tradition of Menger and Böhm-Bawerk beyond the 1930s. Black's *Introduction to Production Economics* is especially noteworthy as a popular economics textbook from the late 1920s to the early 1950s, presenting with considerable attention to detail the stages of capitalistic output over time. Beginning with chapter two, "The Nature of Production," Black relied heavily on Menger's idea of stages or orders of goods and Böhm-Bawerk's concepts of capital and roundabout processes. He illustrated these precepts using the genealogy of a suit of clothes-from the sheep ranges of Australia to the wool dealer, the clothing manufacturer, the wholesaler, and ultimately the retail department store where it is sold directly to the customer.[54] Black made a distinction between production and consumption.

> Consumption satisfies human wants directly, and production only indirectly. Thus when I am wearing a suit of clothes, I am satisfying a want of mine directly, but the farmer who produced the wool, and the factories which spun the yarn, wove the cloth and made the suit, were satisfying no wants of their own directly, nor my want directly—they were merely getting something in condition to be used in satisfying a want later.[55]

Black further observed that "[m]any manufacturing plants . . . are so far removed from the actual finished goods that they make only the machines or the materials that are to be used by others in later stages of the manufacturing process. Behind the baker is the miller, the farmer, the manufacturer of milling machines and bake-ovens, the builders of plants, and the manufacturers of the building materials used in plants."[56]

Black, like Jevons, classified occupations according to "The Fields of Production"—from primary to secondary to household occupations.[57]

He also adopted Böhm-Bawerk's roundabout theory of economic progress. "Roundabout production is today the usual form of production. Production has been getting more and more roundabout all the time. A large percentage of the people of modern occidental nations are engaged in making tools and machines and in building factories and railroads. As a result, the per capita product has been very greatly increased, and men are able today to satisfy more varied and more numerous wants than ever before."[58]

Several principles textbooks continued this tradition of introducing Böhm-Bawerkian production economics to students. An introductory textbook by James E. Moffat and C. Lawrence Christenson was published numerous times between 1926 and 1947. The fourth edition (1947) had a large second chapter on roundabout production, which involves elaborate machines and equipment, complicated processes and an extensive amount of time.[59]

An introductory economics textbook by Albert E. Waugh distinguished between primary industries, which take materials directly from natural resources, and secondary industries, which transform these materials on the way to final consumption.[60] *Modern Economics,* by Arthur E. Burns, Alfred C. Neal, and D. S. Watson, had a chapter called "The Process of Production," and told how a can of string beans is made to show how almost "any commodity in common sense is the product of a long series of diverse and complicated production stages."[61] In the case of the string beans: "In these operations, economic resources are put to use, and from this use the thing in production changes its form (from raw string beans), or its location (from the farm to the consumer's home), or it is held (by the wholesaler and retailer) until needed and finally sold to the consumer."[62]

A popular text in the 1940s was *Economics* by Paul F. Gemmill and Ralph H. Blodgett. They redrew Böhm-Bawerk's rings to show the relationship between land, capital, and consumption (see figure 4.2). Between land and consumer goods are "a whole series of intermediate stages."[63] Gemmill and Blodgett proposed a straightforward description of economics: "The problem of economic society is, in large part, to change land—that is, natural resources—into finished goods, and to place those goods in the hands of the persons who will consume them."[64] Rejecting Clark and Knight, they stated that capital is not a fund, but "capital consists of goods, and not of money."[65] Gemmill and Blodgett cite Böhm-Bawerk's example of the farmer seeking the most efficient way to obtain water to show the advantages of roundabout or capitalistic processes. Referring to a city's water supply system as a modern day example, they stated: "where the amount of capital involved is extremely great . . . it takes months or even years to provide the equipment used in our modern water systems."[66]

J. R. Hicks wrote *The Social Framework* during World War II, a basic economics text for British students emphasizing a neo-Austrian time-using economic process. He said that it turned out "to have had the widest circulation of any of my books."[67]

Figure 4.2. Gemmill's and Blodgett's Version of Böhm-Bawerk's Rings

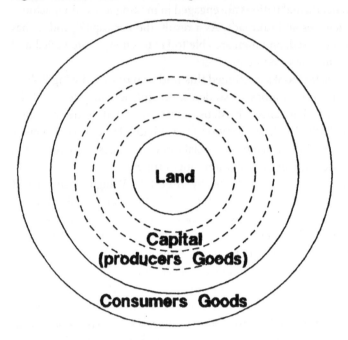

"The Productive Process: This process consists of converting land into consumers' goods, with the aid of labor and capital (or producers' goods). (Production also includes, of course, the creation of non-material goods, or services.)" Gemmill and Blodgett, *Economics: Principles and Problems*, 76. Copyright 1948 by the authors. Reprinted by permission of Harper & Row, Publishers, Inc.

After the war, Hicks joined together with two American professors to write a similar textbook for an American audience, entitled *The Social Framework of the American Economy*. It stressed the "stage" analysis of inputs and outputs, using the simple example of the "history" of a piece of bread, from the wheat crop to the kitchen table. "In our illustration, the bread is a consumers' good; the wheat, the flour, the tractor, the ship, the oven (and so on) are producers' goods."[68] Production takes time, and so does consumption. Hicks and others distinguished between perishable goods and durable goods, and gradually built a more complicated theoretical model of the economy, involving depreciation, services, and durable goods.

Shorey Peterson's 1949 textbook emphasized the time stratification of capital and output. In chapter 2, "The Occupational and Industrial Structure," he divided the levels of employment in a vertical hierarchy. He described the production process as follows:

Any act or process is productive that *helps to make economic goods available....* The product may be any kind of economic good. It may be a tangible, material thing, like a loaf of bread or an automobile, or it may be a nonmaterial service, like the music of an orchestra or the sermon of a preacher. The productive process may be related to the product directly or indirectly and may or may not alter its physical nature. In producing the loaf of bread, farming contributed by raising the wheat, manufacturing by milling the flour and baking the bread, transportation by moving wheat and flour and bread, merchandising by furthering a succession of exchanges, banking by providing funds to mobilize resources.[69]

Peterson gave extensive coverage in chapter 6 to "capitalistic production," highlighting the essential role that inventories play in all lines of production as a reflection of the time element and coordinating process of supply and demand.[70]

Raymond T. Bye and William H. Hewett joined together to write *The Economic Process,* which went through two editions (1952 and 1963). Chapter 5, "The Time Element in Production," is owed mostly to Böhm-Bawerk. Like Gemmill and Blodgett, they illustrated the roundabout process using the example of the building of a city's water system:

In order to provide water for a modern city, men must first extract iron ore from the ground, purify the iron, forge it, cast it, or convert it into steel, make the castings and steel into machinery, then with the machinery and more iron ore make pipes and plumbing fixtures. Prior to most of these operations, rock must be quarried, bricks baked, and cement manufactured, in order that the necessary building may be erected. Finally, reservoirs and pumping stations must be constructed, and pipe lines, sewers, and plumbing systems must be installed. When all this done (but not until then), water flows readily in *every* home, and can be obtained by the mere turning of a faucet.

Months or years must elapse between the first steps in the opening of an iron mine and the eventual flow of water in consumers' homes; and it will be many more years before the total amount of water so obtained is sufficient to compensate for all the preliminary effort that went into the construction of the water system.[71]

Bye and Hewett referred to successive stages as the "vertical stages of production."[72] Some processes are "remote," others "near" to final consumption. They stressed the great amount of time that is often necessary before production finally yields its services. The waiting and production of remote processes are only possible because of "surplus of consumable goods"—i.e., from savers and capitalists. People must use increased income to save and invest in "productive operations at remote stages or in the making of durable goods."[73] Bye and Hewett considered investment an essential factor of production. "Since the extra product obtained by time-consuming methods of production is made possible by saving and investment, investment (also called waiting) may be regarded as a factor of production in addition to land, labor, and business enterprise."[74]

While accepting Böhm-Bawerk's productivity theory of roundabout processes, Bye and Hewett rejected the idea that the average period of production can be measured. It is "a very elusive problem. We can never find the beginning of the production process." However, the "useful life" of capital equipment can be measured. "By calculating the average life of all the manmade wealth in society, then (just as we measured the average length of life of the people constituting a population), we can measure the average period of waiting involved in roundabout production." Bye and Hewett treated the "capital-output ratio" as a measure of the degree of roundaboutness. The higher the ratio, the more capitalistic is the economy. They estimated the U.S. capital-output ratio to be 3.4 in 1955, reflecting a "high degree of roundaboutness" compared to other nations.[75]

Other more recent economics textbooks which mention stages of output over time include Fairchild, Abbott, and Hailstones and Brennan.[76] Hailstones and Brennan compared the economy to a machine:

> The economy can be viewed as a giant productive machine. Inputs of productive resources are fed into one end. The machine rattles and whirs as the various resources are combined and put to work. From the other end of the machine a flow of final goods and services emerges. The process of production, stripped conceptually to its bare bones, is a continuous flow of physical inputs generating a continuous flow of physical output.[77]

Leland J. Gordon, in his introductory book, *Elementary Economics,* defined economics as the study of "the organization and operation of the system which has developed for the purpose of satisfying wants."[78] The organization of his textbook is unique, in that it is organized completely in a time-sequential manner, according to the time-structure of production, starting first with the retailing of consumer goods and ending with the extraction of raw materials.[79] The chapter headings are:

Chapter 4—"The Consumer Goes to the Seller for Groceries."
Chapter 5—"Retailers Buy Food in Wholesale Stores."
Chapter 6—"Wholesalers Buy Food from Processors."
Chapter 7—"Processors Buy Raw Materials from Domestic Farmers" (based on his examples of milk production and bread making).
Chapter 8—"Processors Buy Raw Materials from Foreign Suppliers."

Heinrich von Stackelberg, a German economist who was influenced by Böhm-Bawerk, Strigl, Wicksell, and other members of the Austrian and Swedish schools, wrote favorably of Menger's time flow of goods in *The Theory of the Market Economy.* Like Robertson, he made use of the "period of gestation" in the production formula and developed a one-year model.[80] In contrast to Clark, he suggested that

"As capital is subject to the uninterrupted process of gestation, its composition is continually changing."[81] Stackelberg described the positive effects of a higher savings rate. "Thus with continual saving the average period of gestation is extended, and thus the value of capital and the productivity of industry continually rise."[82] He cited statistics in Germany between 1875 and 1925 (see figure 4.3) to support his thesis that the technical structure of the economy was lengthening as a result of greater savings. During this fifty-year period of time, employment gradually shifted away from consumer-goods output to capital-goods output.

Figure 4.3. Division between Capital Goods and Consumer Goods Industries in Germany, 1875 and 1925

	Employed Persons Percentage Figures	
Industry	1875	1925
Capital Goods Industries	35%	51%
Consumer Goods Industries	65%	49%

Source: Stackelberg, *The Theory of the Market Economy*, 287.

Perhaps the most thorough-going "free market" textbook in the 1950s was John V. Van Sickle and Benjamin A. Rogge's *Introduction to Economics*. Van Sickle and Rogge advocated an international gold standard and were critical of Keynesian economics. They used an elementary Crusoe model (a common device in old-fashioned principles texts) to support the case for increased savings and capital formation as sine qua non for economic growth. Crusoe eventually saves time and increases his standard of living by investing his labor in building a cabin, a water trough and other "round-about methods of production."[83]

Van Sickle and Rogge were highly critical of Keynesian economics in a chapter called "The Theory of Effective Demand." A countercyclical spending policy by the government to increase "effective demand" during a recession was unnecessary, they argued, because "a reasonable amount of flexibility in wages and other cost elements is adequate to prevent widespread unemployment."[84]

The Keynesian critique was followed by the detailed chapter "Alternative Theories," including the Hawtrey-Simons monetarist position and the Hayek-Mises "structural disequilibrium theory." According to the Hayekian interpretation of the business cycle, fiat monetary inflation results in a situation where "the interest rate is not permitted to perform its proper function," that is, to allocate resources between production and consumption. The business cycle is caused by "unwarranted changes in the production-mix, with first too many, then too few, resources being devoted to the production of capital goods."[85]

According to Van Sickle and Rogge, monetary inflation causes an excessive boom and artificially-inflated incomes.

> When this newly created money reaches consumers, as it must when it is spent to acquire resources, they will use it to bid resources back into the production of consumer goods. This will cause serious difficulty to the investors who have not as yet completed their capital goods' projects, and many of those projects will have to be abandoned with great losses. Moreover, because resources do not move back and forth between the consumer goods and the capital goods industries with complete freedom, there is certain to be some unemployment.[86]

One of the few modern textbooks to discuss the intertemporal structuralist approach to economics is *Economics Made Simple,* by British economist Geoffrey Whitehead. He stresses the vertical stages of production at the outset. He also breaks down various trades and employment by their distance from final consumer needs: primary (directly from nature, such as mining), secondary (manufacturing) and tertiary (commercial and personal services).[87]

In reviewing principles textbooks published over the past fifty years, many of them—perhaps even a majority—begin with a discussion of the concepts of time, capital, and the stages of production. Even Paul Samuelson has a small section on "capital and time," confirming that modern society has witnessed a gradual lengthening of roundaboutness.[88] These are building blocks of a complete macroeconomic model. Unfortunately, most of these economic writers neglect the critical microfoundations of the whole economy, and go on to build an excessively aggregate model based on a Keynesian or monetarist macro system. It is my intention to complete the macroeconomic model that these introductory textbooks in economics began.

RECENT CONTRIBUTIONS BY AUSTRIAN ECONOMISTS

Despite the virtual disappearance of the multi-stage production theory in mainstream economic thinking, a small but growing number of economists have continued the Austrian tradition of Menger, Böhm-Bawerk, and Hayek.

Ludwig M. Lachmann has written extensively on the Austrian theory of capital and market processes since the 1930s when he was one of Hayek's students at the London School of Economics. In an article he wrote on the Austrian theory of industrial fluctuations in 1940, he suggested that "Once 'free capital' has been converted into buildings and machinery, any failure of events to conform to expectations will upset everything."[89]

Lachmann stressed the complementary nature of capital goods. "Hides, leather, and shoes in wholesale stocks, are not just physically similar goods at different points of time, but *products* at different stages of processing."[90] He scorned the idea of capital as a "stock" or "fund." "Our heterogeneous assortment is thus converted into a homogeneous aggregate by using money value as a common denominator. . . . In a homogeneous aggregate each unit is a perfect substitute for every other unit, as drops of water are in a lake." Yet: "Once we abandon the notion of capital as homogeneous, we should therefore be prepared to find less substitutability and more complementarity. There now emerges, at the opposite pole, a conception of capital as a *structure,* in which each capital good has a definite function and in which all such goods are complements."[91]

Lachmann continued his efforts to replace the "macroaggregate 'capital stock'" concept, "to be broken up into small entities responsive to microeconomic forces" in his 1956 book, *Capital and Its Structure.* Lachmann's goal was to develop a "capital *structure* of society" and an "order of capital."[92] Opposing capital as homogeneous, he defined it as the "heterogeneous stock of material resources."[93] He had a considerable discussion of Böhm-Bawerk's period of production, and the meaning of indirect, roundabout methods of economic growth. But Lachmann warned, "If the economic system, as it progresses, evolves an ever more complex pattern of capital complementarity, it is bound to become more vulnerable as it become more productive."[94]

Lachmann defended the Austrian theory of the business cycle against its critics: "The Austrian theory does not, as it often suggested, assume 'Full Employment.' It assumes that in general, at any moment, some factors are scarce, some abundant. . . , the heterogeneity of all resources."[95]

At the same time, however, Lachmann adopted over the years several viewpoints closely connected to Shackle and which may be considered quasi-Keynesian. He repeatedly stressed the idea of the "superior strength of the forces of disequilibrium" and that general market equilibrium is highly unlikely.[96] In fact, he states that "[i]n a world in which prices depend on supply and demand in a multitude of markets, a constant price system is almost inconceivable. Relative prices change every day. . . . A price system implying a uniform rate of profit and wage rate cannot exist. The forces tending to bring it about will always be weaker than the forces of change."[97] In addition, in many cases, savings cannot be equal to investment, a theme echoed by Keynes. "Today there appears to be fairly wide agreement that, in modern industrial society at least, we had better refrain from saying either that savings determine investment or that investment determines savings. In the first place, there is no such thing as *a* rate of interest, there is a structure of interest rates. . . . Put briefly, it is impossible to say that the rate of interest brings savings and investment into equality."[98]

Finally, Lachmann maintained that Keynesian economic analysis may be appropriate under certain circumstances, such as a severe depression or war:

The Keynesian economics is an economics of extreme situations; it fits the circumstances of war and post-war inflation with the universal shortage of labour and material resources just as much as it did the world of the early 1930s with almost universal unemployment and "excess capacity." In other words, the Keynesian model fits reasonably well any world in which we find the various classes of factors of production in approximately the same condition, and where they therefore can be treated *as though* they were homogeneous.[99]

Israel M. Kirzner, like Lachmann, also addressed the issues that have divided economists over capital theory. In his textbook, *Market Theory and the Price System,* Kirzner contrasted the "vertical" with the "horizontal" structure of the market. Figure 4.4 demonstrates Kirzner's simplest notion of vertical relationships.

Under Kirzner's system, the market consists of two parts: "a market for products (in which entrepreneurs are the sellers and consumers are the buyers); and a market for productive services (in which resource owners are the sellers, and entrepreneurs are the buyers)."[100] The horizontal market consists of goods or factors within the same vertical stage.

Figure 4.4. Kirzner's Vertical Structure

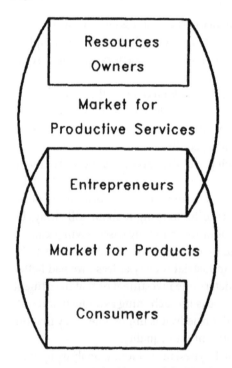

Source: Kirzner, *Market Theory and the Price System,* 19.

Kirzner described the supply and demand conditions for capital goods in terms of time preference. "Demand conditions for capital goods will thus reflect the relatively greater *nearness* in time to the final production goal, which command of these goods confers. Supply conditions for capital goods will reflect in turn, among other costs of production, the sacrifice of *time* that went into their production."[101]

In a short work entitled *An Essay on Capital*, Kirzner began with a discussion of Crusoe economics and the significance of "multi-period plans" of entrepreneurs. In this regard, capital plays a vital role. "The revision of plans cannot be understood without reference to the stocks of equipment, raw materials, half-finished products and finished products, that are available at the relevant dates."[102]

He was critical of Knight's "permanent fund" thesis and Clark's "synchronization" of production and consumption, which meant no time lag between inputs and outputs. In defense of Böhm-Bawerk's period-of-production concept, Kirzner argued:

As soon as one recognizes that periods of production are important only insofar as they are taken into account in the forward looking multi-period plans of acting individuals, the entire Knightian objection falls away. If the operator of a Roman iron mine did not introduce into his planning any of the implications of the fact that some of the ore may find its way into the pocket knife of a twentieth-century school boy, then no production period extending from Roman times to those of the schoolboy is relevant for the theory of capital, either as applied to Roman industry or to that of the twentieth century.[103]

Murray N. Rothbard, one of the foremost leaders of the Austrian school of economics, has constructed a whole theory of the economy based on the time structure of production. In his monumental work, *Man, Economy, and State*, Rothbard developed an "aggregate production structure" based on the Misesian "evenly rotating economy."[104] Since the interest rate is the same for the ERE at every stage of production, according to Rothbard, the value of all firms at each stage can be aggregated. "Money moves from consumers' goods back through the various stages of production, while goods flow from the higher through the lower stages of production, finally to be sold as consumers' goods."[105] He made extensive use of Hayek's triangles and used his macro model to analyze the effects of monetary inflation and the business cycle.[106]

Like Mises, Rothbard was critical of Böhm-Bawerk's "average period of production," which he called a "mythical concept."[107] He also objected to Böhm-Bawerk's term *roundaboutness*: "Calling these methods 'roundabout' is definitely paradoxical; for do we not know that men strive always to achieve their ends in the most direct and shortest manner possible?"[108] But lengthier processes are necessary, Rothbard maintained. Using oil as an example, he described how, when oil is discovered in the ground, it required the production of wells and drilling machinery. "In other words, the only way to obtain more oil now is to invest more capital in more machinery and lengthier production periods in the oil-drilling business."[109] There is no doubt that Rothbard has carried the Menger-Hayekian theory of production further than any other economist in modern times.

Rothbard applied the Mengerian economic structure and the Hayek-Mises theory of the business cycle to the Great Depression of the 1930s in his immensely successful book, *America's Great Depression*. He argued that "business cycles and depressions stem from disturbances generated in the market by *monetary intervention*."[110] The government, not private enterprise, was responsible for the boom-bust cycle.[111] The boom, created by an expansion in government fiat credit, causes "a period of wasteful malinvestment . . . the depression *is* the 'recovery' process. . . . The boom, then, *requires* a 'bust'."[112] Rothbard was critical of alternative theorists of the business cycle, including Keynesians and the underconsumptionists. "A favorite explanation of the crisis is that it stems from 'underconsumption'—from a failure of consumer demand for goods at prices that could be profitable. But this runs contrary to the commonly known fact that it is *capital goods,* and not consumer goods, industries that really suffer in a depression."[113] According to Rothbard, the Keynesian prescription of more consumption is just the opposite of what should be done to reverse the depression: "More consumption and less saving aggravate the shortage of saved capital even further."[114] Rothbard advocated policies which are frequently in opposition to the view of establishment economists, but which conform more to pre-Keynesian free-market economics: encourage savings, curtail government spending, reduce taxes, return to a gold standard (i.e., stop inflating the money supply), and encourage flexibility in wages.[115] In the last half of the book, Rothbard applied his "Austrian" perspective specifically to the 1929–33 economic debacle, arguing that the Federal Reserve's inflation during 1921–29 led inevitably to the crash and ensuing depression during 1929–33.

THE AUSTRIAN EXPLANATION OF "INFLATIONARY RECESSION"

In the second edition of *America's Great Depression*, Rothbard was one of the first economists to offer an explanation of the contemporary phenomenon of an "inflationary recession" using the Mengerian stages of production.

Neither the Keynesians nor the contemporary "monetarist" schools anticipated or can provide a satisfactory explanation of this phenomenon of "inflationary recession." Yet the "Austrian" theory contained in this book not only explains this occurrence, but demonstrates that it is a general and universal tendency in recessions. For the essence of recession . . . is a readjustment of the economy to liquidate the distortions imposed by the boom—in particular, the overexpansion of the 'higher' orders of capital goods and the underinvestment in consumer goods industries. . . .

In short, the prices of consumer goods always tend to rise, relative to the prices of producer goods, during recessions. The reason that this phenomenon has not been noted before is that, in past recessions, prices have *generally fallen*. . . . The result of the government's abolition of deflation, however, is that general prices no longer fall, even in recession. . . . Hence, the prices of consumer goods still rise relatively, but now, shorn of general deflation, they must rise absolutely and visibly as well.[116]

The subject of inflationary recession continued to interest Austrian economists in the late 1970s. In one of the most succinct articles on the subject, two economists, Gerald P. O'Driscoll, Jr. and Sudha R. Shenoy, applied the Austrian time hierarchy of production to the problem of inflationary recession along the lines of Rothbard. They pointed out the inadequacies of the Keynesian and monetarist models, and how monetary inflation creates "maladjustments" in the structure of the economy, thus bringing about the concommitant ill effects of inflation and a decline in real output.[117]

O'Driscoll, as part of his published dissertation, *Economics as a Coordination Problem,* analyzed the economics of Friedrich A. Hayek, especially with reference to his macroeconomic theories of the 1930s. Overall his review was sympathetic, but he criticized Hayek for adopting a most "un-Hayekian" procedure in *Prices and Production*. "He treated consumer goods as homogeneous if they are available in the same time period. . . . He in effect adopted a one output-good model, though he was quite explicit at other places about the difficulties that arise from the existence of heterogeneous capital goods."[118] O'Driscoll also offered an unusual explanation of the Phillips curve trade-off between inflation and unemployment using Hayek's Ricardo effect.[119]

In a more general way, Roger W. Garrison made the first attempt to contrast Austrian macroeconomics and Keynesian macroeconomics in a diagrammatical fashion. The two-dimensional structure of production (time and output) is, according to Garrison, "one of the most distinctive features of Austrian macroeconomic theory."[120] Using a form of Hayek's triangles, Garrison demonstrated how the structure of production is altered by an expansion of the money supply, the ill effects that follow, and how Keynesian diagrams obscure this distortion in the market processes.[121] Garrison has in fact been in the forefront in publishing articles attacking Keynesian economics.[122]

A little-known exposition on Austrian macroeconomics, *The Economic Axioms* by Howard S. Piquet, was published in 1978. It incorporated the use of

Hayekian-type triangles, except that Piquet employs three-dimensional "cones." Piquet's mentor, Frank A. Fetter, established a "subjective" approach to economics along the line of Menger and the Austrian school.[123] Piquet defined production as "the forward movement of use from the most indirect level through various stages of indirectness to the level of direct (or end) use."[124] This principle is "one of the most basic and most important distinctions in economic thinking."[125] He used the common illustration of iron ore being transformed into iron, steel, the oven, and so on. Figure 4.5 shows how each good is qualified according to three dimensions:

Figure 4.5. Piquet's Three Dimensions of Goods

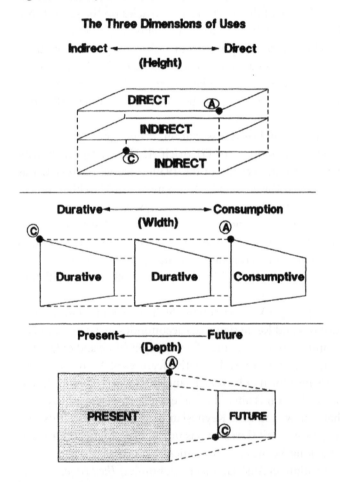

Source: Piquet, *The Economic Axioms*, 13.

1. Degree of indirectness.
2. Degree of durativeness.
3. Degree of futurity.

Piquet reviewed Hayek's *Prices and Production* approvingly, making only minor criticisms.[126]

Three Austrian economists—Gerald P. O'Driscoll Jr., Mario J. Rizzo, and Roger Garrison—attempted a full-scale development of economic theory in *The Economics of Time and Ignorance*, published in 1985. Garrison contributed an important chapter, "A Subjective Theory of a Capital-Using Economy," based on the "Mengerian vision" of "goods in process."[127] He stressed that each stage of production is subjective in concept. "A given stage does not correspond to a particular industry or even to a particular, objectively defined, collection of capital goods."[128] According to Garrison, the coordination between stages—the saving/investment decision—"has always been the central issue in macroeconomics."[129] Moreover: "Modern macroeconomics has virtually ignored the relationship between changes in liquidity preferences and alterations in the multi-stage production process as conceived by the Austrian school."[130]

Building on Garrison's subjective capital concepts, O'Driscoll and Rizzo analyzed the "microanalytics of money" and the Mises-Hayek theory of economic fluctuations. They emphasized the "serious coordination failure" caused by government monetary policy which results in malinvestment or misdirected investment (*not* simply overinvestment).[131] O'Driscoll and Rizzo then referred to statistical evidence in support of the Mises-Hayek interpretation of business cycles, particularly the econometric work of Charles Wainhouse.[132]

CAPITAL THEORISTS AND THE RETURN OF THE MENGERIAN VISION

But it is not just the Austrian school of economics that has recently shown an interest in the Mengerian approach to capital theory and macroeconomics.

Many mainstream capital and growth theorists have shown a decided affinity toward the vertical approach to macroeconomic analysis. Joe S. Bain, for example, adopted an Austrian view of production as a "chain effect through time."[133] He added:

Although "lengthening" and "shortening" are oversimplified one-dimensional concepts as applied to an essentially multidimensional structure of production, the general validity of the idea is clear. It is quite clear that in industrial societies since 1800, for example, there has been a progressive and rapid "lengthening" of the structure of production, as an increasing proportion of resources has been devoted to the production of capital goods.[134]

B. S. Keirstead, in another example, characterized the economy as a "progressive capital-using society."[135] He rejected the Clark-Knight concept of capital as an abstract, mobile, and indestructible fund. For Keirstead, the time lag between investment and consumption is significant, and is too often neglected in growth and trade-cycle theories.[136] Measurement of the period of production is virtually impossible on an aggregate scale, however. "It is in a complex economy when we contemplate groups and series of investments in the making of tools of various periods of production that the problem becomes difficult or impossible to solve."[137]

Keirstead then explained the importance of viewing the economy as a heterogeneous structure of capital:

Economists of our times, however, who have had to deal with the problems of the so-called under-developed nations have found this question of the structure and form of capital of first importance. The first crude attempts to deal with the underdeveloped countries turn on the assumption that they lacked capital and that the only source of capital was from foreign loans or gifts. It was soon apparent, however, that there were local sources of capital supply in many of these countries, that capital was, in fact extensively used, and that one could not simply say "import capital"; one had to specify what kind of capital and for what uses.

The Hayekian theory has been found to fit much closer to the facts as they were revealed in these countries than other western economic formulations. The high rate of time preference, as reflected in rates of interest which to western eyes were usurious, explained the comparatively short-run investments that characterized these economies and the rapid turnover of loanable funds.[138]

Trygve Haavelmo, a Norwegian economist, has also been sympathetic to the Austrian theory of capital. He analyzed the economy in terms of the time element and the instruments of production. "There is no *formal* difficulty in constructing a recurrent chain from a given capital item back to the original factors of labor and land (even if such a calculation may be impossible in practice). There is no denying that this way of looking upon the subject of capital can give us insight into the fundamental relations between capital and the time element, even if the procedure is somewhat artificial."[139] Haavelmo looked at a variety of production processes: Wicksell's wine aging process, the growth of trees in a forest, the growing of apples, cattle feeding, an assembly line, the production of a ship or machine, and the building of a house.[140]

Robert M. Solow, who has attempted to mathematically develop a general equilibrium model, admitted that it is "extraordinarily complicated" to create a capital theory which includes consumer goods, fixed capital, and working capital.[141] In addition, he confessed, "We still do not have a satisfactory specification of the conditions under which the adjustment mechanism of the economy will guide it to its general equilibrium position."[142]

In building a capital-using economic model, Solow adopted a subjective outlook: "Capital problems are inevitably bound up with questions of uncertainty, limited foresight, and reactions to the unexpected."[143] While having misgivings about the Austrian emphasis on circulating or working capital, Solow did accept the Austrian view that a time structure of the economy is essential: "I think the Austrian school overdid the identification of capital itself (and capital theory) with time—it was an inspired simplification that didn't work—but the need for a theory of capital does arise only when we try to take account of production processes which involve time in some essential way."[144] He opted for a "theory of the rate of return," rather than one which requires a measurement of capital.

William J. Baumol's extensive analysis of capital was based almost entirely on time and the period of production. According to Baumol, "the mere passage of time can be a crucial requisite of production." [145] Furthermore:

Any good whose manufacturer makes use of capital must involve the passage of time. For a capital asset is defined as a means of production which was itself produced *before* being put to its current use. Work on today's newspaper must already have been underway when metal was being mined for the production of the linotype machines, when the trees for making the paper were being planted, and so on.[146]

Baumol stated that capital involves three characteristics:

1. Time it takes to produce a good.
2. Quantity of machine units (value).
3. Date of activity.

Baumol criticized Böhm-Bawerk's "average period of production" for making "the error of forgetting the necessity of *discounting* if outlays at different dates are to be compared and added together."[147] He then developed a Böhm-Bawerkian model in which "increasing capital intensiveness always takes the form of a longer (more time consuming) process which permits labor to be saved."[148] He used three processes involving the output of firewood.

In process I, one plants some fast-growing bushes and uses them one year later, with much labor needed to gather the required amount of wood. In process II, one plants two years before using the wood, expending an intermediate amount of labor in watering and weeding one year before the wood is used. In process III, the wood is permitted to grow for three years with small amounts of labor devoted to its care during each of the years of its growth. The processes have been ordered so that each one is more *capital intensive, or roundabout* than its predecessor—each involves an earlier expenditure of preliminary labor than the one before it.[149]

The following figure 4.6 summarizes the three processes:

Figure 4.6.

			Outlays of Labor		
Process	Capital Intensity	t	t + 1	t + 2	Total
I	low	0	0	12	12
II	intermediate	0	4	4	8
III	high	2	2	2	6

Source: William J. Baumol, *Economic Theory and Operations Analysis*, 4th ed., © 1977, p. 658. Reprinted by permission of Prentice Hall, Inc. Englewood Cliffs, N.J.

The three discounted cost figures per unit of output are:

$$C_1 = 0 + 0D + 12D^2 = 12D^2$$
$$C_2 = 0 + 4D + 4D^2 = 4D + 4D^2$$
$$C_3 = 2 + 2D + 2D^2$$

where $D = 1/(1 + i)$, the discount factor, and where i is the interest rate.

Like Wicksell, Baumol concluded that as the interest rate declines, the more roundabout processes become cheaper. Thus, more capitalistic methods are adopted, and the capital-output ratio rises. On the other hand, if the interest rates rise, there is a fall in output because less capital is used.[150]

As mentioned in chapter 1 of this work, Michio Morishima abandoned the neoclassical approach to production in favor of genealogical techniques, or what he calls "blueprints."[151] Morishima attempted to develop an aggregate production structure based on vertical processes using matrix algebra.[152] The "immobility of capital goods" makes "aggregation" difficult if not impossible. Decision-making, even by socialist economies, must be decentralized, according to Morishima.[153]

MODERN CRITICISM OF AUSTRIAN CAPITAL THEORY

Donald Dewey's theory of capital is more in the tradition of Clark's and Knight's. Highly critical of Böhm-Bawerk, he stated: "Even if capital accumulation is associated with an increase in the average useful life of capital assets, this increase has no economic significance. In the construction of a capital asset, the crucial consideration is not time but *cost in relation to income*."[154] Dewey referred frequently to Knight's Crusonia plant as a representation of a homogeneous capital stock which is constantly increasing except for tissue consumed: "Income is the amount by which the size of the plant would increase, in any time interval, in the absence of consumption. . . . An economy so favored by nature has only one economic problem. It must decide how much consumption to forgo now in order to have more income later."[155]

C. J. Bliss warned economists in 1971 that "the most urgent imperative facing the theory of capital at the present time is to get away from steady states, long-run equilibrium, and even the 'essentially timeless' Arrow-Debreu model, and to confront directly the problems of short-run equilibrium in a world in which the future is uncertain."[156] Later, he partially rejected Böhm-Bawerk because "it is not difficult to invent examples where the most productive method does not take longer, but rather takes a shorter time."[157] But then Bliss proceeded to adopt a model "closer" to the Austrian theme than any other! Like the Austrians, he rejected the mainstream view that the interest rate is the price of capital. Dismissing Solow's rate-of-return model, he developed a capital theory based on "intertemporal prices," where consumers set up "intertemporal consumption plans" and firms set up "intertemporal production plans."[158]

Daniel M. Hausman called the Austrian theory of capital "ingenious" and a "particularly intelligible effort." "The Austrian theory is more sophisticated than Clark's work and, indeed, functions as a critique of Clark."[159] He cited Oskar Lange's two-commodities model of the economy, a capital good (axes) and a consumption good (wood). He concluded: "Notice that, despite the fixed periods of production, Lange's model does support the Austrian view that capital is not an independent factor of production and that indirect processes are more productive. When money capital is scarce, less indirect and more direct labor per unit wood output will be used."[160] The U.S. economy, according to Hausman, is a classic Austrian example in that "more roundabout production processes have always been more productive."[161]

Despite these favorable remarks, Hausman concluded that there is "little evidence for its truth." "The problem with the Austrian theory of capital is that it is unfounded. It is not a minor application of the basic equilibrium model, but adds substantive but unsubstantiated claims. Böhm-Bawerk's law of roundaboutness is nicely illustrated by aging wine or by Lange's wood and ax model, but economists have no reason to believe that it is generally reliable."[162] According to Hausman, more empirical evidence is needed to prove that roundabout processes are more productive.

THE DEBATE OVER MODERN AUSTRIAN CAPITAL THEORY

The excessive aggregation and neglect of the time horizon in macroeconomics led to the creation of a "neo-Austrian" capital theory in the 1970s. One of the prominent names in this episode is John Hicks, discussed at the end of this chapter. Another group that focused on this area came from Germany, and includes Malte Faber, Peter Bernholz, and others.

Faber combined his earlier papers with Bernholz's to write an *Introduction to Modern Austrian Capital Theory* in 1979. In it, Faber criticized Hicks' neo-Austrian approach in that, although he included time in his model, he "does not use the Austrian concepts of superiority of roundabout methods, of time preference and of the period of production."[163] He further attacked standard neoclassical capital theory because it adopts a timeless Walrasian view and usually oversimplifies the market by having only one capital good and one consumption good. Hence, "relative prices" play no role.[164]

Using a two-period two-sector model, Faber developed a special case based on redefined Böhm-Bawerkian concepts of superiority and roundaboutness. A superior technical method is defined as one using less labor, and a roundabout method is one which requires a reduction in current consumption. By defining these terms in this way, a roundabout method can be either more or less capital-intensive. Thus, Faber was able to avoid the flawed average period of production problem as well as the sticky reswitching debate, discussed below. Using a generalized von Neumann model of balanced growth, Faber demonstrated that positive net investment necessarily meant superiority, roundaboutness, and a positive rate of interest.[165]

Faber's methodology has not gone uncriticized. Gerhard O. Orosel, an economist at the University of Vienna, argued that Faber's theory is "neither modern nor 'Austrian.'"[166] Faber "is simply using a standard neoclassical model and not the Austrian conceptualization of the production possibilities."[167] "Further, it seems that Faber is not aware that in order to speak of 'more roundabout' methods of production one must have *some* notion of the 'time' that passes between inputs and outputs, i.e., of a 'period of production.' Hence without a concept of a period of production the notion of 'roundaboutness' becomes meaningless."[168]

In his response, Faber justified his position. According to Faber, the "essential" features of the Austrian theory of capital are the superiority of roundabout methods and the time structure of goods. But the Austrian theory must be restructured because of the "unrealistic weaknesses" of Böhm-Bawerk and Menger, including the problems of measuring the production period, circularity and joint production.[169]

In a rejoinder, Orosel denied that a vertical structure of production even existed in Faber's model, adding that the von Neumann model "explicitly displays the *horizontal* and not the vertical structure of production."[170]

Roger W. Garrison criticized Faber for his straitjacket formalism. "Constructing a model that allows for only one capital good and theorizing in terms of units of the capital good serves to skirt, rather than answer, the fundamental questions in capital theory."[171] Garrison noted the severe assumptions Faber required in order to reach his conclusions. For example, the economic model presumed a centrally planned economy.[172] More to the point, Faber used a variety of highly stylized formulations:

> There are no market processes in Faber's model. There are no money prices that convey market information. In fact there is no money in the model. . . . Each investment is immune from risk and uncertainty, and all investments are assumed to be perfectly coordinated. Thus, the model has no use for entrepreneurs. And despite all the discussion about multiple periods, the temporal structure of production, and roundaboutness, Faber is actually offering us a timeless model. It is timeless in the sense that there is no analytical distinction between the past, the present, and the future.[173]

In a recent contribution, Faber extended the formalism noted by Garrison in comparing "modern Austrian capital theory" with Sraffa's neo-Ricardian book, *Production of Commodities by Means of Commodities*. Faber noted that the title is similar to the second section in Menger's *Principles of Economics*, namely, "Capital as Means of Production." Faber stated: "Both point to our main theme, the vertical time structure of production, which is neglected in neoclassical steady state theory. Both are related to each other by bringing to the fore intermediate products and the production process."[174] Nevertheless, despite Faber's comparisons, the similarities are superficial and the differences are substantial. In Sraffa's book, it is clear that there is no real discussion of the production process with his basic commodities, wheat and iron. He rejected the period of production and the linear direction of capital toward consumption.[175] Instead, he opted for the classical circular process.[176] Moreover, as Burmeister noted, Sraffa "implicitly assumes a steady state equilibrium in which prices are constant."[177] No wonder Hausman concluded, "It is not yet clear, however, what, if anything, one can learn from it."[178]

Faber's is the first significant attempt to apply the principles of advanced mathematics to Austrian capital theory, and the above analysis demonstrates the difficulty in doing so. Another effort has recently been made by two other German economists to create a mathematical model for Hayek's macroeconomic concepts in *Prices and Production*. According to Thalenhorst and Wenig,

Prices and Production "contains a brilliant piece of economic theory which is quite distinct from present-day neoclassical and Keynesian economics and which has remained a serious alternative to conventional economic analysis."[179] But this distinction makes it all the more difficult to incorporate Hayek's model into mathematical language. Thalenhorst and Wenig's efforts amounted to an equilibrium analysis only, while Hayek's theory is primarily concerned with disequilibrium analysis. The authors expressed disappointment that they created only a static, not a dynamic, model. Furthermore, Viennese economist Hansjörg Klausinger criticized it as a distorted version of Hayek's theory because it concluded that an increase in thrift reduced the length of the production process, which is precisely the opposite of Hayek's case![180] Comparing their model to a "frictionless barter" case, Klausinger concluded: "It is evident, then, that if one tries to promote a renaissance of Hayekian economics, one must hope that disequilibrium analysis can get beyond the state now prevailing and one will be able to reconstruct formally the typical paths of a Hayekian business cycle. . . . Undoubtedly most of the work still remains to be done."[181]

CAPITAL PARADOXES AND "RESWITCHING": THE CAMBRIDGE CHALLENGE TO BÖHM-BAWERK

The greatest theoretical challenge to the Austrian theory of capital came from the Cambridge school in England in the 1950–60s, led by Joan Robinson and Piero Sraffa, among others. They questioned the classical growth theory of Böhm-Bawerk and the Austrians, which held that a lower interest rate involved more roundabout productive processes and that the interest rate was determined solely by time preference, not productivity.

Accepting the view that capital represents specific tools and equipment and is therefore "heterogeneous," Robinson proposed that capital is often used in fixed combinations with labor and raw materials. This meant that there may be "no room" for factor substitutions except by "switching" from one fixed-proportion technique to another.[182]

Using a Wicksell-type example of wine-making, labor-use may be high in the beginning (picking and sorting), while capital intensity may be low. According to the Cambridge theorists, it may *not* be true that higher interest rates will necessarily lead to a less capital-intensive output. As Richard X. Chase states:

Thus an increase in interest costs would probably tend to induce producers to economize by shortening the aging stage closer to its limits, given the acceptable quality standards for the wine. . . . However, further increases in the rate of interest would, at a point, raise the costs of holding wine so much that producers would find it advantageous to switch to some technique of higher capital intensity that would speed up, that is, shorten the production process.[183]

Samuelson, in a famous 1966 article in which he declared "unconditional surrender" to the Cambridge Switching Theorem, gave an illustration of "double switching" involving two techniques A and B which produce the same good in three years. Technique A involves the application of seven man-years in the second year, while technique B involves two man-years in the first year followed by six man-years in the third year. Figure 4.7 demonstrates this production schedule:

Figure 4.7. Comparison of Two Production Techniques

Technique	Years			Total Inputs of Labor
	t–2	*t–1*	*t*	
A	0	7	0	7
B	2	0	6	8

Source: Samuelson, "Paradoxes in Capital Theory," 568–73. Reprinted by permission of John Wiley and Sons, Inc.

According to this case, at zero or negligible interest rates, only labor costs matter, and technique A has lower total input costs (seven, as opposed to eight for technique B). Mathematically, technique A is in fact preferable and more profitable as long as the rate of interest stays under 50 percent. This is because the interest expense of carrying labor costs is relatively low for A compared to B. However, when the interest rate exceeds 50 percent, technique B has lower overall costs because most of the labor is done in the third year and therefore the interest-carrying charges for the project are relatively less for technique B.[184] Finally, once the rate of interest climbs above 100 percent, technique A again becomes more profitable because at that level, the difference in total interest costs are relatively even, and the principal difference is again one of labor costs. Thus, Samuelson concluded: "The phenomenon of switching . . . shows that the simple tale told by Jevons, Böhm-Bawerk, Wicksell, and other neoclassical writers—alleging that, as the interest rate falls in consequence of abstention from present consumption in favor of future, technology must become in some sense more 'roundabout,' more 'mechanized,' and more 'productive'—cannot be universally true."[185]

Blaug called Samuelson's illustration "the final nail in the coffin" of the Austrian theory of capital, which he labeled "untenable." Furthermore, even though there is no empirical evidence for reswitching, "it appears that we have to give up the idea of a demand curve for capital as a function of the interest rate."[186]

However, other economists have expressed serious reservations about such conclusions and what they regard as Samuelson's premature surrender. For one thing, Samuelson's "straw man" example cannot determine which technique is actually more productive. "Are seven units of labor invested for two time periods more or less roundabout than six units of labor invested for one period and two units invested for three periods of time?" Samuelson himself admitted, "There is no obvious answer."[187] As Garrison reported,

> If two processes are compared strictly in physical terms, it may be unclear which of the two is more roundabout; if capital values are used in gauging the degree of roundaboutness, then the comparison will depend in a critical way on the rate of interest that is used to calculate the capital values. Attempts to spell out the precise relationship between the price of capital and the quantity of capital are bound to run afoul of these difficulties.[188]

Leland Yeager raised the same objections in several articles on the topic. In maximizing the present value of a project, a low interest rate tends to favor investment projects which are more remote from consumption, while a high interest rate favors techniques which take less time. Yeager criticized the Samuelson case:

> In examples of reswitching, neither of the two (or more) options considered has revenues that are unequivocally more remote in relation to outlays than the other option has. In Samuelson's example, technique B employs some of its labor earlier and some of it later than A. Which technique employs its labor earlier on the whole? The answer depends on the weights accorded to amounts of labor employed at different times; and this is a matter of time-discounting, that is, of the interest rate.[189]

Yeager attempted to dissolve the Cambridge paradox of capital reversing and reswitching by using the notion of waiting as a factor of production.

Garrison, commenting on Yeager's paper, focused on what he called the "root problem" of the reswitching debate, "the illegitimate use of the comparative-statics method in the analysis of a dynamic market process."[190] According to Garrison, the case of reswitching is "completely spurious" because no one explains what causes the interest rates to change in the first place. To make Samuelson's example palatable, we must analyze three different interest-rate scenarios as if they occur in three separate economies. One country has 50 percent interest rates, a second between 50 percent to 100 percent, and the third over 100 percent. What causes the difference in interest rates between countries? "The difference in interest rates can be attributed to differences in time preference. . . . The question of transitional outputs simply doesn't arise. . . . Reswitching becomes a very sterile concept. . . . In the comparative-statics mold there is no switching at all."[191]

In reality, the reswitching debate is wrongheaded in its approach. Essentially, Böhm-Bawerk was only drawing the rational conclusion that if a firm is going to consider a longer production technique, the technique must ex ante be considered more profitable. Otherwise, the firm would not go ahead with the project. It may not work out profitably ex post, but profitability must be the firm's intention. The only projects that survive are those that pass the test of profitability—hence, the history of economic progress is, ipso facto, the history of adopting more roundabout processes.

Perhaps Blaug summarized best the current controversy on capital theory when he suggested that "economists are ill-advised to throw away their textbooks . . . just because the models in them frequently imply that a fall in the rate of interest will raise the capital-labour ratio of an economy."[192]

THE ROUNDABOUT PATH OF HICKS

Probably the best example of the roundabout path taken by economists over the past fifty years regarding the time theory of production is John R. Hicks (1904–89). As Lachmann noted, "For forty years Hicks has been the great broker of ideas who has regarded it his main task to accomplish a synthesis of the ideas of the age."[193]

Hicks began his career heavily influenced by Hayek and the Austrians. He said, "I did not begin from Keynes; I began from Pareto, and Hayek."[194] In an article originally published in German in 1933, Hicks offered a Hayekian explanation of the business cycle, referring to "malinvestment" due to an artificially lower interest rate. "The tempo of the boom gets faster and faster, but it can be maintained only if it continues to accelerate."[195] The first edition of his *Theory of Wages*, published in 1932, depended in part on Hayek's capital theory, especially his discussion on "Wage Regulation and Unemployment."[196] But by the second edition, Hicks had abandoned the "physical" description of capital goods in favor of a Knightian "fund" concept, and later wrote that he was "greatly ashamed" of his few mentions of "neutral money" notions based on Hayek.[197] In the late 1940s, along with Alvin Hansen he formulated the "neo-classical synthesis" of the Keynesian and classical positions, the famous IS-LM diagram.

Hicks's first book on capital theory, *Value and Capital*, written in 1939, was by his own admission "a product of the Keynesian thirties . . . being descended from Walras and Pareto."[198] He was highly critical of Böhm-Bawerk and the "average period of production," stating, "The absolute length of the true average period has no significance whatsoever. . . . It will be lengthened and shortened in an entirely arbitrary manner according as we calculate the average period of the same plan at different rates of interest."[199]

Hicks's second book, *Capital and Growth*, published in 1965, was "critical and expository, rather than constructive." He renounced the Keynesian acceleration principle and criticized the idea of homogeneous capital. "If there is just one homogeneous 'capital' . . . there can be no problem of malinvestment—or of saving going to waste."[200] Finally, his third book in the trilogy, *Capital and Time*, returned to some of his Austrian roots. He called his third book a "neo-Austrian" theory because his model was more general than the old model of Böhm-Bawerk and Hayek, which excluded fixed capital and durable goods. Hicks's model uses "an elementary process that converts a sequence (or stream) of inputs into a sequence of outputs."[201] Referring to the tradition of the Austrian time-structure of production theory, Hicks commented:

The "Austrians" were not a peculiar sect, out of the main stream; they were in the main stream; it was the others who were out of it.

The concept of production as a process in time . . . is not specifically "Austrian." It is just the same concept as underlies the work of the British classical economists, and it is indeed older still—older by far than Adam Smith. It is the typical business man's viewpoint, nowadays the accountant's viewpoint, in the old days the merchant's viewpoint.[202]

In his interpretation of "neo-Austrian" economics, Hicks has been at times confusing in his terminology and highly selective in his choice of Austrian themes.[203] For instance, he suggested a new approach to Hayek's theory of the business cycle: "The Hayek theory is not a theory of the credit cycle, the *Konjunktur,* which need not work in the way he describes. . . . It is an analysis—a very interesting analysis—of the adjustment of an economy to changes in the rate of genuine saving. In that direction it does make a real contribution. . . . It is a fore-runner of the growth theory of more recent years."[204]

In a separate article, Hicks elaborated on the "rebirth" of the Austrian theory of capital. Capital theory, he concluded, must include durable instruments as well as "goods that are *in the pipeline,* goods in process of production."[205] But with fixed durable capital, some of Böhm-Bawerk's concepts must be abandoned, said Hicks, such as the period of production, and roundaboutness, which apply only to a working capital model. "What we must not abandon are Böhm-Bawerk's (and Menger's) true insights—the things that are the strength of the 'Austrian' approach. Production is a process, a process in time."[206]

It is time to begin the process anew.

NOTES

1. Uhr, *Economic Doctrines of Knut Wicksell*, 113–14.
2. Boulding, A *Reconstruction of Economics*, 194.
3. Ibid., 195.
4. Boulding, "The Application of the Pure Theory of Population Change," 645–66. Boulding quoted Fisher: "Just as population is correlative to the various rates of births, deaths, marriages, 'coming of age,' emigration, immigration, etc., so capital is correlative to income, expenditure, production, consumption, 'ripening' of goods in process of production, exports, imports, monetary circulation, etc." Fisher, "What Is Capital?" 534.
5. Boulding, "Professor Knight's Capital Theory," 530.
6. Boulding, *Economic Analysis*, 686–719.
7. B. M. Anderson, *The Value of Money*, 38.
8. B. M. Anderson, *Economics and the Public Welfare*, 119, 309–407.
9. L. Albert Hahn, *Volkswirtschaftliche theorie des Bankkredits* (The economic theory of bank credit) (Tübingen: J. C. B. Mohr, 1920). See Ellis, *German Monetary Theory 1905–1933*, 327–33.
10. Hahn, *The Economics of Illusion*.
11. Hahn, *Common Sense Economics*, 26. Incidentally, every book I have encountered with the words "common sense economics" in the title has been categorically "free market" in orientation. See, for example, Philip Wicksteed, *The Common Sense of Political Economy* (London: Macmillan 1910); Gilbert M. Tucker, *Common Sense Economics* (Albany: Economic Education League, 1957); and John A. Pugsley, *Common Sense Economics* (Santa Ana, Calif.: Common Sense Press, 1974).
12. Hahn, *Common Sense Economics*, 31.
13. Ibid., 117,120–24.
14. Ibid., 124–25.
15. Ibid., 177.
16. Stigler, *Production and Distribution Theories*, 26.
17. Ibid., 138.
18. B. B. Seligman, *Main Currents in Modern Economics*, 302.
19. Ibid., 349.
20. Ibid., 350.
21. Ibid., 357.
22. According to Hayek, the Ricardo effect can occur in different phases of the business cycle. When Hayek first introduced the term, he had reference to a depression scenario, where a stimulation in consumer prices (via Keynesian deficit spending) reduced real wages and forced further reductions in capital-goods output as producers switched to labor-intensive techniques. See Hayek, *Profits, Interest and Investment*, 3–37. But the Ricardo effect could also take place in the latter phases of a boom, when consumer prices are rising—again depressing real wages and encouraging businesses to reduce their purchases of capital goods.
23. Seligman, *Main Currents in Modern Economics*, 358.

24. Ibid., 359.

25. Blaug, *Economic Theory in Retrospect,* 541.

26. Ibid., 499.

27. Ibid., 545.

28. Sherman and Evans, *Macroeconomics,* 270.

29. Sherman, *Introduction to the Economics of Growth, Unemployment, and Inflation,* 95.

30. Sherman and Evans, *Macroeconomics,* 270. Sherman, by the way, is one of the few economists to recognize the pioneering work on relative prices by Frederick C. Mills at the National Bureau of Economic Research.

31. Dow, *Macroeconomic Thought,* preface.

32. Ibid., 170–74. On Hayek's idea of privatizing the banking system, see his work, *Denationalization of Money* (London: Institute for Economic Affairs, 1978).

33. Bratt, *Business Cycles and Forecasting,* 157–67.

34. Hansen, *Business Cycles and National Income,* 387.

35. Ibid., 387–88.

36. Ibid., 392–93.

37. Hamberg, *Business Cycles,* 202, 210–11.

38. Estey, *Business Cycles,* 110, 111.

39. Ibid., 228.

40. Ibid., 237, 238.

41. Ibid., 239–40.

42. Ibid., 241–42.

43. Ibid., 243.

44. Ibid., 244.

45. Lloyd M. Valentine, *Business Cycles and Forecasting,* 7th ed., 354–61. Previous editions had been coauthored with the late Carl A. Dauten.

46. Ibid., 357–58.

47. Ibid., 367. Mises rejected the notion that the Austrian business cycle theory was an "overinvestment" theory. "The essence of the credit-expansion boom is not overinvestment, but investment in wrong lines, i.e., malinvestment." Mises, *Human Action,* 599.

48. Ibid., 367–68. Hayek and other Austrians do not deny that both capital and consumer markets can expand at the same time; rather they argue that unemployed resources do not preclude competition between the stages of production. Moreover, the Austrians point out that the only way that demand for *all* goods can increase simultaneously is if the money supply increases.

49. Ibid., 372–73.

50. Achinstein, *Introduction to Business Cycles,* 53.

51. Ibid., 54. Achinstein considered Lachmann's presentation of the Austrian position "much more palatable." See Lachmann, "Investment and Costs of Production," 469–81. Lachmann endeavored to validate the Austrian theory of the trade cycle without reference to the time structure of production, forced saving, and other controversial terminology. He concluded that "the Austrian theory comes out fairly completely vindicated. It is often said that its validity depends on full employment; but we have endeavored to shake this

belief. We have pointed out that in a world of immobile labor and specialized equipment unemployment and idle resources may coexist with scarcity of factors and inelastic supply of output. We have further shown that, if this is so, increased demand for consumption goods by its effects on marginal costs must adversely affect durable investment (the earlier stages of production); and we have tried to show that this result is quite independent of the monetary policy pursued." (480)

52. Carver, *Principles of Political Economy*; Taylor, *Principles of Economics*; Boucke, *Principles of Economics*; Bye, *Principles of Economics*; Brown, *Economic Science and the Common Welfare*; and Rufener, *Principles of Economics*.

53. Johnson, *The Theory of Income Distribution*, 128–29.

54. Black, *Introduction to Production Economics*, 24.

55. Ibid., 25.

56. Ibid., 33.

57. Ibid., 65–66.

58. Ibid., 34.

59. Moffat and Christenson, et al., *Economics,* 29–30.

60. Waugh, *Principles of Economics,* 161.

61. Burns, Neal, and Watson, *Modern Economics,* 61–62. Introduction by H. S. Ellis.

62. Ibid., 62.

63. Gemmill and Blodgett, *Economics,* 76. Blodgett also wrote his own textbook, *Principles of Economics*.

64. Gemmill and Blodgett, *Economics,* 219. This is one of the most precise and accurate definitions of economics I've read. Most economics textbooks define economics in a way that can mean almost anything. The standard definition is that economics is the study of how "society chooses to employ its limited resources, which have alternative uses, to produce goods and services for present and future consumption." M. H. Spencer, *Contemporary Economics* (New York: Worth Publishers, 1971), 2. According to this definition, people could do practically anything with their resources, including waste them, and that would make economic sense. Here's a much improved definition along the lines of Gemmill and Blodgett: "Economics is the study of the best and most efficient way to transform unfinished resources into the goods and services people want."

65. Ibid., 82.

66. Ibid., 81.

67. Hicks, *The Social Framework.* Originally published in 1945.

68. Hicks, Hart, and Ford, *The Social Framework of the American Economy,* 30–32. Hicks's textbook has also been published in India as *The Framework of the Indian Economy,* by J. R. Hicks, M. Mukherjee, and S. K. Ghosh (Delhi: Oxford University Press, 1984).

69. Peterson, *Economics,* 37–38.

70. Ibid., 129–50.

71. Bye and Hewett, *The Economic Process,* 1st ed., 73. Of course, Bye and Hewett neglect the fact that the water system does not really require waiting for the basic ingredients of the waterway to be built. The iron ore, steel and other raw materials as well as the machinery and tools are probably already available on the market, ready to be

purchased or put to use to build the water system. Only the most specific needs are "built to suit." Also, if the building of the water system involved the floating of bonds or stock, investors do not have to wait thirty years to get their money back. They are paid dividends, or they can sell their stock immediately on the market, at a price reflecting the discounted market value of the project at the time they sell. Still, even with capital goods and machinery already in inventory, it may take several years to complete the project. The illustration by Bye and Hewett is valuable in demonstrating the long processes every major capital project involves.

72. Ibid., 74.

73. Ibid., 76.

74. Ibid., 85.

75. Bye and Hewett, *The Economic Process*, 2d ed., 57.

76. Fairchild, *Understanding Our Free Economy*; Abbott, *Economics and the Modern World*; Hailstones and Brennan, *Economics*.

77. Hailstones and Brennan, *Economics*, 25.

78. Gordon, *Elementary Economics*, 3.

79. Ibid., 47–162.

80. Stackelberg, *The Theory of the Market Economy*, 273–90.

81. Ibid., 277.

82. Ibid., 285.

83. Sickle and Rogge, *Introduction to Economics*, 96–98.

84. Ibid., 407.

85. Ibid., 409.

86. Ibid., 410–11.

87. Geoffrey Whitehead, *Economics Made Simple*, 25. Whitehead, however, like most of the textbook writers mentioned above, did not extend the stages of production approach into his analysis of the economy as a whole. Instead, he opted for standard Keynesian and monetarist analysis in the latter part of the book (327–87).

88. Samuelson, *Economics*, 1st ed., 42–43. Similar language still exists in the current edition, Samuelson and Nordhaus, *Economics*, 13th ed., 720–21.

89. Lachmann, "A Reconsideration of the Austrian Theory of Industrial Fluctuations," in *Capital, Expectations, and the Market Process*, 269. Originally appeared in *Economica* 7 (May 1940). Many of Lachmann's most important articles are found in this volume.

90. Lachmann, "Complementarity and Substitution in the Theory of Capital," in *Capital, Expectations, and the Market Process*, 205. Originally appeared in *Economica* 14 (May 1947).

91. Ibid., 198–99.

92. Lachmann, *Capital and Its Structure*, 2d ed., 4. First edition appeared in 1956.

93. Ibid., 11.

94. Ibid., 85.

95. Ibid., 113.

96. Lachmann, "Ludwig von Mises and the Market Process," *Capital, Expectations, and the Market Process*, 190. Originally appeared in *Toward Liberty: Essays in Honor of*

Ludwig von Mises, ed. Friedrich A. Hayek, vol. 2, 38–52 (Menlo Park, Calif.: Institute for Humane Studies, 1971).

97. Lachmann, "Austrian Economics in the Present Crisis of Economic Thought," *Capital, Expectations, and the Market Process,* 31–32.

98. Lachmann, "Austrian Economics Under Fire," 232.

99. Lachmann, "Some Notes on Economic Thought, 1933–1953," *Capital, Expectations, and the Market Process,* 136. Originally in *the South African Journal of Economics 22* (March 1954).

100. Kirzner, *Market Theory and the Price System,* 19.

101. Ibid., 318–19.

102. Kirzner, *An Essay on Capital,* 41.

103. Ibid., 88.

104. Rothbard, *Man, Economy, and State,* 274–76, 333–40.

105. Ibid., 333.

106. Ibid., 314, 470–79, 853–81.

107. Ibid., 412–13.

108. Ibid., 486–87.

109. Ibid., 489.

110. Rothbard, *America's Great Depression* (New York: Richardson & Snyder, 1983 [1963]), 3. There have been four editions: 1st ed. (Princeton, N.J.: Van Nostrand, 1963); 2d ed. (Los Angeles: Nash Publishing, 1972); and 3d ed. (Kansas City, Kans.: Sheed and Ward, 1975).

111. Ibid., 37–38. Changes in industrial output initiated by the free market were classified by Rothbard as "irregular fluctuations," not "cycles" (37–38).

112. Ibid., 19–20.

113. Ibid., 19, 39–77.

114. Ibid., 26.

115. Ibid., 21–33.

116. Rothbard, Introduction to *America's Great Depression,* 2d ed., xxv–xxviii.

117. O'Driscoll and Shenoy, "Inflation, Recession, and Stagflation," in Dolan, *The Foundation of Modern Austrian Economics,* 185–211.

118. O'Driscoll, *Economics as a Coordination Problem,* 72.

119. Ibid., 116–18.

120. Garrison, "Austrian Macroeconomics," 169.

121. Ibid., 172–202.

122. See the recent debate over Keynesian-Austrian macroeconomics in Garrison, "Intertemporal Coordination and the Invisible Hand," 309–19; J. Snippe, "Intertemporal Coordination and the Economics of Keynes: Comment on Garrison," *History of Political Economy* 19 (Summer 1987): 329–34; and Garrison, "Full Employment and Intertemporal Coordination: A Rejoinder," 335–41. Also see the penetrating analysis in Garrison, "Time and Money," 197–213.

123. Piquet, *The Economic Axioms,* xvi.

124. Ibid., 8.

125. Ibid., 9.

126. Ibid., 122–29.
127. O'Driscoll and Rizzo, *The Economics of Time and Ignorance*, 164–69. See also Garrison, "A Subjective Theory of a Capital-Using Economy," ibid., 160–87.
128. Garrison, "A Subjective Theory of a Capital-Using Economy," 167.
129. Ibid., 170.
130. Ibid., 173.
131. O'Driscoll and Rizzo, *The Economics of Time and Ignorance*, 198–202.
132. Ibid., 212–13. More specifically, see Wainhouse, "Empirical Evidence for Hayek's Theory of Economic Fluctuations," 37–71. Wainhouse's article is based on his dissertation, "Hayek's Theory of the Trade Cycle."
133. Bain, *Pricing, Distribution and Employment,* 579.
134. Ibid., 580n.
135. Keirstead, *Capital, Interest and Profits,* 11.
136. Ibid., 25–26.
137. Ibid., 25.
138. Ibid., 47.
139. Haavelmo, *A Study in the Theory of Investment,* 41.
140. Ibid., 50–70.
141. Solow, *Capital Theory and the Rate of Return,* 12.
142. Robert M. Solow, *The Price System* (Englewood Cliffs, N.J.: Prentice-Hall, 1964), 107–8.
143. Solow, *Capital Theory and the Rate of Return,* 13.
144. Ibid., 11, 25. In a review of Hicks's "neo-Austrian" work, *Capital and Time,* Solow indicated that in teaching he used a simplified "point-input-point-output" Austrian model to demonstrate the importance of time in the production process. "My experience is that students learn a lot from this exercise." Although Solow considered the Austrian model to be ultimately a "weak instrument of analysis," he felt it "looks so different on the surface, tells so different a story, that one is first surprised and then enlightened by the fact that the steady-state theorems are recognisably identical to those that come from Sraffa-like circulating capital and growth-theoretic fixed-capital models." Solow, Review of Hicks's *Capital and Time,* 189–92.
145. Baumol, *Economic Theory and Operations Analysis,* 640. See also Baumol, *Economic Dynamics,* 127–41.
146. Baumol, *Economic Theory and Operations Analysis,* 640.
147. Ibid., 642.
148. Ibid., 658.
149. Ibid. Cf. Wicksell's wine-aging illustration, *Lectures,* vol 1, 172–84.
150. Baumol, *Economic Theory and Operations Analysis,* 659.
151. Morishima, *The Economic Theory of Modern Society,* 45.
152. Ibid., 37–53.
153. Ibid., 51–52.
154. Dewey, *Modern Capital Theory,* 42–43. It is not solely cost in relation to income, but profit per time period, per year that matters. Not total profit, but the annual profit rate!

155. Ibid., 52–53. On Knight's Crusonia plant analogy, see Knight, "Diminishing Returns from Investment," 29.

156. C. J. Bliss, "Capital Theory in the Short Run," in Brown, et al., *Essays in Modern Capital Theory*, 187.

157. Bliss, *Capital Theory and the Distribution of Income*, 6.

158. Ibid., 10, 45.

159. Hausman, *Capital, Profits, and Prices*, 37, 39.

160. Ibid., 54. Cf. Oskar Lange, "The Place of Interest in the Theory of Production," *Review of Economic Studies* 3 (1935–36): 159–92.

161. Hausman, *Capital, Profits, and Prices*, 47.

162. Ibid., 192. Hausman is an extreme skeptic, almost to the point of failing to reach any conclusions in capital theory, as if economists have proved nothing: "Economists do not understand the phenomena of capital and interest. They do not understand why the rate of interest is generally positive (and thus how it is that capitalism can work). They do not know how large-scale technological changes will affect wages and interest or how changes in the rate of profits will affect innovation." (190) This is quite an indictment of the economics profession.

163. Faber, *Introduction to Modern Austrian Capital Theory*, v. Cf. Hicks, *Capital and Time*.

164. Faber, *Introduction to Modern Austrian Capital Theory*, 32.

165. For a summary, see Edwin G. Dolan, "Review of Faber (1979)," *Journal of Economic Literature* 18 (September 1980): 1096–98. On von Neumann's model, Garrison writes: "The von Neumann model differs from those of Walras and Cassel in several respects. It recognizes, for instance, the possibility of 'circular production,' e.g., while coal may be used in the production of steel, steel is used in the production of coal. The model also allows for joint production, for the production of intermediate goods, and for the existence of several different production techniques for each good produced. But if the von Neumann model represents a highwater mark in technique, it represents a low-water mark in substantive economic content. The model includes no primary factors of production and permits no consumption! At the end of each period all outputs are employed as inputs for the next period." Garrison, "Review of Faber (1979)," *Austrian Economics Newsletter* 2, 2 (Spring 1980): 5.

166. Orosel, "Faber's Modern Austrian Capital Theory," 141.

167. Ibid., 142.

168. Ibid., 147n.

169. Faber, "Modern Austrian Capital Theory and Orosel's Standard Neoclassical Analysis," 157–76.

170. Gerhard O. Orosel, "Faber's Capital Theory: A Rejoinder," *Zeitschrift für Nationalökonomie* 41 (1981): 177–78.

171. Garrison, "Review of Faber (1979)," 5.

172. Ibid., 11. "In all of these papers, however, it was either assumed that there exists a central planning agency or perfect competition." Faber, *Studies in Austrian Capital Theory, Investment and Time*, 7.

173. Garrison, "Review of Faber (1979)," 11.

174. Faber, "Relationship between Modern Austrian and Sraffa's Capital Theory," in *Studies in Austrian Capital Theory, Investment and Time,* 51.

175. Sraffa, *The Production of Commodities by Means of Commodities,* 38.

176. Ibid., 93.

177. Burmeister, "Synthesizing the Neo-Austrian and Alternative Approaches to Capital Theory," 456 n. 2.

178. Hausman, *Capital, Profits, and Prices,* 184.

179. Thalenhorst and Wenig, "F. A. Hayek's 'Prices and Production' Re-Analyzed," 214.

180. Klausinger, "'Hayek Re-Analyzed,'" 425.

181. Ibid., 428.

182. Robinson, "The Production Function and the Theory of Capital." Also see Chase, "Production Theory," 74.

183. Chase, "Production Theory," 76.

184. Blaug, *Economic Theory in Retrospect,* 523.

185. Samuelson, "Paradoxes in Capital Theory," 568. Also consult Harcourt, *Some Cambridge Controversies in the Theory of Capital.* Baumol criticizes reswitching techniques for the same reason. "There is no unique ranking of techniques as there was in the neoclassical models in terms of the order in which they are favored by successive reductions in interest rates." Baumol, *Economic Theory and Operations Analysis,* 665.

186. Blaug, *Economic Theory in Retrospect,* 524, 523–28.

187. Samuelson, "Paradoxes in Capital Theory," 569–70.

188. Garrison, "The Austrian-Neoclassical Relation," 13–14.

189. Yeager, "Capital Paradoxes and the Concept of Waiting," 189. See also Yeager, "Toward Understanding Some Paradoxes in Capital Theory," 313–46. Hausman rejected Yeager's argument, however. "I find Yeager's conclusion unpalatable and, in any case, mistaken. . . . Whatever the merit of Yeager's aspirations and of his method of calculating the period of investment, he has found no general answer to the problem of capital reversing." Hausman, *Capital, Profits, and Prices,* 79n–80n.

190. Garrison, "Comment: Waiting in Vienna," 222.

191. Ibid., 222–23. High interest rates may also be caused by inflationary expectations, which could severely alter the techniques of investing and the investment period.

192. Blaug, *Economic Theory in Retrospect,* 527. Elsewhere, Blaug added, "there is nothing irrational about the tendency of scientists to hang on to a theory despite anomalies if no better rival theory is available." Blaug, *The Cambridge Revolution,* 43. Paul Samuelson used to consider the reswitching debate of sufficient importance to include it in his popular introductory textbook, *Economics.* However, he dropped the topic in the twelfth edition, perhaps because he wished to downplay the significance of the controversy. Solow, in his Nobel-prize acceptance speech, said the reswitching debate was a "waste of time." Solow, "Growth Theory and After," 307–17.

193. Lachmann, "Comment: Austrian Economics Today," 69. Sheila C. Dow added that Hicks's work "has consistently sparked off new research programmes in a range of fields. Indeed, his contributions could be described as resulting from a creative admixture of ideas from different schools of thought." Dow, *Macroeconomic Thought,* 5.

194. John R. Hicks, "The Formation of an Economist," in *The Economics of John Hicks,* 285.

195. Hicks, "Equilibrium and the Trade Cycle," 523–34. Originally published in *Zeitschrift für Nationalökonomie* 4 (June, 1933): 441–55.

196. Hicks, *Theory of Wages,* 1st ed., 187–207. Hicks indicated that his work was also influenced by Pigou and Walras.

197. Hicks, *Theory of Wages,* 2d ed, 342–48. Also, John Hicks, "Recollections and Documents," *Economic Perspectives,* 136.

198. Hicks, *Capital and Time,* v.

199. Hicks, *Value and Capital,* 223.

200. Hicks, *Capital and Growth,* 35.

201. Hicks, *Capital and Time,* 6–8.

202. Ibid., 12.

203. Hicks made a confusing distinction between "fundists" and "materialists" in a review of capital theory, "Capital Controversies: Ancient and Modern," 307–16. Referring to fundists as those who visualized capital as a fund value, he correctly pointed out: "Not only Adam Smith, but all (or nearly all) the British Classical Economists were Fundists. . . . So was Marx." (309) But then he called Böhm-Bawerk, Jevons, and Hayek "fundists," while calling J. B. Clark a "materialist," one who visualizes capital as physical goods! Kirzner called Hicks's terminology "quite unfortunate and may lead to a misunderstanding of his own thesis." Kirzner, "Ludwig von Mises and the Theory of Capital and Interest," 65 n. 39.

204. Hicks, "The Hayek Story," 210. Of course, Hayek would insist that his theory remains quite relevant to the trade cycle, especially during this era of significant monetary inflation.

205. Hicks, "The Austrian Theory of Capital and Its Rebirth in Modern Economics," 191.

206. Ibid., 193.

PART 2

THE THEORETICAL FRAMEWORK

FIVE

THE STRUCTURE OF PRODUCTION: THE BUILDING BLOCKS

There can be fewer fields of economic enquiry today which promise a richer harvest than the systematic study of the modes of use of our material resources.—Ludwig M. Lachmann, *Capital and Its Structure*

Economists have traditionally visualized the structure of the whole economy in two ways. The first method, the current neoclassical approach, characterizes the economy in a *horizontal* fashion. It pictures the market in a timeless dimension wherein land, labor, and capital are separate coexisting entities. In essence, it is a view which denies any time structure at all. Using this description of the production process, one might see the economy in terms of workers earning wages, employers making profits and losses, landlords collecting rent, and capitalists earning interest on their investments, without examining how they are interrelated.

While this standard method of economic analysis has its advantages, it also has its limitations in that it obscures many critical elements of the economic forces at work (see chapter 1).

The purpose of this chapter is to develop an alternative method of looking at the whole economy, the so-called "vertical" approach, one which John Hicks has appropriately called the "typical business man's viewpoint, nowadays the accountant's viewpoint, in the old days the merchant's viewpoint."[1] L. Albert Hahn calls it "common sense" economics.[2] As I will demonstrate, this revitalized concept resurrects the importance of time in economics. The amount of time it takes to produce and consume goods and services is a key variable that is missing from almost all popular macroeconomic models. Failure to include this critical factor has led to much mischief in macroeconomic analysis and policy recommendations.

THE BUSINESSMAN'S APPROACH AND
THE ROLE OF THE ENTREPRENEUR

What is this "businessman's common sense" approach to economics? It is to visualize the entire market as a long series of production processes that are in various stages of completion. This alternative is far more involved than the simple one-stage distinction that neoclassical economists make between production and consumption goods.

The businessman is an entrepreneur who chooses which area of the hierarchical marketplace he wants to develop, based on his estimation of the risk and profit potential in that particular product or service and what his abilities are as a manager and creator. He sees himself as a mediator between unfinished resources and final products, placing himself somewhere along the conveyor belt of intertemporal activity, whether it be as a retailer, wholesaler, manufacturer, or extractor of natural resources. Whichever position he chooses in the process of production, each businessman undertakes a similar purpose involving three time-consuming steps: (1) to purchase inputs, (2) transform these inputs into a new product or service, and (3) sell the output to the next stage of production.

The factors needed to produce these goods or services may be simple or complex. They may simply involve hiring a secretary and leasing a small office; or hiring hundreds of workers, purchasing heavy machinery and raw products, leasing property, and raising capital. Whatever it takes for the business to produce its goods or services, the important consideration is that the transformed product be sold for more than the cost of the inputs, so that the "value added" is comparable with other business projects. Maximizing short-term profits may not be the overriding objective of a firm—in fact, many companies endure losses or low profit margins for years—but adequate profitability is essential for long-term survival. Otherwise, the producer will stop operating, and will seek alternative opportunities. More often than not, the whole production effort is a discovery process, as Kirzner has emphasized, both in terms of the final products sold to customers and the level of profit or loss.[3]

Piquet explains the risk the businessman undertakes when he is involved in the production process:

> A businessman, knowing the prices of the inputs which he needs to produce something, which he thinks he can sell for a certain price a few months hence, knows how much he is able to pay to acquire those inputs. The price of the inputs incorporates time-discount as a result of market forces in the economy as a whole. Most of the inputs have multiple uses which are reflected in their market prices. Because individual rates of time-discount vary, some of the inputs are either overpriced or underpriced, relative to any particular line of

production. To the extent that they are underpriced, the businessman can make a profit over and beyond the price he must pay for borrowed funds. Conversely, to the extent that inputs are overpriced, he is in danger of incurring losses.[4]

The businessman is, of course, often unaware of the *whole* production process, the transformation process from raw commodities to final consumer goods, unless the firm is "vertically integrated." The book publisher, for example, may not be concerned about the intricate details of paper manufacturing, or where logs are milled. The publisher's principal concern is the supply and price of the paper used to print books. In general, it does not matter where the producer is located along the chain of production as long as the firm's long-term profit margin is achieved. But, as we shall demonstrate, from the perspective of the economist in search of a realistic macroeconomic model, visualizing the whole structure of the economy is imperative.

ECONOMIC ACTIVITY AS A PROCESS IN TIME

All businessmen and entrepreneurs are deeply concerned about the time factor—how long it is going to take to obtain a particular input, complete a project, bring the final product to market, receive payment for services rendered, and so forth. Waiting is a fact of life in the business world.

Commercial builders, for example, are extremely conscious of the time it takes to put up an office building, especially when the builder has financed the construction through a bank loan, effectively increasing his production costs with each passing day. The time period varies, but generally it may take two to three years to construct a major office building.

Waiting is a fundamental factor in nearly every market decision. It may take one year to write a book, four years to earn a degree, seven years to build a major highway, or ten years to realize a return on a long-term investment. The investor, whether seeking a return on a hotel, an apartment building, an oil-drilling project, or a corporate bond, recognizes the universal existence of time and waiting in the real world.

In short, the Clark-Knight theory of the production process as a continuous, repetitious round of synchronized production and consumption is a static model, and as such is a fictitious account of the marketplace. Even companies which have established their markets witness constant change in their products, customer base, and personnel. A firm may have the same number of corporate officers and employees year after year, yet people are aging, their financial status is changing, and they are moving from job to job. Entrepreneurs just starting a business sense change more than anyone, and often expect long periods of investment (waiting) before achieving a return of their funds.

The time dimension is, as management expert Peter F. Drucker has indicated, "man's most perishable resource"—and man's most critical element. Unlike money, which as a store of value can be used at a later date, time must be used immediately or lost forever. Thus time becomes an integral cost of production at every stage.

RELATIONSHIP OF PRODUCTION TO CONSUMPTION:
LOOKING AT THE "SNAPSHOT" ECONOMY

Having noted the basic characteristics of a market economy, let us visualize the overall economy, beginning with a look at final consumption, since that is ultimately the end of all economic effort. Economists from Adam Smith to John Maynard Keynes have recognized this universal principle. The work behind the transformation of resources, the manufacture of tools, machines and instruments, and the retailing of goods and services all have one goal in mind: to fulfill the consumer's demands.[5] Exactly how does this causal nexus of production to consumer demand function?

To see this critical linkage, imagine for a moment that time is at a standstill, with everything and everybody suddenly frozen. If we were permitted to walk around and be bystanders, what would we see in this worldwide snapshot of the economy?

Economists see things from many different perspectives but, from our current standpoint, we will discover that goods and services are at different stages of completion. We may notice first that goods are completely finished, having already been purchased by final users, and are now in varying stages of depletion. They are being used up or consumed.

Next, we may look at items currently being produced and those about to be sold to final users. We note that many goods in our snapshot economy are in retail department stores, grocery stores, car dealerships, and so on, and are ready for *direct* use by consumers. As Taussig states, "Matter reaches the stage of complete utility when it is directly available for satisfying our wants; when it is bread that we can eat, clothes that we can wear, houses from which we can secure shelter and enjoyment."[6]

The automobile may be a good example of the snapshot economy that we envision in this time suspension. Millions of cars have already been built and are being used on the road today, in varying degrees of condition (some cars are old, some are new). Thousands of other cars are in the showrooms, ready to be purchased. Thousands more are in transit to the car dealers. Others are parked temporarily at the production plant waiting to be ordered by the car dealers. And still more are just coming off the assembly line.

THE MARKETING VIEWPOINT

This chain of production is clearly evident in the field of marketing, which deals with a product from the time it is manufactured to the point when it is purchased by its final user or consumer.

Suppose you are in a supermarket. You see the myriad of products on the shelves. But this consumer point of purchase is merely the final stage of a long series of activities which brought the product to this point. As marketing expert Bert Rosenbloom states:

> For behind this commonplace activity of shopping at the supermarket—or most any other type of store for that matter—lies a host of rather complex activities that have made the act of shopping so ordinary and simple. Thousands of people in perhaps hundreds of different organizations have been involved "behind the scenes." These organizations and the people working in them make up the marketing channels that have performed all the tasks and activities necessary to make those products in the store so conveniently available to the consumer.[7]

Rosenbloom portrays a typical marketing channel structure with the following diagram:

Figure 5.1. A Typical Portrayal of Channel Structure for Consumer Goods.

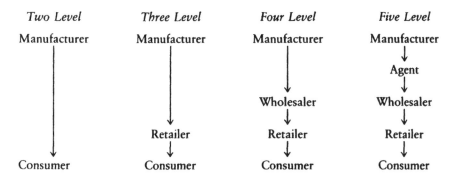

Source: Rosenbloom, *Marketing Channels: A Management View*, 18. Copyright © 1983 by The Dryden Press, a division of Holt, Rinehart and Winston, Inc. Reprinted by permission of the publisher.

Obviously, there are a number of supply stages prior to the manufacturing level. But the field of marketing does not normally concern itself with the construction of the product itself, only with its distribution to the final user once it is manufactured.

THE ASSEMBLY LINE OF PRODUCT TRANSFORMATION

Now let us carry the period of production back further, before the product is manufactured. We wish to develop a more complete model than the overly simplistic neoclassical one, which divides production into only two major groups: consumer goods and capital goods. Consumer goods, such as automobiles and groceries, are the ultimate end product. And to that end, producer goods or capital goods are created and used. They are the *indirect* means to satisfy *direct* individual wants and needs.[8]

Let us return to the case of the automobile industry in our snapshot view of the economy. Besides the cars which are just coming off the assembly line, we note that some are only half built or partially assembled by the car manufacturer. Others aren't built at all, but are only represented by parts in inventory, on order, or being manufactured by secondary car-related industries. If we go back even further, we could look at the rubber producers, the steel plants, and the raw-commodity producers who ultimately make up the components of automobiles and numerous other manufactured goods. The car is the final user good, but literally thousands of capital goods—from steel to plastics—are used to produce the final consumer good (see the vertical column under "transportation" in an input-output table to calculate the components which go into the production of automobiles and other forms of transportation).

WORKING CAPITAL VERSUS FIXED CAPITAL

At this point, it's worth discussing an important distinction made by economists between circulating (or working) capital and fixed capital. The automobile itself, moving from its raw materials to the final product, can be viewed as circulating capital, representing "goods in process." It moves along the assembly line toward ultimate consumption. As Shackle defines it, "Capital is *potential* service and usefulness ... intermediate products, embryonic items *not yet* ready for application or consumption. To make a tool for productive purposes is to take an indirect but ultimately more fruitful route to that production. . . . In short, *capital is time.*"[9]

At the same time, there are numerous machines and tools which are used at specific junctures in the car-making process. These are fixed capital, because they are stationary and do not move along the assembly line. Moulton defines this form of capital as "implements, tools, machines, industrial buildings, railroad tracks, power houses, and the other concrete material instruments which aid man in the processes of production."[10] But one must not forget that fixed and circulating capital are always interrelated, because the precise purpose of fixed capital is to move circulating capital along the conveyor belt toward its final use.

There is another way of comparing circulating with fixed capital. Circulating capital can be defined as essentially *unfinished* goods. Fixed capital may be regarded as *finished* goods. This distinction makes sense because circulating capital, i.e., unfinished goods, tend to *appreciate* as value is added throughout the production process. But when the circulating capital reaches its final stage, to be used as a household product or commercial input, it becomes a fixed good, and immediately begins to *depreciate*. In short, fixed capital, like consumer goods, is consumed.[11]

As the earlier chapters on the history of capital indicate, there are essentially two contrasting views on the nature of capital goods. The neoclassical fundists (Clark, Knight, Harrod, Keynes, et al.) envision all capital as basically "fixed," providing an eternal flow of income or services without moving through stages. The Austrians (Menger, Böhm-Bawerk, Hayek, Machlup, et al.) characterize capital primarily as "circulating," a multiperiod intermediate good moving through stages.[12]

Clearly, a complete macroeconomic model must deal with both kinds of capital. My view is that both fixed and working capital involve significant periods of production, and in this sense, they are more alike than different. In the case of fixed capital, one must consider the time it takes to make machines, buildings, and so forth, and once they are put to use, one must not ignore the years of service such machines and instruments provide in transforming unfinished goods through the pipeline. The manufacturing and marketing of circulating capital goods also involves a considerable period of production, and may provide years of consumer service if the final goods are durable in nature. Since long periods are involved in the production and use of either fixed or working capital, it does not seem appropriate to abandon the idea of an intertemporal capital-using economy.[13]

THE PROCESS AND ORDER OF PRODUCTION

Capital goods and raw materials are used to make other producer goods, in a long chain of economic activity with the ultimate goal of satisfying the final demand of consumers.[14] As Rothbard writes, "At each stage, labor uses nature-given factors to produce capital goods, and the capital goods are again combined with labor and nature-given factors, transformed into lower and lower orders of capital goods, until consumers' goods are reached."[15] Income (in the form of wages, rents, interest, and profits) is paid at each stage for the various factors.

In sum, there is an ordering to the stages of production as they move through time toward final consumption.[16] "The product of one stage of the industrial process furnishes the materials for the next stage, and the product of that stage in turn supplies the materials for the next subsequent stage."[17]

The direction of economic activity can be illustrated as an assembly line sequence, as indicated by Figure 5.2 below.

Another way to look at the transformation of goods through time is as the branches of a tree, per figure 5.3, which Morishima calls the "genealogy of production."

Morishima describes the makeup of economic allocation this way:

> Passing through these vertical processes, the raw materials gradually mature through higher stages of intermediate products in a form approaching the finished product. . . . Operations which have been organized into vertical channels take place simultaneously, and at certain stages the fruits of these several operations are combined. The combined result is then, at the next stage, united with the results of the chain of operations which have been taking place simultaneously in a separate vertical channel.[18]

Note that Figure 5.3 makes several simplified assumptions. First, we are assuming that all capital goods are *specific* in nature, that each capital good is

Figure 5.2. The Industrial Process

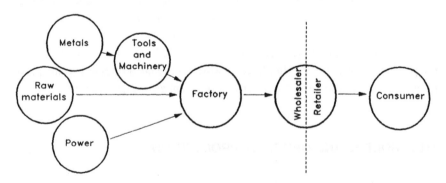

Source: Cornelius C. Janzen and Orlando W. Stephenson, *Everyday Economics* (New York: Silver, Burdett & Co., 1931), 89. Copyright 1931, renewed 1959 by Silver Burdett Company. Used with permission.

Figure 5.3. The Direction of Economic Production

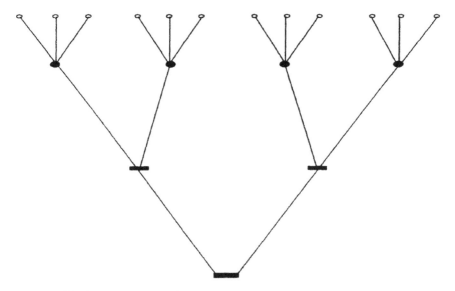

Source: Rothbard, *Man, Economy and State*, 282.

utilized at only one point in time to be used in one specific production process. In reality, capital goods are almost always used in a variety of stages or at various points of production at the same stage (joint production). We will deal with the problem of nonspecificity later on.

Second, we have simplified the number of stages. In figure 5.2 the production process goes through only four stages on the way to making a final consumer good. In modern society, the number of stages is virtually always much greater.

MATRIX OF FINISHED AND UNFINISHED GOODS: THE TABLE OF SYNCHRONIZED PRODUCTION

Economists from Taussig to Baumol have illustrated the sequential branches of production in tabular form.[19] Baumol, for instance, shows this intricate relationship between finished and unfinished goods in what he calls the Wicksellian "dated input approach." It measures capital in values rather than physical quantity, based on the age of the capital good and the interest rate. The production process consists of an output requiring a sequence of outlays over a period of time, which can be months to years depending on the product. Baumol uses the example of a product which takes four years of outlays (x_1, x_2, x_3, x_4) to produce. In an evenly-rotating state, with the firm wishing to have a steady flow of output each year, we have most of the outlays "in the pipeline" as unfinished goods, per figure 5.4.

Figure 5.4. Dated Inputs for Finished and Unfinished Goods

Batch of Goods	3 Years Ago	2 Years Ago	1 Year Ago	Now
Finished	x_1	x_2	x_3	x_4
¾	o	x_1	x_2	x_3
½	o	o	x_1	x_2
¼	o	o	o	x_1

Source: Baumol, *Economic Theory and Operations*, 644.

Thus we see that there is indeed a "synchronized" form of production and consumption, as Clark calls it, but both the Baumol example above and Taussig's example demonstrate that it is not a timeless process. The production of individual goods and services is continuous, but it is not simultaneous.

PRACTICAL EXAMPLES

Economists have used many common examples to describe and categorize how the whole economy is structured. In chapter 2 we noted the examples used by Menger, Clark, and Taussig. Menger refers to the case of wheat, a "good of the third order," being transformed into flour, a "good of the second order," and eventually into bread, a "good of the first order."[20] J. B. Clark uses several illustrations, including the production of bread, clothing, and houses.[21]

Taussig describes the process of transforming iron ore into various metal instruments and materials.[22] Black enumerates the specific stages: "Thus the mining of iron ore is one stage, the concentrating of it is another, the smelting of it is another, the converting of it into steel is another, and the rolling of the car rails is another. . . . The finished product of one establishment becomes the raw material of the next in line in the production process."[23] Alderfer and Michl separate the stages of the iron and steel industry into five general categories:

Stage #1. Mining the raw materials (iron ore, coal, limestone).
Stage #2. Smelting the iron from the ore.

Stage #3. Refining the iron into steel.

Stage #4. Shaping the steel into:

    (a) finished products such as rails, pipes, wires, and nails.

    (b) semifinished products such as steel plates, sheets, and bars.

Stage #5. Fabricating the semifinished products into finished goods such as tractors and railway cars.[24]

BUILDING A SIMPLE MODEL

To build a macro model of the economy, a rudimentary version of making bread can be a useful example. We will make use of several highly simplified assumptions:[25]

First, each stage of production will take an equal amount of time to complete.

Second, the total period of production will take one year or less to complete.

Third, there will be only one producer at each stage of production. No other capital goods will be bought from other businesses to be used in a particular stage.

Fourth, there will be only working capital, no fixed capital.

Fifth, there will be no durable capital goods.

Sixth, there will be no durable consumer goods.

Seventh, there will be no inventories.

Eighth, we assume that the economy will be "evenly rotating," meaning that at each stage of product development, the profit level will be the same. There will be no losses by firms.

After developing this simple model, we will gradually eliminate each assumption as we move toward a more realistic model of the whole economy.

We can use the Hayekian triangles, as outlined in *Prices and Production,* to represent the structure of production for breadmaking. The two key elements are (1) the basic stages of production in the making of bread, and (2) the time it takes to produce bread from the raw commodity (wheat). Figure 5.5 expresses our four simplified stages of breadmaking, based on "gross revenues" for each stage in a year's time.

The horizontal axis measures the gross revenue obtained from the sale of the product at each stage of production during the season (one year). The vertical axis is a measurement of time.

The gross revenue increases at each succeeding stage. At each level of production, value is added as the final consumer good, bread, is approached. Let us assume that the first stage is the farmer growing wheat. This incorporates the

Figure 5.5. Four Stages of Bread Production

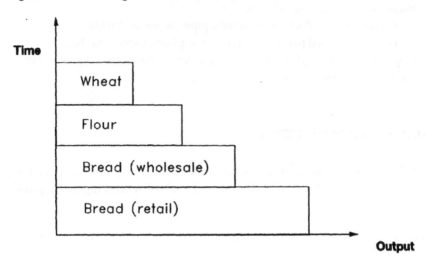

use of a plough in preparing the land. The farmer's cost is the price of the plough used to raise the wheat crop. The farmer plants, fertilizes and harvests the wheat at a certain cost, and then sells the wheat to the miller for a profit. The second stage is the miller's threshing of the wheat and grinding it into flour. Again, the miller must consider the basic costs of the mill equipment to turn the wheat into flour. He then sells the flour to the baker for a value-added price which assures the miller of a profit. The third stage is the baker who takes the flour and makes it into bread, and then sells the bread to the grocer, again at a price higher than his costs. The final stage is the grocer, who sells the bread to the consumer at still a higher price that insures a profit for the supermarket.

The making of shoes may be another rudimentary example. The first stage could be the raising of cattle to make hides. The second stage is tanning the hide and making it into leather. The third is the manufacture of the shoe itself, and the fourth and final stage is selling of the shoe to the retail customer. This production process is diagrammed in figure 5.6.

JOINT PRODUCTION AND THE COMPLEMENTARY NATURE OF PRODUCERS' GOODS

Now let us eliminate a few of our oversimplified assumptions. We know, for example, that every product involves the use of more than one input at each

Figure 5.6. Four Stages of Shoe Production

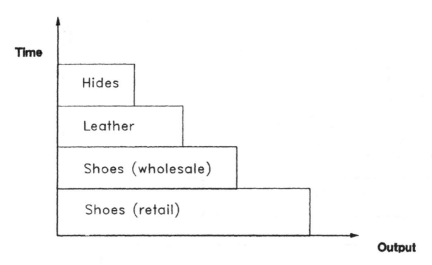

Source: Durbin, *Purchasing Power and Trade Depression*, 54. Reprinted by permission of Jonathan Cape Ltd.

stage. As Menger notes, "We see everywhere that not single goods but combinations of goods of different kinds serve the purposes of economizing man."[26] And Hayek adds: "At each stage of the process from the raw material to the finished product the main stream will be joined by tributaries which in some cases may already have run through a much longer course than the main stream itself."[27]

In many cases, these tributaries are machines, tools and other instruments that facilitate the production process, which we have called fixed capital. Fixed capital is generally specific in nature, i.e., used for a specific purpose at a certain point in time. For instance, in our breadmaking example, the plough and mill are considered a fixed capital good, while wheat seed and flour are working capital.

In order to complete our macroeconomic model of the entire bread industry, we must include joint production in the picture. The best way to include all the stages of the joint factors of production is through a generalized geometric structure.

To show how we can incorporate this new factor of joint production, let us return to our example of breadmaking, this time using an illustration similar to Durbin's example in chapter 3 repeated below.

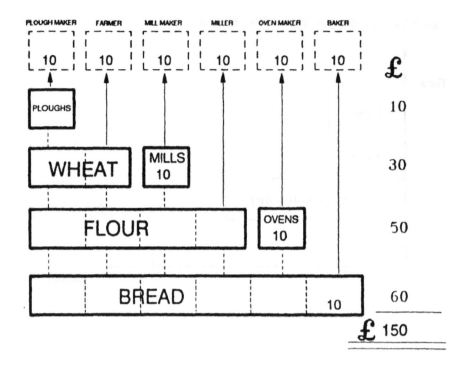

Let us slightly alter Durbin's example by placing the mills in stage two along with the output of wheat, and putting the ovens in stage three, along with flour. We start with the first three stages of the breadmaking industry, i.e., the plough-maker, the wheat farmer, and the miller. Assume that the profit margin is the same at each stage. i.e.,

$$\pi_a = \pi_b = \pi_c = \pi_d.$$

We also assume that we have only one joint input, a mill used by the miller in stage three. But since it is a cost to the miller, we place the mill in stage two, along side the miller.

Let the gross revenue of the ploughmaker (stage one) be *a*, the revenue of the farmer, *b*, the output of the miller, *d*, and the cost of the mill, *c*. Figure 5.7 illustrates the business relationship between the resources and products.

What are we trying to show? We wish to prove that the profit margin is the same at each stage of production even when joint inputs are involved in the supply chain.

The miller's cost of the mill, *c*, becomes the revenue of the millmaker. But the millmaker also has his own costs in manufacturing the mill. In order to make

Figure 5.7. Joint Production with Three Stages

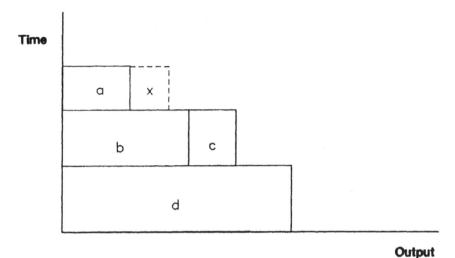

Time

Output

the bread industry a complete model, we must include the stages necessary to produce a mill. Let us assume in this algebraic example that the cost of producing a mill is x, and that the mill is produced in only one stage. Therefore we place x at stage 1 along with the ploughmaker.

If we assume that the profit margin for the millmaker is the same as it is for other businesses (a hypothetical assumption we can only make in the case of a risk-free, evenly rotating economy), we can then show that the *profit margin* at each stage is also the same, regardless of whether joint production exists at any level. We also make the important assumption that the time periods are the same for each stage. To prove that the profit margin is equal at every stage, we define the profit margin as,

$$\text{Profit margin} = \frac{\text{total profit}}{\text{total cost}} \text{ or } \frac{\text{revenue} - \text{cost}}{\text{cost}}$$

Therefore,

$$\pi = \frac{b - a}{a}$$

and

$$\pi = \frac{d - (b + c)}{b + c}$$

If x is the cost to produce c, and the profit margin for c is the same for other producers, then we must prove:

$$\frac{(b + c) - (a + x)}{a + x} = \frac{b + a}{a} \qquad \text{(Eq. 5.1)}$$

Proof: Since the profit margin on c is $\dfrac{c - x}{x}$, and the profit margins on all businesses are equal, therefore

$$\frac{b - a}{a + x} = \frac{c - x}{a}$$

Reduced,

$$x \frac{ac}{b}.$$

Therefore, substituting $\dfrac{ac}{b}$ for x in equation 5.1, we obtain,

$$\frac{b + bc - ab - ac}{ba + ac} = \frac{b - a}{a}.$$

Reduced,

$$\frac{b(b + c) - a(b + c)}{a(b + c)} = \frac{b - a}{a}.$$

The $(b + c)$ cancel out in the left side of the equation, and the proof is complete.

The proof can be applied to more than one joint input, although it becomes more complex. Ultimately, the point is reached in an industrial economy where there are many stages of production with a multitude of inputs. Thus, the Hayekian triangle for the whole economy shows a smooth "profit margin" line running from top to bottom, per figure 5.8.

Figure 5.8. Sector Model with Joint Production

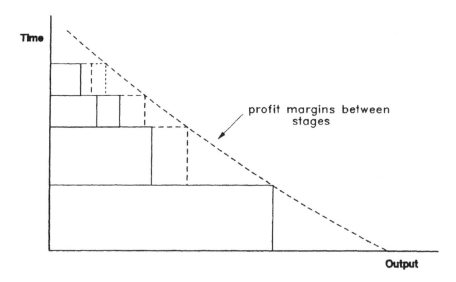

DIFFERENT TIME SCHEDULES

Another of our initial assumptions was that each stage takes the same amount of time, which is contrary to the real situation. In the case of breadmaking, the planting and harvesting of wheat may take four to five months, while the milling process may be less than a month, and the baker's time for making bread may be only a few days. The alteration in the triangular production figure can easily account for differences in the period of production. Figure 5.9 below shows how the breadmaking industry could look under the above differences in time schedules.

In this case, the revenue for the wheat farmer (indicated by stage one) remains the same as in Figure 5.5, but the vertical axis is longer (reflecting the longer time involved) and the horizontal axis is shorter. Note that the profit margin between stages is the same as when all the stages took the same amount of time. Thus we see that longer or shorter periods of production do not present a problem in creating an aggregate economic model.

THE PERIOD OF PRODUCTION: HOW LONG IS IT?

In our simplified example of breadmaking, we also assumed that the whole production process took one year or less. One of the major debates in capital theory

Figure 5.9. Sector Structure with Different Time Schedules

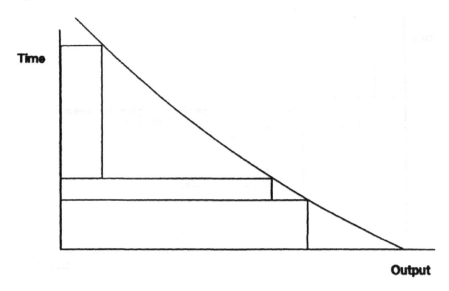

is to determine the time it takes to produce a final good from its original matter. Is it possible to measure the period of production? Many economists, including Clark, Knight, and Stigler, have dismissed the entire concept of a time-oriented structure of production because of this difficulty. They argue that the period of production is virtually infinite.

Taussig explains the dilemma: "Bread is made with flour, and flour from grain; the sowing of the seed is our starting point in the process of production; but seed was grown a season before, and comes from an earlier stage of effort. The plough, too, was provided before the seed was sown, and that plough was made with tools which came from still an earlier application of labour. . . . If we would be mathematically accurate, we should need to carry it ages back, to the time when the first tool was made."[28] Knight flatly states that "the production period has no beginning and no end."[29] And recently Earl Rolph asks sardonically, "What is the period of production of a kilowatt hour of electricity, the transportation of a ton of freight from Chicago to Seattle, a computer printout, a seat on a Boeing 747 flying from New York to San Francisco? . . . It is purely arbitrary to date the beginning date of production of wine—the Austrians' favorite illustration. . . . Trees—another Austrian illustration—grow from smaller trees that are rooted in the soil."[30]

Böhm-Bawerk was well aware of this problem of infinite time length. He admitted that "the production period of almost any consumption good could, in any strict calculation, trace its beginning back to early centuries. . . . The cracking of nuts with a hammer which might chance to be made of iron brought from a mine opened by the Romans would perhaps be the most 'capitalistic' kind of production."[31] He therefore adopted the concept of the average period of production, arguing that past work constitutes "such a small element" that it "will scarcely influence the average, and may in most cases be simply neglected."[32]

However, Böhm-Bawerk's controversial solution is not only wrong, but it is unnecessary. It has been rightly criticized by economists, even by sympathizers. Rothbard calls the average period of production a "mythical concept."[33] Mises states: "The length of time expended in the past for the production of capital goods available today does not count at all. These capital goods are valued only with regard to their usefulness for future want-satisfaction. The 'average period of production' is an empty concept."[34] And Machlup adds the important point that the average period of production may obscure significant changes in an economy's structure. The economy could switch resources from "uses with quick maturity" to "uses with later maturity" *without* changing the average, depending on the weight given to the resources involved. Thus: "The 'shape of the investment function' would tell what the single 'average investment period' conceals."[35]

The dilemma is resolved by treating the first stage of production at the point where a new undertaking actually begins, not when the first joint capital good was produced. For example, in the case of breadmaking, the first stage is when the wheat is planted, *not* when the plough is manufactured or the fertilizer is made. Such resources have already been produced and are ready to be used. We do not need to go back to the time when a machine is made. Every extractive industry today uses heavy industry in the first stages of production, and it is quite appropriate to consider this the beginning of production, and not to fall back on endless genealogies of the mass of capital goods used to extract natural resources. Thus, the first stage of iron ore production is mining with heavy machinery, not with a shovel and wheelbarrow.

Of course, the heavy machinery involved in iron ore production as well as all other higher-order tools also have their own sequential process of manufacturing apart from the iron ore operation, but we must make a sharp distinction between *current* production of these higher-order capital goods and *past* production of these machines which are now being used to extract iron ore.[36]

The first stage of constructing a building, therefore, does not have to be traced back to when the cranes and other tools to be used were manufactured. These capital goods have already been made and are in inventory, ready for use. The period of construction is actually measured from the point when the company directors, having decided to construct the building, call in the architect to make the plans. The production period ends when the building is finished and ready to open for business. Typically a large multi-level building will take three to five years from the time of conception to its grand opening.

However, suppose a major machine necessary in the building of a new project is not in inventory, but has to be ordered. Its construction must then be included in the period of production. This is often the case with specialized expensive projects that are "built to suit." Examples include turbine engines used in dams and jumbo jets ordered by airline companies.

In response to Rolph's objection, quoted above, the appropriate period of production for trees begins when the smaller trees are planted. Such "seed" trees are already in inventory, ready to be planted whenever the tree grower decides. Therefore the time it takes for the seed plants to grow themselves (and for their parent trees to grow, ad infinitum) is *not* part of the production process as far as the tree grower is concerned.

Or, what about the period of production of, say, a seat on a Boeing 747 flying from New York to San Francisco, another Rolph example? We could discuss this situation in terms of the period of consumption rather than production, since the airplane has already been built. In fact, a seat occupied by a tourist could be regarded as a period of consumption equal to the time it takes to fly to the tourist's destination. If we look at the seat in terms of a capital good—e.g., a vehicle for a businessman to use getting from New York to San Francisco—then we can see that the period of production is the time it takes to make a transcontinental flight (five to six hours). It need not include the time it took to build the airplane.

Despite the hostility expressed by many mainstream economists toward the concept of the period of production, the time it takes for a project to be completed is very much on the minds of the capitalist. Cost of materials and labor is not the only factor. Time is also a cost, as reflected in the necessity of waiting and the interest paid before the project can be completed and revenue received. As Mises states, "Hence acting man must always take into account the period of production and the duration of serviceableness of the product."[37]

Rothbard also makes the important point that the period of production should not include the cost of any permanent improvements that result from the project. In fact, according to Rothbard, these permanent changes should be treated as *land,* as if they were an original factor of production. "Land that has been irrigated by canals or altered through the chopping down of forests has become a present, permanent *given.* Because it is a present given, not worn out in the process of production, and not needing to be replaced, it becomes a *land* factor under our definition."[38]

Once "the permanent are separated from the nonpermanent alterations, we see that the structure of production no longer stretches back infinitely in time, but comes to a close within a relatively brief span of time."[39]

THE QUESTION OF SPECIFICITY OF CAPITAL
GOODS AND THE CIRCULARITY OF PRODUCTION

A major critique of the concept of stages of production is that stages are meaningless because it is impossible to tell in which stage a particular production technique belongs. This is the problem of "circularity," where a particular type of capital good may be used in many intertemporal levels of output. Paper and nonferrous metals are two examples. "In both cases, the path of the product from the primary materials stage to finished goods are long and complex. Both are one stage removed from raw materials—wood pulp and ores. Both are used in literally thousands of other products."[40]

Shackle notes,

> Production in an advanced industrial society needs for its description a Leontief table of input coefficients, where, in principle . . . every operation or every industry or sector is deemed actually or potentially to contribute means of some kind to every other, both directly and indirectly. Such sectors as transportation, the telephone system and the electric power industry plainly have a hand to some degree in everything that is done by anybody anywhere.[41]

We have previously mentioned those economists who ultimately rejected the hierarchical approach because of the circularity problem, such as Marshall, Knight, Stigler, and Sraffa. Because of the "very complicated pedigree" of consumption and capital goods, Jevons rejects the intertemporal classification of goods as "hopeless."[42] Hawtrey is even more adamant: "Every commodity belongs to a variety of different stages, and every stage contains a variety of different commodities, and it is quite impossible even in theory to say what commodities belong to what stages."[43]

This is precisely the point Sraffa makes in his critique of economic theory. How does one deal with the "production of commodities by means of commodities"? Sraffa uses the Ricardian example of corn as "the one product which is required both for its own production and for the production of every other commodity." The classical position of a circular process, as espoused by Quesnay, Smith, and Ricardo, stands "in striking contrast to the view presented by modern theory of a one-way avenue that leads from 'factors of production' to 'consumption goods.'"[44]

And, finally, referring to the Austrian capital theory as a "fairy tale," Earl Rolph challenges advocates to "ask themselves precisely how they wish to define a period of production in a context where horses produce horses, trucks are used to produce trucks, electricity is used to pump water back into a reservoir to produce electricity, crude oil is used to produce crude oil, used beer cans are used to produce beer cans."[45]

Certainly these economists demonstrate the complexity of the industrial process. They raise a critical issue which cannot be ignored or swept under the Böhm-Bawerkian rug. Does the circularity of capital goods destroy the vertical stage-of-production concept? It certainly does complicate the problem of classification, but it does not destroy it. As Shackle declares, "These considerations by no means destroy Hayek's theme, but that conception needs to be seen in their light."[46] Hayek himself responded to this difficulty:

It may be mentioned here, since this has occasionally been a cause of confusion, that any given capital good need not, and usually will not, belong to any one given "stage" of production only. If it is used to produce other capital goods employed in different stages, and still more if it helps to produce durable goods, or is itself durable, it belongs to as many different "stages" as different periods of time elapse from the moment in which we consider it, to the moments when the different final products which it has helped to produce are consumed. This, however, so far from making the concept of stages useless, is only a necessary distinction in order to explain the different ways in which the value of individual capital goods will be affected by changes in the supply of capital, the rate of interest, or other factors affecting the structure of production.[47]

What kind of conclusions can we make about the general nature of capitalistic production? Certainly, all goods are transformed into final consumption through multi-stage development, but not all are multi-staged in terms of final use. Many capital goods are highly specific in their use, especially in the earlier stages of output (raw materials, producers' goods, etc.). Their distance from final consumption can generally be identified.

It is a different matter for nonspecific goods, such as paper products, electricity, telephones, trucks, and other goods used in a wide variety up and down the industrial sectors. Actually, all goods vary in their degree of specificity. Some goods are extremely specific, others are very non-specific and are used in virtually all sectors of the economy.[48] But rather than abandon the idea of stages entirely, it is better to try to identify in a general way where along the time-structure hierarchy these nonspecific goods belong.

The very essence of the market economy is the specificity of capital goods. Suppose, for the sake of argument, that all capital goods were completely non-specific and totally versatile. This would mean that they could be transferred from one project to another at no cost. If this were the case, there would be no structure to the economy, and therefore no lags, no structural unemployment of resources or labor—in short, no business cycle. In short, capital goods are *specific* in nature, although some are more specific in use than others. This is the crux of macroeconomic analysis, and the reason that Lachmann and others stress the importance of the heterogeneity of capital goods (and, I might add, the labor market, although to a lesser extent). But the degree to which producer's goods and machinery are nonspecific—that is, useable in more than one stage—is the degree to which the economy will be flexible in adjusting to monetary disequilibrium.

Basically, goods should be classified according to intertemporal *use*, not physical attributes; they should be identified by what they *do*, not by what they *are*. As Howard Piquet states, "Difficulties arise when attempts are made to classify goods instead of their uses." He takes the example of coal, which is used as either a consumer good when used to produce heat in a house, or as a producer good if used in a factory to produce electricity, "A ton of coal, therefore, can be either a producer good or a consumer good. It is not the coal that should be classified, but the use to which it is put."[49] Moreover:

> Degrees of indirectness shade into each other, as shades of gray blend into each other between the extremes of black and white. What is important is not that rigid categories between the two extremes be established, but that the degrees of difference be identifiable. It is important that any use can be compared with any other use as being either *more,* or *less,* indirect.[50]

Where should the nonspecific goods be located along the industrial transformation belt? This is a quantitative question which cannot be answered without referring to an input-output table and other historical statistics. The I-O table might be helpful in determining the degree of specificity of any particular good or machine. For example, according to the 1982 I-O table 38.8 percent of transportation vehicles manufactured in 1982 were used in intermediate commercial concerns. Hence, it would be appropriate to classify 38.8 percent as intermediate capital goods, specifying as far as practical which vehicles went toward "higher" stages and which went toward "lower" stages. As Hayek indicates, the degree of specificity and the location of the goods' uses along the industrial hierarchy is significant because that location will affect the stability or volatility of the goods' own volume of output from year to year.

Does the fact that "crude oil is used to produce crude oil" present a problem, as Rolph suggests? I do not believe it does. First, oil companies use very little crude oil directly to discover, drill, and refine oil. They do use processed oil and gasoline products to pursue their business interests in the machines, trucks and other forms of transportation that they use, and to the extent that crude oil is an ingredient of their costs, a small percentage of crude oil should be treated as a "higher order" producer good. It is highly significant that only a *small percentage* of raw material is used to produce raw material, just as only a small percentage of the corn crop is kept back to be used for seed corn. If this were not the case, raw commodities would not be extracted in the first place. It would not be cost effective.

The fact that many completed capital goods are used as intermediate goods to further the production of higher-order goods implies that the period of production is becoming even more lengthy! If 38.8 percent of all transportation vehicles are used in assisting the production of other intermediate markets, this fact signifies that the supply of vehicles in general is not dependent solely on the demands of consumers, but that markets must also be responsive to the ups and downs in the highly volatile capital-goods markets. In the forthcoming section on business cycles, we will discuss the implications of this lengthening process insofar as it affects the stability of the entire economy.

In any case, the relative specificity of capital goods should not lead us to deny the basic transformation process from raw materials to final consumer goods. Even the specific machine or tool is used for that purpose—to move the circulating goods along the production assembly line. Thus, Rothbard concludes, "The pattern of production is not changed by the fact that both specific and nonspecific factors exist. Since the production structure is aggregated, the degree of specificity for a *particular product* is irrelevant in a discussion of the time market."[51]

THE DURABILITY PROBLEM

The next major challenge to the time-structure theory of production is the durability problem. Durability of capital and consumer goods is a common feature in all economies. Can this fact be represented in the Hayekian triangles? Hayek himself assumed in *Prices and Production* that all goods were circulating intermediate goods on their way to becoming consumer goods. Moreover, he assumed that the consumer goods were used up in a short period. Shackle comments that the simplified Hayekian model "makes no explicit provision for durable goods, and . . . uses the single-track, isolated process of production without contributory streams or any hint of the complexity of the production net."[52]

Bellante and Garrison point out that Hayek's triangles are heuristic in nature, i.e., "a deliberate fiction used to facilitate the logical development of a theory."[53] "This particular assumption [multi-period inputs and a point output] allowed for the abstraction from many complexities while it retained the essential element—the time element—in the analysis."[54]

Faber suggests that the durable goods problem is a special case of joint production. "The main reason why fixed capital is so difficult to analyze is that its use in the production of other goods is a special case of joint production, namely, over time. After they have been produced, capital goods yield a flow of usages which can be distributed variously over the individual time periods."[55]

Arthur Smithies dismisses the durability of goods as a nonexistent problem. "The durability of an instrument has no relevance in considering the technique of production apart from cost. Provided the service is the same, it matters not whether it is rendered by an instrument of long or short durability."[56] Only the durable goods' "services per unit of time" are what matters, according to Smithies.[57] Rothbard, in essence, argues the same thing, figuring that durable goods "are themselves only discounted embodiments of their nondurable services and are therefore no different from nondurable goods."[58] According to this view, then, one might see the distinction between durable and nondurable goods as one of degree rather than definition.[59] All goods vary in degrees of durability—-e.g., fresh fish (one day), canned goods (one year), automobile (ten years), house (one hundred years). The solution, according to Rothbard, is to capitalize their value over time, where their price (rent or lease) is equal to their discounted marginal product. Obviously, a building would be discounted more than a car or canned goods.[60]

If a capital good is 100 percent durable, of course, it is no longer a capital good but *land,* as Schumacher points out.[61] It becomes a permanent good with no cost of maintenance. Thus, as figure 5.10 shows, one may compare land, capital and consumption on an intertemporal continuum.

Despite the effort of mainstream economists to minimize the impact of durability, one can see that it is critically important to recognize the distinct attributes of durable capital goods and how such characteristics affect the aggregate structure of production.

First, durable capital equipment and machines provide services in the transformation of raw materials and the manufacture of intermediate goods over a long period of time, typically anywhere from five to fifty years. As such, machines and tools—fixed capital—cannot be treated the same as is labor, which is applied over a shorter period of time. As Uhr states, reflecting the ideas of Wicksell, "Labor can only yield its services in an unchangeable *day-to-day* sequence over a finite period of years, and the same applies to land with the

Figure 5.10. An Intertemporal Continuum

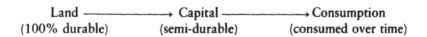

Land ⟶ Capital ⟶ Consumption
(100% durable) (semi-durable) (consumed over time)

additional qualification that it yields an infinite rather than finite series of services. Furthermore, neither the services of labor nor those of land can be stored *as such;* they can only be stored indirectly in the form of real capital."[62] Based on this Wicksellian concept of capital as "stored labor," Hahn adds:

> The labor incorporated in the machine differs, however, from the labor added in the current production period in that it is work done long before the current period, and that its result is normally not consumed during the immediately following production period but a later one. On the average, the machine remains in the production process much longer. It is consumed only over long periods. . . . Even if the worker can thus produce more quickly with the help of the machine than he could without it, the entire production process lasts much longer. It starts not with the current work of the worker using the machine but with the production of the machine itself, and it ends not with the goods completed currently with the help of the machine but with the last goods which the machine is still able to turn out.[63]

Because of the long-term use of capital goods and their relatively high price, durable equipment and machines (especially in heavy industry) are bought occasionally, not regularly, by most firms. The high price of heavy equipment often requires firms to lease them instead of buying them. Frederick C. Mills notes: "In buying capital equipment a manufacturer is, of course, concerned with the relation between the price he pays for the equipment and the prices at which goods to be manufactured will be sold. But the connection is much more remote than that between the prices of materials and prices of goods made from them."[64] Demand for capital goods is a "derived demand" of final consumer goods. "Such derived demand (especially where durable goods are involved and where stocks may be accumulated) is variable, subject to wider fluctuations than is the demand for ultimate consumers' goods."[65] This is not to say that entrepreneurs cannot respond to this increased volatility in the capital-goods market, but it is a high-risk business.

Since many durable goods are more specific in nature, they may be assigned to a precise stage of production. For example, large dump trucks may be custom-designed and used almost exclusively in the extraction of minerals and other raw materials. They lack standardization and flexibility and are more difficult to use in other stages of output.[66]

How do we place durable capital goods along the aggregate production function? It is necessary to bear in mind that we are always looking at the structure of *current* output, not what has been produced in the past. Naturally, the more durable all capital goods are (as well as consumer goods), the better off the economy is. A lower rate of depreciation means that fewer durable goods need to be produced and manufacturing tends to be more efficient.

The stages-of-production theory does not include past output of fixed capital goods, just as it does not include past manufacturing of intermediate goods, or consumer goods. But it does include the current output of individual durable capital and consumer goods. These must be allocated according to their period of production in the intertemporal capital structure. Admittedly, many of these durable factors take several years to complete. If our aggregate production structure only measures what is produced in one year, per our assumptions in the simplified model, how do we include two-year or five-year projects? We can, of course, include the value of such investment projects during the year they are completed and sold to their users. But this does not mean that we should exclude incompleted projects. Unfinished long-term undertakings must also be included, because they involve purposeful human action. As Hawtrey asserts, "The expression, Structure of Production, is used to mean the totality of productive processes employed by the community."[67] Though the long-term project has not yet been sold to a buyer, the buyer has contracted for the work to be done and, while the work is in progress, wages, rents, and other manufacturing costs are being paid. Therefore, the annual cost of working on the project should be included in the appropriate stage of production, based on its estimated time length from the final consumption stage.

In analyzing the meaning of the aggregate production structure, then, it is essential to distinguish between *past* production of consumer durables and *current* output. Past production does not belong in the aggregate production structure unless it has occurred during the "current time period" that we have selected for the aggregate production structure. We have selected a one-year time frame in our model because it fits conveniently with the accounting procedures of businesses, and with statistical gathering in general.[68] This one-year time frame means that the value of the output at each stage (measured horizontally) represents the amount of production accomplished by each firm during the calendar year. For products which can be completed in only a few months, the one-year aggregate includes a multiple number of sales. For products that take several years to finish, the one-year aggregate includes only the amount of work completed on the long-term project during the calendar year.

This one-year limitation should not be confused with the vertical axis of the aggregate production structure, which measures the time it takes for any particular investment project to be completed before reaching the final consumption stage. The vertical axis can extend back to ten years, twenty years, and even longer.

To make this clear, let's look at an example in the automobile industry. All car manufacturers have ongoing research and development projects, which undoubtedly represent one of the most remote higher-order goods in the whole economy. Suppose it normally takes ten years before a new car design becomes a reality in the showroom. The vertical axis of the aggregate production structure would therefore indicate a figure of ten years away from final use for research and development projects.

But at the same time the car company spends a certain amount of money *each year* on research and development. This amount represents the horizontal axis of the ten-year R&D stage. It would show how much of this research and development was carried out *during a one year period* based on the annual expenditures made by the automobile industry.

THE CASE OF CONSUMER DURABLES

How do we include consumer durables—houses, automobiles, appliances, and so on—in the whole production matrix? In many cases, it takes longer for consumer goods to be used up than it takes to produce them. A house may be built in six months, but the basic framework and foundation will provide services for fifty to one hundred years, and perhaps longer. An automobile may take three to six months for its period of production, from the point of assembling basic components to its sale by a car dealer. Yet it may serve the car owner for ten years or more before it is sent to the wrecker. Canned goods may take a year to produce (if one includes the length of the season to make the fruits, vegetables, meat, and other components of the canned goods), but may have a two- to three-year shelf life.[69] Graphically, this fact can be shown as a single-line continuum of time, demonstrating the variation between the period of production and the period of consumption. I have indicated several examples in the economy, some with periods of short production and long consumption, others with long production and short consumption, to suggest the incredible variety and complexity of goods and services within the economy.

Number 3 in figure 5.11 is the typical case of a durable consumer good. Many economists, such as Wicksell, excluded durable consumer goods from their economic models, almost as though they were an anomaly; something that did not matter in the overall scheme of things. But again, such a view makes the model highly inadequate, since the output of durable consumer goods is a significant part of gross national product and economic variables such as interest rates have a critical impact on their output.

The solution to the durability problem is to treat durable consumer goods as if they were higher-order investment goods which take a long time both to produce and to use up. In this manner, durable goods are not different from products which have a relatively long "period of production" and are distant from final consumption (as illustrated in number one category in figure 5.11).

Figure 5.11. Periods of Production and Consumption

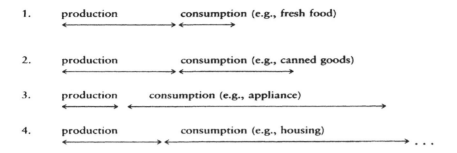

Several other economists have shown why this adaptation is not a distortion of economic reality. In stating that consumer durables should be treated as remote goods, Bye and Hewett argue:

> The creation of durable goods must be regarded as production remote in time from ultimate consumption, even though the goods are to be used directly by the consumer. A dwelling house, for instance, yields services directly to its occupant. However, these services are released so gradually that most of them are not enjoyed until long after the house is built. The major part of the productive activity that goes into its construction is directed toward a quite distant future, and is remote from final consumption.[70]

In general terms, Bye and Hewett consider the use of the terms *consumers' goods* and *producers' goods* to be inexact, especially because consumers' goods are defined as "all goods sold to consumers," even though some are quite remote from final consumption. According to Bye and Hewett's definition, consumer goods are "near goods . . . which can be wholly consumed in the near future for the direct satisfaction of wants."[71] Food, clothing, and an automobile "nearly worn out" fit into this category. On the other hand: "All very durable wealth is to be classed with investment goods, even if it is being partly consumed for direct satisfaction in the present (as in the case of an occupied dwelling), for most of its services will not be released until the future."[72]

Garrison also emphasizes that marketability, not durability, should be the principal factor in distinguishing capital goods from consumer goods. He points out the general lack of effective markets for most secondhand goods. Only the exceptions, those goods which offer well-established secondhand markets, such as automobiles and houses, should be considered an important factor in the production of current goods and services. Thus, Garrison explains:

This is to suggest that in dealing with goods in the hands of the consumer, remarketability, and not durability, should be the basis for the distinction between capital goods and consumer goods. That is, goods that are readily remarketable are not necessarily in the hands of their *ultimate* consumer. Goods such as houses and automobiles, for which there are effective secondhand markets, should be considered to be capital goods even from the Austrian point of view. Such remarketable goods *can* be shifted back into business inventories (the second lowest maturity class) in response to changing supply and demand conditions. They may even be absorbed in even higher maturity classes, as in the case of a secondhand automobile that is purchased by a business firm.[73]

No doubt Garrison is correct in emphasizing the effect of secondhand markets in the production of current consumer durables, especially in situations where the cost of new production increases, thus causing more consumers to enter the secondhand markets. Obviously, durability has a lot to do with the fact that automobiles and houses have such a good secondhand market, although many consumer durables such as furniture, household goods and jewelry sell at a much greater discount compared to retail prices. Thus, durability is a necessary but not sufficient condition for remarketability.[74]

The proposal to treat remarketable consumer durables in the same manner as remote capital goods can also be shown in graphic form. As stated earlier, consumer durables increase in value or marginal utility over a long period of time. This can be demonstrated in figure 5.12.

Figure 5.12. Marginal Utility of Consumer Durable Goods over Time

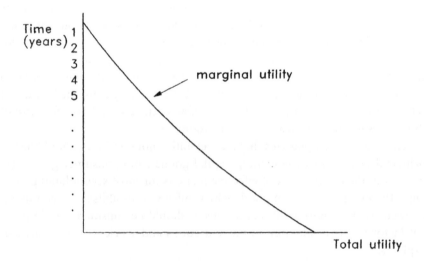

The horizontal axis is a reflection of the gradual increase in "total utility" or satisfaction obtained from the use of a consumer durable as the period of consumption ends. As can be seen, this diagram is similar in nature to the triangular production functions we have been using throughout this chapter. And, as economic variables such as interest rates change, the effects on the discounted value of consumer durables will produce similar effects on the production of remote higher-order capital goods. For example, an increase in real interest rates will, other things being equal, tend to restrict current output of distant capital goods as well as consumer durables. Thus it comes as no surprise that both consumer durables and higher-order capital goods are "interest sensitive."

In sum, consumer goods in general must not be treated as homogeneous, any more than capital goods can be treated as homogeneous in nature. Their intertemporal production schedules are supremely important. The Hayekian triangles, which show the consumption stage as a single monolithic stage, are only homogeneous in terms of aggregate monetary value. It should not lead one to the conclusion that only capital goods are heterogenously distinct. Consumer goods are also nonuniform. They are not solely goods of the first order, as Menger and Böhm-Bawerk suggested, but differ widely according to their durability and remarketability. Food and fuel are almost immediately used up, for example, but houses and cars are not.

In a sense, we can now interrelate all three time-oriented goods, i.e., fixed capital, working capital, and consumer durables. Each type of good can be compared according to its *combined* period of production and consumption.

THE CLASSIFICATION OF LAND AND LABOR

Land and labor, the two original factors of production, are applied at each stage of product transformation, and can therefore, like capital goods, be classified according to their role in the production architecture. If land is used for the production of lower-order consumer goods, then it is a first order good. If the land consists of minerals and other natural resources, then it is a higher-order good.[75] As Röpke notes, referring to labor,

Just as specialization and division of labor characterize production on any one level (horizontal division of labor), so also we find a division of labor between the different levels of production (vertical division of labor). In other words, there is not only a division of labor between the production of shoes and the production of paper, but also a division of labor between the production of shoes and the production of fore-products (tools, machines, leather, hide, etc.) which enter into the manufacture of shoes.[76]

Jevons divides labor and landowners into six "classifications of trade" in his principles textbook, which he describes as "the principal orders of industry, or ranks of traders, as it were, who successively contribute some operation to the complete production of a commodity."[77] Jevons' six levels of industry are:

First, sources of raw materials—landowners, mine-proprietors, lessees of fishing rights, etc.

Second, producers of raw materials—farmers and agricultural laborers, shepherds, gardeners, fishermen, miners, woodsmen, hunters, etc.

Third, dealers in raw materials—corn merchants, cotton traders, hide dealers, timber agents, raw material importers, etc.

Fourth, manufacturers—the miller, the baker, the tanner, the bootmaker, the brewer, the cabinetmaker, pig iron manufacturer, etc.

Fifth, wholesale dealers—shippers of finished goods, warehousers of manufactured goods, etc.

Sixth, retail dealers—shopkeepers, bakery owners, tailors, clothiers, food stores, etc.[78]

In a more up-to-date economics text, Geoffrey Whitehead divides the labor market into three categories:

—Primary (from natural resources).
—Secondary (manufactured goods derived from natural resources).
—Third, tertiary (commercial and personal services).

WHAT ABOUT SERVICES?

Many of the categories listed above involve the selling of services instead of producing material products. How do they fit into the vertical production scheme? Whitehead defines personal services as "intangible utilities" provided by the dentist, the surgeon, the television personality, or the hairdresser. Commercial services involve trade, banking, transport, insurance and communications, among others.[79] While Whitehead categorizes all commercial and personal services in the tertiary division of production, it is clear that many commercial services are provided at the higher-order industries as well as final consumption. Barber services generally apply to final consumer demand, while accounting services are primarily business-oriented (though some are used to prepare individual tax returns).

Hence, services are just as much part of the transformation process as anything else. As Rothbard declares, "It must be understood that 'factors of

Figure 5.13. Three General Types of Labor

| | The Production of Goods | | The Production of Services | |
| | | | Tertiary | |
Primary	Secondary	Commercial	Personal
Coal miner	Engineer	Wholesaler	Doctor
Gold miner	Electronic engineer	Retailer	Dentist
Tin miner	Builder	Banker	Nurse
Lead miner	Decorator	Insurance agent	Teacher
Oil driller	Cabinet maker	Stockbroker	Lecturer
Lumberjack	Carpenter	Importer	Policeman
Farmer	Plastics engineer	Exporter	Detective
Fisherman	Refinery technologist	Transport driver	Entertainer
Shepherd	Stillman	Merchant-Navy captain	Vocalist
Pearl drier	Potter	Ship's crews	Clergyman
Herdsman	Tailor	Communications engineer	Undertaker
Fur trapper	Steelworker		Editor
etc.	Aeronautical engineer		Author
			Psychologist

Source: Whitehead, *Economics Made Simple,* 12.

production' include *every* service that advances the product toward the stage of consumption. Thus, such services as 'marketing costs,' 'advertising,' etc., are just as legitimately productive services as any other factor."[80]

GROWING COMPLEXITY OF THE INDUSTRIAL ECONOMY

In building our aggregate economic model, we have addressed some of the most complex issues in capital theory. I have attempted to incorporate these complexities into the aggregate production structure rather than ignore them. Clearly, the modern economy is a difficult subject to examine. Even the simplest of commodities, such as bread and shoes, involve a long chain of processing techniques. Taussig points this out:

The labor of the tailor but gives the finishing touch to the work previously done by a long series of persons—the shepherd who tended the flocks, the wool shearer, those who transport the wool by land and sea, the carder and spinner and weaver, not to mention those who made the tools and machinery of these workers. Similarly the carpenter is the last of a succession of persons who worked toward a common end—the lumberman in the woods, the sawyer in the mill, the trainman and the engineer on the railroad, and so on. Many laborers, arranged in long series, combine in making even the simplest commodities.[81]

Leonard Read uses the classic example of the ordinary pencil to illustrate how complex and seemingly unending the process of making a pencil can be, even to the point that Read asserts that "not a single person on the face of this earth" knows to make a pencil on his own! In "I, Pencil," Read describes the genealogy of the pencil from its raw components to the pencil being used by a student, writer, or businessman. The illustration begins with a wide variety of raw materials: a cedar cut down in Northern California, the graphite mined in Ceylon, and a rubberlike substance made from the Dutch East Indies. Read emphasizes the wide variety of tools and machines used just to extract the raw materials. In the pencil factory, wood slats are cut and grooved, glue is applied, and reformulated lead molded and inserted into each "wood-clinched" sandwich, all accomplished with speed and precision by highly complex machines. Six coats of lacquer and finally the "crowning glory" (the "rubber" plug) are added to complete the everyday pencil. Read's story ends at the pencil factory, but the full account of pencil production does not end there. It continues through the extensive distribution channels until it reaches its final destination: the pencil customer.[82]

Figure 5.14 and 5.15 show the complex constellation and direction of two major industries, textiles and petroleum. One might conclude from all this that industrial production is so convoluted that it is impossible to make any generalized structural formula out of it. One might be tempted to throw up one's hands in Jevonian fashion and adopt a timeless, stageless fundist approach. As Keynes put it, it is easy to get "lost in a haze where nothing is clear and everything is possible."[83] But the patient analyst can see that stages can be generalized, even in Read's pencil example. Trees, graphite, and zinc are all remote materials that eventually become part of the pencil.

Nevertheless, we can still make certain general characterizations about the whole economy that will allow us to construct an aggregate production structure. The complexity of the production process should not deter us from recognizing that each and every good or service has a linear genealogy behind it—a series of production stages, each adding value, until the finished good is complete and ready for immediate or gradual consumption, whether it be a consumption good, fixed capital or circulating capital. It may be extremely difficult to trace this genealogy, or to determine where along the time structure a particular good belongs, but the fact remains that the supply chain exists for every good and service in the economy.

Figure 5.14. Production Stages in the Textile Industry

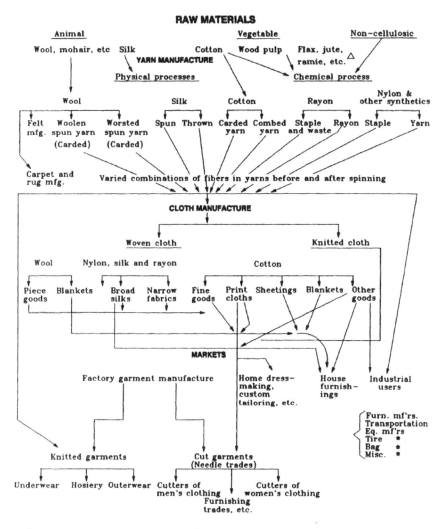

△ Of minor importance in domestic manufacture.
* Some woven felt goods; others "felted" by special machines; major market–industrial users

Source: Alderfer and Michl, *Economics of American Industry,* 324.

INDUSTRIAL OUTPUT: FOUR BASIC CATEGORIES

In examining the aggregate structure of the industrial economy, Matilda Holzman identifies the "technical schematization of the economy" in a linear fashion, dividing the production of materials into four basic categories:

Figure 5.15. Production Stages in the Petroleum Industry

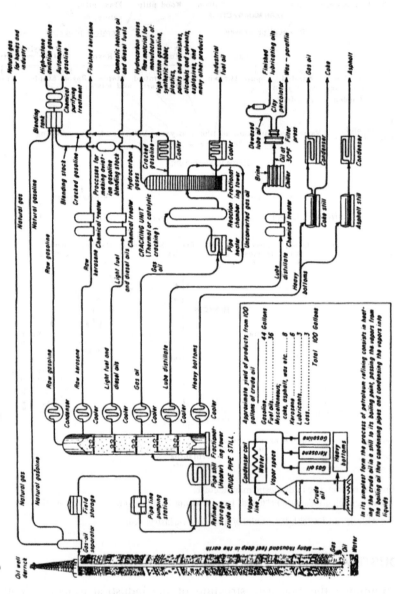

Source: Alderfer and Michl, *Economics of American Industry,* 272–73. Reprinted by permission of the American Petroleum Institute.

1. Cultivation or extraction of raw material
   a. growing and harvesting of crops,
   b. mining of minerals.
2. Purification or conversion into an economically useful form (such as cleaning fruits and vegetables for household consumption). "For most materials there are two stages of purification, a series of mechanical operations followed by chemical processing involving some degree of chemical change. This stage ends when the material reaches the purest form which is desirable."[84]
3. Combination of purified materials into basic materials of industry, designed for a wide variety of uses. Examples: alloys, steel ingots, papers, cotton gray goods, window glass, cement, canned and frozen foods, basic plastics, manufactured gas, electricity.
4. Fabrication of these basic materials into final products. "Fabrication consists of three sets of processes: the forming of product parts, whether by cutting as for textiles, or stamping, pressing, forging, and machining for automobiles; the assembly of the parts into final products; and finally whatever finishing—painting, dyeing, etc.,—must be reserved until after assembly."[85]

Holzman adds: "For many materials, fifteen or twenty separate processing stages may be observed, however, and there are borderline decisions which are not clear cut whether a particular process is part of one of the above-mentioned operations or of the operation immediately following."[86]

Essentially, then, there is a structure to the economy, albeit it is not always easy to pinpoint exactly in what stage each technique takes place.

Based on the general categories of resource production and retailing, we may build the following stylized aggregate model:

Stage #1: raw agricultural and industrial commodities.
Stage #2: manufactured or produced goods.
Stage #3: wholesale goods.
Stage #4: final retail goods.

Figure 5.16 shows the breakdown in the aggregate model.

On of the best evidences that this general triangular form can be applied to the whole economy is the annual revenue obtained by these stages of production. For instance, H. J. Pick figured the gross value of output at various processing stages for world aluminium production in 1963 (see figure 5.17).

This kind of exercise can be performed for many industries, demonstrating strong evidence of a triangular portrayal of the economy.

Figure 5.16. General Stages in the Aggregate Production Structure

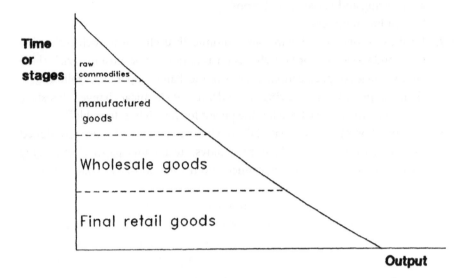

Figure 5.17. 1963 World Aluminium Production at Various Stages

Product	Gross Value (millions)	Value Added (millions)
Mining	$240	$240
Ore refining	900	660
Aluminum	2,700	1,800
Fabricating and casting	6,000	3,300

Source: Pick, "Materials, Resources and Production: An Engineer's View."

STAGES AND THE MEASUREMENT OF TIME

In the above general taxonomy of stages, it must be understood that the vertical axis is solely a measure of the period of production, measured in months, years, or decades. This can easily be misinterpreted, resulting in fallacious interpretations. One may seek to imply from this time arrangement that the earliest stage of *all* production processes should somehow be categorized in the most remote region of the vertical time axis. For example, under this misinterpretation, you might conclude that raw agricultural products (wheat, corn, soybeans, and so on) should be contained in the higher-order stage along with all other natural resources (iron ore, copper, and so forth). But the reality of the matter is that iron ore may be three years from final use while agricultural goods may be only one year away from consumption. It is therefore proper to place iron ore far above wheat and corn in the timetable. The first stage of the transformation process is not the same for every good. In fact, it may differ widely. It may even differ widely within industrial groups, such as mining. Only quantitative studies can estimate the intertemporal distance between first-stages.

THE IMPORTANCE OF INVENTORIES

Until now, we have not discussed in any detail the critical role that inventories play in the market system. Yet inventories represent the largest portion of the production process. Most working capital is not actually "circulating," as the economists state, but is simply waiting to be processed into another form along the transformation chain. As Reavis Cox states, "The great mass of goods undoubtedly spend most of the time that elapses between their appearance as raw materials and their disappearance as consumables simply waiting somewhere for somebody to do something to them."[87] These inventories "impose costs of storing, financing, and risking which someone must bear."[88] The balance sheets of all manufacturing, wholesale, and retail companies show the holding of great quantities of wealth in the form of stock inventories. Shorey Peterson, who writes extensively on this major factor in production, states: "The manufacturer needs plant and equipment, but he also must have his piles of raw materials and fuels, his accumulation of purchased parts and office supplies. In addition, he will have a considerable stock of 'goods in process,' of partially manufactured goods moving through the successive operations of his plant. Finally, he will usually have on hand a stock of finished products from which orders can be filled. Measured in dollars, these various stocks are a large item in the manufacturer's wealth. Many a balance sheet shows a higher total for inventories than for fixed capital."[89]

As an economy advances, stock inventories play a greater and greater role, since the ability of firms to hold finished and unfinished goods in reserve reduces the risk of shortages and permits commercial and individual customers to have a greater variety of products from which to choose. As Peterson notes,

Primarily, goods are found in them [inventories] because of the sheer impossibility of producing physical products instantaneously, including all processes from the mining or growing of materials to the final sale of finished products. But stocks must also be larger than otherwise because successive steps in production cannot be coordinated perfectly, and reserves must be available to draw on at each stage to insure continuous operations. More-over, stocks are necessary, especially in merchandising, to permit customers to be served promptly and to have some choice in their buying.[90]

At any one time, a large sector of crude materials, intermediate goods, and produced products are held in reserve, waiting to be used in the manu-facturing process or to be sold to customers. Stock inventories are prevalent in all lines of production, and sometimes, as in the cases of wholesaling and retailing, exceed the value of fixed capital. Abramovitz concludes that stocks are so significant that "a very large share of cyclical changes in gross national product has regularly taken the form of changes in the volume of inventory investment."[91] Typically in a business cycle, an inventory build-up or draw-down occurs prior to any change in the amount of goods and services actu-ally produced.

Does the existence of inventories increase or decrease the overall period of production? Clearly, in measuring the length of the transformation process, one must include the time during which goods are in inventory. It is quite possible that the total amount of time between the extracting of raw materials and the selling of final consumer product will be longer as inventories are built up. This would be particularly true if interest rates decline, thus making the holding of stocks less expensive. At the same time, however, the expansion in inventory would increase the efficiency and reduce the waiting time of the capitalistic process for each indi-vidual firm operating along the path of economic activity. The overall effect would be beneficial.

NOTES

1. Hicks, *Capital and Time*, 12.
2. L. A. Hahn, *Common Sense Economics*.
3. Kirzner provides an excellent description of the role of the entrepreneur *qua* producer in "translating resources . . . into products in the market baskets of the consumers." Israel M. Kirzner, *Competition and Entrepreneurship* (Chicago: University of Chicago Press, 1973), 44, 43–52.
4. Piquet, *The Economic Axioms*, 55.
5. Smith: "Consumption is the sole end and purpose of all production." *The Wealth of Nations*, book 2, 179. John Maynard Keynes: "All production is for the purpose of ultimately satisfying a consumer. . . . Consumption . . . is the sole end and object of all economic activity." *The General Theory*, 46, 104. Eugen von Böhm-Bawerk: "All human production has as its object the acquisition of consumption goods." *Capital and Interest*, vol. 2, *Positive Theory of Capital*, 79. Such statements are not to suggest that consumption is more important than production—in fact, just the opposite is

true. Increased consumption will not necessarily increase production, but higher production—of the right kind—will bring about higher consumption in the future.

6. Taussig, *Wages and Capital*, 3. Taussig also notes that after the completion of physical production, middlemen take weeks if not months to deliver the final goods to the consumer. "Months elapse, on the average, between the time when goods are finished, in the everyday sense of the word, and the time when they reach the stage of enjoyment." (14)

7. Rosenbloom, *Marketing Channels: A Management View*, 3.

8. Piquet, *The Economic Axioms*, 8–9.

9. Shackle, *Epistemics & Economics*, 304. Machlup distinguishes between fixed and working capital as follows: "The individual entrepreneur regards as working capital that part of his capital which is released when he stops producing; fixed capital, in contrast, remains tied up even after he has stopped producing." Machlup, *The Stock Market, Credit and Capital Formation*, 202.

10. Moulton, *The Formation of Capital*, 8. For cotton shirts, the "fixed" capital requires plows, mechanical cotton-pickers, sacks, locomotives (to move the cotton), spinning machinery, looms, warehouses, retail stores, and so on. "The complete list would be staggering." Abbott, *Economics and the Modern World*, 179.

11. Black, *Introduction to Production Economics*, 35–36. I wish to thank Royal Skousen for making this point clear to me.

12. According to Martin Hill, the Böhm-Bawerkian view of capital is that "there is no place for the distinction between fixed and circulating capital: all intermediate products are regarded as passing more or less quickly into consumers' goods." Hill, "The Period of Production and Industrial Fluctuations," 600. Cf. E. F. Schumacher, "Inflation and the Structure of Production," 406. Böhm-Bawerk considers capital to include both fixed and working capital. His view of capital is "organic," like a seed that is planted, absorbs primary services, and over a period of time, is harvested as a consumption good. See Kuenne, *Eugen von Böhm-Bawerk*, 20. Hayek's model in *Prices and Production* excludes fixed capital. Machlup criticizes Hayek's implication that "there is one stage of production at which no tools and no instruments, but only the 'original' services of land and labor, are employed." Machlup calls this assumption "entirely unrealistic." Machlup, "Professor Knight and the 'Period of Production,'" 587. However, I do not see any insurmountable problems in incorporating fixed capital in the joint production of intermediate goods.

13. Haavelmo concludes that "the distinction between working capital and instruments of capital is not as profound as one might think." Haavelmo, *A Study in the Theory of Investment*, 78–79.

14. Piquet defines production as "the forward movement of use from the most indirect level through various stages of indirectness to the level of direct (or end) use. . . . To illustrate, iron ore is transformed into iron, which is made into steel, and then manufactured to form an oven which is used to bake bread for direct use. Together with labor, transportation, etc., these represent various use levels." Piquet, *The Economic Axioms*, 8.

15. Rothbard, *Man, Economy and State*, 282–83.

16. Gemmill and Blodgett refer to this transformation process as "form utility," which "consists of taking raw materials, or partly finished goods, and making them more desirable by changing their form." Gemmill and Blodgett, *Economics*, 71–72.

17. Hansen, *Business-Cycle Theory*, 125.

18. Morishima, *The Economic Theory of Modern Society*, 34–35. Morishima's representation of the "tree" process of production is the reverse of Rothbard's figure 5.2, so that unfinished goods move *higher* toward final consumption. But the analysis is essentially the same.

19. See also Taussig, *Wages and Capital*, 23–25. Machlup analyzes an agricultural example from the work of N. J. Polak, *Grundzüge der Finanzierung, mit Rüchsicht auf die Kreditdauer* (Berlin-Vienna: Industrieverlag Spaeth and Linde, 1926) to illustrate the synchronized production process. In the case of wheat, it is sowed in March, harvested in September, processed in two successive stages, and held in inventory so as to sell to consumers continuously throughout the year. See Machlup, *The Stock Market, Credit and Capital Formation*, 217–18.

20. Menger, *Principles of Economics*, 55–57.

21. Clark, *The Distribution of Wealth*, 268–69.

22. Taussig, *Principles of Economics*, 60.

23. Black, *Introduction to Production Economics*, 34.

24. Alderfer and Michi, *Economics of American Industry*, 28. Also see the chart on 54.

25. "Any scheme, or diagram, or classification of the stages of production must have a rigid and arbitrary character, and cannot conform to the endless complexities of the living industrial world." Taussig, *Wages and Capital*, 25.

26. Menger, *Principles of Economics*, 118–19.

27. Hayek, *The Pure Theory of Capital*, 25.

28. Taussig, *Wages and Capital*, 2.

29. Knight, "Capitalistic Production, Time and the Rate of Return," 338.

30. Rolph, "On Austrian Capital Theory," 502.

31. Böhm-Bawerk, *The Positive Theory of Capital*, 88, 90.

32. Ibid., 89.

33. Rothbard, *Man, Economy and State*, 412–13.

34. Mises, *Human Action*, 489.

35. Machlup, "Professor Knight and the 'Period of Production,'" 588.

36. "It is really not necessary that we go back to a point in history where there was no capital." Haavelmo, *A Study in the Theory of Investment*, 42.

37. Mises, *Human Action*, 480.

38. Rothbard, *Man, Economy and State*, 414. "Resources that are being depleted [coal, oil, gas, and so forth] obviously *cannot* be replaced and are therefore *land*, not capital goods" (460n.15). However, once these natural resources are processed in any way, they become "working" capital goods, not land.

39. Ibid., 414.

40. Elliott-Jones, *Input-Output Analysis: A Nontechnical Description*, 3.

41. Shackle, "F. A. Hayek," 239.

42. Jevons, *The Principles of Economics*, 115.
43. Hawtrey, *Capital and Employment*, 240.
44. Sraffa, *The Production of Commodities by Means of Commodities*, 93.
45. Rolph, "On Austrian Capital Theory," 502. David McCord Wright uses the analogy of a group of ships to represent the economic structure. They are all "sailing *roughly* in the same direction," but it is a "disorderly huddle," not an organized military convoy. "They cross each other's bows. They signal back and forth. They even sometimes ram and sink one another. . . . They constantly observe and feel each other's behavior, they also read each other's reports." Wright, "What Is the Economic System," *Quarterly Journal of Economics* (1958): 207–8.
46. Shackle, "F. A. Hayek," 239. Harold Moulton notes the problem of some commodities acting as both productive and consumptive, "such as an automobile, a house used also as an office, or a hotel used alike for pleasure and business purposes. . . . But this fact does not alter the general principle with which we are concerned; it merely complicates the problem of classification." Moulton, *The Formation of Capital*, 8n.
47. Hayek, *Prices and Production*, 142n.
48. On the specificity of capital, Lachmann writes, "Every capital good exists in a specific form which limits the range of its possible uses: it has limited versatility. Each capital good therefore depends for its efficient use on the support of other capital goods complementary to it." Lachmann, *Capital, Expectations and the Market Process*, 330. Money is, by definition, the most nonspecific of all goods.
49. Piquet, *The Economic Axioms*, 7.
50. Ibid., 8.
51. Rothbard, *Man, Economy and State*, 333. Or, to use Wright's analogy of ships (see n. 45), the fact that the ships zigzag and move occasionally in the opposite direction does not prevent them from reaching their final destination.
52. Shackle, *Epistemics and Economics*, 328.
53. Bellante and Garrison, "Phillips Curves and Hayekian Triangles," 238.
54. Ibid., 224. Cf. Kuenne, *Eugen von Böhm-Bawerk*, 64–65. George Malanos, following Ragnar Frisch, suggests three types of output:
    1. point-input, point-output case (circulating capital).
    2. continuous-input, point-output case.
    3. point-input, continuous-output case (fixed capital).
    According to Malanos, the Austrians use the first type in most cases. See Malanos, *Intermediate Economic Theory*, 321–90.
55. Faber, *Introduction to Modern Austrian Capital Theory*, 42.
56. Smithies, "The Austrian Theory of Capital," 129.
57. Ibid.
58. Rothbard, *Man, Economy and State*, 343.
59. Referring to durability in capital goods as a "vague term," Montgomery D. Anderson states: "This distinction is one of degree rather than of kind, and it is an unimportant difference at that." Anderson, *Capital and Interest*, 14.
60. Rothbard, *Man, Economy and State*, 417–20.

61. Schumacher, "Inflation and the Structure of Production," 407.

62. Uhr, *Economic Doctrines of Knut Wicksell,* 78–79.

63. L. Albert Hahn, *Common Sense Economics,* 30–31.

64. Mills, *Prices in Recession and Recovery,* 354n, 355n.

65. Ibid., 355.

66. Schumpeter suggests that higher-order capital goods tend to be more specific in nature than lower-order capital goods. "The higher up we go in the order of goods, the more they use their specialisation, their efficacy for a particular purpose; and the wider their potential use, the more general their meaning. . . . This simply means that the further away from consumption goods we choose our standpoint, the more numerous the goods of the first order become which descend from similar goods of higher orders. When any goods are wholly or partially combinations of similar means of production, we say they are related in production. Therefore we can say that the productive relationship of goods increases with their orders." Schumpeter, *The Theory of Economic Development* 16–17.

67. Hawtrey, *Capital and Employment,* 22.

68. Hawtrey raises a "fundamental difficulty" with the structure of production concept if it goes too far beyond a one-year time frame: "When the calculation of the period of production is based on *data* extending over a long period of time, the structure of production is sure to change in the course of it." Hawtrey, *Capital and Employment,* 24. Restricting the time period of national output to one year does not eliminate entirely this dynamic effect, but its distortion is minimized.

69. Piquet suggests that durability should not be defined simply as physical durability, but the repetition of use. For example, canned peaches have a long shelf life, but are not economically durable. They can only be used once. Real durable goods include land, buildings, automobiles, furniture, clothing, radios, televisions, and so on. See Piquet, *The Economic Axioms,* 10.

70. Bye and Hewett, *The Economic Process,* 1st ed., 75.

71. Ibid., 79n.

72. Ibid., 79. In *The Economic Process,* 2d ed., Bye and Hewett add: "This is not a very satisfactory classification, because it includes in consumers' goods some remote wealth that represents investment (e.g., owner-occupied dwelling), while it includes in producers' goods some wealth that is very close to consumption (e.g., milk in a dairy)."

73. Garrison, "The Austrian-Neoclassical Relation," 45.

74. Garrison observes: "An automobile and an overcoat, for instance, may be equally durable, but we tend to think of the former as a capital good and the latter as a consumer good." "The Austrian-Neoclassical Relation," 54n.28.

75. Menger, *Principles of Economics,* 165. On the distinction between land, labor and capital, Carl Uhr states the Wicksellian interpretation: "Labor can only yield its services in an unchangeable *day-to-day* sequence over a finite period of years, and the same applies to land with the additional qualification that it yields an infinite rather than finite series of services. Furthermore, neither the services of labor nor those of land can be stored *as such;* they can only be stored indirectly in the form of real capital."

Uhr, *Economic Doctrines of Knut Wicksell*, 78–79. But Rothbard argues that certain types of finite natural resources can also be treated as land: "Resources that are being depleted [coal, oil, gas, and so on] obviously *cannot* be replaced and are therefore *land*, not capital goods." Rothbard, *Man, Economy and State*, 460n.15.

76. Röpke, *Economics of a Free Society*, 43–44.
77. Jevons, *Principles of Economics*, 108. Jevons, like J. B. Clark, used such classifications, but later rejected the whole concept as a macroeconomic model.
78. Ibid., 108–13.
79. Whitehead, *Economics Made Simple*, 2–3. Cf. Black, *Introduction to Production Economics*, 65. Black classifies "the fields of production" according to "primary" (extractive and genetic) and "secondary" (manufacturing and services) categories.
80. Rothbard, *Man, Economy and State*, 452n.8.
81. Taussig, *Principles of Economics*, 15.
82. L. E. Read, "I, Pencil," 40–42.
83. Keynes, *The General Theory*, 272.
84. Holzman, "Problems of Classification and Aggregation," 328–29. It is almost impossible to figure out the distance from final use for certain classifications made by the U.S. Commerce Department and the U.S. Bureau of Labor Statistics. Unfortunately, many of their categories (motor vehicles, machines and equipment, intermediate materials, and so on) include both consumer and commercial use. See Wainhouse, "Hayek's Theory of the Trade Cycle."
85. Ibid., 329.
86. Ibid.
87. Cox, *Distribution in a High-Level Economy*, 33.
88. Ibid.
89. Peterson, *Economics*, 132.
90. Ibid., 132–33.
91. Abramovitz, "The Role of Inventories in Business Cycles," 1. A new theory of demand for inventories by stages-of-processing has recently been proposed. In previous models, studies were made of total inventories and their relationship to economic fluctuations. Under this new model, inventories are disaggregated by components: retail, wholesale, and manufactured finished and manufactured input inventories. The empirical evidence indicates that inventories in the earliest stages are the most volatile. See Ramey, "Inventories as Factors of Production and Economic Fluctuations."

APPENDIX

THE STRUCTURE OF PRODUCTION UNDER CENTRAL PLANNING: A CONTRIBUTION TO THE SOCIALIST CALCULATION DEBATE

The concept of the structure of production is a valuable tool in the ongoing debate over economic calculation in the socialist economy. In the 1930s, a major dispute developed between the Austrian economists, led by Ludwig von Mises and Friedrich A. Hayek, and the socialist economists, led by Oskar Lange and Fred M. Taylor. In his critique of socialism, Mises argued that central planning would not work because, without competition between firms, prices could not logically be calculated, and without market prices, firms could not produce goods and services efficiently.[1]

Oskar Lange rebutted Mises' view by contending that central planning boards under socialism could determine prices through "trial and error." A price could be set and the market of supply and demand could be observed. If shortages occurred, the price should be raised. If surpluses abound, the price should be lowered. Lange even went so far as to state, "Let the Central Planning Board start with a given set of prices chosen *at random*. . . . If the quantity demanded of a commodity is not equal to the quantity supplied, the price of that commodity has to be changed."[2]

Surprisingly, most economists concluded that Lange and the other "market" socialists adequately answered the Austrian challenge, although the issue is still debated today.[3]

However, the literature on the socialist calculation debate tends to ignore in large measure the problems arising out of the structure-of-production concept. The debate seems to focus on a "micro" approach of supply-demand factors of individual consumer and factor markets rather than the critical interrelation of economic processes. Specifically, how could a central planning board successfully use a "trial and error" method at each stage of production wherein each successive level of output depends on earlier produced inputs and working capital? After all, the setting up of a socialist state, whereby government controls the means of production, does not eliminate the intermediate stages of output. As Mises states, "Capital conceived as the intermediate products, which arise at the different stages of production by indirect methods, would not, at any rate at first, be abolished by Socialism. It would merely be transferred from individual to common possession."[4]

Setting prices at random would undoubtedly create massive shortages and surpluses. But the deficiencies in one market are never isolated—they lead to disequilibrium in other related markets before and after the specific market. Moreover, it takes time to eliminate shortages and surpluses—the industrial system under central planning cannot create equilibrium overnight. Random pricing would therefore result in delays and shortages in the long and complex chain of production.

Let us use the example of shoe production to demonstrate the inherent problems with central planning. Suppose a price is set too low for the production of cowhide, causing inventories to decline and a shortage to arise. As the incentive to produce cattle declines, cattlemen fail to build up their herds for future slaughter. The central board realizes its mistake and raises the price for cowhide. This is the right decision, but it takes time for cattle producers to rebuild their herds. Meanwhile, there is a current shortage of cowhides, even at the higher price. The next level of production, leather making, is severely restricted in its output because of the cowhide shortage. It must look for substitutes, or expensive foreign imports, but the search may not be entirely successful, especially in the short run. It also takes considerable time to find synthetic leather or other substitutes.

Now we come to the final stage of shoe production. Suppose a shoe factory has been given a quota (demand) to produce ten thousand shoes in a given time period to satisfy consumer demand. The factory possesses all the tools, labor, and materials necessary to achieve its quota *except* the shoe manufacturer has only enough leather to produce five thousand shoes due to the shortage of leather.

How many shoes will be produced? Only five thousand. Half the consumer demand will be met. Output is always limited to the availability of *each* complementary capital good. As Menger puts it, "With respect to given future time periods, our effective requirements for particular goods of higher order are dependent upon the availability of complementary quantities of the corresponding goods of higher order."[5]

In sum, the shortage of cowhide leads to a shortage of leather and eventually to a shortage of shoes. In addition, those capital goods and labor associated with the shoe industry will be underemployed because of the shortage. Thus, delays, shortages and underemployment of labor and resources are inevitable under such a random pricing system. The shortage problem is intensified even more when the process of transformation involves a wide variety of complementary factors. Thus a shortage of a widely demanded complementary factor can create more havoc as the production process moves toward final consumption.

Given the length and complexity of the production chain, from raw materials to final consumption, it would be almost impossible for this random system not to cause artificial shortages somewhere along the supply line and, therefore, to create disequilibrium in all successive stages toward final consumption. This has in fact been the chief characteristic of command economies—intermittent delays, shortages and underemployment of machines, material and labor. Moreover, the more intricate and capitalistic the economy becomes, lengthening the number and variety of stages, the problem is exacerbated. Mises notes that it does not help when the socialist regime owns all producers' goods in common without established prices, without market exchange, because

> the money prices of goods inform not only the consumer, they also provide vital information to businessmen about the factors of production, the main function of the market being not merely to determine the cost of the *last* part of the process of production and transfer of goods to the hands of the consumer, but the cost of those steps leading up to it. The whole market system is bound up with the fact that there is a mentally calculated division of labor between the various businessmen who vie with each other in bidding for the factors of production—the raw material, the machines, the instruments—and for the human factor of production; the wages paid to labor. This sort of calculation by the businessman cannot be accomplished in the absence of prices supplied by the market.[6]

There are several reasons why the competitive marketplace minimizes these shortages. First, price can change almost instantaneously when a shortage or surplus arises, as competitors are always seeking to respond to new supply and demand factors, while central planning decisions can easily get bogged down in bureaucratic red tape. Second, if one source of cowhides or leather experiences a temporary shortage, the shoe manufacturer can quickly contact another source to obtain the necessary materials to keep up with demand, even if it means paying a higher price. By contrast, state-run industries are by their nature monopolistic, which severely limits alternate sources for scarce materials. As a result, the government-run plant often seeks input from foreign or free market sources. Under a competitive system, there are always myriad avenues for materials and supplies. Moreover, the market process encourages the holding of extensive inventories in *all* areas, which help allay occasional shortages at various stages of production.

NOTES

1. Mises, "Economic Calculation in the Socialist Commonwealth," 87–103.
2. Lange, "On the Economic Theory of Socialism," 86. Lange's following comment is wishful thinking at best: "The Central Planning Board has a much wider knowledge of what is going on [in] the whole economic system than any private enterpreneur can ever have and, consequently, may be able to reach the right equilibrium prices by a *much shorter* series of successive trials than a competitive market actually does" (86). On the contrary, it is much more likely that the central board has only a broad general knowledge of market conditions and very little specific information about individual markets known by private entrepreneurs.
3. Lavoie, *Rivalry and Central Planning.*
4. Mises, *Socialism: An Economic and Sociological Analysis,* 124.
5. Menger, *Principles of Economics,* 85–86.
6. Ludwig von Mises, *Economic Policy, Thoughts for Today and Tomorrow* (Chicago: Gateway, 1979), 32. See also Butler, *Ludwig von Mises,* 42–43.

SIX

TIME AND THE AGGREGATE PRODUCTION STRUCTURE

All economic activity is carried out through time. Every individual economic process occupies a certain time, and all linkages between economic processes necessarily involve longer or shorter periods of time.—F. A. Hayek, "International Price Equilibrium and Movements in the Value of Money," *Money, Capital and Fluctuations*

In the previous chapter, we derived the building blocks of a macroeconomic model. The result was the construction of what I call the Aggregate Production Structure (APS). The APS contains several characteristics that are worth noting in order to avoid confusion over the meaning of the term:

1. The APS represents an economy's output in a disaggregated fashion, according to intertemporal stages of production.
2. The APS figures the total output of an economy during a one-year period of time, measured in terms of a country's monetary unit of account.
3. Although APS is a measurement of economic activity during one year's time, it also includes projects which take more than one year to complete. However, only that portion of the project which is completed during the year is included in the APS, based on the costs of land, labor, and capital expended.
4. The APS includes the combined value of goods and services which can be reproduced several times during the year.
5. Inventories and any other products manufactured but which have not yet been sold are still covered in the APS, thus including *all* forms of production for which factors have been paid.
6. The APS comprises the production of machines and other durable capital goods, durable consumables, and nondurable consumables, regardless of how long it takes for such goods to wear out or be consumed.
7. Capital goods manufactured prior to the current year are *not* incorporated in the APS even though they may be used in the production of current goods and services.

In short, the Aggregate Production Structure measures the value of *all* goods and services produced during a specific calendar year. It represents total spending by business, consumers, and government, not just final goods and services.

It should also be noted that the APS used throughout this work represents the world economy, or a closed economy, so that all stages of production take place. Many countries, such as Britain, are so small that the complete process of production does not occur within the country's boundaries. They may depend heavily on imported raw commodities and foreign trade, for example. Many stages of production may take place in other countries. Other nations, such as the United States, have such a diversified amount of resources that practically every stage is represented. Still, the level of foreign trade has been increasing significantly recently.

GNP NOT AN ACCURATE PICTURE OF ECONOMIC ACTIVITY

One might conclude that the Gross National Product (GNP) is similar to the Aggregate Production Structure, but in fact the two are quite distinct. The APS's portrayal of national output is a far cry from the definition of national output as developed by the government's statistical gatherers. Their purposes are similar, but the GNP figures are not at all a true reflection of the economic structure, as I will demonstrate.

First of all, the APS does not lump all capital goods into a single category such as "gross investment" or "gross capital expenditures." Current GNP figures, as developed by Kuznets and other pioneers in the field of economic statistics, utilize a Keynesian-style aggregative approach, whereby capital goods are lumped together. The APS, on the other hand, emphasizes a stratification of the capital-goods markets, at least on a theoretical level, as indicated in figure 5.16 (raw commodities, producers' goods, wholesale goods, and so on). A heterogeneous intertemporal hierarchy of capitalistic production is established instead of a timeless homogeneous lump-sum.

Even more significantly, current GNP figures do not represent the total spending of all sectors of the economy. GNP takes into account only the production of goods and services sold to "final users." They take a "value added" approach only. No "intermediate goods" are included in GNP figures because final goods and services contain the valued added by all previous stages.

This means that all consumption goods and services, but only a small portion of capital goods, are contained in annual GNP figures. GNP encompasses the gross purchases of durable capital goods, such as machinery and tools, because they are treated as final products. But they do not include *nondurable capital goods or intermediate products*. In short, GNP takes into account fixed capital, but not circulating capital. By contrast, the APS comprises the gross output of all capital goods as well as all consumer goods.[1]

To demonstrate the difference between the two macroeconomic measures of national output, let us use an example taken from Rothbard. Figure 6.1 reproduces a slightly altered APS from Rothbard's illustration.

In Rothbard's example, there are six general stages of production. The first five stages represent the output of intermediate goods, while the sixth stage is final consumption. The breakdown of social income, by factor, in such an economy is as follows: "Total expenditures on production are: 100 (Consumption) plus 318 (Investment = Savings), equals 418 ounces. Total gross income from production equals the gross income of capitalists [of total consumer goods] (100 ounces) plus the gross income of other capitalists (235 ounces) plus the gross income of owners of land and labor (83 ounces), which also equals 418 ounces."[2]

Figure 6.1. Rothbard's Illustration of the Aggregate Production Structure (Revised)

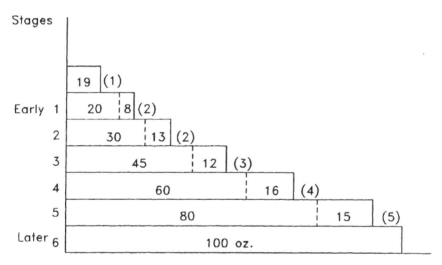

Consumer Expenditures

Note: In Rothbard's illustration, the production process takes up to six years (six stages). Total gross income is 418 oz. Total gross savings/investment is 318 oz. Net (new) savings/investment is 0. Total consumption is 100 oz. Net income to factors are: 83 oz. to land and labor (19 + 8 + 13 + 12 + 16 + 15 = 83 oz.), 17 to capital owners (1 + 2 + 2 + 3 + 4 + 5 = 17 oz.).

Source: Rothbard, *Man, Economy and State,* 314.

Thus, in terms of gross figures in the APS, the total amount of business outlays (as reflected in gross savings-investment) in the economy is 318 ounces, compared to 100 ounces of consumption. Hence, it is clear that the capital-goods industry is considerably larger than the consumer-goods industries. In Rothbard's example, capitalists spend more than three times the amount spent by final consumers on goods and services.

Many economists before the Keynesian revolution noted this fact in modern society, especially with regard to employment. M. A. Abrams notes, "In most modern countries only a minor part of the community's resources is devoted to the production of consumption goods. Most of our energies and equipment are applied to earlier stages of production. The labours of the miner, the cotton spinner, the shipwright, the mechanic, the engineer produces what can be called intermediate goods—goods that are only part way on the road to becoming consumption goods."[3]

Röpke adds, "It is apparent that a large part of a country's total production serves for the production of capital goods and not for the production of consumer goods, and that the production of capital goods must itself become a specialized branch of manufacturing."[4] Black states, "Roundabout production is today the usual form of production. Production has been getting more and more roundabout all the time. A large percentage of the people of modern occidental nations are engaged in making tools and machines and in building factories and railroads."[5] And Taussig says that a great majority of our wealth is in the form of capital output, or what he calls "inchoate wealth." "The great mass of workers are engaged in producing tools, materials, railways, factories, goods finished but not yet in the place where the consumer can procure them— inchoate wealth of all sorts."[6]

Unfortunately, when one examines current figures for the Gross National Product, this fundamental characteristic of modern society is completely lost—in fact, it appears as just the opposite. If one looks at a breakdown of GNP, consumer spending always appears as by far the largest sector of the economy. For example, in 1987, total personal consumption expenditures in the United States came to $3,012 billion, while "gross private domestic investment" totaled only $713 billion and government spending amounted to $925 billion. How does one explain this discrepancy, which shows consumer spending to be four times larger than capital expenditures?

What is happening is that the gross private investment figure in GNP is not really a gross number after all. It is actually a net measure and purposely excludes "intermediate goods" that are purchased to be used as inputs in producing other goods and services. It is strictly a value added figure. Thus, if one were to apply this net income approach to Rothbard's example, the net return to capitalists (interest income) would amount to only 17 ounces, less than one-fifth of the 100 ounces of total consumer spending. But if one looks at the total amount of capital expenditures, the gross investment comes to 318 ounces. Thus, the value added approach to GNP gives the appearance that consumption plays a much larger role than is really the case.

Actually, in Rothbard's example there is *no* net savings or private investment (nor government revenues). The Rothbard economy is in a steady state, meaning that "there is just enough gross saving to keep the structure of productive capital intact, to keep the production process rolling, and to keep a constant amount of consumers' goods produced per given period."[7] Thus, while "net" savings is zero, gross savings (or total savings) amounts to 318 ounces, equal to "the aggregation of all the present goods supplied to owners of future goods during the production process."[8]

Current GNP figures represent gross private investment as the "value added" to the nation's capital stock in a year. In reality, the number has not been adjusted for losses due to depreciation and obsolescence. Gross private investment minus an allowance for depreciation and obsolescence is called "net private investment," which is a more accurate reflection of new capital stock than the gross figure. The capital consumption allowance was estimated to be $402.9 billion in 1984, so that net private investment in the U.S. in 1984 was about $134.4 billion. This lower figure makes capital expenditures appear to be even less significant in the economy compared to consumption.

In short, the GNP data exclude the critical intermediate stages of production. Advocates of this traditional approach do so because, they say, they wish to studiously avoid the problem of "double counting." Dolan's introductory economics textbook uses a simple example of breadmaking to demonstrate the double counting problem. See Figure 6.2 below.

Regarding this method, Dolan adds, "This table shows why GNP must include only the value of final goods and services if it is to measure total production without double counting. The value of sales at each stage of production can be divided into the value added at that stage and the value of purchased inputs. The selling price of the final product (a $1 loaf of bread, in this case) is equal to the sum of the values added at all stages of production."[9]

Yet this well-meaning but specious exercise by mainstream economists dangerously misconceives the true nature of the economic process. It almost implies that the manufacturers, producers and middlemen (e.g., those whose services transform the wheat into bread), are not worth counting. From the businessman's point of view, however, the firm has to have the income and resources to pay for the *gross* costs of production, not just the value added. Thus, if we add together the value of production at all stages, the APS of the bread example

Figure 6.2. Value Added and the Use of Final Products in GNP

Final stage: baking		
Value of one loaf of bread	$1.00	
Less value of flour	–.60	
Equals value added in baking	$.40	$.40
Next to final stage: milling		
Value of flour	$.60	
Less value of wheat	–.35	
Equals value added in milling	.25	$.25
Second from final stage: farming		
Value of wheat	$.35	
Less value of fuel, fertilizer, etc.	–.20	
Equals value added in farming	.15	$.15
All previous stages		
Value added in fuel and fertilizer industries, etc.	$.20	$.20
Total value added		$1.00

Source: E. G. Dolan, *Economics,* 4th ed. (Chicago: Dryden Press, 1986), 174. Copyright © 1986 by The Dryden Press, a division of Holt, Rinehart and Winston, Inc. Reprinted by permission of the publisher.

Figure 6.3. Producers' Contribution to Bread Production

Inputs	*Value*	
Previous inputs (fuel, fertilizer, etc.)	$ .20	
Wheat	.35	= $1.15
Flour	.60	
Bread	1.00	

comes to $1.15 for the producers' goods and $1.00 for the final consumer good. (See Figure 6.3 above.)

In actuality, we should also add the $1.00 price of bread to the producers' sector instead of the consumers' sector, because in today's world the baker is usually a wholesaler who sells the bread to a retail store, which in turn sells the loaf of bread to the final consumer for $1.50. Thus, the value of all producers of the bread should total $2.15, and the final product has a value of $1.50.

In sum, the double counting argument is a hollow one. As Rothbard comments, "The net-income theorists implicitly assume that the only important decisions in regard to consuming vs. saving-investing are made by the factory-owners out of their net income. Since the net income of capitalists is admittedly relatively small, this approach attributes little importance to their role in maintaining capital in gross expenditures and gross investment and not net investment."[10] Thus, the net approach to national income leads to a Clark-Knight concept of capital as a perpetual fund. "To maintain this doctrine it is necessary to deny the stage analysis of production and, indeed, to deny the very influence of *time* in production."[11] Further, the net method (GNP) greatly exaggerates the role of consumption in the economy, giving the deceptive impression that most of the national output is in consumption goods rather than investment. Such thinking encourages economists and government officials to form the misleading idea that consumer spending, being the largest sector of the economy, must be stimulated in order to get the economy out of a slump.

The APS, on the other hand, accurately reflects the activities in the whole economy. As Hayek notes, "the amount of money spent on producers' goods during any period of time may be far greater than the amount spent for consumers' goods during the same period. . . . Most goods are exchanged several times against money before they are sold to the consumer."[12] Thus, as figure 6.4 shows, "whenever we draw the line between consumers' goods and capital goods by far the greater proportion of the goods existing at any moment will always fall into the latter category."[13]

Figure 6.4. Division between Consumers' Goods and Producers' Goods in Aggregate Production Structure

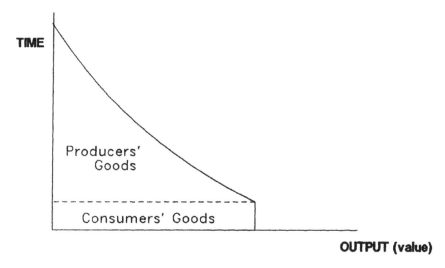

GROSS NATIONAL OUTPUT: A MORE ACCURATE DEFINITION

It is possible to construct a more complete picture of total spending in the economy by using input-output data. Unfortunately, raw data for inputoutput models are compiled only every five years in the United States, based on an economic census made twice each decade. Intermediate inputs are determined for each industrial classification. Total intermediate output is figured by adding the intermediate inputs for each industry. Figure 6.5 details the total spending by sectors in 1982, the latest data. I have called the total output in the economy, "Gross National Output," to distinguish it from GNP.

Several observations are worth noting. First, Gross National Output (GNO) was nearly double GNP, thus indicating the degree to which GNP underestimates total spending in the economy. Second, consumption represents only 34 percent of total national output, far less than what GNP figures suggest (66 percent). Third, business outlays, including intermediate inputs and gross private investment, is the largest sector of the economy, 56 percent larger than the consumer-goods industry. GNP figures suggest that the capital-goods industry represents a miniscule 14 percent of the economy. Fourth, government spending as a percent of economic activity is substantially less than GNP data indicates. Government outlays represent only 11 percent of GNO.[14]

THE AGGREGATE PRODUCTION STRUCTURE IN A STEADY STATE

Let us examine the features of the APS in a steady state, or what Mises calls the "evenly rotating economy" (ERE). Even though the "no change" static environment

Figure 6.5. U.S. Gross National Output, 1982 (in billions of dollars)

Personal consumption expenditures		$2,046.4
Business expenditures		$3,196.7
Intermediate inputs	$2,745.6	
Gross private investment	451.1	
Government purchases		641.7
Net exports		27.0
Gross National Output (GNO)		$5,911.8
Gross National Product (GNP)		$3,166.2

Source: "Annual Input-Output Accounts of the U.S. Economy, 1982," Survey of Current Business (April 1988): 31–46.

can never be realized in real life, the evenly rotating economy is an important pre-cept.[15] As Mises states, "We cannot do without this notion of a world where there is no change; but we have to use it only for the purpose of studying changes and their consequences, that means for the study of risk and uncertainty and therefore of profits and losses."[16] This detailed account will make it easier for us to see what happens when dynamic changes occur in the economy, which may involve shifts in savings, economic growth, technology, government policy, and so forth.

The steady state of the evenly rotating economy is a point of general equilib-rium, where values, technology and resources stay constant. As Rothbard indi-cates, "In that case, the economy tends toward a state of affairs in which it is *evenly rotating*, i.e., in which the same activities tend to be repeated in the same pat-tern over and over again."[17] Under this system, there would be no entrepreneur-ial profit-seeking. Mises defines equilibrium as a point where "no capital goods are idle, no opportunities for starting profitable enterprises remain unexploited and the only projects not undertaken are those which no longer yield a profit at the prevailing 'natural interest rate.'"[18] Of course, even in an ERE, the economy would be characterized by (a) factors which are specific and nonspecific in nature, (b) production involving numerous stages, and (c) many firms at all stages.

EQUALITY IN THE ERE INTEREST RATE

The primary characteristic of the ERE is that the rate of net return would tend to be the same in every line of production, and the rate of return would be equal to the pure rate of interest—what Wicksell calls the "natural rate of interest" and Roth-bard calls the "social rate of time preference."[19] We see why this is so by considering the contrary. Suppose that the profitability of one industry in a particular stage of output is greater than one in another stage. Assuming mobility of factors in *inter* stages as well as *intra* stages, resources will shift from the less profitable sector to the more profitable sector until there is a more or less equal rate of return.[20]

POSITIVE YIELD CURVE?

One debatable point is whether the rate of return or interest rate will, *ceteris paribus,* tend to be higher in the earlier industries furthest from final demand. In other words, in a stationary economy, is it natural for long-term interest rates to be slightly higher than short-term interest rates? Is there is a natural positive yield curve? Figure 6.6 illustrates the choices.

Economists have debated this question for many years. Rothbard argues that in the ERE, the pure rate of interest "must be uniform for every stage of every

Figure 6.6. Yield Curve between Long Term and Short Term

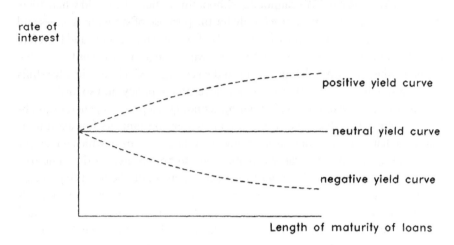

good."[21] Competition, both interstage and intrastage, makes it so. But Wicksell suggests that longer-term projects (i.e., investment plans furthest removed from final consumer use) involve a higher risk premium than projects closest to final use. "Interest rates for long and short periods do, in reality, tend to be equal; the difference which actually exists should be regarded partly as an increased *risk premium* for long-term loans, partly as due to the fact that, under existing economic conditions, short-term debts on good security are largely used as cash (money substitutes)."[22]

Historically, under normal market conditions, the yield curve has tended to be slightly positive. The yields on long-term debt securities are typically higher than on short-term instruments. But such a phenomenon appears in a dynamic setting, where risk is much more apparent than it would be in a stationary no-change environment.

Theoretically one would think that an investor would need to be compensated with a higher guaranteed rate of return in order to induce him to invest for a longer period of time. For example, if the choice is between a 5 percent one-year bank deposit and a 5 percent five-year deposit, wouldn't the investor always choose the shorter maturity? Not necessarily. He may think that interest rates could decline in the coming year, and therefore he will invest in the five-year certificate in order to lock in a guaranteed 5 percent rate for five years.

What about the alleged higher risk involved in the "higher order" industries involved in the transformation of raw commodities and natural resources? Don't they take greater chances because they are so far removed from final consumption? Wouldn't investors in such "higher order" projects need to be compensated more? Undoubtedly there would be a marked risk premium on such long-term debt if there were no secondary market for such securities. But the fact is that there is a ready market for such debentures, discounted according to the maturity of the debt instrument. Such discounting and liquidity are what makes the yield curve highly elastic and minimizes the risk involved in long-term investments. In short, there is no a priori reason why yields should rise with longer maturities.

ANALYSIS OF THE AGGREGATE PRODUCTION STRUCTURE

Once we have established the uniformity of the rate of return in the evenly-rotating economy, we can legitimately aggregate the value of production in each stage of the economy. The Aggregate Production Structure is the proper representation of the economic process.[23] Figure 6.7 is a theoretical representation of a general APS of an economy.

Figure 6.7. Idealized Aggregate Production Structure

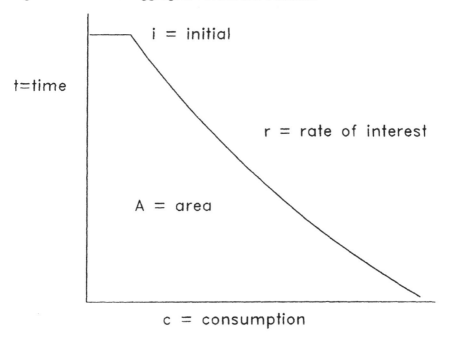

The number of stages is numerous and unspecified, reflecting a large and broad-based economy. Thus, the APS curve is a relatively smooth line from the beginning point on the vertical axis to the final point on the horizontal axis. The concave nature of the APS curve occurs even when the rate of return remains the same throughout the economy. This is due to the compounding effect when the transformed product moves from one level to the next as it eventually reaches final use.

We can represent the APS mathematically. Let A be defined as the area of the APS in the evenly-rotating economy. Thus, A represents the gross output of an economy during the year. If we assume that the rate of return, r, is constant throughout all stages, therefore

$$A = (i/r)\,(e^{tr} - 1) \text{ when } r \neq 0. \quad \text{(Eq. 6.1)}$$

Also, c, the total consumption value in any one year, is measured as follows:

$$c = i \cdot e^{tr}. \quad \text{(Eq. 6.2)}$$

THE DUAL NATURE OF THE APS

The APS is an extremely versatile economic function. It embodies in a single diagram the annual value of all raw materials, intermediate products, and final consumer goods and services produced in one year.

Second, the APS is valuable in demonstrating two separate aspects of economic activity. On the one hand, it can show how much production is occurring simultaneously (during the current year) at each intertemporal branch of the economy: the value of raw materials produced, tools and machines manufactured, wholesale goods sold, and retail products and services purchased by consumers, all during one year. But, in a steady state, the APS can also reflect the complete genealogy of the transformation process, i.e., the successive stages along the assembly line of production, in the same way the snapshot economy was described in chapter 5. As Hayek notes, "we may conceive of this diagram not only as representing the successive stages of production of the output of any given moment of time, but also as representing the processes of production going on simultaneously in a stationary society."[24]

Taussig utilizes the following (slightly altered) diagram to show the two ways of looking at the stratification of current output:

Figure 6.8. Production Process over Five-Year Period

In First Year	A_0	B_0	C_0	D_0	E_0
In Second Year	A_1	B_1	C_1	D_1	E_1
In Third Year	A_2	B_2	C_2	D_2	E_2
In Fourth Year	A_3	B_3	C_3	D_3	E_3
In Fifth Year	A_4	B_4	C_4	D_4	E_4

Source: Taussig, Wages and Capital, 23.

In the above case, A is the earliest commodity, and E is the final end product. A through E represents the successive stages of production. But each stage is being produced simultaneously in each year. The *horizontal* line represents current simultaneous production. But the *diagonal* line reflects the transformation of A to E over a five-year period of time, each stage taking one year to complete.

The APS is similar in nature. The horizontal direction represents current reproduction of each stage, while the diagonal downward direction represents successive stages of output.

In this sense, the APS can be viewed as a representation of the economy in the past, present, and future. In a steady state, with no changes in human action, the value of past (and future) stages of a particular good is the same as the value of current output. But the dual view of the APS is also extremely useful in a dynamic setting. Such a versatile diagram allows us to analyze the effects on the economy in the future when variables such as time preference, interest rates, and government policy change.

ALTERNATIVE TO THE CIRCULAR FLOW DIAGRAM

The APS triangle also incorporates both the production and expenditure sides of economic activity. The APS representation of the movement of commodities and money is far more accurate and complete than the standard circular flow diagram used in most textbooks. As indicated in chapter 1, the circular-flow diagram is a timeless, one-dimensional view of the economy which obscures the transformation process of goods and services.

In reality, goods flow downward from the higher to the lower stages of production until they are finally sold to consumers, while money moves from consumers' goods back through the various stages of production. Hayek notes, "While goods move downwards from the top to the bottom of our diagram, we have to conceive of money moving in the opposite direction."[25] Several other economists have commented on this important aspect of the APS. For example, Foster and Catchings describe the process as follows:

> For the most part, raw materials are grown, extracted and graded, moved on to factories and prepared for final consumers, moved on to wholesalers, thence distributed to retailers, and finally turned over to consumers. At the same time, streams of money are moving in the opposite direction—a main stream becoming smaller and smaller as it flows from consumers to retailers, from retailers to wholesalers, from wholesalers to manufacturers, from manufacturers to producers of raw materials, and thence, mainly in the form of payments for personal services, back once more to consumers.[26]

Piquet maintains that this principle is one of the most basic and most important distinctions in economic thinking. That is, "production is primarily a physical phenomenon, and signifies movement *forward* from indirect uses to direct uses. Values, on the other hand, from the point of view of the overall economy, are essentially psychological phenomena and reflect anticipated future direct uses *back* through various levels of indirectness, to the most indirect level."[27]

Finally, Albert Hahn describes the interrelationship between production and consumption: "Production creates income for the factors of production and the spending of this income leads to consumption. . . . Consumption, in its turn, depends on the size and distribution of income from production. Production again depends on consumption, because the consumer by his demand determines what is to be produced. Production influences consumption, and consumption influences production."[28] But this interdependence does not make the system indeterminate, however. "A logical chain leads from production to consumption and back. To determine the beginning of that chain is just as impossible as to establish the priority of the chicken or the egg. Every phase presupposes a preceding phase—which, however, can only be described subsequently."[29]

Rothbard illustrates the fact that the economic activity involves one continuous round of supplying and demanding (see figure 6.9).

THE MEANING OF SAY'S LAW

The meaning of Say's law, "supply creates its own demand," becomes apparent in this context. As purchased production moves from raw materials to final consumption, income is paid out to the factors of production in the form of wages, rents, and profits, which in turn is used to purchase the goods and services being produced by business. As J. S. Mill generalizes, "All sellers are inevitably, and by the meaning of the word, buyers."[30] B. M. Anderson also explains:

Figure 6.9. Supply and Demand at Each Stage of Production

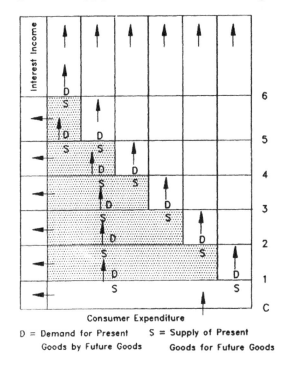

D = Demand for Present   S = Supply of Present
Goods by Future Goods   Goods for Future Goods

Source: Rothbard, *Man, Economy, and State,* 334.

"The great producing countries are the great consuming countries. . . . Supply of shoes gives rise to demand for wheat, for silks, for automobiles and for other things that the shoe producer wants. Supply and demand in the aggregate are thus not merely equal, but they are identical, since every commodity may be looked upon either as supply of its own kind or as demand for other things."[31] Say's law was fashioned in response to the "overproductive" theorists who argued that a general glut of excess commodities could occur from time to time. But if prices are allowed to fluctuate freely, how could such an event occur when the selling of one good always gives rise to a demand for another?

Actually, however, it is possible to have disequilibrium on an economy-wide scale. As will be shown shortly, Say's law is not a universal law, at least in the short run, once a nonneutral fiat monetary system is created. Certainly, under barter conditions and a pure gold standard, it is an immutable law. But as Anderson notes, "But this doctrine [Say's law] is subject to the great qualification that the proportions must be right; that there must be equilibrium."[32]

In an effort to understand the full implications of the APS, let us look more closely at the two ways of visualizing the economic structure, aggregate supply and aggregate demand.

THE AGGREGATE SUPPLY VECTOR

First, let's look at the Aggregate Supply schedule, which I have called the Aggregate Supply Vector (ASV). It is a vector because it has both direction and distance. As we have concluded beforehand, economic production generally works its way from the raw materials stage to final consumption as follows:

Raw commodities
↓
Manufacturers' goods
↓
Wholesale goods
↓
Retail goods

All firms transform inputs into outputs in a downward direction, toward final consumption. As production moves from one stage to the next, the aggregate revenue increases according to the profitability of each stage. Thus the Aggregate Supply Vector can be demonstrated to be a downward-sloping schedule as illustrated in figure 6.10.

The direction and length of the ASV is determined by several factors. The direction or slope of the ASV is determined by the profitability of each stage of output. As each stage is more profitable, the slope of the ASV decreases. The length of the ASV is determined by several factors, such as (a) the technology of indirect methods of production, and (b) the amount of saving-investment which can be applied to the production of machines, tools and other capital necessary to produce more goods.

THE AGGREGATE DEMAND VECTOR

To visualize the income-expenditure effect of the economic process, we must look at the Aggregate Demand Vector (ADV). Aggregate demand is also a vector with direction and distance. However, demand must be in the opposite

Figure 6.10. Aggregate Supply Vector

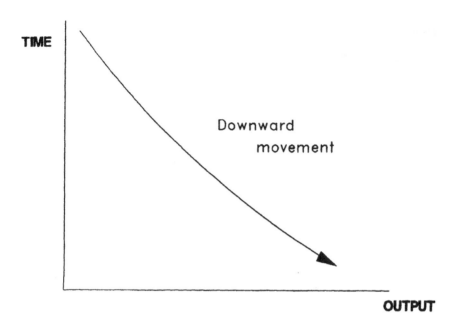

direction from the ASV, upward instead of downward. Since final demand is at the last stage of production, the consumer-goods market, the movement of money must begin at the consumption stage and work backwards. Figure 6.11 illustrates the demand function for the whole economy.

Hayek states, "every change in demand, from the moment of its appearance, propagates itself cumulatively through all the grades of production, from the lowest to the highest."[33] This principle is what Menger called the "imputation of value" of all goods and services. As B. M. Anderson explains,

> It is the one great contribution of the Austrian economists to have shown that the causation in value runs, primarily, from consumption goods to the goods of higher 'orders' which are concerned with their production. . . . The value of wheat is based on the value of bread, the value of land on the value of wheat. The value of the stock of United States Steel rests in part on the value of iron lands, which rests on the value of ore, which rests on the value of pig iron, which rests on the value of steel rails, which rests on the value of the service of transporting building materials, which rests on the value of a building, which rests on the value of the services which a dentist performs in an office in the building.[34]

What factors influence the demand for final consumption? They are:

Figure 6.11. Aggregate Demand Vector

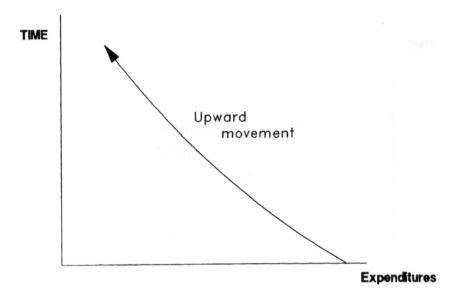

a. the income earned by the factors of production (rent, interest, wages, and profits), and
b. the savings/consumption ratio, i.e., how much income is allocated toward investment and how much is spent on consumer goods.
c. expectations of future prices, earnings, profits, and so on.

In short, the combined time preference of individuals determines the upward direction of the Aggregate Demand Vector.

EQUILIBRIUM BETWEEN AGGREGATE DEMAND AND AGGREGATE SUPPLY

If we combine the ASV and the ADV on the same graph, we note that they move in the same direction with a negative sloping curve. In fact, if we are in an evenly rotating state, the ASV and the ADV are one and the same, as B. M. Anderson noted earlier. They are not only parallel, but coincidental at every stage of production.

We see why this must be so by first considering the opposite example. If demand exceeded supply at a particular point along the transformation chain

Figure 6.12. Equilibrium between Aggregate Demand and Supply

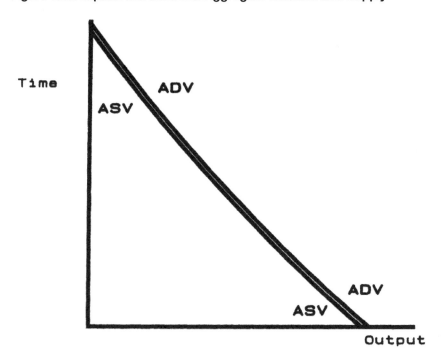

of activity, excessive profits would be made by those producers in that particular stage, higher than other stages. Therefore, assuming mobility of resources, firms would move out of other stages and into the stage with a higher level of profit. As a result, the profit margin would decline in that particular economic sector until it was equal to the others.

If supply exceeded demand in one sector, just the opposite would occur. Resources would move out of that stage of production and into the others which appear more lucrative.

THE CRITICAL ROLE OF INTEREST RATES

What keeps aggregate supply equal to aggregate demand in general equilibrium? If the ASV is determined primarily by the profitability of individual firms, and the ADV is determined by the time preference (consumption/ savings ratio) of individuals, how can these two variables cause a tendency toward equilibrium throughout the whole economy?

The answer is the interest rate—the economy's "regulator."[35] Without market interest rates operating throughout the economy, producers would be unable to determine what quantity of resources should be devoted to the various intertemporal market sectors and consumers would not know how much of their disposable funds should be devoted to savings and investment. Without freely fluctuating interest rates, the market would be destabilizing.[36]

In short, the money system must be arranged so that the structure of production, which Machlup calls the "time distribution of productive services," corresponds with the structure of expenditures, Machlup's "time distribution of purchasing power."[37] How does the interest rate determine the proper balance between production and consumption, and how do variations in the interest rate keep them from going into imbalance indefinitely? Abrams correctly raises the all-important issue: "Now, the most important task for those in charge of production today is to decide correctly the proportions between the production of consumption goods and the production of intermediate goods."[38] How does the interest rate assist the producer in making this decision?

Let us begin by examining the supply and demand for capital funds as reflected in the loanable funds market. The loanable funds market permeates the whole economic system because money is used almost universally throughout the world.[39] Figure 6.13 represents this supply and demand function.

In this diagram, we have SS, the supply of capital, which comes from business and personal savings. The SS schedule has a positive slope, because as the interest rate climbs, savers earn a higher yield and are encouraged to invest more. We also have II, the demand for capital by business firms. The II schedule has a negative slope because as the interest rate increases, business is less likely to borrow the more expensive money.

The figure also shows three interest rates in Figure 6.13–i_1, i_e, and i_2. In the first case, suppose the government artificially set the interest rate at an excessively high level, i_1. The result would be that individuals would alter their consumption/savings habits in favor of saving more money and consuming less. Even though more funds are thus available to invest, producers would not be willing to utilize the full amount because of the high cost of borrowing. The result is a surplus of savings over investment. Moreover, the real economy would suffer. Consumers spend less than normal, thus cutting back on the demand for final products, and business would cut back on production plans throughout the economic structure because of the high cost of business loans. In fact, businesses in the remote stages would cut back even further since they are more sensitive to interest-rate changes.[40] The subsequent decline in economic activity would be a strong incentive for the government to abandon its "pro-savings" stance and reduce interest rates.

Figure 6.13. Supply and Demand for Loanable Funds

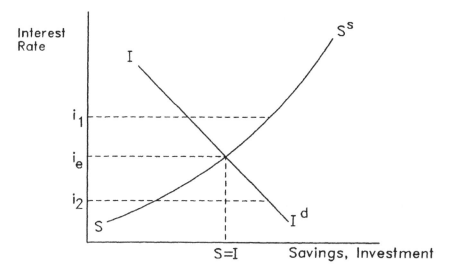

On the other hand, suppose the government imposed an artificially low interest rate, i_2, perhaps in an effort to stimulate trade. In this case, business would be encouraged to borrow large amounts of funds and expand operations at every level. Higher-order industries furthest from consumption would particularly benefit because they tend to be capital-intensive. Yet the lower interest rate would greatly discourage savers from placing funds in the banks and other financial intermediaries. The result is a shortage of loanable funds. Moreover, the low interest rate would encourage consumers to stop saving and start spending, thus exacerbating the demands for higher production even more. The increased competition to obtain funds for expansion would become intense, forcing interest rates to rise, despite the objections of government officials.

Thus, we see how "the prime significance of movements in the rate of interest is that they indicate *relative* changes in the demand for consumption goods and the demand for intermediate goods."[41] Hence, there is a tendency toward a "natural rate of interest," where the supply of savings equals the demand for investment, where S=I, denoted as i_e. The natural interest rate occurs when "the demand for loan capital is just equal to the supply of savings."[42] O'Driscoll adds, "This natural rate is the rate of interest at which the flow of consumer and producer goods being produced and sold on the market is the same as the flow of expenditures on such goods. It is the rate at which the ex ante decisions of producers and consumers are mutually consistent."[43]

As Garrison concludes, "the rate of interest is the key coordinating link that allocates capital goods in such a way as to match the intertemporal utilization of resources with intertemporal consumer demands."[44] Furthermore: "The entrepreneurs, whose decisions are guiding the production process, are in effect constantly assessing and reassessing the importance that consumers attach to goods in the more remote future as compared to goods in the near future. They then tailor the production process as best they can in accordance with their assessments and expectations. Disappointed expectations will lead to a retailoring of the production process."[45]

STANDARD MODELS OF AGGREGATE
SUPPLY AND DEMAND INACCURATE

It is important to note the dramatic difference between the above aggregate equilibrium model and the traditional aggregate model found in standard economics textbooks. The standard neoclassical model shows the aggregate demand curve as a negative downward-sloping curve, and the aggregate supply curve as a positive upward-sloping curve which becomes highly inelastic as production approaches capacity and full employment (see figure 6.14). However, neither curve reflects a relationship to time.

The neoclassical model of macroeconomics indicates only one point of equilibrium, while the structural model shows that in order to achieve equilibrium,

Figure 6.14. Comparison of Aggregate Production Structure and Neoclassical Model of Aggregate Supply and Demand

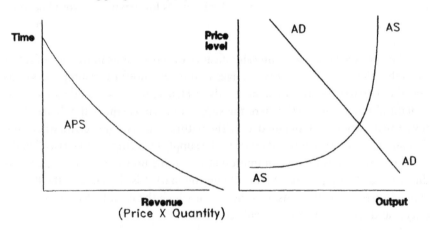

supply and demand must be equal *at every point* along the Aggregate Production Structure. Thus, we see how the APS format is far more complete as a macroeconomic model.

In a period of disequilibrium, supply and demand can be expressed as opposites to each other *at each stage of production*. At the micro level, the neoclassical supply and demand cross is certainly appropriate since there is competition between industries and between stages. But on the macro scale, the model must change to a whole new blueprint. The standard supply and demand schedules cannot be used to express the whole economy as a single unit. What can the "whole economy" compete against?

The APS, unlike aggregate supply and demand curves, introduces the time element into the diagram. The supply and demand schedules are provided at *each stage* of production in the APS. Time is measured on the vertical line, while *both* price and quantity combined (i.e., total revenue) for each stage is measured along the horizontal line.

Even when there is a difference between aggregate demand and aggregate supply (macroeconomic disequilibrium is discussed in later chapters), the ADV and the ASV *both* tend to move in a negative-sloping manner, upward for the ADV and downward for the ASV, although in a divergent pattern. Only when one looks at one particular stage of production can one discuss intelligently the oversupply or excess demand of a group of goods, because one can then compare relative prices with other sectors of the economy. This distinction will become apparent in the next few chapters.

Market forces are always seeking to achieve a resting point of equilibrium, but there are factors which constantly disrupt this goal. In the remainder of this work, we will examine the wide variety of ways in which the economy undergoes constant revision and how these changes can alter the Aggregate Production Structure.

HALFWAY HOUSE BETWEEN MICRO AND MACRO

Let us review what we have accomplished in creating the Aggregate Production Structure. We have aggregated *intra*stage firms and industries, but have not aggregated all *inter*stage firms and industries. We have aggregated within stages, but not between stages. The economy has only been partially aggregated (or partially disaggregated, depending on your point of view). In this way, we have in essence made *time and money* the critical factors in developing the macro model for the economy.[46] The link between the micro and macro economy is accomplished by partially aggregating—not aggregating all capital goods into a single-dimensional homogeneous soup, as the neoclassical economists do, but aggregating within stages of production only, leaving each time-age sector disaggregated and a function of its time distance from final consumption. For some stages, the distance is short, perhaps a few months, for others the distance is long, perhaps several years.

Thus, the APS is a halfway house between micro and macro—it is the "missing link" for which economists have long been searching.[47] The flaw of the orthodox macro economists is that they have always carried aggregation too far. It is proper to aggregate to some extent in order to analyze the actions of money, government, and other agents in the economy. But excessive aggregation of capital goods into a single unit completely obscures the structural intertemporal relationship, which is critical to understanding how government-made money interferes with macroeconomic equilibrium. The only appropriate aggregation in macro analysis is at each stage of production, but not on an *inter*stage basis. Nor is it helpful in analyzing macro theory to disaggregate partially on a horizontal basis, i.e., dividing the economy into general factors of production (land, labor, and capital). Rather, the appropriate vehicle for macroeconomic analysis is the *time* structure of economic output: the Aggregate Production Structure, which measures the value of current output against its time distance from ultimate consumption.

DECENTRALIZED NATURE OF THE ECONOMY

One further characteristic that should be emphasized about the APS and the economy, is the decentralized nature of the markets. Surprising though it may seem, national economic statistics often have little meaning to the individual entrepreneur and producer. To the owner of a small company it often does not seem to matter if GNP grew at a specific rate last year, whether a recession has hit the nation, or what the inflation rate is. What really concerns him is the price he can get for the products in his own business, and the costs of land, labor, and capital to produce those products. He may be unaware that prices are rising or dropping in other unrelated markets, but he will know if they are rising or dropping in his market. Inflation may be raging nationwide, but if demand for his own product wanes he may not be able to raise his prices. The expected profit margin is the key indicator to him, nothing else.

Nor does he usually concern himself with the structure of production for the whole economy. He has only the vaguest notion how the economy works.

It is of little interest to him how raw materials turn into intermediate goods and eventually final consumer goods and services, nor is he necessarily knowledgeable about the driving force that brings about a maximization of consumer goods and services. All he is interested in is discovering a window of opportunity, a chance to increase his profit margin in a previously unexploited market, whether it is in the capital or consumer markets. He is a demander of inputs and a supplier of products, and he seeks a profit. If he incurs losses, or sees a more profitable opportunity, he will shift his resources to it. Schumpeter comments:

> All products are only products and nothing more. For the individual firm it is a matter of complete indifference whether it produces means of production or consumption goods. In both cases the production is paid for immediately and at its full value. The individual need not look beyond the current period, even though he always works for the next. He simply follows the dictates of demand, and the mechanism of the economic process sees to it that he also provides for the future at the same time. He is not concerned with what happens further to his products, and he would probably never begin the process of production if he had to follow it to the end.[48]

It is the very decentralized pattern of economic behavior that fulfills the needs of individuals. Supply and demand weave a systematic pattern, via the ever-present structure of interest rates, leading to economic growth and harmony.

No corporation or business, no matter how large, can conceive of producing a good from raw materials to final consumer product. Vertical integration has its limitations. A carmaker buys steel, or plastics, but it would be foolish for the company to produce steel or plastics itself. It would probably be very costly to do so because of the economies of scale and technical expertise required. In the end, very few producers visualize the whole picture of what is really happening in the economy. As Garrison states, "Those working in the early (higher-order) stages, such as the extraction industries, need not ever know what the output will ultimately be used for. In many circumstances it will be enough that they know the cost of their inputs and the demand for their immediate output. No single entrepreneur, or group of conspiring entrepreneurs, has knowledge about the production process as a whole."[49]

This is not to say that a study of the whole economy and the APS should be left to the armchair economist and the government planners. On the contrary, business men as well as employees should be knowledgeable about "macro" economic trends, because these trends may well affect their own "micro" situation. Major corporations employ economists to determine the outlook for the economy in general and their products in particular. Moreover, individual and institutional investors are often searching for speculative opportunities, which are frequently created by dramatic changes in government activity. An independent, disinterested observer can learn a great deal about the inner workings of the capitalistic system by analyzing the structure of production, and can determine the harmful or beneficial effects of certain public and private actions.

LIMITATIONS OF THE APS

Like any macroeconomic model, the APS has its limitations as well as its advantages. It can demonstrate disequilibrium in the macroeconomy, but it cannot necessarily prove any relationship between monetary inflation and a *general* rise in prices. It can show relative changes in prices and output between broad-based stages of production, but it cannot show the overall change in the general price index or national output. Figure 6.15 demonstrates the difficulty.

In Economy A, prices and output have risen throughout the economy, although it appears that they have risen more in the higher-order industries than in the consumer-goods industries. It is clear that nominal output and prices have risen across the board. The general price index and current national output have risen.

But what about Economy B? In this case, prices and output have risen in the higher-order markets, but have fallen in the consumer industries. It is impossible to say what has happened to the general price level or to nominal output.

Thus, we see how the APS is best suited for making relative price and output comparisons and is not very useful in measuring changes in the general price level and real national output.

Figure 6.15. Relative versus General Change in the Economy

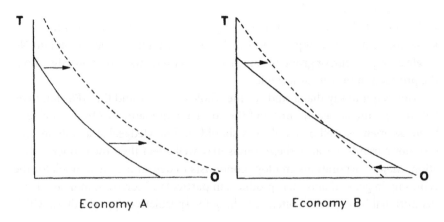

Economy A   Economy B

NOTES

1. Rothbard comments, "It is completely illogical to single out durable goods, which are themselves only discounted embodiments of their non-durable services and are therefore no different from nondurable goods." *Man, Economy, and State*, 343.
2. Ibid., 340.
3. Abrams, *Money*, 11.
4. Röpke, *Economics of a Free Society*, 43.
5. Black, *Introduction to Production Economics*, 34.
6. Taussig, *Wages and Capital*, 6. However, a review of employment figures by industry in a highly developed country like the United States indicates that employment in the consumers' goods industries has expanded much more rapidly than in the capital-goods industries since Taussig and others wrote their views. The breakdown depends on how one categorizes certain industries. In 1979, the breakdown by industry was as follows:

	(in thousands)
Producers' Goods Industries	38,661
Agriculture, forestry, fisheries	3,455
Mining	865
Construction	6,299
Manufacturing	22,137
Wholesale trade	3,775
Business services	2,200
Consumers' Goods Industries	38,613
Retail trade	15,898
Nonbusiness services	17,659
(automobile, personal, entertainment, recreation, hospital, health, welfare)	
Public administration	5,056
Industries in Either Category	18,974
Education (including universities)	7,416
Finance, insurance, real estate	5,779
Transportation, communication, and other public utilities	5,779
Total Employment	96,248

Source: "Employment, by Industry: 1970 to 1979," *Statistical Abstract of the United States* (U.S. Department of Commerce, 1980), 406.

Based on these figures, it appears that it is no longer true that "the vast majority of employees" in the U.S. work in the producers' goods markets, as Taussig, Black, and other earlier economists have suggested. Of course, most of the above statements were made in the early twentieth century, before the U.S. and other Western nations became a "consumer society."
7. Rothbard, *Man, Economy and State*, 339.
8. Ibid., 340.
9. Edwin G. Dolan, *Economics*, 4th ed. (Chicago: Dryden Press, 1986), 174.

10. Rothbard, *Man, Economy and State,* 341. Input-output analyst M. F. Elliott-Jones comments, "Aggregate econometric models seldom consider production as anything but aggregates of final output. Intermediate transactions are aggregated until they disappear. Production of commodities which are to be used in the making of other commodities is, however, a major part of economic activity. For some purposes, therefore, the convention of avoiding double counting by excluding intermediate transactions is unsatisfactory." Elliott-Jones, *Input-Output Analysis,* 2.

11. Rothbard, *Man, Economy and State,* 343.

12. Hayek, *Prices and Production,* 47, 48.

13. Hayek, *The Pure Theory of Capital,* 74.

14. As far as I am aware, the only earlier attempt to measure the total flow of economic activity was made by Reavis Cox and his associates in a project funded by the Twentieth Century Fund in the mid-1960s. Based on an I-O model, they estimated total spending of $676 billion in the United States in 1947, approximately three times larger than GNP. See Cox, *Distribution in a High-Level Economy,* 265–81.

15. "In reality there is never such a thing as an evenly rotating economic system." Mises, *Human Action,* 247.

16. Mises, "My Contributions to Economic Theory," in *Planning for Freedom,* 231.

17. Rothbard, *Man, Economy and State,* 275.

18. Mises, *On the Manipulation of Money and Credit,* 124.

19. Rothbard, *Man, Economy and State,* 299–301. The rate of profit will tend to be the same as the pure rate of interest in the ERE because competition would eliminate any differences. If some firms were making a higher return than what they could make in the loanable funds market, resources would shift into that particular industry until the difference was eliminated.

20. Interstage competition, i.e., competition between industries at different distances from final use, is just as important as intrastage competition, but often neglected in economics textbooks. Yet economists must realize that steel companies do not just compete with other steel companies, but with department stores and banks. They all are in competition for investment funds. In short, there is horizontal and vertical competition going on all the time.

21. Rothbard, *Man, Economy and State,* 315, 316, 337.

22. Wicksell, *Lectures on Political Economy,* vol. 1, 161.

23. "Furthermore, the fact that the ERE interest rate will be the same for all stages and all goods in the economy especially permits us to aggregate the comparable stages of all goods." Rothbard, *Man, Economy and State,* 337.

24. Hayek, *Prices and Production,* 40.

25. Ibid., 45.

26. Foster and Catchings, *Money,* 299.

27. Piquet, *The Economic Axioms,* 9. Piquet uses this principle to show the fallacy of the "marginal productivity theory of distribution," which seeks to explain prices through the costs of production and wages through past productivity instead of anticipated future values.

28. L. A. Hahn, *Common Sense Economics*, 35. Hahn's description of the economic system has elements of Say's law in it, "supply creates its own demand," although one could easily fall into the Keynesian trap of suggesting, "Demand creates its own supply."

29. Ibid.

30. J. S. Mill, *Principles of Political Economy,* book 3, chap. 14. Quoted in Keynes, *The General Theory*, 18.

31. B. M. Anderson, *Economics and the Public Welfare*, 390.

32. Ibid.

33. Hayek, *Monetary Theory and the Trade Cycle*, 63.

34. B. M. Anderson, *The Value of Money*, 38–39. It would be more accurate to state that the value of the higher order goods depends not only on the value of a building or the services of a dentist, but on the value of *all* buildings, services of dentists, and so forth, which require the use of steel.

35. Hayek states that "interest forms a sufficient regulator for the proportional development of the production of capital goods and consumption goods, respectively." *Monetary Theory and the Trade Cycle*, 91–92.

36. "To keep the economy in equilibrium, it is necessary that the factors of production be utilized so as to produce a pattern of production that corresponds to the pattern of consumption." Valentine and Dauten, *Business Cycles and Forecasting*, 426.

37. Machlup, "Professor Knight and the 'Period of Production,'" 621. Similarly, Richard Strigl states, "The process of a market economy moves between two poles: on the one hand from the supply of factors of production, and on the other hand, from the demand for consumer goods." Strigl, *Capital and Production*, 43.

38. Abrams, *Money*, 11.

39. "Money, the general medium of exchange is precisely nonspecific," says Rothbard (*Man, Economy and State*, 298). It is neither a producer nor consumer good, except in the case of gold and silver, which have nonmonetary uses. "Money being a commodity which, unlike all others, is incapable of finally satisfying demand." Hayek, *Monetary Theory and the Trade Cycle*, 44. It is because of the nonspecific, nonconsumable nature of money that allows it to become so universal in the economy. As a result, interest rates and the loanable funds market play a critical role in all market economies.

40. According to Piquet, the interest rate is central to businessmen's plans: "Interest is the price that is paid for time in the sense that money in hand enables one to acquire inputs which will 'mature' into a product, the price of which will exceed the costs of the inputs by the time-discounts involved in the prices of the inputs." *The Economic Axioms*, 56.

41. Abrams, *Money*, 21.

42. Valentine and Dauten, *Business Cycles and Forecasting*, 291.

43. O'Driscoll, *Economics as a Coordination Problem*, 75.

44. Garrison, "The Austrian-Neoclassical Relation," 81.

45. Ibid., 82.

46. For an excellent summary of the significance of time and money in macroeconomics, see Roger Garrison's profound article, "Time and Money: The Universals of Macroeconomic Theorizing," 197–213. Garrison's theme is taken from Hayek's comment (*The*

Pure Theory of Capital, 408–10) that money is a "loose joint" in the self-equilibrating market system. In contrast, members of the monetarist and rational expectations schools seem to take a "tight joint" attitude toward money, while extreme Keynesians and Marxists appear to have a "broken joint" view of money in the economy. In this sense, the Austrians represent the middle ground.

47. "If productivity and capital formation are its focal points, a microeconomic theory can also do what never before could be done in economics: to tie together microeconomics and macroeconomics, if not make them into one." Drucker, "Toward the Next Economics," 14–15. It is my contention that Drucker's vision is fulfilled in the Aggregate Production Structure.

48. Schumpeter, *The Theory of Economic Development*, 43–44.

49. Garrison, "The Austrian-Neoclassical Relation," 83.

SEVEN

SAVINGS, TECHNOLOGY, AND ECONOMIC GROWTH

The study of individual thrift and aggregate saving and wealth has long been central to economics because national saving is the source of the supply of capital, a major factor of production controlling the productivity of labor and its growth over time. It is because of this relation between saving and productive capital that thrift has traditionally been regarded as a virtuous, socially beneficial act.[1]—Franco Modigliani, "Life Cycle, Individual Thrift, and the Wealth of Nations," Nobel Prize Lecture, 1985.

The preceding chapter established the value of the Aggregate Production Structure in a stationary economy. The purpose of this chapter is to analyze dynamic changes in the economy, especially with regard to advances in technology and changes in consumption/savings patterns, to discover how they might affect aggregate supply and aggregate demand in the APS.

The role of savings and technological advancement in a free society have been a controversial issue since the 1930s. In the depths of the Great Depression, Keynes and his followers debunked savings as a "leakage" from the economic system. Furthermore, they contended that the world had reached a permanent level of stagnation. Since World War II, the United States, West Germany, Japan and many other countries have rebounded spectacularly from the dismal depression years, and as a result, economists have rejected the stagnation thesis and have gradually overcome the anti-saving bias in neoclassical economics. In fact, many economists have concluded that savings are beneficial and critically necessary to achieve significant economic growth. Unfortunately, the theoretical development in support of increased savings and technological growth has often been lacking in economics, as witnessed by the fact that the Keynesian antisavings doctrines are still taught in the textbooks. This chapter aims to demonstrate the benefits of savings from a purely theoretical framework, and to show how savings and technological advancement work hand in hand.

The major economic goal of any country is to increase its standard of living for all its citizens. That is the real meaning of "economic growth" and the "wealth of nations." How can such universal and permanent economic prosperity be achieved? In this chapter, we will analyze the effects of two techniques often considered essential for economic growth: (1) technological improvements in the capitalistic process, and (2) increases in savings, i.e., expanding the base for capital formation. There is no question that the two major forces of the industrial revolution since the eighteenth century have been technological breakthroughs and a massive build-up of capital as a direct result of private savings and investment.

IMPACT OF TECHNOLOGICAL CHANGE

In the market system, there is always a monetary incentive to reduce costs or to create new or better products for consumers and business. Either way, the entrepreneur seeks to increase his net return on his investment. Efforts to reduce expenses may take the form of using cheaper labor, moving to another location to take advantage of lower office rents, or developing a new process that eliminates stages of production altogether. The elimination of stages is, in effect, a way of shortening the manufacturing process, and thus reducing the waiting time before the final product can be sold.

Wieser states, "the progress of the technical arts should reduce the duration of production periods just as it elsewhere reduces the cost of production."[2] Shackle remarks how "discovery and invention" may decrease the average period of production.[3]

At the turn of the twentieth century, Gustav Cassel pointed to many examples of technological changes which shortened the period of production. Modern methods of distribution, communication, and transportation have substantially reduced the time it takes to make a machine, building, or ship. He stated that, at the time, "about 27 hours are needed to transform iron and coal (from the rough state of nature in which they are found) to steel rails (without holes) loaded on board ship." A modern cargo steamer can be built, on average, in twelve months. In the case of growing sheep for wool and mutton, "the decrease is reported to be from eight to ten years in the beginning of the [nineteenth] century to two to three years at the end."[4] Horace White, in criticizing Böhm-Bawerk's argument that economic progress involves ever-lengthening processes, says that "the most marked and distinguishing feature of the modern industrial world is *not* the lengthening of processes of production or the employment of larger capital and more roundabout ways to produce a given quantity of products, but the shortening of processes, the employment of less capital and less roundabout ways."[5] Examples: drilling for oil instead of sending ships to catch whales; using electric power instead of steam machinery; printing with mechanized presses instead of writing longhand; making steel in a modern mill.

Taussig uses several historical examples of how new production techniques and machines have replaced older, less productive methods. But, in each case, he asserts, producing the labor-saving device involved *more* time and capital to build than did the older, less productive tool: "The spinning wheel and the hand loom, easily and simply made, have given way to the jenny and the mule and the power loom, fixed in a great building, and moved by complicated machinery; all involving a longer stage of preparatory effort, and yielding the enjoyable commodity in the end of easier terms."[6] Taussig uses other examples: the grist mill was replaced by the modern steam mill, the creation of which involved a much longer time in the production process than the grinding of corn, but which resulted in a "great increase in efficiency."

Both the critics and apologists for Böhm-Bawerk are, in my view, arguing about two aspects of the same phenomenon. In Taussig's as well as White's examples, there are two steps to new capitalistic methods: first, there is the building of the capital good, and second, the increased productivity that follows its implementation. It takes a great deal of time to set up a steam mill, to use Taussig's example, but once in place, it makes the grinding of corn more productive. Initially, as Taussig says, these inventions have all "taken the form of greater and more elaborate preparatory effort. The railway, the steamship, the textile mill, the steel works, the gas works and the electric plant." But once established, they provide a much higher degree of efficiency and productivity. This higher level of efficiency is what other economists refer to as the shortening of the period of production: "The railway, the telegraph, and the telephone, have served to shorten many steps in production; and elaborate machines, though it takes time to make them, do their work, once made, more quickly than simpler tools."[7]

Commenting on this two-phase nature of new capital investments, Black notes in his important work, *Production Economics*, "Whenever production is carried on with machinery, tools and buildings, the production process is prolonged. The machines have to be completely manufactured before production of the commodity itself can be started. . . . The reasons for such production is the hope of securing ultimately a larger product, or of satisfying in the end the same wants with less effort."[8] H. G. Brown uses an illustration of two towns where a railroad is to be built between them. "The building [of the railroad] requires three years, during most of which period the rails can not be used to carry goods. At the end of three years, the possible trade may be, indeed, much greater than before and the carriage of goods swifter; but the labor of building the railroad will still be contributing to community welfare long after those who built the road have ceased to be able to lift a spade or carry a tie."[9]

Machlup, commenting on how inventions tend to reduce the period needed for production, states, "Sewing by hand is a much slower method of making dresses than sewing by machine."[10] Machlup concludes, "New inventions may suggest new sorts of equipment which compete with, and render obsolete, existing equipment. This may cause major losses of sunk investment; the investment period may be shortened (in case replacement funds have to be attracted from other industries) or may be left unchanged (in case new savings are just sufficient to finance the new investment) or lengthening in a smaller degree than would otherwise have been possible."[11]

MISCONCEPTIONS OF BÖHM-BAWERK'S ROUNDABOUTNESS

Machlup and many other economists sympathetic to the Austrian theory of capital criticize Böhm-Bawerk for his narrow focus on economic growth as an extension of the average period of production, and his failure to see how technology can shorten the production period once it is in place. In the case of a sewing machine, for instance, "Böhm-Bawerk had a hard time to explain that sewing of the dress was only the last part of the process, while in the process as a whole services were invested in iron production and machine shops and in the sewing machine and only finally in the dressmaking."[12]

Rothbard concurs, adding that Böhm-Bawerk made a mistake in using the term *roundabout*: "Calling these methods [accumulation of capital] 'roundabout' is definitely paradoxical; for do we not know that men strive always to achieve their ends in the most direct and shortest manner possible?"[13] Haavelmo says that Böhm-Bawerk had it all backwards. "Certainly it is not the delay in output which itself is 'productive,' but the fact that the more time we spend, the more capital we can construct."[14] Finally, Keirstead adds that Böhm-Bawerk's views are wrongheaded. "It is not because using tools is round-about that it enhances production. Rather the increased use of tools and the improvement of tools directly enhances productivity and for this reason it is socially worthwhile to wait for their production."[15]

A THEORETICAL REPRESENTATION OF TECHNOLOGICAL CHANGE

What does Böhm-Bawerk mean when he suggests that "the adoption of roundabout methods of production leads to greater returns from the productive process"?[16]

A simple Böhm-Bawerkian example of roundaboutness makes his principle clear. Take, for instance, a man alone on an island whose main source of sustenance is fishing. He could spend all day fishing and sunbathing. But by foregoing sunbathing (pleasure) for a few days, he can build up several days of fish supply. This build-up of fish inventory will then allow him the time to build a net, a capital good, which will increase his productivity. He goes from

$$Man{\rightarrow}Fish{\rightarrow}Consumption$$

to

$$Man{\rightarrow}Net{\rightarrow}Fish{\rightarrow}Consumption.^{17}$$

While the man is building the net, he is reducing his consumption of fish, and is depleting his fish inventory. But he is not unemployed. Instead of fishing, he is building a capital good. Once completed, the net will make the man far more proficient at fishing, and soon he will be catching far more fish per hour than he did before the net was made. Consequently, because of the capital good, the man can now spend less time fishing and more time sunbathing and pursuing other activities. In short, his long-term standard of living has increased sharply because of his short-term sacrifice (saving) and investing in the time and effort to build a net.

One can demonstrate the trade-off between current production methods and new more productive techniques in graphic form:

The graph illustrates a typical production function of product A, where the company's net income (C_p) increases with time (t). When a new, more efficient method is introduced to produce A, t amount of time is required to implement the technology before it can start producing. But once established, it produces greater output per time period than the old production function. Thus, the slope, $\dfrac{\delta C_k}{\delta t}$, is greater for the new production function than the slope, $\dfrac{\delta C_p}{\delta t}$, of the older method:

$$\frac{\delta C_k}{\delta t} > \frac{\delta C_p}{\delta t}.$$

However, this is not to conclude that all new production techniques will be adopted if they are more productive than the old ones. For example, a business would probably not try to implement a new technique which takes two years to set up but only improves productivity (profit margin) by 5 percent.

Figure 7.1. Effect of New Technology on Production Function

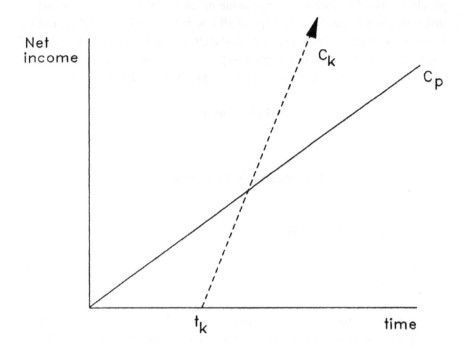

Thus, it is proper to recognize a trade-off between productivity of the new technique and the period of production of the capital good. We can show this graphically by adding a time preference schedule to the current production function. For simplicity's sake, we have expressed the current production function, C_p, as a linear function, when in fact it would likely have a declining marginal productivity. The time preference schedule is superimposed on the current production function. In terms of intertemporal choice, the production function represents current income, while the higher line represents future income. The trade-off between current and future income is a reflection of time preference: at any point in time t, the entrepreneur (who owns and produces product A) is willing to give up a net income of X for a period of time T in order to obtain a higher net income Y. Obviously, the longer the waiting, the greater the disparity between X and Y, current and future income (see figure 7.2).

Note that the time preference schedule is an exponential curve, while the current production function is linear. The time preference schedule is the current interest rate, which we assume to be equal throughout the economy (although longer-time rates may involve a higher risk premium, as noted in chapter 6). Even

Figure 7.2. Time Preference: Current Income versus Future Income

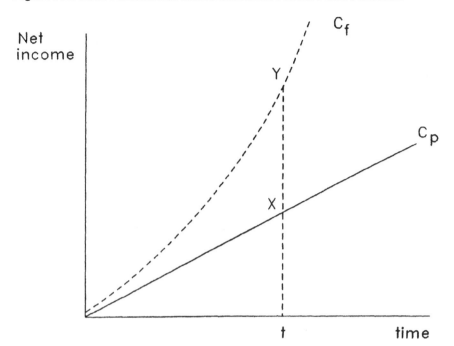

when interest rates are the same thoughout the economy, the time-preference curve will be exponential because of the compounding effect. (I thank Royal Skousen for making this crucial point.)

In figure 7.3 below, I have noted the *minimum* rate of return on a new technique in order for a business to consider its implementation. Any new technologies earning a higher expected return will be instituted, while those earning less will be rejected.

In short, no new investment will occur in the marketplace unless the expected rate of profit on the project exceeds or at least matches the current interest rate.

The production function of a new technique validates Böhm-Bawerk's position. We note, first, that the period of production has lengthened while a new method is instigated, i.e., if we measure the time from the point when construction of the capital good begins to the point where new production equals the old level; second, the new method results in greater productivity, or higher net income at some point in the future compared to the old method of production. In essence, Böhm-Bawerk is simply stating that in order for a firm to consider a new technique of producing its products, the new method must have a higher

Figure 7.3. Minimum Net Return on New Project

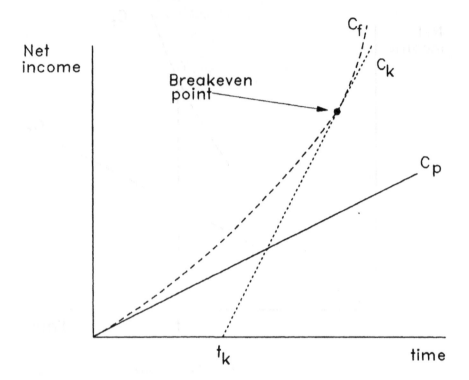

expected rate of return than the current method. Moreover, the rate of return must exceed the opportunity cost (i.e., interest rate) of the company's capital investment, or the cost of borrowing from a financial institution.

In referring to figure 7.3, it should also be noted that all technical developments involving shorter processes and higher productivity have already been undertaken by entrepreneurs. Therefore, any new processes being considered must either involve a more lengthy period of production or be more profitable than current processes.

The fact that new operations and new capital are being instituted all the time in modern society supports the Böhm-Bawerkian thesis that the total production structure is being lengthened and, as a result, becoming more productive. As Joe S. Bain concludes, "It is quite clear that in industrial societies since 1800, for example, there has been a progressive and rapid 'lengthening' of the structure of production, as an increasing proportion of resources has been devoted to the production of capital goods."[18] Carl Uhr agrees that, "looking at the economy as a whole, introduction of laborsaving methods have as a rule meant subdivision of former single processes into a greater number of production stages. This has expanded the time dimension of production as a whole, with an attendant increase in output, as experience shows."[19]

TECHNOLOGICAL DEVELOPMENT OF THE AUTOMOBILE

The technical progress of automobile manufacturing offers a modern-day example of the Böhm-Bawerkian thesis. The simple horseless carriage has gradually, over several decades, become a highly complex, intricate piece of workmanship, accomplished by the application of many innovations which have taken a great deal of time and money. What once took several hundred steps to complete now takes hundreds of thousands of operations to finish. New technology has been a constant and integral part of the automobile's changing and improving character over the past century. Initially, little capital or financial requirements were necessary to build an automobile, and the marketing structure was simple. But once cars began to be manufactured in large quantity, starting at the turn of the century, physical capital and financial requirements ballooned. Technical innovation occurred in every aspect of automobile manufacture: switching from steam engines to internal combustion gasoline engines, from one cylinder to four cylinders, and from the mechanical hand-cranked starter to the electric starter (which historian John Rae says "may be regarded as the decisive factor in the triumph of the gasoline over the steam automobile").[20]

The dramatic rise in the demand for passenger cars and trucks also had a vast impact on other industries. The petroleum market was virtually revolutionized. Not unexpectedly, the discovery of vast oil fields in Texas and other parts of the world came at the same time that the demand for gasoline were rising rapidly. At first the techniques of oil refining yielded less than 20 percent of gasoline from crude, but, after spending four years and one million dollars, Standard Oil Company developed the Burton cracking process, which doubled the yield of gasoline. Eventually, new techniques such as catalytic cracking and hydrogenation replaced the Burton process, increasing efficiency even more. In the early 1920s, after years of experimentation, scientists discovered that the mixing of tetraethyl lead with gasoline reduced engine knock.

Rubber has a similar story to tell. The bicycle clincher tire, which made road travel unreliable at best, was soon abandoned for the straight-sided tire. Meanwhile, rubber manufacturers constantly searched for new ways to develop stronger tires. Eventually, the industry adopted cotton cord as the base fabric and then introduced a low-pressure balloon tire.

During this period, the chemical industry discovered new quick-drying paints, useful in fast-moving assembly lines, and antifreeze for car use during cold weather. The steel industry developed the continuous-strip mill for rolling sheet steel and the glass industry used the continuous-process technique for manufacturing plate glass, both in response to demands for the automobile. Road construction went through dramatic improvements, from gravel and cobblestone to smooth, hard surfaces using asphalt or concrete. All of these innovations required years of research and millions of dollars to accomplish.[21]

But by far the most significant example of technological revolution came from Henry Ford's assembly-line method of mass production. It took many years in the early twentieth century for Ford to perfect this remarkable technique, which involved tremendous initial risk but which paid off so handsomely that by 1920 the Model T Ford comprised half of all automobiles on the road. Rae reports, "In order to achieve the price level Ford desired, it was necessary to make a large number of units at a low cost per unit, and this process demanded a heavy initial investment in specialized equipment and tools. To justify this investment there had to be a market capable of absorbing all these units. As it turned out there was, but Ford could have been catastrophically wrong."[22]

Ford took his company public in June, 1903. Five months later, the first automobile came off the assembly line. Sixty years later, in the spring of 1964, Ford introduced a new model, the now-popular Mustang. This time, it took three and a half years from the time of conception until the first finished model was ready for a test drive. Thus, Ford provides a classic example of the increasing span of time required to create a new product. Commenting on this lengthening time span, Galbraith notes:

The manufacture of the first Ford was not an exacting process. Metallurgy was an academic concept. Ordinary steels were used that could be obtained from the warehouse in the morning and shaped that afternoon. Nothing associated with this basic material required that the span of time between initiation and completion of a car be more than a few hours.

The provision of steel for the modern vehicle, in contrast, reaches back to specifications prepared by the designers or the laboratory and proceeds through orders to the steel mill, parallel provision for the appropriate metal-working machinery, delivery, testing and use.[23]

In the late 1920s, new technical challenges forced the Ford Motor Company to shut down and revamp its whole plant. In essence, Ford faced the same prospect as shown in figure 7.1. In the mid-1920s, due to increased competition by General Motors and Chrysler, the famous Model T had become obsolete, falling way behind in sales. By May 1927, Ford had stopped output altogether, shutting down production for nearly a year to devote all its efforts toward designing a new, technically improved Model A. Sixty thousand workers were temporarily laid off. Salesmen quit. Ford customers looked to GM. Investors waited. Meanwhile, Ford spent one hundred million dollars developing the new model which, once designed, required the redesigning and creation of thousands of new machine tools, dies and fixtures, and so on. It was a gigantic capital undertaking. Fortunately for Ford and its investors, the waiting was worthwhile. The Model A proved to be extremely popular when it finally appeared in late 1928. "By 1933 Ford sold fewer cars than either General Motors or Chrysler, but the bottom had been reached and there was no danger of extinction. In a mere six years, from Model T to V8, Ford had caught up and surpassed, technically, his competitors in many respects."[24] Ford's shutdown was an exceptional case, occurring at a time when the automobile industry was still in relative infancy. Today automobile and other large manfacturers do not generally close down all their operations to incorporate new designs and other changes—they conduct their research and development on new models while current production continues. This means that consumers and final purchasers usually do not have to wait for the products they need. As Moffat and Christenson explain:

There appears to be some danger of a misunderstanding regarding the results of the roundabout process of production. Much stress is ordinarily placed upon its indirectness and upon the time element, or waiting, involved. However, these features do not mean that the capitalistic production process is a slow one. It is true that a long time may elapse between the beginning of a series of productive stages, and the delivery of the product to the final consumer. But once capitalistic production is organized and the equipment is in operation, the supply of the product to the consumer normally becomes highly regular, speedy, and dependable. To the consumer the important consideration is not how long the productive process has taken, but rather the availability of the product and its quality and cost. . . . As a general proposition it may be said that, while waiting is essential where roundabout methods of production are employed, the waiting is done by the savers and investors, and not by the consumers.[25]

THE QUESTION OF WAITING

The point expressed by Moffat and Christenson needs to be emphasized. The lengthening of the period of production by continual applications of new capital and technology does not mean that each improvement in a product's design involves a longer waiting period by final users or consumers. Such would be the case if a manufacturer had to start from scratch and build the product completely himself—but he does not have to do so. Over the years the industrial economy has built up innumerable levels of production in order to facilitate the production of a wide variety of goods, goods which become inputs at various points along the chain of economic activity. The furniture buyer does not have to go to North Carolina to furnish his house; he can to to a retail outlet in his own home town. The furniture maker does not have to own a lumber yard or cut down his own trees; he can purchase a variety of wood products and other inputs from a lumber company. The publisher of this book does not even need to have his own printing press; he can subcontract it. And even if he did print the book, this does not mean that he manufactured the printing press. Undoubtedly he ordered it from a manufacturer who specializes in the making of printing presses. In short, inputs are readily available at virtually every level of the economy—at the raw commodity, manufacturing, wholesale, or retail level. Each firm usually has an inventory of raw, semifinished, or finished products which can be marketed further down the line toward the consumer. As a result, a complex consumer product such as an automobile, which involves hundreds of thousands of intricate steps to complete and which would take literally years to duplicate from scratch, can be built by a car manufacturer in a matter of hours.

But, of course, the time it takes for an assembly line to put together an automobile is not an accurate accounting of the whole period of production. There are hundreds of other items—tires, small machines, mirrors, upholstery, and so on—that have previously been made and are held in inventory to be included in the carmaking process at some point in time. We have not included the time it took to make these products. The car manufacturer himself is not concerned with the time it took to build the radios, mirrors, steel, and other factors of production which he will use. He is only concerned with how long it takes him to assemble those components into a car. Of course, if there is a shortage of a particular input, then he will suddenly be concerned about how long it will take before he can get it in stock, or whether a suitable substitution is available. Otherwise, he is not concerned. The market economy does its best to minimize this waiting period.

To give a full account of the period of production, we must also include the time these inputs remain in inventory, which can be weeks, months, perhaps years, before they are actually used in the manufacturing process. In the case of automobiles, for instance, the time the car sits in the parking lot waiting to be sold should be included.

To measure the actual full period of production of, say, an automobile, one must start with the basic raw materials—digging iron ore from the ground, planting the rubber tree, shoveling the sand on the beach (to make glass), and so on—and count the number of days, months, or years it takes before they all come together in the final shape of an automobile purchased by a consumer. Economists do not generally gather such statistics because they do not attach any importance to such intertemporal measurements. Renewed interest in the vertical structure of production may cause researchers to begin such studies. How long does it take to construct an office building? An automobile? A mature redwood tree? A book? Obviously, these are extremely important questions to the businessman, but the mainstream economist seems uninterested.

TECHNOLOGY AND THE APS

The APS can be very helpful in demonstrating the economic benefits of a technological breakthrough. If a new technology reduces the costs of inputs or the price of outputs, more time and resources are freed up to expand in other areas. The reduction in prices and the increase in the volume of business would occur at stages closer to consumption. Ultimately, then, a technological advancement should mean an expansion in consumer goods through lower prices, increased volume, higher incomes, and better quality. The amount by which consumption increases depends on many factors. Because consumer prices are lower, consumer demand increases. Consumers pay less but buy more, so that total spending on final consumer goods may actually remain the same, even though people are clearly better off. In real terms the volume of consumer goods has definitely increased, and probably in nominal terms as well. Thus, the standard of living improves.

If the new products are universally useful in both industrial and consumer sectors, such as computers and word processors, then the standard of living increases almost universally—and the real APS increases throughout the structure.

An increase in the production of technologically advanced equipment and products will also encourage a dramatic increase in savings and capital formation. As Böhm-Bawerk argues, savings and innovation are "interrelated."[26] A sudden increase in profit margins by firms tends to increase corporate dividends, wages and salaries, and so forth. In addition, higher profits lead to greater corporate savings, an increase in capital investment activities and expansion into new markets. These new funds may well be used to research other projects which were previously considered unthinkable as investment opportunities because the length of time to reach fruition made them unprofitable. Moreover, higher wages and salaries are not just spent on more consumption goods, but also result in greater individual savings and thus a greater pool for investing.

Henry Ford's voluminous output of mass-produced Model Ts is a classic example of the widespread benefits that new technology in one area can bring to the whole economy. As Rae concludes, "[Ford] believed that the gains made by improving techniques of production should be passed on to society as a whole in three ways: to stockholders in the conventional form of dividends, to consumers in the form of lower prices, and to labor in the form of higher wages."[27]

Thus, ultimately, we may describe the final effect of widespread technological advancement as an expansionary APS, but even more expansive in the "higher order" industries. As Böhm-Bawerk asserts, inventions which reduce costs set capital free "for the utilization of other circuitous methods which have been neglected because of the lack of funds"[28] (see figure 7.4).

TECHNOLOGY AND THE RATE OF INTEREST: TIME PREFERENCE VS. PRODUCTIVITY THEORY OF INTEREST

Does an increase in productivity, as a result of technological improvement, cause a reduction in the natural rate of interest? Such a question has been the point of heated debate over the years. Is the interest rate determined by productivity or by pure time preference? Böhm-Bawerk attacked the "naive" productivity theories of interest in *Capital and Interest,* but later relapsed into

Figure 7.4. Ultimate Impact of New Technology on APS

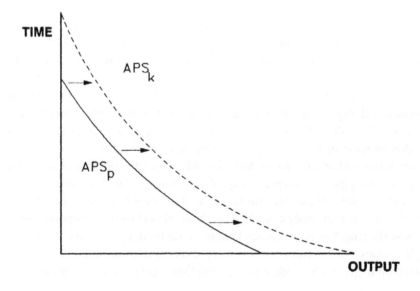

a physical productivity explanation of interest. His third reason for a positive rate of interest was based on the phenomenon of the superiority of roundaboutness, that "methods of production which take time are more productive."[29] Based on Böhm-Bawerkian groundwork, Schumpeter contended that the interest rate in a circular flow steady state (no growth) would be zero. In essence, he denied the existence of pure time preference.[30] Frank A. Fetter, on the other hand, chided Böhm-Bawerk for his productivity interpretation of interest, and instead adopted a pure time-preference theory of interest.[31] Other economists who have accepted a purely subjectivist theory of interest include Mises, Rothbard, and Garrison, all of whom maintain that time preference alone is sufficient to preserve a positive rate of interest at all times.

We have seen in the above analysis that new technology and increased productivity are likely to increase the standard of living. Insofar as a higher living standard encourages individuals to save more—i.e., at a higher rate—interest rates are likely to fall. Thus, in an indirect sense, increased productivity can lower interest rates—but only if the general populace decides to save relatively more than it has done in the past. There is no requirement that they do so, however. It is almost as reasonable to suppose that people will spend *more*. They may be tired of constantly sacrificing for future consumption. They may be ready to finally consume their income.

In short, it is ultimately time preference, and time preference alone, that determines the natural rate of interest. Increased productivity is a factor, though certainly not the only factor, in determining time preference.

The amount of capital held by an individual or a country will not necessarily determine the interest rate. One country may have a lot of capital, but if it is consuming its capital, or has a declining low rate of saving, the interest rate may be very high. On the other hand, a smaller country may have less capital, but a high degree of saving, and thus have a lower interest rate. Bliss has correctly pointed this out:

Even people who have made no study of economic theory are familiar with the idea that when something is more plentiful its price will be lower, and introductory courses on economic theory reinforce this common presumption with various examples. However, there is no support from the theory of general equilibrium for the proposition that an input to production will be cheaper in an economy where more of it is available. All that the theory declares is that the price of the use of an input which is more plentiful cannot be higher if all other inputs, all other outputs and all other input prices are in constant proportion to each other.[32]

As long as life is finite and resources are limited, a zero interest rate will be impossible.

THE CRITICAL IMPORTANCE OF SAVINGS

Mises and other Austrian economists argue that the level of savings and investment is far more important than technical know-how, especially in developing countries. "It is not a lack of 'know how' that prevents foreign countries from fully adopting American methods of manufacturing, but the insufficiency of capital available," Mises told an American audience in 1952.[33] Rothbard concurs in the view that the supply of capital is much more significant than technology: "[T]echnology, while important, must always *work through* an investment of capital."[34] "The African peasant will gain little from looking at pictures of American tractors; what he lacks is the saved capital needed to purchase them."[35] In all countries, including the advanced Western nations, companies continue to use outmoded equipment and machines, not because they prefer the older technologies, but because they lack the capital funds to purchase and install them. Even Ford's remodeling from the Model T to the Model A in the late 1920s could not have been accomplished without the $100 million Ford had saved from his previously accumulated profits. If he had spent this money as it came in rather than saving it, he would have had to borrow money from banks at high interest rates in order to pay for the necessary product transition. Such a large amount of capital may have been difficult to borrow at that time.

Peterson concludes: "Even if all the technical knowledge required for modern production were available, the difficulty of saving, and thus of diverting resources to capital-goods production, would remain."[36]

Let us now examine the impact of increased savings on economic growth. Assume a situation where technology is given. There are, nevertheless, an unlimited number of additional investment opportunities that could be undertaken, but are not because of the limited supply of personal and business savings available. If more savings became available, how would they be invested? Given a specified amount of investment funds, the shortest, most productive projects will be addressed first. Then if additional funds are made available—say, through increased individual savings—those new funds can then be invested in longer processes. Mises indicates, "for capital is of course always invested in the shortest available roundabout processes of production, because they yield the greatest returns. It is only when all the short roundabout processes of production have been appropriated that capital is employed in the longer ones."[37]

Now, longer processes will only be considered if the cost of doing them is so reduced as to make it relatively profitable (compared with current projects) to do so. As Shackle notes, "Unless the marginal productivity of capital is raised by new discovery or invention, such increased specialisation will be profitable only when the rate of interest has declined relative to the cost of labour."[38] One way for this to happen is for the financial institutions to obtain more lending capital from the public, thus reducing interest rates to borrowers and expanding their loan portfolio. Such an expansion of loanable funds would greatly enhance the profitability of longer-term investment projects.

SAVINGS AND INTEREST RATES

Interest rates are determined ultimately by individuals' time preferences, i.e., how much current spending they are willing to sacrifice in order to gain a higher level of spending in the future. It is a question of present income versus future income. This concern over time preference is unavoidable because resources are finite. If resources were infinite, there would be no need for time preference; a person could consume now, knowing that he could consume again at any time from the unlimited supply. But when resources are severely limited, a choice of time preference must be made between current and future consumption. As Irving Fisher states:

> [T]he rate of interest is the common market rate of preference for present over future income, as determined by the supply and demand of present and future income. Those who, having a high rate of preference, strive to acquire more present income at the cost of future income, tend to raise the rate of interest. These are the borrowers, the spenders, the sellers of property yielding remote income, such as bonds and stocks. On the other hand, those who, having a low rate of preference, strive to acquire more future income at the cost of present income, tend to lower the rate of interest. These are the lenders, the savers, the investors.[39]

One way in which interest rates can be reduced on a permanent basis is if there is an increase in the savings rate pattern in the community, so that the supply curve for autonomous savings shifts outward (see figure 7.5).

Another way of looking at the effect of lower interest rates is to refer to the production functions illustrated at the beginning of this chapter. Suppose an investment project, C_k, is expected to return a net-income schedule that falls well below the time preference schedule, as noted in figure 7.6 below.

Under current conditions, the project, C_k, will not be implemented. Its expected rate of return is below the rate of interest; projects currently in progress are more profitable. As Rothbard indicates, "The existence of time preference acts as a brake on the use of the more productive but longer processes."[40]

But what happens if the social time preference becomes more future-oriented, so that interest rates fall? Then the time preference level falls (from

Figure 7.5. Effect of Outward Shift in Supply of Savings

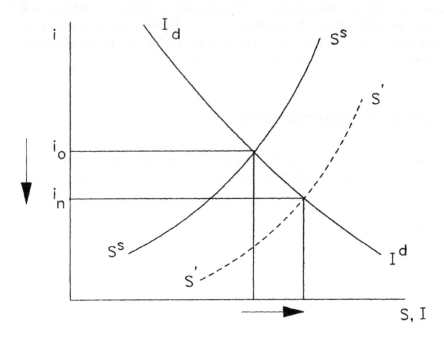

C_f to the dotted line, $C_{f'}$, per figure 7.7) and the new investment project, Ck, suddenly becomes viable, according to business expectations. As Mises states, "If, other things being equal, the supply of capital increases, projects which hitherto could not be undertaken become profitable and are started. There is never a lack of investment opportunities."[41] There are always unlimited investment opportunities; it is only investment funds which are limited. And it is the interest rate—the opportunity cost—which keeps business from doing every project imaginable.

THE TRANSMISSION MECHANISM OF INCREASED SAVINGS

How is this development of new savings reflected in the whole economy, the APS? The genuine, permanent shift in consumption/savings patterns toward a higher level of savings will initially cause a disequilibrium in the economy. Let us consider the step-by-step effects of an autonomous decision by consumers to save and invest more.

Figure 7.6. Time Preference Excludes Profitable Projects

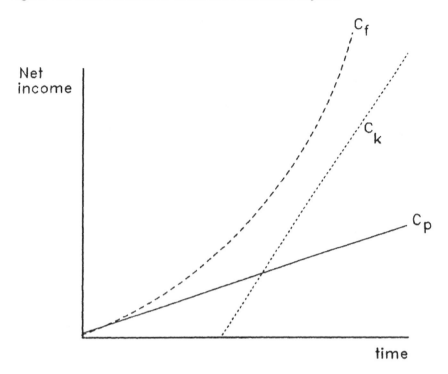

Reduction in Consumer Demand?

First, the aggregate demand vector will change direction if there is an autonomous increase in savings. That is, as discretionary income is redirected, there may be a temporary reduction in the demand for final consumer goods in money terms. (See figure 7.8A.) Many economists have mentioned this possibility. Hayek suggests that the demand for consumer goods declines at first, but that ultimately there results a decline "in still greater proportions" in prices in final consumer goods due to increased production efficiency. In the long run, the consumer is better off in real terms as a result of an increase in savings.[42] Moulton suggests, "For the moment there may have been a decrease in the amount of consumption goods that might have been produced during the hours devoted to the creation of capital; but as a result of the temporary sacrifice an expansion of consumption satisfaction was realized in the future."[43] Röpke says that the reduction in consumer demand is essential when savings rise. It "would have ensured that investment, compensated by a corresponding reduction of consumption, would not

Figure 7.7. Lower Time Preference Makes New Investments Profitable

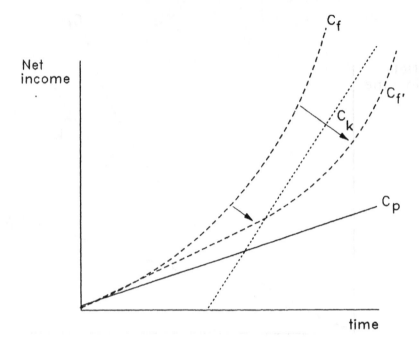

have overstrained the economy and thus led to the well-known consequences of inflationary pressure and balance-of-payments difficulties."[44]

However, for a variety of reasons, it is unlikely that consumer spending will actually decline in absolute terms when savings rates rise. One reason is that, in a dynamic setting, increased savings are likely to occur at a time when incomes are rising. Such a situation would increase the propensity of individuals to save, rather than having to reduce their customary expenditures temporarily, which consumers might be adverse to doing. Even in the case where rising incomes are not a major factor, Hayek suggests that a reduction in the demand for *all* consumer goods is "highly unlikely" and that only a "few kinds of such goods" would be so affected.[45] However, while consumer spending may not decline in absolute terms, it will decline relative to capital-goods output. (See figure 7.8B)

Expansion in Investment

Second, although the increased savings may create a temporary contraction in the final consumer markets, lower interest rates will encourage an expansion

Figure 7.8. Effect of Increased Savings on APS

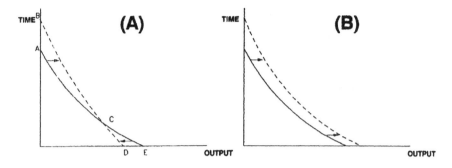

in the producers' goods industries. Prices for capital goods would tend to rise (or not fall as much as before). But the effect would not be uniform, as Hayek notes. The rate of expansion would increase as stages move further from final consumption, with raw materials stages being affected the most. This is due to the "interest-rate effect." In chapter 6 we demonstrated that the ASV is affected directly by changes in interest rates, as well as by changes in technology. A reduction in interest rates benefits most those industries that are furthest removed from the final stages of production. Interest rates have a greater effect on the value of fixed capital and higher-order producers' goods. L. Albert Hahn states that "the demand for fixed capital is much more sensitive with respect to interest rates than the demand for variable capital. Whether credits are available at 3 percent or at 4 percent makes hardly any difference if they are used for wage payments, but a great deal of difference if they are used to buy real estate and build factories."[46] One of the reasons for this interest-rate sensitivity is that most higher-order capital goods (e.g., heavy machinery, trucks, turbines, and so forth) are expensive durable goods and require long-term financing. An increase in the long-term interest costs on a project, say, from 3 percent to 4 percent, can double the total cost of the project.

Myrdal also notes, "The greater the remaining life of the capital goods, the more the capital value increases, since they then represent receipts in the more distant future, discounted at the now lower money rate. The increase of capital values is only an expression of the greater profit possibilities of longer, more roundabout processes of production, which follow immediately from the relatively low money rate of interest."[47]

The net effect of an increased savings rate causes a gradual shift in the aggregate supply vector, as figure 7.8A illustrates.[48]

As the graph 7.8A indicates, the increased savings and lower interest rates affect different intertemporal segments of the economy in varying degrees. As

Wicksell notes, "the technical dimensions and composition of capital" have changed.[49] There is a trade-off between lower and higher order industries, giving the appearance of a "twisting effect." Regarding the industrial sectors closest to the consumer-goods market, Wainhouse comments, "In the stage of production immediately preceding that in which the consumption good is finished, the impact of the decline in the relative price of consumers' goods will be more pronounced than the effect of the increase in invested funds available for producers' goods of every kind. . . . The price of the output from this stage of production will decline, but it will decline less than the price of final consumers' goods."[50] That is to say, the profit margins between stages begin to narrow, a reflection of the fact that interest rates are lower. In addition, specific factors involved in the later stages would be hurt relative to specific factors in earlier stages, and nonspecific factors would tend to shift to the "higher order" industries.

At a certain point somewhere in the middle of the APS, the positive forces of the aggregate supply vector equal the negative forces of the aggregate demand vector, and there is no change in output at that central point (C). Above point C, an expansion of higher-order production takes place. Below point C, there will be a decline in lower-order production. Wainhouse gives an example of the intermediate producer good, specialty steel, which should increase in demand as a result of lower interest rates:

> The rise in the price of the product of any given (producers') stage of production, (i.e., specialty steel), will provide an incentive for increased output in those industries (e.g., machine tools, electricity) which provide input to specialty steel. The products of those stages of production which feed steel will rise in price both due to the general rise in the demand for producers' goods, (as a consequence of the initial autonomous increase in savings), and as a result of the rise in prices in those industries (e.g., coal mining) which in turn supply machine tools and electricity. The rise in prices in basic stages of production (coal mining) will tend to increase the relative profits in machine tools and electricity, reenforcing the incentive to produce the latter. The dynamics of this process will result, via the fall of prices in later consumption stages, (say home appliances), and the rise of prices in earlier stages of production, (say steel, plastics, etc.), in a reduction of price margins throughout the system.[51]

Capital Widening

The increase in capital goods above point C represents capital widening in the economy. Capital widening occurs when more of the same type of capital is used. This is different from capital deepening, which involves the switching to processes involving longer investment periods. For example, capital widening would involve increasing the number of shovels in a project from twenty to one hundred, while capital deepening would involve substituting power-digging equipment, which requires more time to produce, for shovels.[52]

Capital Deepening: Addition of New Stages

As you can see from figure 7.8, the increase in savings lengthens the structure of production, or as some economists put it, deepens it. Wicksell refers to the greater "height" of the APS.[53] Bye and Hewett state, "As production methods have become more roundabout, a greater proportion of our economic resources has been devoted to remote stages. In other words, the vertical structure of industry has been lengthened, and there has been a 'deepening' of investment."[54]

There are several practical aspects to the deepening or lengthening of the APS. First, modernization takes place. Lower interest rates will permit many firms to replace obsolete equipment and methods with technology and automation that are already in existence but which may have been financially prohibitive prior to this time. In this case capital deepening does not involve developing new technologies, but simply means that more companies are able to adopt previously developed technologies. The adoption of already-established "new" technology is a major consequence of permanently lower interest rates.

Second, goods can be made more durable, by adding more stages to the manufacturing process, or by using higher-quality materials. Machlup explains: "This lengthening of the period of maturing can be done in many ways, one of which is the making of goods and instruments of higher durability, another is the making of a greater amount of durable goods and instruments."[55]

Third, inventories are likely to expand. Lower interest rates reduce the cost of waiting, thus permitting longer holding periods for goods in process, durable capital goods, and so on. Inventories expand because the cost of holding stocks of goods has been reduced.

New Stages

Are there practical examples of these "new links into the chain of technical production," as Fetter calls them, which did not exist before the new savings took place?[56] Fetter uses the railroads as an example. "Expensive improvements on railroads . . . [and] . . . the replacement of lighter by heavier rails, have been made possible by a fall in the rate of interest."[57] Fetter says that an increase in traffic was also responsible, but not as much.

Another example of new levels of production is the increase in research and development, the hiring of scientists and design engineers, which may be regarded as the furthest removed from final use. Take the automobile, for example. As profits flourished and new capital poured into this budding industry, car manufacturers gradually added new features, such as a completely enclosed cabin (as opposed to the open touring car), which required many additional stages and greater complexity in the manufacturing process. No doubt an integral part of providing additional features is extensive research and development by the auto manufacturers. Virtually all major industries engage in research and development. When interest rates, especially long-term rates, decline, firms have an additional incentive to engage in R&D with more extensive time horizons. Some research projects involving extremely long investment periods of ten years or more now finally become viable as interest rates and the cost of waiting decline.[58]

The additions of new links into the structural chain are, in essence, technological innovations. Research and development always bring about inventions and advanced changes in goods and services. Shackle notes, "The longer period [of] production allows the deployment of finer, more subtle, complex and specialized technical methods."[59] This consequence of new investments is separate from the increases in the production of durable goods which were already being produced prior to the change in consumption/savings patterns. Lachmann is quite right when he says that the "deepening" of capital formation is an innovative process causing "a complete re-arrangement of the existing productive apparatus, including depreciation of specific factors, and possibly a change in the character of the final product."[60]

Shackle comments on the meaning of the lengthening process:

Lengthening the process of production really consists in rearranging and multiplying the connections between streams of intermediate products and introducing new sections of the "grid," so that a given unit of original resources goes a longer way round, and is embodied in a larger number of different products and stages before it emerges as a consumable good. The purpose of this lengthening is to realise the economies of a higher degree of specialization: typically, special plant and equipment will be created for turning out a single product which before was an "internal" product of a more generalised plant, where its production was carried on with less capital but more labour per unit of output.[61]

According to Peter F. Drucker, the historical evidence is overwhelming that roundaboutness has occurred. "In the first place, it is the essence of economic and technological progress that the time span for the fruition and proving out of a decision is steadily lengthening." He gives several examples: "Edison, in the 1880s, needed two years or so between the start of laboratory work on an idea and the start pilot-plant operations. Today it may well take Edison's successors fifteen years. A half century ago a new plant was expected to pay for itself in two or three years;

today, with capital investment per worker twenty times that of 1900, the payoff period often runs to ten or twelve years. A human organization, such as a sales force or a management group, may take even longer to build and to pay for itself."[62]

A RETURN TO THE BÖHM-BAWERKIAN VISION

Thus, we have come full circle. We began the chapter discussing the effects of technical advancement as a way of achieving economic growth. We noted the Böhm-Bawerkian theory that correctly envisioned how higher productivity could be achieved through a prolonged investment in new methods. Then, assuming no change in technical innovations, we see how an autonomous increase in savings and investment lowers interest rates, expands the capital relative to consumption, and then reignites innovation in new sectors of the capitalistic hierarchy. Again, a new version of Böhm-Bawerk's thesis is proven correct: new longer processes of production (especially in research and development of new products and better techniques) are finally made profitable, thus bringing about a resurgence in technological advancement. As J. R. Hicks correctly observes, the Austrian theory of saving, as espoused by Böhm-Bawerk, Mises, and Hayek, "is a fore-runner of the growth theory of more recent years."[63]

To summarize the transition period of an autonomous increase in the savings rate, *ceteris paribus*, we have the following:

1. Reduction in consumer spending relative to capital expenditures.
2. Increase in savings.
3. Decline in interest rates.
4. Increase in output of producers' goods.
5. Increase in the number of "higher order" stages, especially in research and development and other forms of technological advancement.
6. Tendency of inventories to expand at each stage of production.
7. Increased profits gradually leading to higher wages and rents.[64]
8. Gradual expansion in real consumer spending and an increase in the standard of living.

THE BENEFITS OF INCREASED SAVINGS

In summary, we may say that when the public voluntarily increases savings, it initially *decreases* production for *current* consumption while *increasing* production for *future* consumption. Rothbard concludes, "A lower time-preference rate will be reflected in greater proportions of investment to consumption, a lengthening of the structure of production, and a building-up of capital."[65] Hahn adds: "If the factors of production save part of their income and put it at the disposal of entrepreneurs, purchases of products for more or less rapid consumption are replaced by entrepreneurs' purchases of capital goods or intermediate products. After a transition period . . . this will result in a lengthening of the production detours by adding, as it were, a lengthening piece to all production detours."[66] Franz Wien-Claudi summarizes: "The final result of saving will always be an increase in capital-goods (intermediate products) and an increase in consumption goods. Some time will have to pass, however, until the decline in prices of the finished product will be followed by a proportionate decrease in moneycosts."[67] Such a change in people's savings habits can be "self-perpetuating," as Hayek calls it. He summarizes as follows:

The increased savings activity . . . must soon cause on the one hand a falling off in the demand for consumption goods, and hence a tendency for their prices to fall (a tendency which may merely find expression in decreasing sales at existing prices) and, on the other hand, an increase in the demand for investment goods and thus a rise in their prices. The extension of production will have a further depressing effect on the prices of consumption goods, as the new products come on the market, until, finally, the difference between the respective prices has shrunk to a magnitude corresponding to the new, lower, interest rate.[68]

But it is also important to note that the increase in investment, which lengthens the capital structure, must not be a one-shot decision. In order to preserve the new APS, a constant stream of new savings and investment at the new higher level must be maintained. A temporary increase in savings would not have a permanent effect. Hayek points out, "What is particularly important in this connection, the period is not lengthened only while *new* investment is going on; it will have to be permanently longer if the increased capital is to be maintained, i.e., *total* investment (new and renewed) will have to be constantly greater than before."[69]

In general terms, Moulton concludes: "In short, the formation of capital under a capitalistic system involves a complex and roundabout process: Individuals and business corporations set aside money income for investment; business enterprises float bonds and stocks in exchange for these funds and then labor and materials are employed in the construction of new capital equipment which, it is hoped, may yield profits in the future."[70]

WHAT WOULD CAUSE AN INCREASE IN THE SAVING RATE?

But increased savings by individuals and businesses seldom occur in a vacuum. It is conceivable that a wave of public enthusiasm spawned by a nationwide government sectarian revival of old-fashioned thrift could increase the average savings rate in the nation without any specific goal in mind but, while such a campaign would be financially beneficial in most circumstances in the long run, it is unlikely to occur on a regular basis.[71]

Nevertheless, a compulsory government saving policy is probably not necessary. As Friedman states, "The important thing is that what is needed to encourage saving and investment is not a policy of increasing saving through compulsion but a policy of giving individuals an opportunity to use their own resources in a way that will promote their own objectives. Not only can development occur without a deliberate governmental policy of increased savings, so far as I know development has never in any free country been produced or accompanied by such a policy."[72]

The most likely circumstances favoring increased national savings during peacetime would be the prospects of new "windows of opportunity" in the business world. New investment opportunities might come from a universally applicable technological breakthrough, such as we saw with the advent of personal and business computers; the opening of new foreign markets, due in part to a reduction in trade barriers; or it could come from a sharp reduction in tax rates. Such a favorable turn of events would enhance both consumer and business savings. The saver might increase his stock market holdings in expectation of higher capital gains in a rising market. Small businessmen, sensing new opportunities, would undoubtedly cut spendthrift plans to the bone in order to use every resource possible to invest in this new enterprise. Corporations would find new ways to raise funds for the same purpose.

Economists have had difficulty in separating which comes first, economic growth or increased savings: Modigliani, for example, concludes that the evidence supports the thesis that higher economic growth leads to higher savings rates, not the other way around. "Between countries with identical individual behavior, the aggregate saving rate will be higher the higher the long-run growth rate of the economy. . . . By now it is generally accepted that growth is a major source of cross-country differences in the saving rate."[73] Other economists argue that economic growth is the result of increased savings, especially if the government exempts investment from taxation. Increased savings may be induced by lower tax rates or expectations of a higher investment return, but ultimately the entrepreneur must increase his savings (capital) *first* before productivity can be advanced. Friedman states that people are "induced by the prospect of a high return on their investment to save and invest."[74]

Under most circumstances, assuming no change in the tax structure, people and businesses do not increase their net savings until a financial goal is clearly evident. A profitable enterprise is discovered, and expectations of higher returns prompt an increase in savings. L. Albert Hahn comes to the conclusion, that the only way to increase the overall savings rate in a community is "through increased work or increased productivity of labor."[75] But the relationship between savings and return on investment must be closely linked. Postwar Japan is a classic example of economic growth and higher savings rates that are linked together. The opportunistic Japanese saw how they could take advantage of their cheap labor to produce inexpensive products for foreign markets, especially the United States. As tax-free profits increased, the Japanese boosted their savings materially in order to increase production and expand their markets. It was not simply in response to a Keynesian mindset, i.e., where increased income led to a higher propensity to save.[76] In many countries, such as the United States, where economic growth has not been so spectacular and where the "consumer society" is the primary motivation, there is no indication of increased propensity to save—in fact, it appears to be just the opposite. As Hahn states, "A sort of inverse psychological law seems to induce at least Americans of today to spend more of the present, once a certain provision for the future has been secured."[77]

Historically, there appears to be a direct correlation between economic growth and savings rates over time. Research by Franco Modigliani and others indicates a strong correlation between savings rates and economic growth rates in cross-country comparisons. Figure 7.9 shows the remarkable results.

KEYNES AND THE "PARADOX OF THRIFT"

The Keynesian revolution in economic theory, which began in earnest in the 1930s, dramatically reversed the positive approach most economists and government leaders had taken toward savings and thrift. Although a strand of anti-savings thought has existed throughout the history of economics (Mandeville, Hobson, Marx, Veblen, Foster and Catchings, et al.), it did not become the mainstream way of thinking in academic and government circles until after the Great Depression.

Keynes's attack on the long-standing virtue of thrift came during the depths of the Great Depression in the 1930s. Fear and uncertainty gripped many investors as well as directors of financial institutions. There appeared to be a dearth of investment opportunities. Many banks held "excess reserves" while savers allegedly turned into "hoarders." Keynes and his followers lashed out at the hoarders and thrifty consumers. In his *Treatise on Money*, published in 1930, Keynes suggests that savings could be "aborted" when not invested, resulting in depression.[78] He said that the interest rate was not an "automatic mechanism"

Figure 7.9. Historical Relationship between Savings and Economic Growth

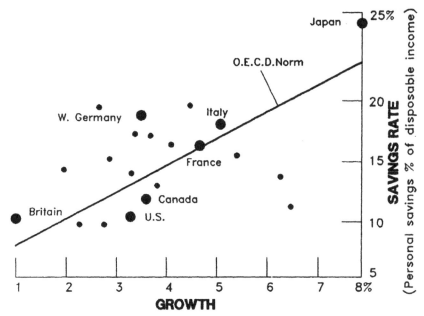

(Compound annual growth in per capita disposable income)

Source: Modigliani, "Life Cycle, Individual Thrift, and the Wealth of Nations," 303. © The Nobel Foundation 1985.

that could keep the rate of savings and the rate of investment equal—they can "get out of gear."[79] Responding to traditional views that increased savings during the depression would help employment, Keynes made a radio broadcast in January 1931, suggesting that increased savings under the circumstances can only cause a "vicious circle" of poverty. "For the object of saving is to release labour for employment on producing capital-goods such as houses, factories, roads, machines, and the like. But if there is a large unemployed surplus already available for such purposes, then the effect of saving is merely to add to this surplus and therefore to increase the number of unemployed."[80] The British economist bluntly told his audience that if "you save five shillings, you put a man out of work for a day." He encouraged housewives to go out on a buying spree to stimulate the economy, and government to engage in massive public works. He seriously suggested, "why not pull down the whole of South London from Westminister to Greenwich, and make a good job of it. . . . Would that employ men? Why, of course it would!"[81]

By 1936, he referred to traditional views of savings as "absurd." He boldly wrote, "The more virtuous we are, the more determined by thrift, the more obstinately orthodox in our national and personal finance, the more our incomes will fall when interest rises relatively to the marginal efficiency of capital."[82] He went on to suggest, "Pyramid-building, earthquakes, even wars may serve to increase wealth."[83] Thus virtue becomes vice in the Keynesian world, and tragedy becomes hope.

Concerning Keynes' anti-savings mentality, B. M. Anderson states, "Where economists generally have held that saving and avoiding unnecessary debt and paying off debt where possible are good things, Keynes holds that they are bad things. He deprecates depreciation reserves for business corporations. He deprecates amortization of public debt by municipalities. He deprecates additions to corporate surpluses out of earnings."[84]

Keynes's views on savings, consumption, and government spending, while initially considered reactionary, were gradually adopted by the academic world after World War II. Mainstream economists, especially Alvin Hansen and his student Paul Samuelson, led the way. Keynes's anti-savings sentiments became imbedded in the "neo-Keynesian" theory of aggregate demand, and could even be expressed graphically and mathematically in Samuelson's development of the "Keynesian cross." The "paradox of thrift" doctrine, as it has come to be known, is still an integral part of the "neoclassical synthesis" and is included in most of the current introductory economics texts.[85] While the anti-savings concept is no longer given the universal blessing it enjoyed during the 1940s and 1950s, it is still considered applicable whenever there is less than full employment. And since it is hard to conceive of a time when is there are not unemployed resources, the anti-thrift attitude has prevailed, at least on a theoretical level, by most orthodox economists.

AN ANALYSIS OF THE "PARADOX OF THRIFT"

According to the "crude" Keynesian theory of aggregate demand, an increase in savings reflects a reduction in consumer spending. This in turn reduces the demand for investment or capital goods, which are used to produce consumer goods. The decline in investment demand forces a reduction in wages and salaries paid to workers and other factors of production. As a result, workers and capitalists have less income, and therefore must reduce spending as well as savings. Hence, by this reasoning, an increase in savings ultimately results in a decline in savings: The paradox of thrift!

To this day, most conventional economists accept this paradox in one form or another and conclude that consumer spending is always good for the economy and increased savings can often, especially during an economic slowdown, be deleterious. Economists admit that such a policy of "more spending, less saving" would be disastrous on a personal level, leading to bankruptcy, but they often justify their anti-saving theory by invoking the "fallacy of composition": That which is good for the individual may not be good for the country. For example, if one farmer increases his wheat crop, his revenue will increase; but if all farmers increase their output, the price of wheat drops and no one is better off. It is the same with savings, they say. If one person saves more, he is better off; but if everyone does it, it could hurt the whole economy. "Under some circumstances, private prudence may be social folly."[86] To demonstrate the "paradox of thrift" in the simple Keynesian theoretical framework, Samuelson uses the following graph (figure 7.10).

Samuelson titles this graph, "Savings-and-investment diagram shows how thriftiness can kill off income." He explains: "In an underemployed economy,

Figure 7.10. Samuelson's "Paradox of Thrift"

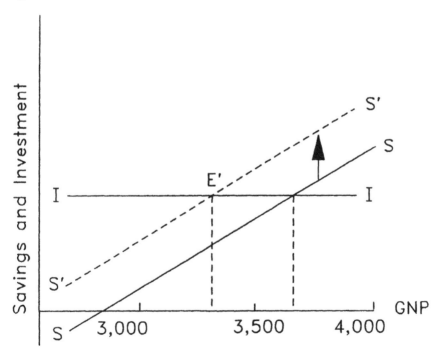

Source: Samuelson and Nordhaus, *Economics,* 171.

desire to consume less at every income level will shift the savings schedule upward. With the II curve unchanged, equilibrium drops to the E' intersection. Why? Because income has to fall-and fall in a *multiplied* way—until people feel poor enough so that they again want to save the amount of planned investment at II."[87]

Samuelson "resolves" the paradox by suggesting that the only case when thrift is a virtue is during full employment—when "output could be assumed to be always at its potential."[88] Today the vast majority of economists apparently agree that increased savings would be bad during a serious recession or depression.

Actually, however, the paradox of thrift is a fallacious doctrine based on an oversimplified construction of the aggregate structure of the economy by neoclassical theorists. And it is not just the Keynesian economists who make this fatal mistake in macroeconomic theory. The monetarists have never, to my knowledge, attempted to resolve the Keynesian paradox of thrift directly. Their rejection of the paradox is based on Friedman's "natural rate of unemployment" hypothesis, which is designed to show that the economy is almost always at full employment. Therefore, the paradox of thrift is resolved by defaulting to the Keynesian full employment case. This resolution of the problem once again points to the similarities between the monetarists and Keynesians.[89]

It appears that the basis for the neoclassical (Keynesian and monetarist) theory of consumption and investment is an overly simplified construction of the APS which does not take into account the time factor. The neoclassical construct might look like figure 7.11 below.

As we can see, this macro view divides the economy into only two stages: investment goods and consumer goods. If we adopt this timeless holistic view of the economy, then it quickly follows that a shift in consumer demand should shift investment production in the same direction, rather than the opposite direction, as demonstrated in figure 7.12. This is consistent with the Keynesian multiplier and accelerator principles, which argue that a rise in consumer spending stimulates investment in a multiple way. (Figure 7.12 indicates how the value added to investment is larger than the value added to consumption.) It is also consistent with the Keynesian monetarist view that an inflationary expansion, through fiscal and monetary policy, would expand both the investment and consumption sectors of the economy.

Conversely, when saving increases and consumer spending declines (the paradox of thrift case), investment also declines, as figure 7.13 demonstrates. Moreover, this graph shows the effects Keynesians expect when the government adopts a deflationary fiscal and monetary policy (surplus budget and contraction of the money supply).

Figure 7.11. Neoclassical View of the Aggregate Production Structure

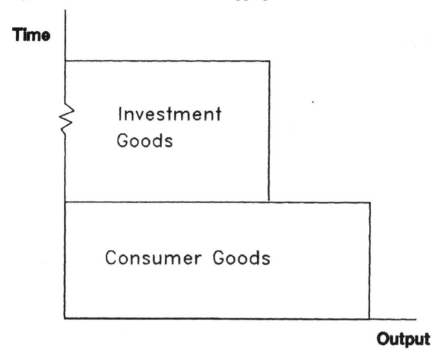

Figure 7.12. Effect of Increased Consumer Spending under the Simple Keynesian Model

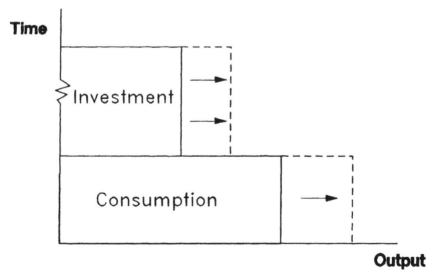

Figure 7.13. Effects of Decreased Consumer Spending (Higher Savings) under the Simple Keynesian Model

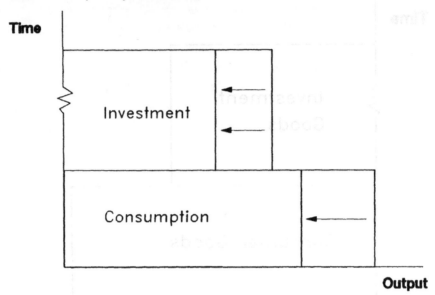

Samuelson appears to support this simplified two-stage setup when he states, "High consumption and high investment are then hand in hand rather than opposed to each other."[90] Keynes argues the same thing: "An increased propensity to save will *ceteris paribus* contract incomes and output; whilst an increased inducement to invest will expand them."[91] Hayek concludes that this two-stage view (or, as he calls it, "single-stage production") is the basis for Foster's and Catchings' anti-savings schemes.[92] Durbin suggests that this is the view of all "underconsumptionists":

> Saving is a peculiarly dangerous and self-defeating process, for it withdraws money from the purchase of finished commodities and makes their production less profitable, while at the same time it seeks to set up still further capital resources with which the production of finished commodities is to be increased. It is this paradoxical process which makes a deficiency of purchasing power inevitable. It increases the supply and diminishes the demand for the products of the industrial system to the point at which production cannot be continued any longer with profit and at that point crisis and depression begins. Hence depression can always be prevented and relieved either by reducing the amount of saving or by stimulating consumption by the issue of new money.[93]

The monetarists, who also endorse a two-sector model of the economy, may not disagree much with the Keynesian theoretical framework; but their policy

240   THE STRUCTURE OF PRODUCTION

recommendations differ.[94] While the Keynesians stress fiscal policy as a way to stimulate aggregate demand in a recession or depression, the monetarists stress monetary policy, or the creation of new money, as a way to get the country out of a slump. Both are demand-oriented, and tend to ignore the supply side.

THE SOURCE OF THE FALLACY

Unfortunately, the paradox of thrift doctrine is a prime example of how "macro" economics can obscure the real events that occur in the economy when the consumption/savings pattern shifts. The Keynesian-monetarist monolithic approach ignores the multi-stage architecture of "higher-order" capital goods, "lower-order" intermediate goods, and the multitude of stages throughout the whole intertemporal conveyor belt. It neglects the critical time element in the production process. Even a division into three or four stages would resolve the paradox of thrift dilemma. In fact, the neoclassical theorists could maintain their two-story structure if they would allow the second stage "investment" sector to become a higher, but narrower, building. The investment building should also grow more in height than it has lost at the base, signifying that total investment has increased (see figure 7.14). But since they disregard varying production periods altogether, they do not envision an investment sector that could be more remote from consumption. Structural change is not even considered in their model of the whole economy. The essential flaw in the Keynesian macroeconomic model is that aggregate demand refers only to *final* aggregate demand and ignores the *intermediate* aggregate stages necessary to produce final demand.

Another possibility for using the standard neoclassical model is to show an upward shift in the investment schedule as the interest rate declines. But, unfortunately, the crude Keynesian model assumes an unchanging interest rate.

The standard two-dimensional vision of a timeless, structureless economy that pervades modern macroeconomic theory can be traced back to Clark-Knight's static concept of capital (see chapters 2 and 3) and contains a fatal error. It is a critical mistake to view the capital markets as an aggregate fund without examining the time it takes to produce the fund. Macroeconomists are unable to visualize how resources are reallocated as a result of changes in the consumption/savings patterns because of what Boulding calls the "fallacy of aggregation."[95] This fundamental error occurred when the economics profession accepted the "macro" fundist orthodoxy of Clark and Knight over the "micro" heterogeneous approach of the Austrian-Swedish school in capital theory. Lutz

Figure 7.14. Effect of Increased Savings in the Neoclassical Model with Time Structure (A) and with a Lower Interest Rate (B)

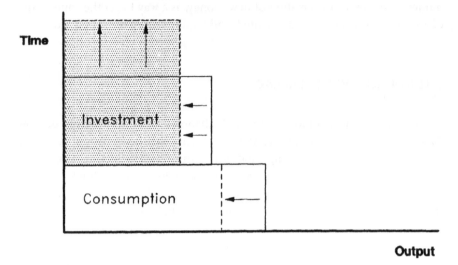

makes a clear comparison between the two schools, characterizing the Austrian-Swedish approach, as adopted by Menger, Hayek, and Lindahl, among others, as a system in which "[i]nvestments in each period are identified with those inputs which are directed toward the production of consumption goods that will ripen out at various times in the future, the length of these investment periods being subject to the choice of the investors. . . . This is clearly a different world from that of some of the aggregate models, where relative prices play no role and where investments are considered as an undifferentiated mass of capital goods added to the existing stock, a mass which will bring forth more or less output according to the magnitude of the capital-output ratio."[96]

Lachmann is also critical of the Clark-Knight concept of capital, which is homogeneous and perfectly substitutable. In reality, however, "we should expect individual capital instruments to be substitutes for some, and complements to some other instruments." Hence, capital goods are "heterogeneous."[97]

A MORE REALISTIC VIEW OF SAVING

The effect of increased savings on the economy is actually quite different from the superficial view held by the Keynesians and other underconsumptionists.

Taken to its extreme, the Keynesian conclusions are absurd. As Böhm-Bawerk answers, "If every attempt to curtail consumption must actually result in an immediate and proportionate curtailment of production, then indeed no addition to the accumulated wealth of society could ever result from savings."[98]

The Keynesian analysis is only correct in the first phase of the paradox of thrift story. An increase in savings may have a short-term depressant effect on the consumer goods industry. But the decline should only be temporary, and may not occur at all if the increase in savings is endogenous, occurring as a result of recent economic growth. Now the extreme Keynesians, still thinking in terms of savings as a "leakage" out of the economic system, overlook the beneficial effect the increased pool of investment funds will have on the economy, as increased savings are invested in the capital markets through banks and other financial intermediaries. As Böhm-Bawerk says, "There will not, however, be a smaller production of goods generally, because the lessened output of goods ready for immediate consumption may and will be offset by an increased production of 'intermediate' or capital goods."[99] Thus, savings are just as much "spending" as consumption is, in the sense that they go toward the production of goods and services, and eventually are paid out to factors of production in the form of wages, salaries, rent, profits, and interest. The only difference is in the type of spending. Savings is spent on investment goods, primarily higher-order capital goods.

Moreover, as we have shown, increased savings will have a far more beneficial impact on the standard of living than regular consumer spending. As the new capital works through the economic system, new investment projects and new income are created. The result is a higher degree of productivity—meaning higher wages and lower prices for practically everyone. Exogenous increases in consumer spending, especially by government deficit spending, cannot accomplish this goal.

The most difficult aspect of the savings/consumption controversy is to explain how there can be a rise in the demand for capital goods concurrent with a decline or a slowdown in consumer spending, since "consumption . . . is the sole end and object of all economic activity."[100]

Pro-savings advocates such as Hayek and Rothbard are well-aware of this dilemma. Hayek says in a footnote that "many people find it so difficult to understand how a general decrease in the demand for consumers' goods should lead to an increase in investment."[101]

To explain this dilemma, let us refer to Rothbard's model used in chapter 6 (see figure 6.1). In the case below, following Rothbard's assumption of increased saving, the APS shifts away from final consumption and toward greater investment.

See figure 7.15. In this diagram, net savings/investment goes from zero to twenty, while consumption falls from one hundred to eighty. That is, the volume of money income directed to capitalists involved in the final stage, the consumer-goods industries, drops from one hundred to eighty because the aggregate demand vector has shifted—final consumer demand has declined.

At the next level, the money income to capitalists in stage two (directly above the consumer goods level) also declines, but by a smaller percentage. The reason is that there is *another force* working in the other direction from aggregate demand—the aggregate supply vector. In this case, the *cost* of producing stage two goods has declined slightly because interest rates have fallen. We noted previously that interest costs are not as significant a factor in the final level of consumption. But the further removed from final use, the more significant the savings in the cost of interest become, especially with regard to inventory costs. By stage three, the decline in demand is neglegible, and by stage four, the "interest rate effect" in the ASV exceeds the "final demand effect" in the ADV, so that output in stage four increases slightly. With each higher level, the expansion is greater. Also note that two stages are added, so that there are now eight levels in

Figure 7.15. The Impact of Net Savings

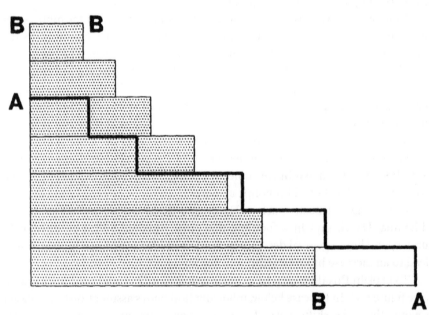

Source: Rothbard, *Man, Economy and State*, 472

the aggregate hierarchy. Overall the ratio of gross investment to consumption has widened—from 318:100 to 338:80. The decline in interest rate has forced a reduction in price margins between stages. Prices in the lower-order industries have declined, while prices in the higher-order industries have increased. The net effect long term is a substantial increase in the standard of living. The end result is a new structure of production, based on two forces working against each other.

In short, the neo-Keynesians focus their macro analysis solely on one level, the final demand sector, while neglecting the all-important time and interest rate factor which affects the capital-goods hierarchy. This is why Keynesian economics is correctly identified as short-term demand economics as well as "depression" economics. In a severe depression, Keynesians foresee interest rates at extremely low levels and unlikely to fall any further.

Keynes believed that the interest rate was a minor determinant of investment compared to the expected profitability of investment. The increased savings is, in the Keynesian model, merely a residual of the decreased consumption, the crucial factor in an economic recession/depression. Expected business profitability is a function of expected demand. With current consumption falling for final goods, derived demand for all factors of production, including capital goods at earlier stages of production, will fall as well. The interest rate, according to Keynesians, has a trivial effect on investment relative to expected demand, particularly during a recession/depression. They ask, "Why would a businessman invest in a new plant just because interest rates are falling if demand for his product is falling too?"

The answer is, of course, that in a recession or depression he probably would not build a new plant. He would rely on his old plant, repair his equipment, retrench and cut costs. He may even shut down his business, and go into some other sector of the economy that is doing better (e.g., food industry and other traditionally defensive markets). In short, it is not *price* (or demand) alone that determines profitability, but *costs* (or supply) as well, i.e., the difference between price and cost. Many firms have survived a recession or depression by cutting costs and living off accrued savings.

But in the case we have been discussing, which involves normal business conditions, interest rates can decline *without* a reduction in demand for higher-order goods. If demand for his product remains high, a lower interest rate may make the difference in deciding to build a new plant.

SAVINGS, HOARDING, AND THE 1930s DEPRESSION

But this raises the query: Are Keynes and his followers correct in stating that the interest rate effect becomes less and less important as the economy moves away from full employment, and in fact, is negligible during a full-scale depression? In such cases, would not an increase in savings have a negative impact on the economy?

In the main, the neo-Keynesian analysis is wrongheaded, even in the case of a full-scale depression. There are several reasons. First, unemployment of resources and labor always exists to some extent in a dynamic economy as factors search out their most efficient alternatives. Changes in interest rates always have an effect on the structure of production, whether there are unemployed resources or not. This is because, as Hayek notes, "the alternative always exists of investing the available productive resources for a longer or shorter period of time."[102] Unemployed resources may make the economy less responsive to interstage competition, but the competition cannot be eliminated. During a recession, for example, higher-order industries may be facing losses of 10 percent annually on average, while consumer-goods markets may be breaking even. Because they are relatively more profitable, there will be a tendency to shift surplus resources from the higher-order sector to the lower-order. In fact, the only condition that would lead to a nonchanging economy would be the highly unlikely scenario where there are *no* changes in *relative* prices between goods. During a depression, such a static economy would require that all prices fall by the same percentage at the same time, which is contrary to all historical data.

Let us take the case of the 1930s Great Depression, certainly the most difficult historical example to make a case for saving. At a time when businessmen are desperate for customers, does it make any sense to encourage individuals to retrench, get out of debt, build a strong cash position, and engage in all the defensive measures traditionally recommended during hard times? While retrenchment may make sense individually, is such action socially beneficial? Today most economists would say, "No." Their recommendation would probably be to stave off bankruptcies by encouraging consumer and government spending, and expanding the money supply. Nevertheless, it is my intention to show that individual savings is a sensible action to take at all times, even during periods of economic depression.

To understand why, other things being equal, an increase in savings during a slump is beneficial, we must first recognize what happens during a depression. In almost all economic downturns, the greatest reductions in economic activity, as measured by the volume of trade, employment, and prices, occur in the higher-order capital goods industries such as raw materials, mining, and manufacturing, rather than the lower-order consumer industries, such as retail, clothing, food, entertainment, and services. A depression is never universal in nature. All prices may decline in an economic contraction, but the average price index of some industries will drop more than others. During 1929–33, the capital markets were hit much harder than were the consumer industries. Personal consumption expenditures declined from $77 billion to $46 billion, a 40 percent reduction. Meanwhile, capital investments declined more steeply, from $16 billion to $1.4 billion, a collapse of over 90 percent.[103]

Given this environment, suppose consumers decide at the depths of the depression to retrench and increase their savings relative to consumption. Suppose that these savings are invested in the economy via banks, brokers, and other traditional avenues. (Here we are talking about genuine savings which are invested, not hoarded.) What would be the initial impact? Clearly, such savings would provide a certain degree of liquidity to these depressed industries. It would reverse the *relative* trend of failing capital markets and rising consumer markets. The depression is characterized by a "glut" in the producer-goods market, or the demand for capital goods, which suggests insufficient savings. In short, increased savings/investments would seek to end the depression, and allow countries to start on the road to recovery. Even though the consumer markets might suffer slightly because of consumer retrenchment, the overall effect would be positive, since, as we have noted earlier in chapter 6, the capital-goods industries are substantially larger than the consumer-goods markets.[104]

What about the alleged problem of hoarding in the 1930s, which served as the basis of Keynes' theory of liquidity preference? Isn't increased savings bad for the economy if the funds are held in cash ("hoardings") and not invested? Not at all. Hoarding may, in fact, be a sensible short-term decision by individuals to increase their demand for cash based on a legitimate fear of a banking crisis and expectations of lower prices in the future. Hoarding in sufficient numbers will actually bring about the collapse in the banking system, but this should not be a criticism of hoarding per se, but of the defective fractional reserve banking system and the government's harmful economic policies. Unstable banking and government actions led to increasing uncertainty and panic by the public. In this context, the temporary move toward hoarding by individuals and excess reserves by the banks was an eminently sensible act of self-preservation during an uncertain monetary climate based on fractional-reserve banking, monetary inflation by the central banks, and major nations departing from the gold standard. If banks had been operating on a sound monetary program instead of an inflationary fractional reserve system, the banking system would not have failed and the money supply would not have shrunk by a third. If citizens had maintained their faith in the U.S. monetary system, the 1930–31 recession would not have turned into a full-scale depression. The problems that resulted from hoarding, excess bank reserves, and other destabilizing effects would have been minimized.

In any case, hoarding and idle bank reserves would not have lasted forever. At some point, individual boarders would have recognized that prices have probably dropped enough, and would start buying products again, just as investors start buying stocks again when they think the market has dropped long enough. It is precisely at this time that the economy turns around.

It should be pointed out that the United States government committed a number of blunders that prolonged the depression into a decade of stagnation— artificially propping up certain hard-hit industries (such as farming), encouraging industries to maintain relatively high wages, raising taxes, imposing exorbitant tariffs, and adopting an unsound quasi-gold standard which applied only internationally. On the other hand, if it had lowered tax rates, cut tariffs, allowed all industries to liquidate bad investments, encouraged wages to fall to market levels, and adopted a genuine gold standard both domestically and abroad, citizens would have responded, savings would have been invested in the hard-hit capital markets, and bank reserves would have returned to normalcy. In short, a lengthy plunge into the economic abyss could have been avoided in the 1930s. Blaming the depression on savers who hoarded their money is like blaming a fire in a theater on the people in the audience who are trying to escape.

Moreover, if the government had adopted these free market measures, the level of unemployment would not have been as severe or prolonged. W. H. Hutt, in his pathbreaking work, *The Theory of Idle Resources*, makes the case that the only reason for resources and labor to be unemployed for extensive periods is that the resource-owners are asking too high a price for their services. In the short run, factors of production may be idle because they are specifically suited toward one particular industry, and cannot be transferred to another market without involving high mobility costs. But eventually the price of withheld resources must drop if they are to be reemployed in an efficient manner. The only cause of permanent unemployment would be government-outlawed employment by minimum wage laws, subsidized unemployment through welfare payments, unemployment compensation, and so forth.[105]

SHORT-TERM ADJUSTMENTS DUE TO THRIFT

We have concluded that an increase in savings is beneficial to the economy, even during times of unemployed resources. An autonomous increase in the savings rate should not cause a significant disturbance to the economic system. As Estey notes, the adjustments in vertical production due to thrift should not be any more difficult than horizontal adjustments due to technological competition.[106] Böhm-Bawerk argues that entrepreneurs may have difficulty in knowing in advance what kind of consumer goods will be demanded in the future, but such a situation is "not at all serious" and capitalists will do their best to "anticipate" the demand "in advance." That is the role in essence of the marketing department and the entrepreneur. "Its knowledge of the amount, the time and the direction of the demand for consumption goods does not rest on positive information, but can only be acquired by a process of testing, guessing or experimenting." Entrepreneurs would have to draw "inferences for the future from the experiences of the past." Mistakes may occur, but readjustments can be readily introduced because of the "great mobility" of capital goods.[107] Durbin, on the other hand, is quite skeptical. Following Keynesian thinking, he argues that an increase in the savings rate can cause a "temporary, general depression" if investment falls or fails to rise as much as the savings rate.[108] However, returning again to the fact that the capital markets are significantly larger than the consumer-goods industry, the impact of increased savings and reduced interest rates should be beneficial overall, despite interim adjustments.

In sum, it is time we unyoked the Keynesian cross, and reenthroned the virtue of thrift as a forerunner of economic growth and technological advancement.

NOTES

1. Modigliani, "Life Cycle, Individual Thrift, and the Wealth of Nations," 297.
2. Wieser, *Social Economics*, 72.
3. Shackle, *Epistemics and Economics*, 322.
4. Cassel, *The Nature and Necessity of Interest*, 125–26.
5. Horace White, "Böhm-Bawerk on Capital," *Political Science Quarterly* 8:144.
6. Taussig, *Wages and Capital*, 9.
7. Ibid., 10.
8. Black, *Introduction to Production Economics*, 33–34. Hayek states, "By lengthening the production process we are able to obtain a greater quantity of consumers' goods out of a given quantity of original means of production." *Prices and Production*, 38.
9. Brown, *Economic Science and the Common Welfare*, 274–75.
10. Machlup, "Professor Knight and the 'Period of Production,'" 614.
11. Ibid., 615.
12. Ibid. 614. Machlup may not be correct on this point. Böhm-Bawerk did respond to the sewing machine example: "for instance, a tailor takes three days to sew a coat by hand, and one day to do it with a sewing-machine. For it is clear that the machine sewing forms only one part, and indeed the smaller part, of the capitalistic process; the principal part falls to the making of the sewing-machine, and the total process lasts considerably longer than three days." Böhm-Bawerk, *The Positive Theory of Capital* (Smart translation), 84.

13. Rothbard, *Man, Economy and State,* 486, 487. Garrison also adds: "Of course, the notion that it is the length or roundaboutness *per se* that makes a process physically efficient is absurd." Garrison, "The Austrian-Neoclassical Relation," 154.

14. Haavelmo, *A Study in the Theory of Investment,* 40.

15. Keirstead, *Capital, Interest and Profits,* 21. In a similar vein, Mises states: "For capital is of course always invested in the shortest available roundabout processes of production, because they yield the greatest returns. It is only when all the short roundabout processes of production have been appropriated that capital is employed in the longer ones." Mises, *The Theory of Money and Credit,* 361.

16. Böhm-Bawerk, *Capital and Interest,* vol. 2, *Positive Theory of Capital,* 12.

17. See Fink, "Economic Growth and Market Processes," 375–76.

18. Bain, *Pricing, Distribution and Employment,* 580.

19. Uhr, *Economic Doctrines of Knut Wicksell,* 112.

20. Rae, *The American Automobile,* 48.

21. For a summary of the technological advances brought about by the automobile revolution, see Rae, *The American Automobile,* 1–104.

22. Ibid., 62.

23. Galbraith, *The New Industrial State,* 11, 14.

24. Hughes, *The Vital Few,* 336.

25. Moffat and Christenson, et al. *Economics: Principles and Problems,* 30.

26. Böhm-Bawerk, "The Function of Savings," 69. Böhm-Bawerk usually envisioned new savings leading to greater capital efficiency, not vice versa.

27. Rae, *The American Automobile,* 63.

28. Böhm-Bawerk, "The Positive Theory of Capital and Its Critics III," 133.

29. Böhm-Bawerk, *The Positive Theory of Capital,* 260.

30. Schumpeter, *The Theory of Economic Development.*

31. Fetter, *Capital, Interest, and Rent,* 89–91.

32. Bliss, *Capital Theory and the Distribution of Income,* 85.

33. Mises, "Capital Supply and American Prosperity," *Planning for Freedom,* 4th ed., 197. Mises also states dramatically, "Every step forward on the way toward prosperity is the effect of saving." *The Anti-Capitalist Mentality* (Spring Mills, Pa.: Libertarian Press, 1981), 39. Similarly, Alderfer and Michl add, "The single most important cause of technological progress and its most spectacular manifestation is the increasing use of capital in the form of plant and equipment." Alderfer and Michl, *Economics of American Industry,* 669–70.

34. Rothbard, *Man, Economy and State,* 490. However, this is not to say that an increase in capital will solve all the economic problems of less developed countries. Capital must fit within the economy's complex structure. As Bauer and Yamey state, "Merely to supply a backward country with capital funds or with supplies of the most modern equipment will not ensure economic development even if the capital is given away. . . . Indeed, it is not unlikely that inexperience, lack of training and acquired skills in the population and inappropriate social and economic institutions curb the economic

development of backward countries more effectively than lack of physical capital assets." (Bauer and Yamey, *The Economics of Under-developed Countries,* 127,129.)

35. Ibid., 491.
36. Peterson, *Economics,* 138.
37. Mises, *The Theory of Money and Credit,* 361.
38. Shackle, "Some Notes on Monetary Theories of the Trade Cycle," 35.
39. I. Fisher, *The Rate of Interest,* 131.
40. Rothbard, *Man, Economy and State,* 488.
41. Mises, *Planning for Freedom,* 211.
42. Hayek, *Prices and Production,* 50–54. Hayek assumes no change in the money supply. Elsewhere, Hayek suggests, "The first effect will be that *less* consumers' goods are sold at existing prices. This does not mean that their prices must fall. . . . Actually, the first effect will probably be that the sellers of consumers' goods, being unable to retail as much as before at existing prices, will, rather than sell at a loss, decide to increase temporarily their holdings of these goods and to slow down the process of production." Hayek, "Reflections on the Pure Theory of Money of Mr. J. M. Keynes (continued)," 27–28. Cf. Hayek, *Monetary Theory and the Trade Cycle,* 216–17.
43. Moulton, *The Formation of Capital,* 11.
44. Röpke, *Against the Tide,* 157. Röpke's comment implies boom conditions, which may not be the case.
45. Hayek, *Prices and Production,* 50n.
46. L. A. Hahn, *Common Sense Economics,* 49.
47. Myrdal, *Monetary Equilibrium,* 25–26. Myrdal's comment is in reference to a credit expansion, but the same principle applies to a genuine increase in savings.
48. Economists who have used similar illustrations showing how changes in the saving rate alter the APS include: Hayek, *Prices and Production,* 56 (known as Hayek's triangles); Lundberg, *Studies in the Theory of Economic Expansion,* 91; Uhr, *Economic Doctrines of Knut Wicksell,* 98–99; Rothbard, *Man, Economy and State,* 472; Garrison, "Austrian Macroeconomics: A Diagrammatical Exposition," 183; and Blaug, *Economic Theory in Retrospect,* 553.
49. Wicksell, *Lectures on Political Economy,* vol. 1, 202.
50. Wainhouse, *Hayek's Theory of the Trade Cycle,* 21.
51. Ibid.
52. Baumol, *Economic Theory and Operations Analysis,* 641.
53. "As the growth of real capital, other factors constant, reduces the rate of interest, this induces expansion preponderantly in the 'height' dimension." Uhr, *Economic Doctrines of Knut Wicksell,* 135.
54. Bye and Hewett, *The Economic Process,* 2d ed., 56.
55. Machlup, "Professor Knight and the 'Period of Production,'" 594–95.
56. Fetter, *The Principles of Economics,* 168.
57. Ibid.
58. For a discussion of the economics of research and development as it applies to the pharmaceutical industry, see Clarkson, *Intangible Capital and Rates of Return,* 41–57.

59. Shackle, *Epistemics and Economics*, 313.

60. Lachmann, *Capital, Expectations and the Market Process*, 272.

61. Shackle, "Some Notes on Monetary Theories of the Trade Cycle," 34–35.

62. Peter F. Drucker, *Management: Tasks, Responsibilities, Practices* (New York: Harper and Row, 1985), 44.

63. Hicks, "The Hayek Story," 211.

64. Rothbard, *Man, Economy and State*, 482.

65. Rothbard, *America's Great Depression*, 17.

66. Hahn, *Common Sense Economics*, 83.

67. Wien-Claudi, *Austrian Theories of Capital, Interest, and the Trade Cycle*, 153.

68. Hayek, *Monetary Theory and the Trade Cycle*, 214, 216–17.

69. Hayek, "Reflections on the Pure Theory of Money of Mr. J. M. Keynes (continued)," 43.

70. Moulton, *Formation of Capital*, 15.

71. According to research by Simon Kuznets in 1946, the savings ratio in the United States has remained relatively unchanged since the middle of the nineteenth century, despite the large rise in per capita income. This finding did much to demolish the Keynes-Hansen "stagnation thesis" that oversavings played a major role in the Great Depression of the 1930s. See Kuznets, *National Income*.

72. Friedman, *Dollars and Deficits*, 41.

73. Modigliani, "Life Cycle, Individual Thrift, and the Wealth of Nations," 300, 303. See also Modigliani, "The Key to Saving is Growth, Not Thrift," 24–29.

74. Friedman, *Dollars and Deficits*, 41.

75. Hahn, *Common Sense Economics*, 86.

76. For an excellent explanation of Japan's superior saving rate, and its relationship to post-war economic growth, see Morishima, *Why Has Japan 'Succeeded'?* 52–87. For a review of the factors which led up to Japan's economic boom, especially from the important Meiji era, see W. W. Lockwood, *The Economic Development of Japan*, 2d ed. (Princeton: Princeton University Press, 1968), especially 268–304.

77. Hahn, *Common Sense Econmics*, 86.

78. See especially Keynes's parable of the bananas in *Treatise on Money*, vol. 1, 158–60, which concludes that increased savings results in no production at all.

79. Keynes, "The Pure Theory of Money. A Reply to Dr. Hayek," 393.

80. Keynes, *Essays in Persuasion*, 151, 152.

81. Ibid., 152, 153–54.

82. Keynes, *The General Theory*, 111, 211.

83. Ibid., 129.

84. B. M. Anderson, *Economics and the Public Welfare*, 394.

85. See, for example, Paul A. Samuelson and William D. Nordhaus, *Economics*, 12th ed. (New York: McGraw Hill, 1985), 171–74. William J. Baumol and Alan S. Blinder, *Economics: Principles and Policy*, 3d ed. (San Diego: Harcourt Brace Jovanovich, 1985), 168; Paul Wonnacott and Ronald Wonnacott, *Economics*, 3d ed. (New York: McGraw Hill, 1986), 196–98; James D. Gwartney and Richard Stroup, *Economics: Private and Public Choice*, 2d ed. (New York: Academic Press, 1980), 194–95.

86. Samuelson and Nordhaus, *Economics,* 170. Foster and Catchings stated in 1927: "Individuals as well as corporations *must* save; yet savings tend to thwart the social object of thrift. For the individual as well as the corporation, a penny saved is a penny earned; but for society, a penny saved is a penny lost if it results in curtailed production. And often it does. For every dollar which *is saved and invested,* instead of *spent,* causes one dollar of deficiency in consumer buying unless that deficiency is made up in some way." Foster and Catchings, *Business Without a Buyer,* 48. For a critique of Foster and Catchings' anti-savings doctrine, see Hayek, "The 'Paradox' of Saving," in *Profits, Interest and Investment,* 199–263.

87. Samuelson and Nordhaus, *Economics,* 171.

88. Ibid., 172.

89. On the natural unemployment rate hypothesis, see Milton Friedman, "The Role of Monetary Policy," *American Economic Review* 58 (March 1968):117. I thank Kenna Taylor for citing this reference in relation to the "paradox of thrift" controversy.

90. Samuelson, *Economics* 8th ed. (New York: McGraw-Hill, 1970), 224.

91. Keynes, *The General Theory,* xxxiii (preface to the French edition).

92. Hayek, "The 'Paradox' of Saving," 224ff.

93. Durbin, *Purchasing Power and Trade Depression,* 22.

94. Thus Peter F. Drucker is correct in part when he says that monetarist Milton Friedman is essentially an epistemological Keynesian. "His economics is pure macroeconomics, with the national government as the one unit, the one dynamic force, controlling the economy through the money supply. Friedman's economics are completely demand-focused. Money and credit are the pervasive, and indeed the only, economic reality. That Friedman sees money supply as original and interest rates as derivative, is not much more than minor gloss on the Keynesian scriptures." (Drucker, "Toward the Next Economics," 9.) Interestingly, the foremost British monetarist in the 1930s, Ralph G. Hawtrey, rejects Hayek and joins Keynes in taking an anti-savings position based on similar views of capital and the macro economy. See Hawtrey, *Capital and Employment,* 270–86.

95. Boulding, *A Reconstruction of Economics,* 188.

96. Lutz and Hague, eds., *The Theory of Capital,* 14. See also Baumol, *Economic Theory and Operations Analysis,* 641.

97. Lachmann, *Capital, Expectations and the Market Process,* 199. Bauer and Yamey add, "Capital, once it is invested, ceases to be a homogeneous factor of production. The word capital includes a wide variety of types of productive facilities, equipment and reserves, differing in their specificity and durability and in the demand *they* make on various complementary resources." Bauer and Yamey, *Economics of Under-developed Countries,* 130–31.

98. Böhm-Bawerk, "The Function of Savings," 61–62. In this 1901 article, Böhm-Bawerk demolished most of the anti-savings arguments in a debate with L. G. Bostedo.

99. Ibid., 62.

100. Keynes, *The General Theory,* 46, 104.

101. Hayek, *Prices and Production,* 50n. Rothbard queries, "And how can a *reduced* consumption profitably support an *increased* volume of expenditures on producers' goods?" Rothbard, *Man, Economy and State,* 471.

102. Hayek, *Money, Capital and Fluctuations*, 142.
103. "Gross National Product," *Historical Statistics of the United States*, ser. F 47–70, (Washington, D.C.: U.S. Department of Commerce, 1975). For a general discussion of the volatility of the capital markets in a business cycle, see Estey, *Business Cycles*, 228–48.
104. The only other economist I know of who has argued in favor of increased savings during a depression is Rothbard, *America's Great Depression*, 24.
105. Hutt, *Theory of Idle Resources*.
106. Estey, *Business Cycles*, 230–31.
107. Böhm-Bawerk, "Function of Savings," 66–68.
108. Durbin, *Purchasing Power and Trade Depression*, 114, 95.

EIGHT

THE THEORY OF COMMODITY MONEY: ECONOMICS OF A PURE GOLD STANDARD

The eminence and usefulness of the gold standard consists in the fact that it makes the supply of money depend on the profitability of mining gold, and thus checks large-scale inflationary ventures on the part of governments.—Ludwig von Mises, *Planning for Freedom*

Until this point in our discussion, we have assumed a constant medium of exchange in the economy. In chapter 7, we discussed the effects on the macroeconomic landscape of changes in both technology and the savings/consumption habits of individuals without reference to changes in the monetary *numeraire*.

Now we wish to move closer to the real world by describing the impact of changes in the stock of money, first under a pure commodity standard and second under a fiduciary paper money standard. This chapter examines the short-term and long-term effects of monetary changes under a pure species standard.

FRAMEWORK OF A PURE GOLD STANDARD

Let us first define what we mean by a pure gold standard, to distinguish it from a variety of pseudo gold standards that were adopted by Western nations in the nineteenth and twentieth centuries. Even the classical gold standard which existed between 1815–1914 (after the Napoleonic War and before World War I) in the Western world involved a certain degree of fiduciary elements, i.e., paper money combined with a specie base.

A real gold monetary standard, however, would consist of the following attributes:[1]

1. Gold bullion serves as the official monetary unit of account, measured in troy ounces. Silver bullion may also be used as a monetary standard, but

the exchange rate with gold is not fixed; it fluctuates according to market conditions.

2. Gold circulates as a general medium of exchange; full-bodied gold coins are used for medium transactions, gold bullion for *very* large transactions. Smaller transactions involve the use of silver, copper, and token coins.

3. Paper banknotes, token coins, checking accounts, and other money substitutes are treated as general warehouse receipts, equivalent to an equal amount of gold coins or bullion stored at the issuing banks. Hence, a true gold standard is a 100 percent banking reserve system and rejects the practice of fractional reserve banking and claims unbacked by specie.

4. National currencies (dollars, pounds, francs, and marks) are defined as specific weights of gold bullion. Thus, the exchange rate between currencies is fixed by definition.

5. The role of government in banking is limited to certifying coins of a fixed weight and the minting of coins. No central bank is necessary. The government and commercial banks are prohibited from issuing banknotes without the full backing of gold bullion. The metal is mined by private firms. Private mints may also be permitted as an alternative to government minting.

Under this narrowly-defined gold standard, the increase in the supply of gold would be strictly determined by the amount of gold produced each year, that is, according to the profitability of gold mining. If fifty million ounces were mined one year, the stock of monetary gold could increase by fifty million ounces, and no more.[2]

THE NATURAL INELASTICITY OF MONETARY GOLD

Gold has a peculiar trait that makes it relatively ideal as a monetary *numeraire*. It is virtually indestructible. Unlike other metals used for industrial purposes, gold is hardly ever consumed. It simply changes form. The amount of unrecovered gold in industry, or in lost buried treasures, is relatively minuscule. As Roy W. Jastram states, "Gold has two interesting properties: it is cherished and it is indestructible. It is never cast away and it never diminishes, except by outright loss. It can be melted down, but it never changes its chemistry or weight in the process. The ring worn today may contain particles mined in the time of the Pharaohs. In this sense it is also a constant."[3]

This fact leads to a significant characteristic of gold as a monetary metal: its supply is always increasing. In the millenia of recorded history, the total stock of gold has never declined from year to year. While the annual production of gold has moved up and down over the centuries, the total aboveground stocks of gold have never diminished. There have been periods of substantial growth in the supply of the yellow metal, especially during the gold rush years of 1849–60 and 1890–1910, but there has never been a time when the stock of gold has declined in absolute terms.[4] Figure 8.1 shows the increase in world monetary gold stocks between 1810 and 1934, when the world officially abandoned the classical gold standard. Note that the figures do not include gold used for jewelry and industrial purposes.

It is entirely appropriate, therefore, to concentrate solely on the impact of monetary expansion—rather than contraction—under a pure gold standard. While a fiat money system may involve occasional sharp declines in the stock of fiduciary money (as in 1929–32 in the United States), such reductions in commodity money are highly unlikely.

DISTINCTIONS BETWEEN SPECIE AND FIAT PAPER MONEY STANDARDS

The framework of a full-bodied specie standard is distinctive from a fiat monetary system in three ways:

1. The quantity of money is unlikely to decline under a pure gold standard, while the supply of fiduciary paper can and does decline at times.
2. The increase in the quantity of money depends on the profitability of mining operations and varies from year to year, while fiat money can be increased or decreased at will, or set to increase at a set rate (monetary rule).
3. Increases in the specie money supply can originate only from the gold-producing countries, while fiduciary paper can be produced by all countries.

MONETARY EXPANSION UNDER GOLD

The annual growth in gold supplies has varied over the centuries. A monetary system based entirely on gold as the monetary base could therefore not be expected to have an exact or fixed rate of growth in the money supply *year* after year. Therefore, Friedman's rule of a steady monetary expansion of 3 to 4 percent per year would not apply to a monetary system based on the precious metals. Historically, it appears that annual gold output has been unable to keep

Figure 8.1. World Gold Stock and Gold Production, 1800–1932

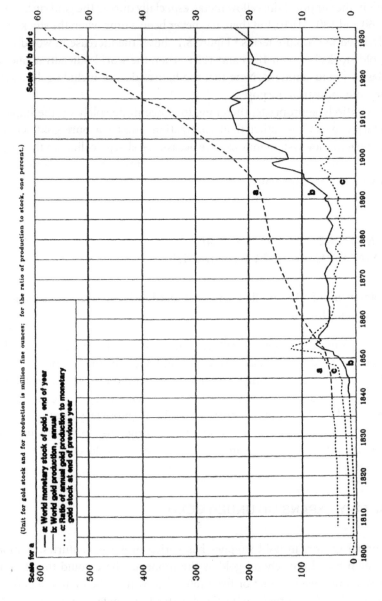

Source: Refus S. Tucker, "Gold and the General Price Level," *Review of Economics and Statistics* (July 1934). Copyright President and Fellows of Harvard College.

up with the 3 to 4 percent average annual growth rate in GNP, except during the gold rush years 1848–60 and 1890–1910. This fact explains in part why average prices have tended to be slightly deflationary during the period when the U.S. and England were on the classical gold standard (1821–1914).[5]

Based on several historical studies on gold production since 1492, annual gold output never increased the total supply of gold by more than 5 percent in any one year, including the gold rush years. While there are no precise figures on the total amount of metal held by governments, individuals and industry, estimates of growth rates in gold supplies can be made based on fairly exact production statistics since the fifteenth century. Based solely on gold output figures since 1492,[6] I estimate that the level of gold holdings increased at an annual rate of less than 1 percent between 1492 and 1840. The gold discoveries in California and Australia in the 1850s added substantially to the supply of gold. Miners extracted more metal in the next 20 years than they had during the previous 350 years! Despite this prodigious outpouring, production never expanded the aggregate stock by more than 5 percent during the height of the gold rush. The opening of new mines in South Africa and other areas of the world in 1890–1910 resulted in annual growth rates of only between 3 to 4 percent. Since 1910, yearly increases in the stock of gold have varied between 1 to 3 percent. Even with the tremendous rise in the price of gold since 1971, when the world went off the gold standard and fixed exchange rates, production has generally lagged behind GNP growth. Gold output actually declined throughout the inflationary 1970s. In the 1980s, the mining industry finally responded to lower production costs, new technical methods of findings and extracting metal, and higher prices. Nevertheless, while gold production has increased an average 20 percent per annum since 1980 (see figure 8.2), mining companies have been hard pressed to increase the aggregate gold stock by more than 1 to 2 percent per annum.

A more liberal interpretation of monetary expansion under a pure gold standard can be obtained by comparing annual production figures with the world monetary stock of gold. The world monetary stock of gold is defined as the amount of specie held by governments and the public for the purpose of exchange and store of value, in either coin or bullion form. It does not include metal used in industry, art, and jewelry. According to a study by Refus S. Tucker covering the years 1800–1932, annual gold production varied between 1 and 12 percent of world monetary gold supplies (see "c" line in figure 8.1). The California-Australian discoveries increased the ratio to over 10 percent in the early 1850s, and South African output increased the ratio to 7 percent around the turn of the century. Under normal times, the ratio was typically below 5 percent. Since the opening of the South African mines, the percentage has declined gradually.[7]

Figure 8.2. World Gold Production, 1820–1980

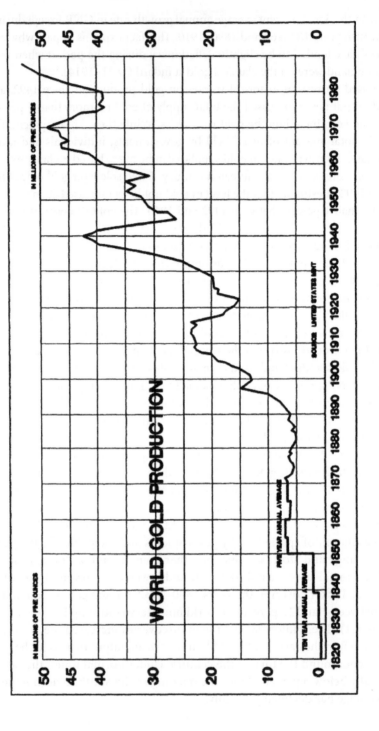

Source: U.S. Mint

Assuming that the newly mined gold is sold entirely to government mints for monetary purposes, it is possible that new gold production could create annual monetary inflation of 7 to 12 percent for brief periods of time in countries which mine the yellow metal. However, gold used for nonmonetary purposes could significantly reduce the degree of monetary inflation.[8]

Finally, it is important to realize that gold inflation, though probably creating a small impact worldwide, may have a much more pronounced effect in the gold-producing countries. For example, the California discoveries in the nineteenth century made the United States a major gold producer for the first time, significantly affecting its money supply. During the gold rush years, 1849–54, the total U.S. currency increased an average annual rate of 13.9 percent.[9] The increase was partly fiduciary, but new gold output obviously had a material influence.

IS GOLD LESS RESPONSIVE OVER TIME?

Because gold is virtually indestructible, new additions to the monetary stock have a declining impact over time. The discovery of new mines must be more and more dramatic as the aboveground levels of the yellow metal grow. Therefore, it is not surprising that the secular trend of new gold production in relation to total supplies has tended downward since 1910.

To demonstrate how increased production tends to have less of an effect on the total supply of gold, consider the following example: Suppose there exists approximately 100,000 metric tons in the total aboveground supplies of gold in Year 1, and that current output is 1,000 fine tons. That is, the annual growth rate is 1 percent. Now assume that gold production increases by 50 percent to 1,500 tons in Year 2. What is the annual increase in the gold stock in Year 2? The total gold stock at the beginning of Year 2 is 101,000 tons. The annual growth rate has risen to only 1.48 percent. In order for the total amount of gold to expand by 4 percent in Year 2, mining companies would have to increase output by 4,000 tons, a 300 percent increase in one year!

Harrison H. Brace comments on this unique feature of the gold standard:

> The supply of gold consists primarily of all the mass of the precious metal which has been stored up during the world's previous history. When there is a new influx from the miners, it merely augments the ancient supply, which has been continually added to from the earliest times. Each addition to the supply, however, after it has had its price effect, tends to make the value more stable as it takes its place in the permanent stock. And each subsequent increment of a given amount is less and less percentage of it, so, in the latter part of a great influx of gold, the effects of additions grow smaller and smaller.[10]

GOLD'S BACKWARD-RISING SUPPLY CURVE

We have seen that the pure gold standard does not provide an absolute fixed supply of money and that the money supply tends to increase over time. But the rate of increase has historically been slow, usually 2 to 3 percent annually, an amount insufficient to match the long-term economic growth of most nations. Such gentle deflationary pressure should not be harmful, however. In fact, it could be regarded as beneficial in that an increasing standard of living (as reflected in lower prices) spreads to everyone.

The constant deflationary pressure on prices of goods and services under a pure gold standard should increase the profit margin of mining operations, thus encouraging an increase in gold production. Van Sickle and Rogge state, "To some extent, the economics of gold mining tends to check price declines. In periods of falling prices the profit margin in gold mining widens."[11] The increased real price for gold should also stimulate the meltdown of jewelry and scrap metal.

Historically, however, the response to higher profitability does not take place until several years down the road. As Jurg Niehans explains, "Since the annual flow of new gold typically is only a fraction of the stock of monetary gold, even a moderate increase in the stock demand for money may require many years of temporary above-equilibrium production of gold to be satisfied. . . . While gold discoveries will certainly tend to push prices up, it would be a coincidence if the money supply and commodity prices moved up in proportion."[12]

The mining industry has never been very sensitive to business conditions on a short-term basis. In fact, when gold becomes more valuable (either through a rise in the price of gold, or a decline in prices in general), there is a tendency for mining companies to *reduce* gold output temporarily as miners shift operations toward deeper shafts and less rich ore bodies that might have been previously cost-prohibitive. This may explain why the inflationary 1970s resulted in a short-term reduction in gold output, but eventually led to a higher production in the 1980s.[13]

This so-called "backward-rising" supply curve for gold is not really perverse, as some economists have suggested. It reflects the important distinction between the short run and long run in the mining industry. If the real price of gold is perceived to have risen permanently, the mining industry tends to cut back on *current* production in order to devote more resources to digging deeper and expanding exploration efforts in an effort to maximize profits in the long run. The mining industry's approach is remarkably similar to the attitude of savers: temporarily reduce current consumption in order to save and invest, earn a return, and consequently increase consumption in the future. The ultimate effect of this "backward-rising" supply curve is to maximize long-term profits.

THE NEUTRALITY OF COMMODITY MONEY?

Although it appears that a pure gold standard would be a much "harder" currency than a fiat paper money system, we must still evaluate the effect an expansion of monetary gold, however small, would have on the economic system.

Traditionally, gold-standard bearers have argued that increases in the gold money supply offer no social benefit except for gold used in industry. Mises states, "An increase in the quantity of money can no more increase the welfare of the members of a community, than a diminution of it can decrease their welfare. . . . Production goods derive their value from that of their products. Not so money; for no increase in the welfare of the members of a society can result from the availability of an additional quantity of money."[14] Hayek adds, "the absolute amount of money in existence is of no consequence to the well-being of mankind."[15]

Gold inflation can of course result in distributive changes within the community; those who get the new money first are benefited the most, while those who receive it last are benefited the least or are actually hurt.[16] As Mises indicates, "An increase in the stock of money in a community always means an increase in the money incomes of a number of individuals; but it need not necessarily mean at the same time an increase in the quantity of goods that are at the disposal of the community, that is to say, it need not mean an increase in the national dividend."[17] In short, commodity money is socially "neutral" and increases are relatively "harmless."

GOLD INFLATION AND THE STRUCTURE OF PRODUCTION

The concept of the neutrality of money suggests that the structure of the economy would be essentially unchanged as a result of gold inflation. Figure 8.3 reflects this neutrality.

Is there any possibility that a gold rush may alter time preference in favor of a more capitalistic economy?

The first-round effect of new gold discoveries is an increased level of profitability in the mining industry. The gold rush also increases the prospects for higher returns to the factors of production associated with the mining industry, i.e., higher wages to miners, higher dividends to mining shareholders, and higher land and lease values in the gold fields.

Within the mosaic of the structural economy, clearly the increased profitability and allocation of resources have shifted to the higher order capital goods area, where the mining industry is located. Not only will there be a shift toward

Figure 8.3. Neutral Effects of Gold Inflation on Economy

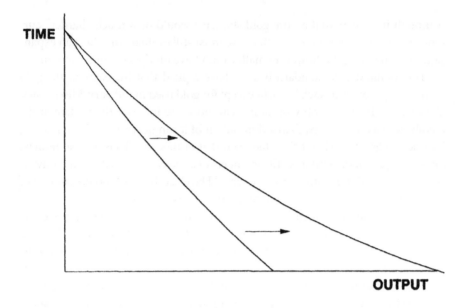

gold production within the raw commodity stage, but there will be a shift from lower order stages to the higher order stages as more mining equipment is produced, more workers become miners, etc. In his study of the gold discoveries in Australia and the United States, John E. Cairnes demonstrated that the price and production effects of the new mines were not uniform. Cairnes indicated, among other things, that the prices of crude products rose more rapidly than manufactured goods. Raw products, especially those of animal derivation rather than vegetable, tended to rise more rapidly. He also stated that prices advanced more rapidly in the gold-producing countries.[18]

But this shift in the structure of the economy may only be temporary; when the gold rush eventually dies out, the monetary inflation subsides to normal levels within a few years. Whether the structure of production is permanently lengthened into a more capitalistic economy depends ultimately on the time preference of those who stand to benefit the most in higher income and those who stand to be hurt by rising prices from the gold inflation. If the gold miners and related income-receivers do not alter their consumption/savings ratio in response to the new gold discoveries, no structural change will take place and the new money can be treated as socially neutral. If they use their increased income to boost their level of savings, the economic structure could lengthen, as shown in figure 8.4, but only if their change in time preference is greater than the rest of the community. If, however, their time preference increases, the structure of production will shorten.[19]

Economists have expressed differing views on the spending/savings habits of miners and mine-owners during a gold rush. In his study of the Australian and American gold rushes in the 1850s, John E. Cairnes argued that "the persons who will chiefly benefit by the gold discoveries belong to the middle and lower ranks of society; in a large degree to the lowest rank, the class of unskilled labourers."[20] Cairnes concluded that the vast majority of new income was spent on perishables, nondurables, and consumption goods in general. Cairnes also suggested that the gold rushes raised the rate of interest because miners spent the money instead of saving it.

> If it comes into the hands of persons who prefer lending to spending it, the increase of money will depress the rate of interest. If, on the other hand, the new additions come into the hands of persons who prefer spending it to lending it, their effect will be to raise the rate of interest. It does this by raising prices and thus increasing the needs of the borrowers. The latter was what happened in the gold countries. The new gold came in the first instance into the hands of miners, who either spent it unproductively or employed it in carrying on mining operations; in either case the effect was to raise prices, and thus to increase needs of borrowers without increasing the loan fund.[21]

Figure 8.4. Lengthening of the Economy Due to Gold Inflation: An Alternative View

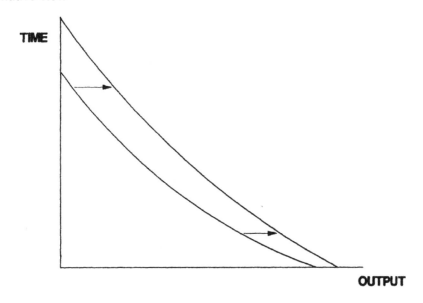

On the other hand, William Newmarch, a classical economist antagonistic toward Cairnes's views, argued that the gold inflation increased real income of workers and capitalists in the mining industry, causing a fall in the interest rate. In short, the gold expansion increased the level of prosperity in the gold-producing countries and foreign trading partners as well.[22]

One might argue that miners and capitalists are by their nature more entrepreneurial and adventuresome than the typical wage-earner. These rugged individualists were willing to take high risks in order to better their material lives. While undoubtedly there were many short-sighted individuals who considered gold digging as a shortcut to quick riches, the real wealth was made by those who took a long-term view and refused to squander their newly earned income on liquor and a hot meal. Moreover, there were severe limitations on the level of consumption that could be achieved in the relatively primitive conditions that existed in California, Alaska, and Australia during the nineteenth century.

Keynes argues that entrepreneurs tend to have a higher marginal propensity to save.[23] This is because, as we indicated in chapter 7, individual business owners always have a specific monetary goal in mind, and tend to increase their capital as much as possible to achieve this goal, especially when profit margins expand. The same kind of attitude would undoubtedly apply to the gold-mining industry. Mises suggests the same possibility: "If a depreciation of the monetary unit favors the wealthier members of society at the expense of the poorer, its effect will probably be an increase in capital accumulation, since the well-to-do are the more important savers. The more they put aside, the more their incomes and fortunes will grow."[24] Although Mises is referring to a fiat money inflation, the same principle should apply under a gold inflation. Nevertheless, one must not ignore the negative effect on the savings habits of the rest of the community, which may well decline in response to the gold-induced inflation.

GOLD AND THE BUSINESS CYCLE

The final question of interest with regard to a pure commodity currency is whether gold inflation is destabilizing, causing a classic boom-bust business cycle of high inflation followed by deflation.

Obviously, the world economy has suffered from boom-bust business cycles even when countries have been on a gold standard. In many cases, such economic debacles occurred when countries went off the gold standard. But this is not the issue here. Nor are we asking whether a return to an ideal commodity standard would cause a depression. We are concerned strictly with the question of economic stability under a 100 percent specie monetary system without the presence of fiduciary elements.

Several points are worth considering. First, as indicated by the historical studies referred to above, the amount of inflation is not likely to be significant. Major gold discoveries have added at most 12 percent to the total monetary supply, and that figure is generous and applicable in only one year.

Second, once the gold inflation follows its course through the economy, a deflationary relapse is unlikely if the monetary system is based on a 100 percent banking reserve system. Cases of declining prices following an inflationary blowoff typically occur under a fiduciary paper money system where the rise in the money supply is followed by a decline in the money supply. In the case of the 1929–32 economic contraction, the money stock declined by a third because banks depended on an unstable fractional reserve system. When the public panicked, the banks were unable to meet the demands for cash, to convert deposits into currency. However, under a pure gold standard, a decline in the quantity of money is highly unlikely. Fractional reserve banking is prohibited and, consequently, bank customers have no need to create a run on the banks. Even if all customers wished to withdraw their money in full, the total amount of monetary gold would not diminish. It would simply change location. The likely result, therefore, of a sharp increase in a commodity currency would be a rise in general prices that would eventually end in a permanently higher plateau.[25]

Nevertheless, there is no doubt that a gold inflation would initially create disturbances in the economy. Hayek calls such changes "harmless," but perhaps he speaks as an economist, not as a businessman or consumer.[26] Dramatic changes could take place depending on the amount of resources shifted into the mining industry and on how the new higher income was spent by the recipient markets. The impact would be felt both domestically and internationally. But there is no indication that the initial boom, alteration in values and reallocation of resources would be followed by a depression that would reverse the positive initial changes. As Rothbard concludes, "Bank credit expansion distorts the market's reflection of the pattern of voluntary preferences; the gold inflow embodies changes in the structure of voluntary time preferences."[27]

SAY'S LAW UNDER A PURE GOLD STANDARD

In sum, we conclude that there is little or no chance of a depression following a gold rush. While it is true that some individuals and industries may be hurt (or benefit less) by the expansion of the money stock, other individuals and industries will benefit more, thus offsetting any decline in another area of the economy. There is little likelihood of a universal decline in economic activity. The same conclusion is appropriate in the case where economic growth exceeds the annual expansion of monetary gold as long as prices are not artificially held high by government policy. Only in the situation of government-induced price controls (in this case, keeping prices and wages from declining) could a general depression and unemployment be likely.

Another factor to consider is that gold mining involves the production of a universally demanded good, money, which is used at every stage of production. It is the most nonspecific of goods, and therefore can be assimilated into every corner of the economy with great felicity. Gold inflation should cause few bottlenecks.

Essentially, we have reached the conclusion that Say's law of markets, "supply creates its own demand," applies to a 100 percent gold economy. Since the product of the mining operation is money itself, there is no question that supply creates its own demand.

New additions to the money stock must involve the use of real resources at their full value. Specie cannot be manufactured at a fraction of its cost, as paper money can, nor can it be created out of thin air. There is no "something for nothing" approach to creating a commodity-backed currency. Gold must be discovered, mined, refined, and manufactured to its specific use, all at substantial costs and requiring the use of labor and machinery, which is drawn from the savings pool. It is this expansion in the use of real resources that *embodies* the increase in the savings pool. While this characteristic may seem to be a disadvantage compared to a paper money standard, involving far fewer resources, it is in fact an essential feature to preserve the validity of Say's law. As the next chapter demonstrates, a paper money standard can invalidate Say's law when it is not fully backed by gold or by another appropriate commodity.

NOTES

1. On the differences between a "real" gold standard and "pseudo" gold standards, see M. Friedman, "Real and Pseudo Gold Standards," *The Journal of Law and Economics* 4 (October 1961), reprinted in Friedman, *Dollars and Deficits*; Michael David Bordo, "The Gold Standard: Myths and Realities," in *Money in Crisis*, ed. Barry N. Siegel, 197–237 (San Francisco: Pacific Institute, 1984); Murray N. Rothbard, *What Has the Government Done to Our Money?*, 2d ed. (Novato, Calif.: Libertarian Publishers, 1981).

2. For a more complete description of a pure gold standard, see my book, *Economics of a Pure Gold Standard*, 53–76. Gary North has suggested a major advantage of a pure

gold standard over the current fiat money standard: the total money supply is easier to calculate.

3. Actually, the addition to the money supply would be substantially less than fifty million ounces because a percentage of the newly mined gold would be used for jewelry and industrial purposes.

4. Roy W. Jastram, *The Golden Constant* (New York: John Wiley and Sons, 1977), 189.

5. Bordo, "The Gold Standard," 211–14.

6. For annual production figures for gold since 1492, see Jastram, *The Golden Constant,* 221–25. Also, see J. D. Magee, "The World's Production of Gold and Silver from 1493 to 1905," *Journal of Political Economy* (May 1909): 50–58. I do not wish to imply that price deflation is necessarily bad. On the contrary, a gently falling price level can be highly beneficial.

7. Refus S. Tucker, "Gold and the General Price Level," *Review of Economics and Statistics* (July 1934): 12.

8. The percentage of gold used for nonmonetary purposes has been growing in significance since the world abandoned the gold standard. According to data compiled by Consolidated Gold Fields, fabrication demand for gold and gold scrap for nonmonetary uses reached 1,339 metric tons in 1986, compared to a total new supply of 1,967. If one considers the making of gold jewelry from new supplies excluding the use of scrap, fabrication of gold jewelry amounted to 827.7 metric tons, still a sizeable figure. It is likely, however, that official mints would capture a much larger percentage of new gold production if a specie standard existed today. Cf. Mises, *The Theory of Money and Credit,* 106.

9. U.S. Department of Commerce, *Historical Statistics of the United States, Colonial Times to 1970,* ser. 10 (Washington, D.C.: Government Printing Office, n.d.), 420–23, 993.

10. Harrison H. Brace, *Gold Production and Future Prices* (New York: Bankers Publishing Co., 1910), 112–13. See also F. A. Walker, *Money* (New York: Holt, 1891), 43, 158, and Milton Friedman, *A Program for Monetary Stability* (New York: Fordham University Press, 1960), 5.

11. Van Sickle and Rogge, *Introduction to Economics,* 284. Van Sickle and Rogge discuss a 100 percent gold reserve model on 282–85.

12. Niehans, *The Theory of Money,* 146, 147.

13. For a discussion of this phenomenon, known as the "backward-rising supply curve," see Jastram, *The Golden Constant,* 186–87.

14. Mises, *The Theory of Money and Credit,* 85–86.

15. Hayek, *Prices and Production,* 31.

16. For a study on the effects of the Australian gold discoveries on prices, wages, exchange rates, etc., see Cairnes, *Essays in Political Economy,* 20–52, 57, 65.

17. Mises, *The Theory of Money and Credit,* 138.

18. Cairnes, *Essays in Political Economy,* 20–74. See also his appendix of price indices, 345–71. Regarding the effect of new spending patterns on prices, Cairnes states, "When an increased amount of money comes into existence, there is, of course, an increased expenditure on the part of those [into] whose possession it comes, the immediate

effect of which is to raise the prices of all commodities which fall under its influence. It is obvious, however, that the advance in price which thus occurs will be, in its full extent, temporary only; since it is immediately followed by an extension of production to meet the increased demand, and this must again lead to a fall in price." (57).

19. Rothbard suggests the possibility that the savings rate might increase and then decline as a result of gold expansion, but he does not elaborate how this could occur. Rothbard, *America's Great Depression*, 38.

20. Cairnes, *Essays in Political Economy*, 60–61.

21. Cairnes, "Lectures on Money," unpublished manuscript (1864/65), quoted in Bordo, "John E. Cairnes on the Effects of the Australian Gold Discoveries, 1851–73," 342.

22. Thomas Tooke and William Newmarch, A *History of Prices* (London, 1857), 189. Quoted in Bordo *supra*, 356. However, Newmarch's views may be colored by his inflationist approach.

23. Entrepreneurs have an "individual marginal propensity to consume probably less than the average for the community as a whole." Keynes, *The General Theory*, 121.

24. Mises, *On the Manipulation of Money and Credit*, 121.

25. Machlup supports this conclusion. See Machlup, *Stock Market, Credit and Capital Formation*, 244–45.

26. Hayek, *Prices and Production*, 30.

27. Rothbard, *America's Great Depression*, 38.

NINE

ECONOMICS OF A FIAT MONEY STANDARD: A THEORY OF THE BUSINESS CYCLE

Mismanagement in the capital sector will be seen to be the chief trouble with postwar economic development.—Wilhelm Röpke, *Against the Tide*

The purpose of this chapter is to analyze the effects of a monetary inflation (or deflation) under a fiat money standard. We define a fiat money standard as a monetary system controlled by the government and based on paper money and other fiduciary elements unbacked by gold or any other commodity. Thus, the creation of new money is no longer dependent on the supply and demand for gold, but upon the decision made by government authorities and based on the needs of business or other criteria. The supply for paper money is entirely under the supervision of the government's central bank or treasury.

Historically, arriving at a purely fiduciary medium of exchange involved a gradual separation of money and specie over many centuries. The world moved from a pure metallic standard to a gold coin standard, then to a gold exchange standard (where specie represented a reserve asset and circulated between governments only), and ultimately to a total abandonment of the official link between currency and gold. The analysis below is based on a modern capital-intensive, market-oriented economy where the *numeraire* is entirely fiduciary, without any specie backing. However, many of the characteristics of a boom-bust business cycle were in evidence during earlier periods when fiduciary elements were a major part of the various gold standards in existence during the nineteenth and twentieth century.

EFFECTS OF MONETARY INJECTION: IS THERE A GENERAL THEORY?

Suppose, under a pure fiat money standard, that the government desires to increase the money supply.[1] The effect of this inflation on the structure of production, and whether it creates a business cycle, depends on the way this new money is used. In this sense, there can be no such thing as a general theory of business cycles. Every period of expansion and contraction is singular in nature and can never be duplicated exactly as before. The only generalized statement that can stand the test of time is to say that the seeds of instability are planted by government fiat money. The course of the business cycle is in large part determined by the points of entry of the monetary injection (who gets the new money first) and the degree of inflation.

There are at least three ways that monetary inflation can take place, each of which produces different effects:

> *First, the universal "cash balance" approach.* Monetarists typically view the expansion of the money supply in terms of a cash balance approach, as if the newly created money is added to the cash balances of all market participants in an equal manner, so that there is a simultaneous upward pressure on *all* prices in accordance with the quantity theory of money. This approach is often referred to as the "helicopter" or "airplane" method of monetary expansion, based on the imaginary example of a helicopter or airplane spreading currency indiscriminately across the country.[2] Such monetary expansion has little long-term effect on the real structure of production since all sectors of the economy supposedly increase by the same amount and, therefore, the relationship between production and consumption remains virtually unchanged. However, based on cyclical trends within the economy, the cash balance appears to be an unrealistic interpretation of how inflation is actually transmitted or injected.

> *Second, the "consumer spending" approach.* To stimulate business on the retail level, the government could take its newly created money and spend it directly on goods and services, welfare payments, buildings, military contracts, and so forth. Mises calls it simple inflation. Such a direct method of inflation, conducted through the Treasury Department instead of a central bank, could significantly alter the intertemporal pattern of economic organization. While this is a fairly common approach among less developed countries and in wartime among industrial nations (it happened in the U.S. during World War II), most Western governments in advanced industrial countries now rely on the credit markets and central banks to carry out open-market operations. We will return to the consumer spending approach in the next chapter as a possible alternative method of government finance.

> *Third, monetary expansion through the credit markets.* Without question the most common approach today, this is the system we will address in this chapter.

The important point to reemphasize is that the economy is affected differently depending on how the new fiat money is spent. Mises suggests that an increase in the quantity of money can affect either consumer goods, producer goods, or both, depending on "whether those first receiving the new quantities of money use this new wealth for consumption or production."[3] Echoing Mises, Percy Greaves states:

> The effects on the economy differ in each case, according to how the new monetary units make their step-by-step appearances on the market. When the expansion is to underwrite current government deficits, the effects depend upon how the government spends the newly created monetary units. When the expansion arises from the monetization of previously privately held government debt, the effect depends on how the previous holders spend the newly created funds. Likewise, the effects are different when banks expand credit for loans to consumers for the purchase of automobiles and real. estate.[4]

Hayek adds, "Everything depends on the point where the additional money is injected into circulation (or where the money is withdrawn from circulation), and the effects may be quite opposite according as the additional money comes first into the hands of traders and manufacturers or directly into the hands of salaried people employed by the State."[5] Hayek's theory examines the effects of a credit expansion through the commercial credit markets and business. His pathbreaking analysis is the best microeconomic explanation of the classic business cycle.

MONETARY INFLATION AND INTEREST RATES

Suppose new money is introduced through open-market operations by the government's central bank. In this case, the central bank purchases government securities from member banks and pays for the debentures by issuing credits on its own account. Thus, new money is created by the central bank through the commercial banking system. Financial institutions now have additional cash with which to make loans to businesses around the country. Under a fractional reserve banking system, the purchase of government securities by the central bank can result in a multiple expansion of the money supply through the credit markets. These new loans create additional deposits at other financial institutions. The use of the credit markets to achieve monetary inflation is a critical part of modern monetary policy.

The primary activator of this new borrowing power is the interest rate. In determining the movement of interest rates, we will assume that this credit creation is at the beginning stages and that an inflationary psychology has not pervaded the economy yet. Later we will abandon this assumption. We shall also assume for the time being that most of the loans are used for business purposes.

Assuming no current inflationary expectations, the interest rate will tend to decrease as the supply of money expands. Generally, the expansion of fiat money will reduce both long-term and short-term interest rates. Some have argued that if the expansion takes place in T-bills (discounted notes of ninety days or less), only short-term loans would be affected.[6] However, as Machlup has pointed out, the lending of funds for "short term" purposes only (such as "working capital" for businesses) does not preclude businesses from using these funds for long-term projects, since increased working capital often must be used in conjection with fixed capital. If short-term and long-term rates differ by too much, arbitrage will tend to equalize them.[7]

Figure 9.1 demonstrates the short-run effect of this inflation.

Note how the increase in the money supply appears to have the same initial effect as figure 7.5 in chapter 7, where we noted the effect of an increase

Figure 9.1. How an Increase in the Money Supply Affects Credit Markets in the Short Run

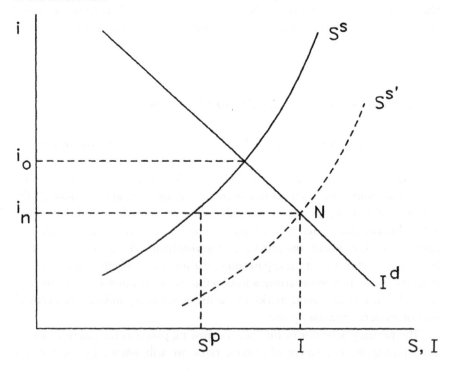

in savings on the credit markets. However, there are some critical differences. The lower interest rate causes a slight reduction in private savings, since the inducement to save has been reduced. In essence, planned (ex ante) investment exceeds planned savings. The gap between private savings and total available credit is filled by government fiat money. In this sense, the new money "drives a wedge between saving and investment."[8] Keynes argues that the creation of government bank credit is "just as genuine as any other savings."[9] But while the primary effects appear to be the same, the creation of new government bank credit cannot be a permanent addition to the stock of savings. The comparative statics of figure 9.1 cannot show this conclusion; although point N appears to be at a resting point, it is actually at a point of disequilibrium or, more to the point, is a movement away from equilibrium! (Hence, the limitation of comparative static analysis in supply and demand schedules for investment.) To demonstrate this, we must turn again to the Aggregate Production Structure.

Because the expansion of the money supply occurs through the credit markets, an economic expansion will occur chiefly in the intermediate and higher order industries, where big borrowers exist. Firms will begin more intensely to build machine-tool factories and more commercial buildings, for instance, rather than retail stores and recreational vehicles. The lower interest rate is more stimulative to the higher-order stages of production than to the lower-order stages near final consumption, because of the time value of money. As Hayek notes, "The price of a factor which can be used in most early stages and whose marginal productivity then falls very slowly will rise more in consequence of a fall in the rate of interest than the price of a factor which can only be used in relatively lower stages of production or whose marginal productivity in the early stages falls very rapidly."[10] More projects far away from final consumption become relatively more profitable compared with projects closer to final consumption. Robbins states, "The longer-lived the capital instrument, or the greater its distance from consumption, the more its value is affected by the change in the rate of interest. The shorter-lived it is, or the less its distance from consumption, the less it is affected. The value of flour in the baker's shop is hardly affected by a cheapening of the cost of borrowing. The value of mines, forests, houses and heavy factory equipment is enormously affected."[11]

The effect of lower interest rates on capital projects of varying maturities can be demonstrated using the discount formula for a capital asset,

$$V = \frac{Y}{(1+r)} + \frac{Y}{(1+r)^2} + \frac{Y}{(1+r)^3} + \cdots + \frac{Y}{(1+r)^n} \qquad \text{(Eq.9.1)}$$

where,

$$V = \text{present value,}$$
$$Y = \text{future income from the capital asset,}$$
$$r = \text{interest rate, and}$$
$$n = \text{number of years.}$$

Clearly, changes in the rate of interest (up or down) affect future incomes much more than those near the present. Interest charges become a more important factor as the investment project is more remote from completion or final use.

Another aspect of the lower rate of interest is the lengthening of the production process. The reduced cost means that long-term projects that were previously put on the shelf can now be initiated. In chapter 7, we discussed the possibility of projects which involved longer periods of research and development, new instruments and more intricate forms of construction. New plants and factories are constructed which may involve long intervals before completion. New types of durable capital goods are developed which may reduce the costs of manufacturing. Techniques of production may be altered to include more materials, such as more steel in cars. All such efforts increase the proportion of resources allocated to higher-order capital markets. As Robbins observes, "When the rate of interest drops from 4 to 3 percent, a whole range of enterprises, which were not worthwhile when 4 percent was the rule, now become attractive. Factories can be built, machines constructed, transport facilities extended, housing provided, which, when the higher rate prevailed, were out of the question."[12]

THE BOOM PHASE

The extent of the economic expansion in the capital-goods industries depends on the degree and duration of monetary inflation. It can vary from a small-scale expansion to a full-scale boom. Moreover, the higher the level of monetary inflation, the more the economic expansion will appear to be universal in all stages of production, even though the higher-order capital markets should expand at a greater rate than the consumer-goods industries. Again, this is assuming the monetary inflation takes place primarily through the business-credit markets only, not as a result of direct consumer spending by the government or through bank credit to consumers.

Because the demand for capital goods will tend to rise more rapidly than consumer goods in the first stage of monetary inflation, resources will shift toward the capital-goods markets. This circumstance is what Hayek and the classical economists called "forced savings," meaning that individuals feel compelled to shift away from consumption toward what appears to be more profitable higher-order investments projects.[13] Figure 9.2 reflects the shift in resources toward the capital goods markets.

While the earlier, capital-intensive stages of production enjoy the highest degree of profitability, the later consumer markets are likely to increase too. Rothbard, for example, believes that credit expansion does not reduce consumption expenditures as savings does, at least in the early stages of inflation. "The production structure has lengthened, but it has also *remained as wide,* without contraction of consumption expenditures."[14] Robbins supports the same thesis.[15] Another reason consumption is not likely to be suppressed is because banks have become more and more willing to lend large amounts of credit for consumer purchases (vacations, appliances, boats, cars, and so on.) And with the increasing use of credit cards, even for perishable items at the grocery store, the continued expansion of the consumer goods industry is even more likely.

IDLE RESOURCES AND UNEMPLOYMENT

The capital-goods expansion will occur even if there are idle resources and labor unemployment. One does not have to assume full employment for resource

Figure 9.2. First Phase: The Capital-Goods Boom under Inflation

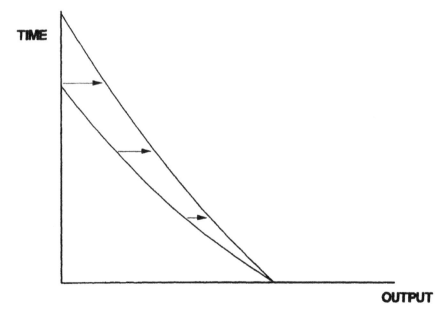

shifting and macroeconomic distortions to take place, as many critics claim.[16] If one stage of economic production is more profitable than another, resources will move into the more profitable stage, whether the resources were unemployed previously or not. Idle resources may well prevent the prices of capital goods from rising much, but they will not keep the resources from shifting to better uses. The resources may not come from the consumer-goods industries, a point well taken by critics, but this does not necessarily mean the expansion is therefore balanced and healthy.

The idea that a disproportionality between production and consumption can only exist under conditions of full employment misconceives the nature of the capitalistic system.[17] Unemployed resources, in terms of land, labor and capital, always exist in some form or another. As Mises says, in the "unhampered market, there are some unemployed workers, unsold consumers' goods, and quantities of unused factors of production."[18]

When unemployed factors are extensive, a shift in demand for more capital goods may hardly affect the consumer-goods market. As Myrdal argues, "Insofar as there were such unemployed factors, they would be employed first in the production of capital without the necessity of a decrease in the production of consumption goods."[19] Thus, there may be no "forced savings," i.e., an absolute reduction in consumption. But there will still be a change in the consumption/ capital relationship. There will be a relative shift in favor of higher order goods over lower order goods because of the relative increased demand for capital goods. Prices may not increase as they would if production were near full capacity, but in relative terms, the prices in capital-goods markets rise in relation to the consumer-goods market. Thus, we see that the argument, made so often by critics of Mises, Hayek, and the Austrians, that the existence of unemployed resources somehow obliterates the overinvestment of producers goods in relation to consumer goods, is fallacious.

But it is historically true, as critics point out, that in an economic expansion both private investment and personal consumption expenditures increase at the same time. This trend is due to the fact that new fiat inflation is typically injected into several areas at once, including both consumer and business credit, to publicly financed projects, and welfare expenditures. Moreover, there is usually some form of genuine economic growth taking place through technological advancements and increased capital expenditures from private savings, which bring about an economy-wide boom. Such circumstances do not negate the fact, however, that the new inflation breeds excessive artificial expansion in the heavier industries.

EFFECT ON SECTORAL PRICES AND OUTPUT

The APS can be used to examine the effect of the inflationary boom on relative prices and output at various stages of production. The APS can be divided into four general categories: raw commodities, manufactured goods, wholesale goods, and final consumer goods (see figure 5.18). Figure 9.3 shows this division.

As the graph indicates, the APS can have more uses than simply demonstrating an expansion in the capital-goods markets in general. There is a whole array of intertemporal sectors of the economy that can be examined. For simplification, we have directed our attention to four areas.

Under the classical business cycle stimulated by bank credit to business, the greatest expansion occurs in the raw commodities sector. Thus, we would expect the raw industrial commodity price and production index to experience the greatest increase during the first phase of the cycle. The producer price and production indices should also experience an increase, albeit less than in the commodity sector. The wholesale sector may experience only a slight rise, if any at all, in either general prices or output, and such a rise may not be apparent until the boom has been in effect for some time. Consumer prices and output are the last to respond, and may not show any change, or may even experience a slight decline, depending on temporary changes in demand.

Figure 9.3. Effect of Monetary Inflation on Four General Stages of Production

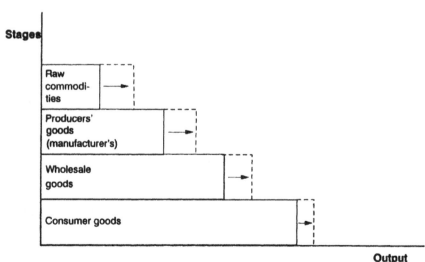

Studies of economic expansions conducted by the National Bureau of Economic Research have confirmed this nonuniform characteristic in most cycles, essentially defining the classic business cycle. Estey writes,

> The rise in prices that is characteristic of the expansion phase is, however, by no means uniform. Wholesale prices rise more than retail prices. Indexes of the cost of living that reflect retail prices rise but modestly. Of the wholesale prices, it would seem that the greater distance from the consumer, the greater and the quicker the rise in price. Thus raw materials rise higher than semifinished goods, and the semifinished goods rise higher than goods ready for the consumer. Prices of farm products tend usually to have the swings of raw materials in general; but they are more erratic and uncertain.[20]

Frederick C. Mills, who conducted extensive price-quantity comparisons at the NBER, identified a number of significant characteristics shared by the classic business cycle. He concluded that in the average expansion period, raw materials prices expand the most, producer prices the next most, and consumer prices the least.[21] There have been exceptions to the rule (as in the 1950s and 1980s), which may not have reflected the classic business cycle pattern due to several factors, including a surplus in raw materials from foreign countries and a broad switch to a consumer-oriented boom. This does not mean, however, that the disinflationary environment of the 1980s cannot be represented in the APS; indeed it can. Figure 9.4 shows a situation of a "disinflationary consumer boom" like the one the U.S. experienced during most of the 1980s. During this decade, the price of raw materials rose the least, followed by producer prices; consumer prices rose the most.

A STUDY OF PRICE AND OUTPUT VOLATILITY IN THE U.S.

My own research (with the assistance of Royal Skousen at Brigham Young University) confirms that historically production and prices tend to be more volatile in production stages which are further and further away from final consumption. We investigated three types of comparative studies in the U.S., each of which reflected to some degree the hierarchy of the transformation process. This study covered prices and production during the post-World War II period, without respect to economic expansions or contractions.

The first set of data compared suitable output figures for the U.S., 1948–70. They included: (1a) gross private domestic investment, (1b) the index of industrial production, and (1c) personal consumption expenditures. Comparing the standard deviation of each series, we concluded that gross investment was less

Figure 9.4. Disinflationary Consumer Boom and Its Effect on Four Stages of the APS

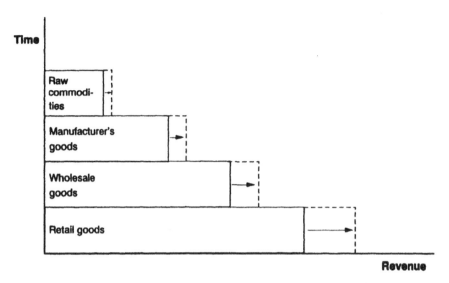

volatile, and consumption was the most stable. The relationships were highly significant to the 0.001 level.

$$F: la/lb = 9.198 \quad 0.001$$
$$F: lc/lb = 6.740 \quad 0.001$$

In the second test, we compared three types of price indices within the narrowly-defined producer price index, 1952–85, using an intertemporal mode: (2a) crude materials for further processing; (2b) intermediate materials, supplies, and components; and (2c) finished consumer goods. A similar relationship was found, although the degree of significance was not as high. Crude materials prices tended to vary the most, followed by intermediate materials prices, and finally finished consumer goods. However, the difference between intermediate materials and finished consumer goods prices was not particularly significant, as indicated below.

$$F: 2a/2b = 2.371 \quad 0.01$$
$$F: 2b/2c = 1.432 \quad \text{between } 0.25 \text{ and } 0.10$$

The third test involved a broader series of prices, 1952–84: (3a) index of spot market prices, raw industrial materials; (3b) producer price index, all commodities; and (3c) consumer price index, all urban consumers. Again, raw industrial materials prices proved to be the most volatile, consumer prices the most stable, and producer prices somewhere in between. The conclusions were quite significant.

$$F: 3a/3b = 6.565 \qquad 0.001$$
$$F: 3b/3c = 1.880 \qquad 0.05$$

THE INFLATIONARY 1970S AS A CLASSIC EXAMPLE

The 1970s was a typical example of the inflationary business-cycle pattern. Monetary expansion following the short recession in 1970 occurred at a considerable rate. The United States abandoned the gold standard entirely in 1971, and the Federal Reserve expanded the money supply at a rapid pace in 1970–72 and 1975–79. The dollar fell sharply on foreign exchange markets while commodity prices, especially for oil and agricultural products, skyrocketed in 1973–74 and 1978–80. During the 1970–74 period, the index of spot market prices of raw materials rose 92.3 percent, while the producer price index went up 45.0 percent, and the consumer price index climbed only 27.0 percent. It was a classic inflation-induced expansion.

After a short recession, during which commodity prices corrected down temporarily, 1975–80 saw another round of inflation. This time the rise in prices spread more evenly throughout the market—raw commodities rose an average 65.2 percent, producer goods increased 53.7 percent, and the CPI went up 53.1 percent. Significantly, this was also a time when the general public became much more mindful of inflationary expectations.[22]

Not surprisingly, this dramatic expansion was also seen in two other markets that both reflect higher capital values and are sensitive to changes in interest rates: the stock market and the real estate market. Common stocks that represent the capital-goods industries tend to rise during early stages of an inflationary boom. The construction industry also participates fully in the boom, stimulated by lower long-term interest rates and readily available mortgages.[23]

PHASE 2: EFFECTS ON LABOR AND MONEY INCOMES

The second phase of the capital-goods boom occurs as resources shift toward the more profitable higher or earlier stages of production. Higher rates of profit in these capital-goods industries stimulate the demand for specific capital goods used in the production of these higher stages.

In addition, nonspecific labor shifts away from lower-order industries to the higher-order industries because employers are demanding more workers. L. Albert Hahn characterizes the effect on labor as follows: "Employment increases because the lower loan costs of capital allow the employment of sub-marginal workers. As the supply curve of capital moves downward, so the demand curve for labor moves upward."[24] Figure 9.5 demonstrates this shift.

Consequently, these factors of production receive higher compensation in the form of higher incomes, rents, and profits.

WHAT ABOUT "VELOCITY" AND THE DEMAND FOR MONEY?

Monetarists point to the rise in velocity, or how quickly money circulates, during an expansion and, conversely, how it falls during a contraction. But to obtain a true perspective of economic activity, it is better to disaggregate velocity according to the stages of production. During a boom, velocity increases first in the capital-goods market. Later, velocity spreads increasingly to the wholesale market and, at the peak of the boom, money circulates more rapidly in the consumer markets. In short, velocity should not be viewed in wholly macroeconomic terms.

Figure 9.5. Inflationary Impact on Employment and Capital Markets

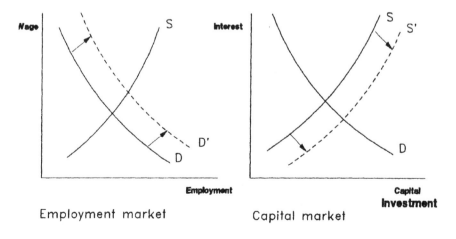

Employment market   Capital market

A far better approach, however, is to focus on the micro demand for money by businessmen, investors, and consumers in the marketplace, and how their individual demands for money vary through the business cycle. In the initial phase of the artificial boom, the demand for money declines as interest rates drop temporarily, continues to decline when consumer prices start climbing, and then finally rises when the credit crunch pushes interest rates up sharply.

THE SHIFT IN CONSUMPTION/SAVING PATTERNS

If the creation of new investment credit came from a shift in people's time preferences, there would be little question how the factors of production would expend their funds. They would divide their money according to the *new* consumption/savings ratio based on a *lower* time preference (see figures 7.3 and 7.8 in chapter 7). Moreover, the more future-oriented attitude of the people would mean that they are now willing to wait the additional time it takes for longer projects to reach fruition.

But when the new capital comes from fiat money creation rather than from increased savings, there will be a strong tendency for the new funds to be spent according to the old, unchanged consumption/savings patterns, creating an artificially-induced imbalance in the economy. The market's *microeconomic* elements will begin to run counter to the government's *macroeconomic* policy. As a result, consumer spending will begin to increase disproportionately as the factors of production receive income, rent, and profits, as figure 9.6 indicates.

However, the level of consumer spending will be extended further than consumer spending under a higher rate of savings. As time progresses, the new income from the investment boom will be spent in the form of higher consumption and lower savings ratios.

WHY THE INFLATIONARY BOOM CANNOT LAST: THE SELF-REVERSIBILITY OF MONETARY CHANGES

Here we have the first indication of the aggregate demand vector moving in a different direction from the aggregate supply vector. They are no longer parallel and coincidental to each other, a necessary condition for macroeconomic equilibrium. They are working at cross purposes. See figure 9.7 below.

Thus, the differential of the aggregate demand vector is no longer the same as the differential of the aggregate supply vector. This disproportionality must

Figure 9.6. Second Phase: Increased Consumption Demand

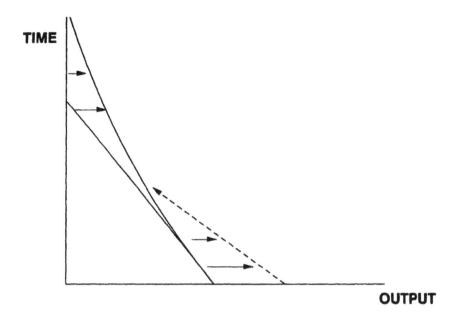

Figure 9.7. Nonuniformity in Aggregate Supply and Demand Vectors: Working at Cross Purposes

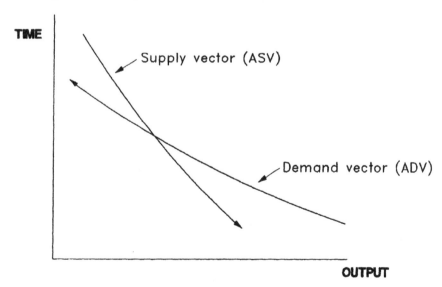

inevitably require a transitional adjustment in the APS, especially in the higher-order capital goods market.

But why wouldn't the increased money incomes received by the factors of production be sufficiently enlarged to pay for the increased production of goods coming down the pipeline, and thus prolong the boom indefinitely? This is the critical test of whether there is disequilibrium in the economy. If the new higher income is sufficient to purchase the increased amount of goods and services being produced, then inflation should not create any false signals and economy-wide maladies. Accordingly, the problem would simply be one of rising prices, not of disequilibrium between production and consumption. This is essentially the claim of the monetarists and other macroeconomists.

The answer to this question is found in the time preferences of the individuals in the economy. In a credit expansion, forces are at work which consist of a "divergence between the individual time preferences (as expressed in the proportions in which the money incomes are saved and invested or spent for consumers' goods) and the time structure of production."[25]

The problem is really one of time, not wealth or income per se. The factors of production do have sufficiently enhanced income to afford the expanded sum of goods and services on their way toward final completion. But it takes time—in fact, more time than the public desires—for the new goods and services to be ready for final use. The individual actors cannot wait! They are demanding goods and services now, sooner than if they had altered their time preferences originally in favor of the future. They lack sufficient patience to support the capital-intensive projects until they are completed. As Mises notes, "Roundabout methods of production can be adopted only so far as the means for subsistence exist to maintain the workers during the entire period of the expanded process."[26] And so, in the words of Machlup, "There is . . . almost no chance that the distribution of expenditures in consecutive phases will adapt itself to the investment structure."[27]

Some individuals, especially business owners, will undoubtedly adopt a higher savings pattern initially as a result of their enhanced wealth, and thus postpone the inevitable contraction. This is Hawtrey's point: "When credit expands, the additional incomes arising are largely additional *profit*, a great proportion of which is likely to be saved and so made available for capital outlay. It is when credit contracts again that profits and savings shrink."[28] According to Hawtrey, the only ill-effect of universal inflation is rising prices. The relative structure of production remains unaffected.

It is critical to note whether the increased savings are permanent.[29] The eventual rise in consumer prices is likely to curtail the initial desires of some individuals to save more, a distinct difference in circumstances between the case of genuine savings (which results in slightly declining consumer prices) and the case of federally-induced bank credit (which results in rising consumer prices). Steadily rising consumer prices cause inflationary expectations and can be highly damaging to traditional savings programs. People adopt the well-known tendency to "buy now, pay later" because prices will be higher later. Simultaneously, the real return on savings is reduced. Thus, as Chapman concludes, "There is little justification for believing, as some do, that the amount of savings will increase during a period of inflation."[30] Robbins adds, "Now there is nothing which justifies us in assuming that the recipients of income will necessarily increase the proportion of the incomes that they save. It follows, therefore, that as the new money becomes income we must expect a strengthening of the demand, not for capital-goods, but for income-goods. The old proportions between demand for income-goods and demand for capital-goods tends to be re-established."[31]

Therefore, in accordance with consumer desires, resources shift back toward the lower-order industries, closest to consumption, as their higher profitability now becomes apparent relative to the lower profitability of higher-order industries. Shackle suggests that "business men will seek by all means to increase their output quickly, and the only way in which they can do so is by adopting shorter, rather than longer, systems of production, drawing the services of men and nature for this purpose away from those who are seeking to build longer systems."[32] Capital, labor, and other resources are reallocated toward the consumer-goods market, too soon to complete the longer-term projects. This is the key to the matter.[33] Thus an inflation-induced economic expansion is "self-reversing."[34]

Abrams summarizes the reason why the inflationary boom cannot last:

> Sooner or later the bulk of this money is paid out as net incomes to consumers—to wage-earners, etc.—and these people use their higher money-incomes to recover their old standards of consumption; since the additional money passes into the hands of consumers before the lengthened process of production has completed itself and turned out a larger flow of consumption goods, the newly enriched consumers can only carry out their wishes through a restoration of the old structure of production.[35]

If somehow the public could restrict their excessive consumer demands until the capital projects could be completed, the bust might not occur, or at least could be postponed for some time. Impetuous Peter needs to change into parsimonious Paul. But as long as laissez faire prevails microeconomically, an inflationary macroeconomic policy is likely to end in a bust.

Lavoie explains why the inflationary policy of the government works against itself. "Thus in the earlier (boom) phase of a monetary expansion, before the price level has fully adjusted, entrepreneurs are catering to the demands of the early recipients of the newly injected money and ignoring the implications of consumer preferences. However, as we approach the later (recession) phase of the expansion, and the money has had a chance to circulate fairly evenly throughout the system, the consumers can reexert their influence, causing the misdirected investments to fail."[36] Machlup concludes, "Though monetary forces help to bring about 'prosperity,' and lead to the excessive length of the investment period, monetary forces do not seem to be capable of maintaining it permanently."[37]

PHASE 3: THE CREDIT CRUNCH

The increase in the demand for consumer goods creates a tug-of-war with the booming capital-goods market. Prices of capital goods and interest rates begin rising in response to the "universal" industrial and consumer boom.

A reduced interest rate originally encouraged the expansion of business into higher-order capital markets, but now the boom appears to have shifted more toward the consumer-goods industry instead. In short, there are too many higher-order capital goods and not enough lower-order consumer goods. The downturn, as Valentine and Dauten observe, comes about because: "It is not merely a shortage of investment funds but a real shortage of capital in the lower stages of production, which is needed to achieve a new balanced pattern of production in line with the additional investment in the higher stages."[38]

Now all levels of production are competing for loanable funds. During this time it is likely that both short-term and long-term rates start rising in tandem. Short-term rates may rise above long-term rates, creating a temporary inverted yield curve, compared to a normal positive yield curve as noted in figure 6.6. As Robbins suggests, the cause may be "the opportunity of speculative gain."[39] Moss and Vaughn argue that increased consumer demand creates a surge in profits on projects investing in consumer goods, which are typically short term in nature. This in turn causes short-term rates to rise dramatically, even more than long-term rates. Moreover, according to Moss and Vaughn, "Entrepreneurs, determined to complete their endangered long-term capital projects, turn to the banks for more bank credit, and a tug of war begins."[40] Figure 9.8 below illustrates a negative yield curve.

Hayek has always referred to his Ricardo effect as the mechanism that triggers the credit crisis. Thus, the boom ends because managers switch from labor-saving methods to labor-intensive methods, due to the rising price of capital

Figure 9.8. Negative or Inverted Yield Curve

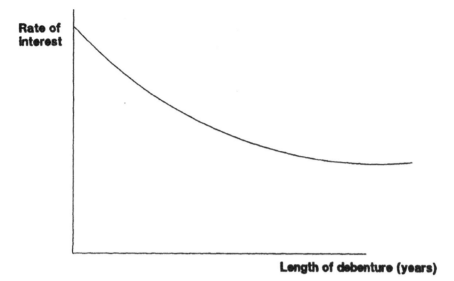

relative to wages during the boom phase.[41] Hayek is really only referring to the fact that raw and semifinished goods markets and other higher-order industries are relatively more capital-intensive than the retail and lower-order industries, which tend to be more labor-intensive.

When demand for capital goods begins to fall and the demand for lower-order consumer goods rises, a credit crunch can be precipitated as businesses scramble for liquidity. The credit crunch is often exacerbated by the decision of monetary authorities to reverse the inflationary course, usually by raising the discount rate or selling bonds on the open market. Credit is tightened because "policies of expanding money and credit could not doggedly persist without threatening unlimited inflation."[42] Figure 9.9 shows the impact of the credit crunch.

PHASE 4: THE RECESSION/DEPRESSION

The industrial boom becomes a bust as the business cycle comes to an end. The capital-goods expansion becomes a capital-goods contraction. Capitalists are reluctant to begin more long-term projects, and are often forced to cut back current projects. Some partially completed jobs may have to be abandoned. Workers are laid off, and orders for machines and materials are cancelled. At higher interest

Figure 9.9. The Credit Crunch Raises Interest Rates beyond Long-Term Equilibrium

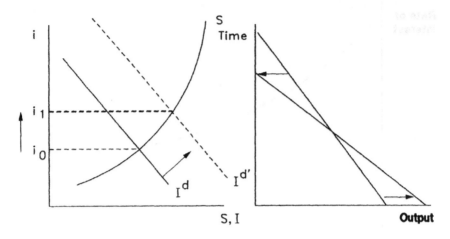

rates and lower demand for their products, businesses tend to use older tools and equipment rather than buy new equipment. Commercial rentals are not renewed and empty office space becomes abundant. Income drops, prices decline, and production is curtailed. Abrams describes the relentless process toward depression:

Consequently there will be a sharp relative rise in the price per unit of consumption goods, and in their turn the producers of these goods will increase their offers of remuneration to the factors of production; those productive resources that are unspecialised will then move from the higher stages of production to the lower stages. The specialised ones—factories, machines, etc.— will be left high and dry since their owners will be unable to pay the higher rates necessary to obtain the services of the complementary factors needed to keep the specialised factors operating. And so the community finds itself with a stock of unemployed plant that has been constructed as part of a degree of roundaboutness of production that was never warranted by the community's real desire for future goods as compared with present goods. This state of affairs is what we know as a depression.[43]

Machlup gives several reasons why a deflationary depression occurs after an inflationary boom:[44]

1. Many capital goods are specific in nature, and thus cannot be easily transferred to another line of business. Shackle observes, "Those high stages which represent the operation of specific capital, incapable of being used elsewhere, will thus find themselves as it were short-circuited, the economies of using

the specific capital being less, now, than the extra cost in interest which its use entails."[45] This factor is precisely why capital cannot be efficiently shifted to the consumer-goods sector without heavy costs. As Van Sickle and Rogge state, "Because resources do not move back and forth between the consumer goods and the capital goods industries with complete freedom, there is certain to be some unemployment."[46]

2. Capital values drop in general due to high interest rates during the credit crunch.
3. Nonspecific complementary machines and equipment may not become finished products in time to be serviceable for consumer-goods production.
4. Wage rates are depressed because the marginal value of productivity of labor is lower in shorter-investment periods (near consumption).
5. Under inflexible wages, unemployment rises.

Mises makes a very important conclusion regarding an artificial boom: "Credit expansion cannot increase the supply of real goods. It merely brings about a rearrangement. It diverts capital investment away from the course prescribed by the state of economic wealth and market conditions. It causes production to pursue paths which it would not follow unless the economy were to acquire an increase in material goods. As a result, the upswing lacks a solid base. It is not *real* prosperity. It is *illusory* prosperity."[47] Mises compares the inflationary boom to a builder who finds out too late that he does not have sufficient funds or supplies to complete the building.

The whole entrepreneurial class is, as it were, in the position of a master builder whose task it is to construct a building out of a limited supply of building materials. If this man overestimates the quantity of the available supply, he drafts a plan for the execution of which the means at his disposal are not sufficient. He overbuilds the groundwork and the foundations and discovers only later, in the progress of the construction, that he lacks the material needed for the completion of the structure.[48]

Hayek comments:

Indeed, it is the experience of all depressions and especially of the present one [1932], that the sales of consumption goods are maintained until long after the crisis; industries making consumption goods are the only ones which are prosperous and even able to absorb, and return profits on, new capital during the depression. The decrease in consumption comes only as a result of unemployment in the heavy industries, and since it was the increased demand for the products of the industries making goods for consumption which made the production of investment goods unprofitable, by driving up the prices of the factors of production, it is only by such a decline that equilibrium can be restored.[49]

RELATIVE CHANGES IN PRICES AND
PRODUCTION DURING A CONTRACTION

Yet neither the expansion nor the contraction in the economy is universal, a concept which is often overlooked.[50] Certain sectors of the economy will be hit harder than others. A "selective" depression (or in the case of the boom phase earlier, a "selective" prosperity) is quite plausible. The degree to which prices, output, and employment are affected is determined by the relative stages of production. Prices and production are generally more volatile in the higher stages of economic production than in the lower stages. Thus, Alvin Hansen is correct when he observes, "The various stages in the productive process (from the raw-material stage up through the various intermediate processes until the goods finally land on the shelves of the retailers) are especially important from the standpoint of the business cycle. The vertical interrelations between producers, in the march of raw materials to the finished product in the hands of the consumer, are of the highest significance."[51] Hamberg adds, "It is a universally recognized fact that during the course of the business cycle the capital goods industries tend to fluctuate much more violently than do those industries which produce for current consumption."[52]

If we return to the four general stages of economic production, we summarize the following effects during the recession/depression phase of the classic business cycle: (1) the most serious decline in prices, production, and employment normally occur in the industrial commodities industry, the furthest stage from consumption; (2) producer goods fall in price and output as well, but by a lesser degree; (3) wholesale markets decline by smaller increments; and (4) consumer markets fall the least, or may continue to rise in the case of a substantial monetary inflation. These relative price, production, and employment changes are apparent as the supply and demand factors vary along the aggregate production function (see figure 9.10 below).

During a contraction, the results will be just the opposite of what occurred during an expansion. As Estey comments, "In contraction, as in expansion, the rate of change in prices is quite unequal. Some goods fall but little; others suffer a veritable collapse. Highly manufactured goods fall less than raw materials or semifinished goods. Wholesale prices fall more than retail prices."[53] Mill's statistical studies in the 1940s confirm this view of the standard business cycle. He found that in the average depression period, consumer prices fell, but producer goods prices fell much more—and raw material prices fell the most.[54]

Interestingly, Lawrence Frank illustrated the same variation in various sectors of the economy in 1923 (see figure 9.11 above).

This pattern also appears in unemployment statistics. The recession or depression is not simply a case of generally rising unemployment, as the

Figure 9.10. The Effect of the Contraction on Four General Stages of Production

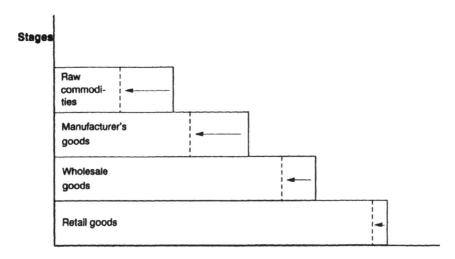

Figure 9.11. Variations in Sectors in Periods of Expansion and Contraction

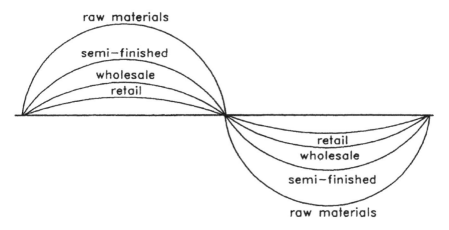

Source: Frank, "A Theory of Business Cycles," 347. Reprinted by permission of John Wiley and Sons, Inc.

monetarists and Keynesians see it, but unemployment principally in the higher-order capital goods and related markets. This is where layoffs are the highest.

IMPORTANCE OF CONSUMER SPENDING IN THE BUSINESS CYCLE

In reviewing the statistical evidence on the business cycle, it is apparent that the focal point of almost all cycles is the capital-goods market, from the raw commodities to the wholesale trade. As one group of cycle analysts concludes, "Indeed . . . the fluctuations in the production of capital goods *are* the business cycle."[55]

Many conventional economists fail to see the fact that the depression is not necessarily all-encompassing or universal in nature, but occurs primarily in the trade or business sector, not in the consumer sector. Thus, economic forecasts and financial analysts who look to retail sales as a sign of the relative health of the economy are bound to be disappointed.

A valuable lesson in looking at business-cycle data, one frequently ignored by contemporary economists as well as by financial journalists, is that the production of consumer goods is relatively stable throughout the ups and downs in the economy. This fact is quite discernible in the theoretical diagrams, figures 9.3 and 9.10, as well as in historical data. As one student of business cycles noted as early as 1923, "It is important to notice that the rate of final consumption varies least of all: that during a period of expansion, final consumption increases slightly, and during a period of contraction decreases but slightly. Because of population growth it has a long term or secular trend upward."[56]

There are several reasons why consumption spending is overemphasized by conventional economists and journalists. First, national income statistics are biased toward the level of consumer spending. As noted in chapter 6, the value added approach to GNP is actually a net figure and does not include the intermediate stages of output. Hence, consumer spending is always by far the largest sector of the economy as measured by GNP, usually between 60 to 70 percent. Government spending is second, and new investment in capital goods is always last. Thus, it is a common mistake to treat consumer spending as the most important element in assessing the future of the economy.

The second reason is related to the first. Keynesian economic theory, which is still very much imbedded in current economic doctrine as well as in the methodology of national income statistics-gathering, emphasizes the consumption function as an integral element of aggregate demand. Theoretically, since the investment side of GNP is so volatile and unpredictable, consumer spending, and more particularly government spending, can serve to stabilize the economy.

But even monetarists have at times fallen into the consumption trap. R. G. Hawtrey, for example, claimed that "the first symptom of contracting demand is a decline in sales to the consumer or final purchaser."[57] Hayek, in a review of Hawtrey's book, *Trade Depression and the Way Out,* sharply criticized Hawtrey as a "purchasing power theorist," saying that his view goes "against all empirical evidence."[58] "In fact, of course, depression has always begun with a decline for capital goods, and the one marked phenomenon of the present depression [1932] was that the demand for consumers' goods was *very* well maintained for a long while after the crisis occurred."[59]

More recently, Leland Yeager, a defender of the "monetary disequilibrium hypothesis," suggests that the business cycle is basically a response of the capital markets to expected changes in consumption. He states:

> Firms invest in view of prospects for profitable sale of the consumer goods and services that will ultimately result, and investment is more susceptible to postponement or hastening than is consumption. In the short and intermediate term, then, investment can exhibit a magnification of observed or anticipated fluctuations in consumption demands. In a world of uncertainty, furthermore—uncertainty exacerbated by monetary instability—hindsight will reveal some investment projects to have been unwise, some even being abandoned before completion.[60]

Yeager's thesis, consistent with the Keynesian "acceleration principle," states that an increase or decrease in investment should *follow* an increase or decrease in perceived consumer demand. It is certainly conceivable to have a business cycle that is consumer-dependent, or more consumer-oriented than investment-oriented. Such a cycle could occur in the case of a credit inflation that operated primarily or entirely through consumer credit, or if government deficits were financed directly by monetary inflation rather than monetized indirectly by the central bank through open-market operations. If such cyclical behavior were apparent, it would show up in the index of leading economic indicators. Consumer spending, therefore, should be a leading economic indicator. But it appears not to be the case.

An examination of the U.S. Commerce Department's Index of Leading Economic Indicators (see figure 9.12) tends to support Hayek's thesis over Hawtrey's or Yeager's. Of the eleven categories, not one records statistics for final retail sales or government expenditures. There is a category called "new orders for consumer goods and materials," but this series deals with manufacturers, not retailers, and includes durable goods, which are more interest-sensitive than demand-elastic, as well as nondurable consumer goods which often have business use (paper and allied products; printing, publishing, and allied products).

The category, "Changes in business and consumer credit outstanding," takes into account some aspect of consumer spending, but again, this category makes no distinction between borrowing by businesses and consumers.

Figure 9.12. Index of Economic Indicators

Cross-Classification of Cyclical Indicators by Economic Process and Cyclical Timing

A. TIMING AT BUSINESS CYCLE PEAKS

Economic Process / Cyclical Timing	I. Employment and Unemployment (15 series)	II. Production and Income (10 series)	III. Consumption, Trade, Orders, and Deliveries (13 series)
Leading (L) Indicators (61 series)	Marginal employment Job vacancies (2 series) Comprehensive employment (1 series) Comprehensive unemployment (3 series)	Capacity utilization (2 series)	Orders and deliveries (6 series) Consumption and trade (2 series)
Roughly Coincident (C) Indicators (24 series)	Comprehensive employment (1 series)	Comprehensive output and income (4 series) Industrial production (4 series)	Consumption and trade (4 series)
Lagging (Lg) Indicators (19 series)	Comprehensive unemployment (2 series)		Business investment expenditures (1 series)
Timing Unclassified (U) (8 series)	Comprehensive employment (3 series)		Consumption and trade (1 series)

IV. Fixed Capital Investment (19 series)	V. Inventories and Inventory Investment (9 series)	VI. Prices, Costs, and Profits (18 series)	VII. Money and Credit (28 series)
Formation of business enterprises (2 series) Business investment commitments (5 series) Residential construction (3 series)	Inventory investment (4 series) Inventories on hand and on order (1 series)	Stock prices (1 series) Sensitive commodity prices (2 series) Profits and profit margin (7 series) Cash flows (2 series)	Money (5 series) Credit flows (5 series) Bank reserves (2 series) Interest rates (1 series)
Business investment commitments (1 series) Business investment expenditures (6 series)			Velocity of money (2 series) Interest rates (2 series)
Business investment expenditures (1 series)	Inventories on hand and on order (4 series)	Unit labor costs and labor share (4 series)	Interest rates (4 series) Outstanding debt (4 series)
Business investment commitments (1 series)		Sensitive commodity prices (1 series) Profits and profit margins (1 series)	Interest rates (1 series)

B. TIMING AT BUSINESS CYCLE TROUGHS

Economic Process Cyclical Timing	I. Employment and Unemployment (15 series)	II. Production and Income (10 series)	III. Consumption, Trade, Orders, and Deliveries (13 series)
Leading (L) Indicators (47 series)	Marginal employment adjustments (1 series)	Industrial production (1 series)	Orders and deliveries (5 series) Consumption and trade (4 series)
Roughly Coincident (C) Indicators (23 series)	Marginal employment (2 series) Comprehensive employment (4 series)	Comprehensive output and income (4 series) Industrial production (3 series) Capacity utilization (2 series)	Consumption and trade (3 series)
Lagging (Lg) Indicators (41 series)	Job vacancies (2 series) Comprehensive employment (1 series) Comprehensive unemployment (5 series)		Orders and deliveries (1 series)
Timing Unclassified (U) (1 series)			

IV. Fixed Capital Investment (19 series)	V. Inventories and Inventory Investment (9 series)	VI. Prices, Costs, and Profits (18 series)	VII. Money and Credit (28 series)
Formation of business enterprises (2 series) Business investment commitments (4 series) Residential construction (3 series)	Inventory investment (4 series)	Stock prices (1 series) Sensitive commodity prices (3 series) Profits and profit margins (6 series) Cash flows (2 series)	Money (4 series) Credit flows (5 series) Credit difficulties (2 series)
Business investment commitments (1 series)		Profits and profit margins (2 series)	Money (1 series) Velocity of money (1 series)
Business investment commitments (2 series) Business investment expenditures (7 series)	Inventories on hand and on order (5 series)	Unit labor costs and labor share (4 series)	Velocity of money (1 series) Bank reserves (1 series) Interest rates (8 series) Outstanding debt (4 series)
			Bank reserves (1 series)

Three other components are almost entirely oriented toward more remote sectors of the economic process: contracts and orders for plant and equipment, changes in manufacturing and trade inventories, and changes in raw material prices. Of particular interest is the category, "Changes in sensitive materials prices," which includes the producers' price index of twenty-eight crude and intermediate materials, and the spot market price index for basic raw industrial materials. Such an indicator reflects economic activity far removed from final use.

The index of new private housing starts is also an indication of future economic activity. While housing may be thought of as a consumer good, it is not actually "consumed" for many decades, and this is one reason new construction acts in the same way as remote capital goods. Like higher-order capital goods, the construction business is highly sensitive to interest rate movements, which in turn are affected by monetary policy (M2 being another leading indicator).[61]

THE INFLEXIBILITY OF SOME PRICES

Business cycle data raises another important issue in economics, the question of inflexible prices of certain kinds of goods. The conventional view is that consumer prices are "sticky," and somehow do not respond as readily to changes in supply and demand, while producer and raw commodity markets are somehow more flexible and hence more responsive to shifts in supply and demand. Some economists explain the problem by suggesting that some markets (such as raw commodities) are "perfectly competitive" while others are monopolistic or oligopolistic. Others, such as Estey and Bordo, blame the inflexibility of some prices as structural in nature, due to custom, regulation, and long-term contractual arrangements.[62] However, we see from the above analysis that the volatility in capital goods markets and relative stability in consumer goods markets is entirely compatible with standard supply and demand analysis, irrespective of structural differences between the market sectors. The supply and demand shifts are distinct for each stage of economic production. The raw commodities sector, for example, is by far the most volatile because it boasts the highest demand in an expansion and the lowest demand in a contraction. At the other extreme, the final consumer market is the least volatile, not because of price stickiness, but because the demand for consumption is least emphasized in an expansion and the most emphasized in a contraction.

THE CASE OF INFLATIONARY RECESSION

One of the characteristics of the fiat monetary business cycle is the universal creation of an inflationary recession. In the recession stage of the business cycle, consumer prices tend to rise *relative* to producer prices. The consumer price index may actually fall during a severe recession, but it will not fall as rapidly as producer or raw commodity prices. In other words, consumer prices do rise, but in *relative* terms to producer prices, although not necessarily in absolute terms. The inflationary recession becomes apparent to the general public only when average consumer prices increase in an absolute sense, which may not occur until the monetary inflation is substantial. Nevertheless, in pure relative terms, the inflationary recession is a universal phenomenon, and not an event that suddenly began in the early 1970s.

The APS is a much more useful tool than the standard neoclassical model for demonstrating *all* aspects of the inflationary recession. Mainstream economists rely on an oversimplified aggregate supply and demand model to demonstrate the inflationary recession, which they say is caused by "supply shocks." The neoclassical model for an inflationary recession and a deflationary recession are shown in figure 9.13.

One of the drawbacks to the neoclassical model is that it can indicate only one price level, which is usually the consumer price index. Thus, the aggregate supply and demand model shows falling output with rising consumer prices.

But the inflationary recession is characterized by changes in several price indices, not all in the same direction or magnitude. In the 1973–74 and 1981–82 inflationary recessions, consumer prices continued to rise, but wholesale prices

Figure 9.13. Aggregate Neoclassical Model Inflationary Recession versus Deflationary Recession

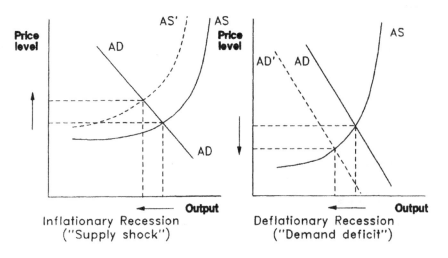

Inflationary Recession
("Supply shock")

Deflationary Recession
("Demand deficit")

rose slightly, and raw commodity prices fell, some sharply. According to U.S. Commerce Department data, in 1975 finished consumer goods rose 9.58 percent, crude materials rose 0.41 percent, and spot raw commodities fell 17.63 percent. In 1982, another recession year, finished consumer goods rose 3.58 percent, crude materials fell 2.89 percent, and spot raw commodities fell 14.43 percent. Unlike the AS-AD curves, the APS can demonstrate these intertemporal price patterns. See figure 9.14 for a generalized case.

We can also contrast a deflationary recession with an inflationary recession in the APS (see figure 9.15).

In the second diagram (b), we see the standard example of a deflationary recession, where prices and output are declining in all stages of production. But note that the drop in prices and output is relatively more sharp in the higher stages (raw commodities, producer prices) than in the final consumer markets.

The same relative pattern occurs in the first diagram (a), the case of the inflationary recession. But in absolute terms, the difference is distinctly observable. In a deflationary recession, consumer prices decline, while in an inflationary recession, consumer prices rise. Meanwhile, output in manufacturing, mining, and other capital markets is falling.

There are actually two situations where an inflationary recession may occur: (1) the recessionary phase of a boom-bust cycle, where past inflation has been sufficiently large to create inflationary expectations in the consumer markets,

Figure 9.14. The APS Model: Inflationary Recession

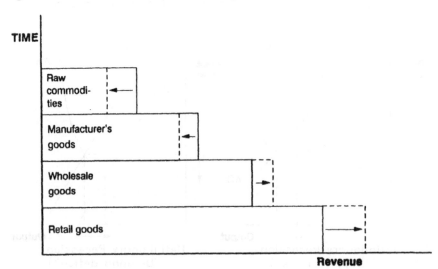

Figure 9.15. The APS Model: Inflationary Recession versus Deflationary Recession

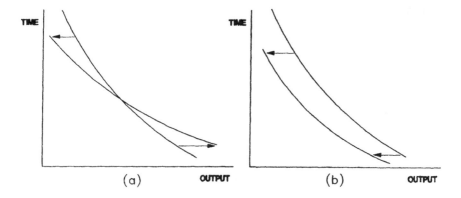

(a)   OUTPUT   (b)   OUTPUT

or (2) where the government engages in inflationary expansion by direct consumer purchases. The latter case is discussed more fully in chapter 10.

PHASE 5: RECOVERY AND STABILITY

Like the expansion, the recession does not last forever. The final stage is reached when the capital-goods market has collapsed and prices have stopped falling. At the same time, consumer demand has declined in response to falling income, but has also reached a stage of stability. Historically, the capital markets recover, followed by a stabilization in consumer spending. As Hayek notes, "It is a well-known fact that in a slump the revival of final demand is generally an effect rather than a cause of the revival in the upper reaches of the stream of production—activities generated by savings seeking investment and by the necessity of making up for postponed renewals and replacements."[63] There are no further declines when the point has been reached where the aggregate demand function is again parallel to the aggregate supply function and equality is reestablished. The cycle need not be repeated unless the government continues to expand the money supply. Figure 9.16 shows the final structure of production after the business cycle is completed.

It should be noted, however, that the inflation-induced boom-bust cycle does not end in a "zero sum" game. The level and configuration of the economy's composition is not the same as before the inflation began. Resources, time and effort have been put into projects that proved unnecessary, induced by artificial

Figure 9.16. Final Phase of Business Cycle

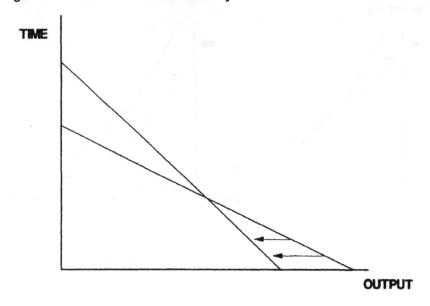

profit incentives. Thus, after the depression has run its course, "A precise re-establishment of the old price-ratios between production goods and consumption goods is not possible."[64] Some capital has been lost forever, property has been redistributed, and many projects have been abandoned. As Rothbard states, "The market will not return precisely to the old free-market interest rate and investment/consumption ratio, as it will not return to its precise pattern of prices."[65] In the end, credit expansion lowers the standard of living by causing the "squandering of scarce resources and scarce capital."[66] There is, as Robbins indicates, a huge "wastage of capital."[67]

A full-blown depression may last for some time, as was the case in the 1930s. Even a severe recession, such as occurred in 1980–82, can have lingering effects and pockets of major weakness. As Estey points out,

Theoretically, there should be a speedy transfer of workers and nonspecific capital from the abandoned higher stages to these lower ones. In fact, this process is slow. Shorter processes still have to be started from the beginning. Goods still have to pass through the necessary stages. In addition, it is possible only gradually, as successive stages are reached in the passage of goods to the consumer, to absorb the labor and nonspecific capital released from longer and more roundabout processes. Moreover, this delay is increased by the uncertainty of producers in respect to appropriate methods in the shortened process where a relatively smaller amount of capital and a relatively larger amount of labor are needed.[68]

In conclusion, it is fiat monetary expansion via the credit markets that creates a business cycle. The inflationary-credit boom is doomed to end because, inevitably, the aggregate supply and demand vectors become non-uniform. Monetary inflation is indeed a "disturbance" in the market economy. The cycle in terms of overall output can be diagrammed in figure 9.17.

SHORT RUN VERSUS THE LONG RUN

Economists frequently distinguish between the short-run and long-run effects of a particular government policy. The short-term effect of an inflation-induced business cycle may be a politically popular economic expansion. But, as we have seen, the long-term effect is a politically unpopular depression. The difference between short term and long term is not just one of time, as in the difference between ninety-day commercial paper and thirty-year bonds. In analyzing the impact of government activities, short term can be best described as a temporary situation which cannot continue to exist. The opposite effect will eventually take hold, i.e., in the long run. Short-term government policies are never permanent in their effects; they are a form of disequilibrium. It is never scientifically possible to predict when the long term will catch up and become the short term, but as Mises states, when it comes to the consequences of government inflationary policies, "We have outlived the short run and have now to face the long run."[69]

Figure 9.17. Classical Business Cycle under Monetary Expansion

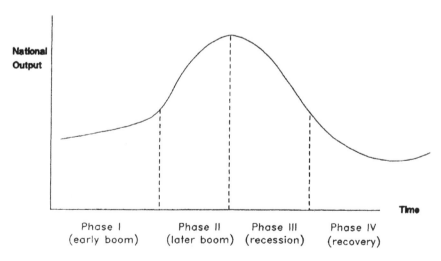

Keynes' famous statement, "In the long run, we are all dead," is largely quoted out of context. His statement was not a fatalistic view of the cosmos, nor was it an indictment of *laissez faire* policies *per se,* but a criticism of economists and political leaders who refused to consider the short-term consequences of their policies. For example, the monetarists, led by Irving Fisher in the first half of the twentieth century, argued that the long-run affects of monetary inflation were "neutral." To this type of thinking, Keynes responded: "In the long run we are all dead. Economists set themselves too easy, too useless a task if in tempestuous seasons they can only tell us that when the storm is long past the ocean is flat again."[70]

RATIONAL EXPECTATIONS UNDER CONTINUED INFLATION

Our analysis thus far has examined the effects of a one-time injection of monetary inflation by the government. The effects of monetary inflation on the structure of production and the business cycle are different, however, when the injection is continuous and fully expected by the public.

We noted in figure 9.2 that a one-time injection of new money would cause an initial basic shift in the intertemporal economic process, resulting in an absolute rise in capital-goods industries at the expense of the consumer-goods industries. When fueled by inflationary expectations, however, prices and revenue are likely to continue rising for the final consumption markets as well. Figure 9.18 below compares the impact of unanticipated inflation and fully anticipated inflation on the macroeconomic mosaic.

Note that I have shown that there is no *relative* change in the production/consumption pattern between the two examples, even though there is an absolute change in the pattern. In essence, I am suggesting that inflationary expectations of the public do not eliminate the distortions created by the inflation, whether it is a case of one-time only credit expansion or continued credit expansion. The credit market will still reflect a bias toward longer-term capital projects under continued inflation. Inflation still causes systematic errors and businessmen will continue to make mistakes as a result.[71]

Inflationary expectations may well prevent longer-term interest rates from falling in response to central bank purchases of treasury bonds on the open market. To keep the new funds from piling up in excess bank reserves, they must be lent out somewhere, and traditionally the short-term market is most affected.

But while long-term rates may remain high, short-term rates may still tend to fall as new money enters the banking system and short-term credit may

Figure 9.18. Initial Structural Impact of Inflation: Two Cases

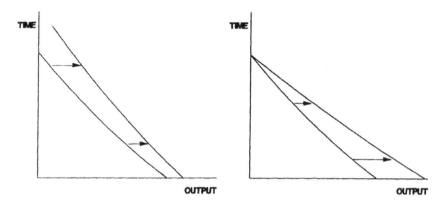

indirectly be used to stimulate long-term projects. Banks normally prohibit the use of short-term loans for fixed capital and other projects involving a long payoff period, preferring short-term funds to be used for consumer purchases, working capital, and inventories in businesses. Machlup suggests a different result, however: "But they [the bankers] forget that by giving the producers these funds for investing in 'working capital' they put those producers in the position of being able to use their own capital in a different way than formerly."[72] Machlup argues that bankers cannot easily stimulate "working capital" without also encouraging fixed capital involved in long-term projects. "Circulating capital will be increased as the result of the credit expansion only to the extent that (1) the fixed capital equipment that is first constructed with the aid of the inflationary credit needs raw materials as complementary goods to go with it, and (2) the increase in demand for consumers' goods, which results in due course from the increase in money incomes, gives rise to a derived demand for working capital."[73] Thus, "New short-term credits usually involve long-term investments for the economy as a whole. The banker cannot know the indirect uses of the funds which he lends."[74]

The rational expectations theory of the new classicists denies any such distortion, however. They argue that the maladjustments of the business cycle can be diffused as the public becomes educated about the inevitable results of inflation. However, there is still a great deal of ignorance as to the precise way in which inflation works its way through the economic system. The new classicist assumption of costless knowledge and market efficiency is a myth. Not only is there is a lack of knowledge by individuals about the whole economy, but their beliefs about how the system works are often erroneous. As Hayek states, "Every explanation of economic crisis must include the assumption that entrepreneurs have committed errors."[75]

Moreover, entrepreneurs cannot resist short-term profits in markets that are showing a relatively high level of profits, no matter how brief they think it will be. They may plan to sell out before the downturn, just as stock market speculators plan to sell at the top. But knowing when the market will turn down is an extremely difficult judgment to make, and not many can do it. In fact, as contrarian theory has demonstrated, it is impossible for everyone to get out at the top. Moreover, many production processes are so complex and specific in nature that they cannot be sold in a moment's time. They are highly illiquid, and only usable when completed.

The effects of monetary inflation are far more complex than economists have realized. The first inflation has simple effects, immediately depressing interest rates and creating an artificial boom in areas where the new money is spent. But if the inflation persists, the market eventually responds. Interest rates no longer decline; in fact, they may well increase as the demand for investment rises. Prices adjust upward more rapidly.

A contraction in the money supply can also have complex results if it happens after a persistent inflation. For example, an unexpected reduction in the money supply may be viewed as a temporary condition, so that prices continue to rise with no accompanying monetary growth. On the other hand, the monetary contraction can be so severe that it breaks the inflationary psychology and a major recession takes hold. The free market forces work at full speed to return order to the inflated debt. In such a disinflationary environment, the central bank authorities may be able to inflate substantially without recreating a consumer price inflation. This situation may last for some time, perhaps years, unless the central bank accelerates its monetary growth to higher than previous levels. The previous malinvestments make the economy less susceptible to the inflationary economy.

THE QUANTITY THEORY OF MONEY
AND NEUTRALITY OF MONEY: A CRITIQUE

The time-dimensional approach to economics demonstrates that the effect of fiat monetary inflation is not uniform. This method is largely ignored by the conventional theory of the macroeconomists or so-called "quantity" theorists who hold to the quantity theory of money.

The quantity theory of money seeks to demonstrate a direct causal relationship between the total quantity of money and the general price level and total output. The equation,

$$M = \left(\frac{1}{V}\right) P \cdot \overline{Q} \quad \text{(Eq. 9.2)}$$

expresses the quantity theory. Assuming the velocity of money (V) is relatively constant over time, and national output (Q) is near full employment, monetarists and quantity theorists argue that in the long run, money is "neutral." An expansion of the money supply (M) increases the price level (P) by the same amount. Indeed, nominal income, prices and production all increase by the same percentage increase in the money supply, so that in real terms, income and production remain the same over the long term. Thus, monetary inflation generally works uniformly throughout the economy, and does not affect real output. If we were to impose the monetary model on the APS, figure 9.19 demonstrates how the structure of production increases by the same percentage at each stage.

Of course, monetarists do not adopt a time-structural vision of the economy. They look at the general price level rather than at relative prices. The aim of monetary policy should be to stabilize prices by increasing the money supply gradually at a constant rate equal to the average growth rate of the economy.

Figure 9.19. A Monetarist View of Change in Economic Structure Due to Inflation

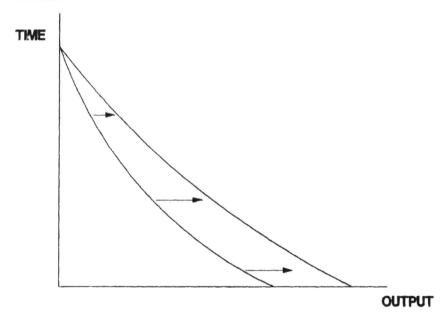

This is based on their view that the only harmful effect of a credit expansion over the long term is the rise in the price level (or, equally as harmful in their eyes, a deflation in the general price level).

Quantity theorists and monetarists, like the neo-Keynesians, fail to recognize the importance of examining relative prices and output rather than the absolute level of prices and output. That is, to look at the Ps and Qs at every level of output, not just the total or average of the aggregate. Or, on the other side of the equation, to consider the *microeconomic* changes made by M or V. The quantity theory of money fails to account for the variance in the prices and production of the various stages of the economy, obscuring the critical fact that a monetary inflation is not evenly spread throughout the economy, nor does the concomitant recession/depression affect all sectors of the economy in the same way. Monetarists fail to recognize that monetary factors affect not only the volume of output, but the direction of production as well.[76] The quantity theory ignores the definite regularly and sequence of producer, wholesale, and consumer price movements in a classic business cycle. Finally, it ignores the effect interest rates have on different sectors of the economy. Its only value seems to be in establishing the long run relationship between inflation and consumer prices. To the monetarists, a business cycle occurs simply as a reaction to the variations in the money supply, causing short-term fluctuations in the volume of output and the general level of prices, with relative price and output changes considered immaterial. The fault of the quantity theorists goes back to their methodology, however, as we indicated in the first chapter. As Garrison notes, "In contemporary macroeconomic models there is no capital structure. There are no stages of production, and the time element in the production process plays no explicit role."[77]

The monetarists frequently fail to analyze the micro aspects of business cycle data. Hawtrey, for instance, once indicated that new government credits granted to producers would create "excess demand" to "*all* goods" to "an exactly equal extent."[78] Obviously, Hawtrey must not have been familiar with business cycle data at the time he wrote.

However, as Estey points out, such generalizations are a major "defect," for they fail to explain critical phenomena in the business cycle. "The most striking feature of the business cycle is the extraordinary variation in the production of capital goods—that is, buildings, machinery, and other instruments of production. No explanation of the business cycle can be regarded as adequate that does not account for the fact that the production of capital goods fluctuates so much more violently than the production of consumption goods."[79]

In contrast to the quantity theory of money, the aggregate production structure does not seek to measure a general price level for all goods and services. It is not necessary to know the general purchasing power of money (price level). In fact, indices can only estimate the price level. One could argue that the general price level has risen if the monetary expansion is sufficiently large so that a nominal expansion in gross revenue is achieved at every level of production (compare figure 9.19). But it is a mistake to concentrate solely on the "macro" effects of the monetary disturbances. Far more important from the viewpoint of the business cycle is to look at the changes in relative prices between various stages of production—between commodity markets, producers' goods, wholesale products, and final consumer goods and services. Too many historical surveys of economic activity are written in terms of general business activity, unemployment, and other large aggregates, ignoring the true cyclical nature of the monetary factors.

Because monetarists view the economy in highly aggregative terms, emphasizing only general prices, output, interest rates and other criteria, they often plead ignorance about the precise transmission mechanism that inflation takes throughout the economy, recognizing only the final results. Thus, Friedman and Schwartz are still uncertain as to how monetary inflation translates into prices and production: "We have little confidence in our knowledge of the transmission mechanism, except in such broad and vague terms as to constitute little more than an impressionistic representation rather than an engineering blueprint."[80] Leijonhufvud is also uncertain about the inflationary blueprint:

The first thing to say, surely, is that we know very little about how inflations work their way through the economy. Our empirical evidence is scant, which becomes less surprising once one notes that the theoretical work needed to lend it analytical structure has been neglected, too. The neoclassical monetary general equilibrium growth model has inflation as "near-neutral" as if it made no difference. The Austrian tradition has inflation associated with systematic and serious distortions of the price system and hence of resource allocation. My own "hunch" with regard to present-day conditions would be that the price distortions are apt to be less systematic than in the Austrian view but none the less serious. There is no good evidence for this view either.[81]

But there is good evidence that an inflation mechanism exists. It is incredible in this regard that Friedman and Schwartz can claim, "Despite repeated assertions by various authors that the first-round effect is significant in this sense, none, so far as we know, has presented any systematic empirical evidence to support that assertion."[82] Nevertheless, this chapter has referred time and time again to inflation's systematic changes in the Aggregate Production Structure, in both the expansion and contraction phase of the economy, as confirmed by such business-cycle specialists as Frederick Mills. Perhaps the monetarists and other macroeconomists have not really taken a hard look at the statistical evidence of business cycle behavior, such as the systematic changes in commodity, producer, and consumer prices in the expansion and contraction phases of the cycle.

The possibility exists that a country could shift from an Austrian business cycle, where higher order capital goods are the primary beneficiaries of new money, to a monetarist business cycle, where both capital goods and consumer markets are stimulated simultaneously through fiat money and credit, government spending, and so on. Under this policy, the business cycle would be more directly connected with changes in the money supply than an imbalance in the capital-consumption relationship. But with such a highly complicated economic structure in industrial nations and continually changing time preferences, it is difficult to conceive of a government policy that could systematically stimulate all sectors of the economy equally.

SAY'S LAW ONCE AGAIN

We noted in chapter 8 how Say's law, "supply creates its own demand," is not likely to be violated under a pure gold standard, or a barter economy. Say's law stated, in essence, that "the supply of every commodity is in itself demand for all other commodities. General overproduction, therefore, is impossible, *ex hypothesi.*"[83] However, the introduction of fiduciary elements into the monetary system can disengage the automatic stability of the whole economy. As Hayek states, "The automatic adjustment of supply and demand can only be disturbed when money is introduced into the economic system."[84] I would alter his statement slightly, to read, "when *fiat* money is introduced into the *credit* system."

In sum, Say's law is violated in the short run by a fiat credit inflation. Of course, the short run may take some time to work itself out! True, the larger supply created by the fiat money also creates its own excessive demand, but it is the *wrong* kind of demand in the case of a business credit expansion, an ephemeral demand which cannot last. Markets lose their sensitive balance as a result of fiat money creation through the bank credit system. Goods will be produced for which, as they near completion, there is no ultimate market. Granted, businessmen undertake new projects all the time which eventually fail because costs exceed demand. Such is a general characteristic of the competitive marketplace, where there is uncertainty and changing product demand. But these mistakes are marginal when compared to the magnified "cluster of errors" that appears in the business cycle, where a majority of entrepreneurs expand operations for which there is no final demand.

At the beginning of the Great Depression, Keynes succinctly wrote, "When investment runs ahead of savings, we have a boom. . . . When investment lags behind, we have a slump."[85] While this notion has a simple ring to it, it is like most aggregate thinking, an incomplete story. First, investment cannot exceed savings unless the government or the banks create fictitious credit. It is basically the government, through government-controlled banks, which causes an excess in investment. Second, the slump occurs not because individuals save too much, but because they consume too soon before the long-term projects are finished. Unfortunately, Keynes' simple statement ignores the critical element of time. In reality, the consumption/savings pattern changes very little over time. What does change, rather drastically, is in the investment sector. It is not so much that savings suddenly exceed investment, but that investment, which previously was booming, has fallen below savings. And this because investment was of the wrong kind. More savings could help the investment markets recover, but people are unlikely to do it.

CONCLUSION: THE HIDDEN COSTS OF A FIAT MONEY SYSTEM

The theoretical justification for a fiat money system, unbacked by any commodity, is that it permits the stock of money to be created with the negligible use of real resources. This is its alleged advantage over the gold standard, which could require 4 to 5 percent of the world's annual national output to produce gold.

But there are hidden costs of the introduction of fiduciary elements which have come to light in this chapter. Fiat paper money permits the monetary system to expand the investment pool without requiring autonomous savings to increase along with it. When the fiat monetary expansion operates through the credit markets, it plants the seeds of a boom-bust cycle, an inflationary bubble that eventually bursts into a depression. Such instability wastes valuable resources which cannot be entirely replaced because of the specific nature of capital goods. In short, we conclude that fiat money's supposed greatest virtue, its low cost of production, turns out to be its greatest vice. At the same time, ironically, the introduction of fiat money has not diminished the search for gold mines and storage of precious metals.

Considering the long history of fiat money inflation, it becomes clear that the present state of the economy, especially in the industrial nations, is inherently unstable and structurally weak. No major government has allowed the deflationary forces to operate fully throughout the economy. Every industrial nation has had to prop up its economy by reinflating. Admittedly some Western nations, such as Switzerland, have not allowed as much monetary inflation and consequently have not suffered as many distortions. But all major nations, including the United States and Britain, have become so complex in their distortions and malinvestments that it seems virtually impossible to alter the structure of production to a stable form.

NOTES

1. According to Percy Greaves, Mises believed that government's first policy step was to reduce interest rates, which was then *followed* by an expansion of money. See Greaves, "Some Misconceptions of the Mises Cycle Theory," in Mises, *On the Manipulation of Money and Credit*, xl–xli. The artificial lowering of the interest rate (by the central bank) increases the demand for bank loans, which is then met by credit expansion (not savings). Such may have been the case in the early history of central banking, when the emphasis was on the use of the rediscount window to effect member bank loans. However, in recent decades, the emphasis has shifted toward the use of open-market operations as an indirect way of influencing interest rates. Mises himself writes of interest rates being reduced by credit expansion in the work edited by Greaves. See Mises, "The Trade Cycle and Credit Expansion: The Economic Consequences of Cheap Money," in *On the Manipulation of Money and Credit*, 221. See also Mises's critique of Haberler, who emphasized lower interest rates instead of increasing the money supply, in *Human Action*, 795n.

2. The helicopter example can be found in Friedman, *The Optimum Quantity of Money and Other Essays*, 4–7. Cf. Patinkin, *Money, Interest, and Prices*, 44–59, for an example where the money supply is doubled for every individual. Monetarists, such as Friedman, Irving Fisher, and Clark Warburton, do recognize short-term nonuniformity in the prices of various assets caused by the creation of new money, but like a swinging pendulum coming to a rest, the long-run result is nothing more than a rise in all prices equally. See I. Fisher, *The Purchasing Power of Money*, 70, 71, 184, 185, 193. Cf. Humphrey, "On Nonneutral Relative Price Effects in Monetary Thought," 13–19.

3. Mises, *On the Manipulation of Money and Credit*, 124–25.

4. Greaves, "Some Misconceptions of the Mises Cycle Theory," xl.

5. Hayek, *Prices and Production*, 11.

6. Greaves, "Some Misconceptions of the Mises Cycle Theory," xl.

7. Machlup, *The Stock Market, Credit and Capital Formation*, 256–57.

8. Garrison, "Hayekian Trade Cycle Theory," 440.

9. Keynes, *The General Theory*, 83.

10. Hayek, *Prices and Production*, 82–83. Bellante and Garrison comment on Hayek's model: "Given the relative volumes of commercial lending and consumer lending, we can say that the new money falls first into the hands of producers and only later into the hands of consumers. This disproportionate distribution of the new money is

consistent with Hayek's story about the effects of a monetary injection on the structure of production: production for *future* consumption is temporarily favored over production for *present* consumption." Bellante and Garrison, "Phillips Curves and Hayekian Triangles," 222.

11. Robbins, *The Great Depression*, 36–37. Surveys of businessmen indicating that interest rates play only a small role in their investment decisions are highly suspect. Much depends on how the question is asked, and what type of investment projects are involved. Heavy construction in the extractive industry may be more affected by credit conditions than retailers, for example. The answer also depends on whether a project is already going on versus one still on the drawing board. An investment halfway finished is likely to be finished despite rising interest rates than one being contemplated only.

12. Robbins, *The Great Depression*, 34.

13. Hayek, *Prices and Production*, 18–31. See also Hayek, "A Note on the Development of the Doctrine of 'Forced Saving,'" in *Profits, Interest and Investment*, 183–97.

14. Rothbard, *Man, Economy and State*, 856.

15. Robbins, *The Great Depression*, 38.

16. See Estey, *Business Cycles*, 244; Hamberg, *Business Cycles*, 274; Valentine and Dauten, *Business Cycles and Forecasting*, 6th ed., 296.

17. Cf. Hawtrey, Review of Hayek's *Prices and Production*, 119–25.

18. Mises, *On the Manipulation of Money and Credit*, 125.

19. Myrdal, *Monetary Equilibrium*, 26.

20. Estey, *Business Cycles*, 101.

21. Mills, *Price-Quantity Interactions in Business Cycles*, 132–33. See also Mills, *Prices in Recession and Recovery*, 46–63, 95–161.

22. Axel Leijonhufvud somehow fails to see the 1970s in terms of an inflationary boom involving excessive capital accumulation. "According to ABC [Austrian business cycle theory], inflation should produce an overinvestment boom. The stagflation decade of the 1970s does not fit: it gave us inflation but no acceleration of capital accumulation and no forced saving. So one cannot accept it as a 'General Theory' (if you will pardon the expression)." Leijonhufvud, "Real and Monetary Factors in Business Fluctuations," 417. If one examines the relative rise in prices of basic commodities, real estate, and equities (especially as measured by the Standard & Poors 500 or other broad index), it is difficult to understand why one would fail to see an acceleration of capital accumulation. The capital-goods market includes titles to capital, such as real estate and securities. Leijonhufvud sees the 1920s as an expression of the Austrian theory, however.

23. Robbins, *The Great Depression*, 39–42. Robbins observed the following ten features of a monetary inflation: (1) the discount rate is reduced; (2) short-term interest rates fall; (3) long-term rates fall; (4) bonds and debentures move up; (5) velocity or money circulation increases; (6) common stocks rise in price; (7) real estate climbs in value; (8) industrial boom occurs, and new issues are floated; (9) prices of commodities and raw materials climb; and (10) stock market booms further in expectation of rising corporate profits.

24. L.A. Hahn, *Common Sense Economics*, 117. In contrasting the Austrian approach to cyclical analysis to the monetarist approach, Bellante and Garrison suggest that

"Friedman focuses his analysis on the market for labor while Hayek focuses his on the market for capital goods." Bellante and Garrison, "Phillips Curves and Hayekian Triangles," 219.

25. Machlup, "Professor Knight and the 'Period of Production,'" 621.

26. Mises, *On the Manipulation of Money and Credit*, 125.

27. Machlup, "Professor Knight and the 'Period of Production,'" 622.

28. Hawtrey, Review of Hayek's *Prices and Production*, 124.

29. L. Albert Hahn argues that there will be a rise in genuine saving during an inflation, not because of Keynes's law but because of a redistribution of income in favor of higher income earners. See *Common Sense Economics*, 138. Machlup suggests the possibility that a credit expansion could cause a temporary rise in voluntary savings, though he considers it "unlikely" because of rising prices, which tends to discourage savings. See Machlup, *The Stock Market, Credit and Capital Formation*, 185–86.

30. Chapman, "Inflation and Investment," in Willis and Chapman, *The Economics of Inflation*, 204.

31. Robbins, *The Great Depression*, 38.

32. Shackle, "F. A. Hayek," 237.

33. "If the 'boom' is to be maintained, there will have to be a rise in saving; what is to happen if the propensity to save does not rise? Only if saving had risen would it be possible to continue producing in the 'boom' manner, with a low rate of interest and high real wages. If saving does not rise, this system of relative prices will be inconsistent with the maintenance of supply-demand equilibrium in the markets; interest will have to rise, in order that supply-demand equilibrium should be maintained-and real wages will have to fall." Hicks, "The Hayek Story," 213.

34. Gerald P. O'Driscoll, Jr., and Sudha R. Shenoy, "Inflation, Recession, and Stagflation," in Dolan, *The Foundations of Modern Austrian Economics*, 199–201.

35. Abrams, *Money*, 33.

36. Lavoie, "Economic Calculation and Monetary Stability," 168.

37. Machlup, "Professor Knight and the 'Period of Production,'" 622.

38. Valentine and Dauten, *Business Cycles and Forecasting*, 6th ed., 295.

39. Robbins, *The Great Depression*, 41.

40. Moss and Vaughn, "Hayek's Ricardo Effect," 554.

41. The other version of the Ricardo effect—that firms switch to more labor because real wages decline in the last half of the boom as prices rise—is less tenable. Statistical evidence does not always support this thesis, especially if labor unions are active in maintaining purchase power of average wage rates. See Seymour Melman, *Dynamic Factors in Industrial Productivity* (Oxford: Oxford University Press, 1956); Lorie Tarshis, "Changes in Real and Money Wages," *Economic Journal* 44 (1939); John Dunlap, "The Movement of Real and Money Wage Rates," *Economic Journal* (September 1938): 413–34.

42. Yeager, "The Significance of Monetary Disequilibrium," 379.

43. Abrams, *Money*, 33.

44. Machlup, "Professor Knight and the 'Period of Production,'" 623.

45. Shackle, "Some Notes on Monetary Theories of the Trade Cycle," 36.

46. Van Sickle and Rogge, *Introduction to Economics,* 410–11.

47. Mises, *On the Manipulation of Money and Credit,* 183.

48. Ibid., 223. Machlup adds, "There is no money system and no credit management conceivable which could permanently maintain a production structure (i.e., time distribution of productive services) which does not correspond to the structure of expenditures (i.e., time distribution of purchasing power). Though monetary forces help to bring about 'prosperity,' and lead to the excessive length of the investment period, monetary forces do not seem to be capable of maintaining it permanently." Machlup, "Professor Knight and the 'Period of Production,'" 621.

49. Hayek, "Reflections on the Pure Theory of Money of Mr. J. M. Keynes (continued)," 43–44.

50. "Depression is a pervasive phenomenon, with customers scarce, output reduced, and jobs lost in almost all sectors of the economy." Yeager, "The Significance of Monetary Disequilibrium," 380. But see Mills, *op. cit.,* on the relative degree of depression in prices, output, employment, and so on.

51. Hansen, *Business Cycle Theory,* 125.

52. Hamberg, *Business Cycles,* 202.

53. Estey, *Business Cycles,* 110. Cf. Frank, "A Theory of Business Cycles," 625–33 and Moore, "The Cyclical Behavior of Prices," 147.

54. Mills, *Price-Quantity Interactions in Business Cycles,* 132–33.

55. Phillips, McManus, and Nelson, *Banking and the Business Cycle,* 121.

56. Frank, "A Theory of Business Cycles," 630–31. This point is also made by Aftalion, "The Theory of Economic Cycles," 165.

57. R. G. Hawtrey in *Trade Depression and the Way Out,* quoted in Hayek, Review of Hawtrey's *Trade Depression and the Way Out,* 126.

58. Hayek, Review of Hawtrey's *Trade Depression and the Way Out,* 126. Hayek characterizes Hawtrey's monetary approach as "a hand-to-mouth system," rather than a complicated time-consuming production process (127).

59. Ibid., 126.

60. Yeager, "The Significance of Monetary Disequilibrium," 382.

61. Richard Band notes that retail sales and consumers' disposable personal income are often used by financial analysts as leading indicators for the U.S. economy, but my reading of these indexes suggests that they are not consistent and often are coincident or lagging indicators.

62. See for example Estey, *Business Cycles,* 110, and Bordo, "The Effects of Monetary Change," 1088–109. After noting greater price volatility in the crude product sector compared to intermediate and final products, Bordo hypothesizes that "if we classify products by stages of processing (crude, intermediate, and final), we would expect to observe more rapid price adjustment in the crude sector, with a higher prevalence of auction markets, than the intermediate and final goods sectors, with a higher prevalence of customer markets." (1106). The agricultural and industrial raw materials sector, according to Bordo, trades in a well-developed auction market with shorter-term

contracts, while the final consumer markets may involve longer-term contracts. But one could just as easily hypothesize that shorter-term contracts and auction markets are only possible because of the tremendous volatility in crude markets, while the relative stability of consumer prices allows longer-term contracts.

63. Hayek, "The Keynes Centenary," 46.
64. Mises, *The Theory of Money and Credit*, 364.
65. Rothbard, *Man, Economy and State*, 858.
66. Ibid., 863.
67. Robbins, *The Great Depression*, 69.
68. Estey, *Business Cycles*, 241.
69. Mises, *The Theory of Money and Credit*, 9–10.
70. John Maynard Keynes, *A Tract on Monetary Reform* (London: Macmillan, 1923), 80.
71. "Interest rates are ratios of relative prices; changes in interest rates accordingly represent changes in relative prices and concomitant changes in the goods produced. Hayek concluded that the changes would be systematic and their general form predictable. Stated briefly, his analysis predicted overproduction of capital goods with relatively long periods of production and underproduction of consumer goods and capital goods with relatively short periods of production." O'Driscoll, "Rational Expectations, Politics, and Stagflation," 166. Lindahl also concludes that with inflationary expectations, "longer investments" continue to expand faster than consumption goods. Eventually there must be a "crisis" to resolve the inflationary spiral. See Lindahl, *Studies in the Theory of Money and Capital*, 182.
72. Machlup, *The Stock Market, Credit and Capital Formation*, 257.
73. Ibid., 256.
74. Ibid., 292, 202–3 1.
75. Hayek, *Profits, Interest and Investment*, 141.
76. Hayek, *Prices and Production*, 4. "In the monetarist view, so long as the price level is stable, monetary expansion is not disruptive. . . . In the Austrian view, monetary expansion is a disruptive force, whether or not the price level is changing as a result of the expansion." Bellante and Garrison, "Phillips Curves and Hayekian Triangles," 227. As far as I'm aware, James Buchanan and the Public Choice school are the only monetarists who recognize the nonneutral effects of inflation: "But monetary changes are not neutral, for such changes affect the behavior of real variables within the economy. It is this nonneutrality of monetary changes that renders the Keynesianist inflationary bias so destructive. Money creation falsifies the signals that operate within the economy. In consequence, labor and capital move into employments where they cannot be sustained without increasing inflation." Buchanan and Wagner, *Democracy in Deficit*, 183.
77. Garrison, "The Austrian-Neoclassical Relation," 110.
78. Hawtrey, *Capital and Employment*, 250.
79. Estey, *Business Cycles*, 228.

80. Friedman, *The Optimum Quantity of Money and Other Essays,* 222. See also Friedman and Schwartz, *Monetary Trends in the United States and the United Kingdom,* 16–72, especially 26–27, 30–31.
81. Leijonhufvud, "Costs and Consequences of Inflation," 287.
82. Friedman and Schwartz, *Monetary Trends in the United States and the United Kingdom,* 31.
83. Myrdal, *Monetary Equilibrium,* 17.
84. Hayek, *Monetary Theory and the Trade Cycle,* 101.
85. Keynes, *Essays in Persuasion,* 117.

PART 3

APPLICATIONS

TEN

IMPLICATIONS FOR GOVERNMENT ECONOMIC POLICY

It is one of the foremost tasks of good government to remove all obstacles that hinder the accumulation and investment of new capital.—Ludwig von Mises, *Planning for Freedom*

Governments have played a major role in national economic policy in virtually every country in the world, especially after the advent of paper money in the late seventeenth century. The state has been an instigator of major inflations, anti-depression measures, wage-price controls, foreign exchange regulations, and other forms of intervention. Today government leaders are searching for answers to world economic problems, contemplating whether to intervene further or to find new ways to open the avenues of economic success. Every major nation now has a central bank, through which it can expand and control its national currency, interest rates, and the credit conditions. The question is: what is the best monetary and fiscal policy for a state to pursue that will maximize national prosperity and minimize the ill-effects of the business cycle and inflation?

Let us examine some of the most popular government economic policies in light of the previous analysis of the structure of production and the aggregate production function.

AN ANALYSIS OF KEYNESIAN POLICY DURING A RECESSION

First, let us examine the effect of instituting the standard Keynesian policy of countering a recession by increasing government spending. Will it work?

In order to answer this question, we must first recall what constitutes a recession or depression. As explained in chapter nine, the credit-induced recession came about through an expansion of the fiat money supply, which artificially lowered interest rates and stimulated a capital-goods boom that could not last. The recession or depression is then created as wage earners, landlords, and businessmen spend their incomes in the old consumption pattern. Ultimately, then, the capital-goods boom is caused by a misspent and misdirected allocation of resources, and eventually turns into a bust. Figure 10.1 shows the recessionary phase.

The recession/depression is the final phase in the business cycle, following a (1) capital-goods boom, (2) an expansion in consumer demand, and (3) a credit crunch. The final result is a sharp drop in capital-goods demand, resulting in layoffs, unemployed resources and a decline in prices and profits, principally in the capital-goods industries.

The Keynesian prescription for a recession is to increase "aggregate demand," to stimulate output in both consumption and capital markets.[1] However, the Keynesians consider capital investment to be volatile and unpredictable, and therefore emphasize stimulating "final effective demand" through autonomous government spending. Keynesians regard government spending as an "honorary investment," taking the place of autonomous investment when necessary. In a full-scale depression, investment is moribund, according to Keynes, and cannot be stimulated on its own by declining interest rates. By increasing

Figure 10.1. Structure of Production in a Recession/Depression

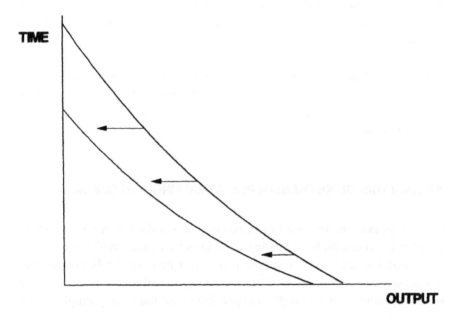

deficit spending, the Keynesians hope to increase consumer spending, a policy aimed at counteracting the declining demand for consumer goods. Once the final consumer-goods market is encouraged, the investment market for capital goods will respond in a favorable manner. (The Keynesian two-stage model of consumption and capital is outlined in chapter 7.) The expected result is an economic recovery.

Unfortunately, the Keynesian goal has been illusory.[2] Figure 10.1 shows why. Such a policy does not deal directly with the central problem of a recession/ depression, i.e., the decline in higher-order capital goods and commodities. As we stated earlier, the recession or depression does not affect everyone universally in the same way. The capital-goods industries, especially the raw industrial commodities and heavy industries, are the worst hit—and it is this decline which precipitates the economic depression. Consumer demand never falls as drastically as capital-goods demand. The Keynesian emergency plan may work wonders for the consumer-goods market, and even for the lower-order capital goods markets required to produce the final consumer goods, but it does little or nothing to enhance the capital goods industry furthest away from final consumption, which is experiencing a massive glut due to falling demand.

So, while the government may increase the demand for consumer goods, a consumer spending policy does little or nothing to address the deficit in the higher-order capital goods markets. A Keynesian government policy may have as its first objective to reverse the falling demand for consumer goods, and thereby make an effort to stimulate the demand for capital goods. But even if the increased output of consumer goods is sufficient to overcome the drop in capital goods industries, it will take considerable time before the effects are seen because the expansion begins at the wrong end of the production process.

THE HIDDEN DRAWBACKS OF PUBLIC WORKS PROJECTS

Furthermore, there is the question of the source of these additional funds. If the government funds come from increased taxes, spending by private consumers and investors will be curtailed by the same amount the government spends. The net effect is negligible. If the government spending comes from borrowing from the public, the capital goods market could drop further as public investment takes the place of private investment. Keynes himself raised this possibility, warning that a public works spending policy "may have adverse reactions on investment in other directions."[3] Durbin discusses the difficulties in getting the economy going again in a depression: "Merely to increase the dole or stimulate consumption by public works will do nothing if it merely offsets the losses which are being made in the production of consumption goods during the second period of depression. That will not really stimulate interest in new capital."[4] Tout and Hansen add:

Again, it may be said that a public works program will stimulate business because it increases the demand for certain raw materials and pays wages to workmen, thus stimulating consumer buying-power. But here again one must not forget that, if the capital market is weak, the moment certain fields are stimulated by public works, a damper may be placed upon private enterprise by a vast issue of public bonds, and so operations elsewhere may be curtailed. The fallacy which lurks here is precisely akin to the familiar tariff fallacy. It is always easy to see the prosperity and activity of the industries protected by the tariff, but what is often overlooked is that at the same stroke the tariff injures and depresses enterprise in other fields.[5]

In fact, the higher-order primary and secondary sectors of the economy may possibly reduce their output further because of the increased relative profitability of the consumer-goods industry, thus shifting its resources to the lower end of the production process. Greater government spending increases the consumption/savings ratio, flattening the aggregate demand vector and thus increasing interest rates or preventing them from falling further. In a sense, there is a negative multiplier, opposite to the multiplier effect Keynes popularized. Figure 10.2 demonstrates the negative multiplier effect on the hierarchy of aggregate production.

Many Keynesians have argued that a more effective route is for government to create the money by fiat through an expansion of the money supply, and then spend it directly on state projects, welfare, transfer payments, subsidies, and military requirements. Another alternative is to argue that government spending be directed toward capital expenditures, such as the construction of highways, buildings, factories, and so forth. As Estey suggests, "If any credit is to be granted at all, it should be to the producers, to encourage them to lengthen the process of production; and this only because the effects of deflation have caused the structure of production to shrink more than the voluntary distribution of saving and spending will eventually justify."[6]

According to this thesis, the state-supported financing of capital projects could serve as an ersatz for private investment. The government projects could not be a perfect substitute for private initiative, since tools, machines and plans tend to be heterogeneous and specific in nature, but an imperfect substitution is possible. Mismanagement will still be a problem, of course, because state projects are usually politically motivated, rather than economically motivated.[7] In effect, the government will have created a subsidy to capital-goods owners. Even

Figure 10.2. Increased Government Spending Makes Economy Less Capitalistic

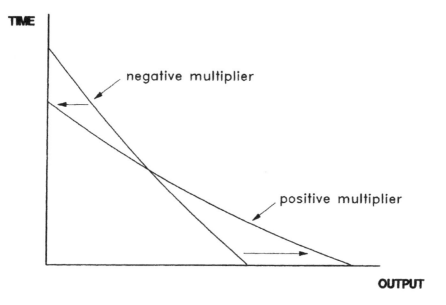

so, the effect can only be temporary, since the aggregate demand vector will continue to be significantly different from the aggregate supply vector. That is to say, the people's time preferences will differ from the government's, creating distortions throughout the economy. Estey concludes, "Credits would do more harm than good if they again caused longer processes to be started than could be maintained in recovery without the help of continued credit expansion. These requirements are so exacting that it would be almost impossible for the authorities to do the job rightly."[8]

A CRITIQUE OF THE PURCHASING POWER DOCTRINE

The Keynesian doctrine of stimulating consumer spending through government edict is part of a broader theory of creating purchasing power. Essentially, their belief is that, if more money can be placed in the hands of consumers and workers, they will increase spending, which in turn will foster economic recovery. Increasing government spending is just one policy measure that purchasing power theorists advocate. Other recommendations include encouraging consumers to spend more of their own money by saving less or by borrowing more, persuading private companies to pay higher wages or at least to maintain nominal wage rates, pushing companies to maintain the same level of dividends, postponing bankruptcies, raising the minimum wage, and setting price support levels on agricultural and other commodities. Keynes himself was a strong advocate of maintaining nominal money wages in the face of deflation.[9]

Such methods, however, often serve to prolong the depression because of a misplaced emphasis on consumption rather than on capital formation. As Estey comments, "It is not lack of consumer purchasing power that is causing the trouble. Quite the reverse, it is the relatively high demand for consumers' goods that is at fault. To add to this demand by advancing funds to consumers makes matters worse. To increase consumer credit at the moment of the crisis intensifies the crisis."[10] Robbins also states, "The maintenance of wage rates and dividends was at the expense of capital. . . . The new savings of the community which takes up the sale of securities that constitute hidden reserves instead of constituting new demand for the products of capital-goods producing industries, is appropriated for the consumption of wage earners and dividend receivers. Consumption is maintained at the expense of capital. The powers of resistance of the capital-producing industries are sapped, and the struggle for liquidity is intensified."[11] Finally, Hahn concludes:

> If more is spent on consumption, entrepreneurs wishing to produce more consumer goods will, it is true, wish to acquire the capital goods necessary to produce the consumer goods in the same capitalistic way. Consumption induces investment, to use the customary expression. But the inducement can succeed only to the extent to which credit supply is elastic. If it is not elastic, entrepreneurs will have to produce the greater amount of consumer goods in a less capitalistic way. More consumption will not lead to more investments—contrary to the reasoning of the acceleration principle.[12]

The 1929–32 depression led many government and corporate leaders, such as Herbert Hoover and Henry Ford, to support the purchasing power concept. Hoover encouraged business leaders to maintain wages and dividends in the early 1930s, an attitude contrary to conventional business response to an economic downturn.[13] Henry Ford was a strong supporter of the idea. He held this view as early as the 1920s. "If we can distribute high wages, then the money is going to be spent and it will serve to make storekeepers and distributors and manufacturers and workers on other lines more prosperous, and their prosperity will be reflected in our sales."[14]

Ford's philosophy was forged a decade earlier when he more than doubled the minimum wage of Ford workers, from $2 a day to $5. The famous "Five Dollar Day" resulted in a tremendous surge in output and skyrocketing morale among

Ford employees. Ford argued that the higher wage rate increased efficiency at the automobile plant. Importantly, the $5 wage also permitted Ford workers to buy their own cars for the first time. The success of the $5 wage made Ford a champion of vulgar Keynesianism. As Jonathan Hughes puts it, "The higher the national wage bill, the more money consumers would be prepared to spend."[15]

But there is a major difference between the Five Dollar Day case of 1914 and the maintenance of high wage rates in 1930. Ford said, "If we can distribute high wages . . ." That is the question—can Ford and other businessmen afford to pay higher wages? *Profits* must *precede* higher wages, for they cannot follow higher wages. Wages must be paid from previous sales, not future sales. Ford was able to double his workers' wages because Ford's total sales grew from $42 million to $89 million in 1913. Net income, which was $13.5 million at the end of 1912, was $27 million at the end of 1913. Ford Motor Company's net assets grew from $21 million to $35 million in only one year. He could afford to double the income of his employees. But if such outstanding profits had not previously been earned, the wage boost would have been a disaster. Increasing the general purchasing power of his workers to stimulate car sales would have been in vain. Moreover, the auto workers may have spent the money elsewhere, defeating the initial purpose of the raise.

The Ford Motor Company itself disproved the purchasing power theory in the 1930s. Cooperating with Hoover, Ford raised wages temporarily. But it didn't work; sales sagged, and he eventually was forced to cut wages. Ford finally admitted, "Country-wide high wages spell country-wide prosperity, provided, however, the higher wages are paid from higher production."[16] Ultimately, the key to prosperity is not spending or consumption, but production and productivity.

Frederick C. Mills explodes the myths of the purchasing power doctrine when he states:

> In a money economy a large portion of the sums that represent disbursements of purchasing power on the one hand represents costs on the other. Salaries and wages on the producers' account books are costs, and must be covered by receipts from the sale of goods produced. *If we could ignore the time lag involved* we might say that in a completely closed system, in which disbursements representing costs of production went to precisely the group of persons who constitute the final market for the goods produced, whether costs (and related prices) stood on high or *low* levels would be a matter of indifference as regards the current movements of goods. But when the disbursements go to a smaller group than those who buy the products, or a different group, the relative levels of costs and of prices may be of profound importance. For the prices necessary to cover higher disbursements may be too high, in relation to the current income of the consuming group at large. Under these conditions an advance in costs and in prices may reduce the physical volume of goods sold, or impede expansion.[17]

CONSUMPTION AND THE IMITATION OF WEALTHY NATIONS

A certain element of mercantilism runs through those who advocate the purchasing power parity. The Keynesian economists and politicians look with envy upon the high level of consumption in wealthy nations and seek to imitate this characteristic by encouraging artificial consumption. Impatiently, they seek to become a consumer society before taking the necessary steps to achieve lasting prosperity. As such, they are often unwilling to adopt measures that underline the real cause of wealth, i.e., a high level of savings, productivity, and technology.

Such an attitude is reminiscent of the mercantilists who, envious of the low rates of interest in advanced countries, sought to imitate them by artificially lowering their own interest rates through expansion of uncollaterized credit. Other mercantilists, in an effort to increase their gold holdings, imposed tariffs and promoted exports, as though the high level of gold holdings was in and of itself the cause of a country's prosperity rather than the effect.

Today's modern mercantilists are wolves disguised in Keynesian fleece. Government leaders promote the appearance of wealth by encouraging consumption and by imposing provincial trade restrictions. But they cannot make their country a wealthy consumer nation without first paying the price to become a productive nation. Production must occur *before* consumption. The Keynesian prescription that consumption must anticipate production is a misconception that must be avoided.

In essence, the whole Keynesian concept that final aggregate demand is the sole motivator of economic activity is greatly mistaken. As H. Parker Willis notes, "No error of the technocratic theorists, or of the Hobsonian school, is more serious than the assumption that demand is always reducible to demand for consumable goods. Every individual, except those upon the barest of subsistence minima, makes some demand for capital goods—even if such demand be only in the form of a demand for housing. The wealthier individuals of a community ordinarily find it impossible to dispose of their income in mere consumption, and incline more and more toward the bestowal of it in the acquisition of titles to capital objects of various kinds."[18]

THE MONETARY SOLUTION: STIMULATE CREDIT EXPANSION

Another common response to an economic contraction is to encourage the central bank to reinflate the money supply via the credit markets. The monetarist school, including R. G. Hawtrey and Milton Friedman, advocates this approach. Theoretically, the new inflation should inject new money into the system, reduce interest rates (if inflationary psychology has been reversed) and reactivate the depressed capital markets. If we examine figure 10.1, it appears that this remedy should be far more effective, in the short run at least, in fighting a recession, than depending on fiscal policy, which has favored the ineffective consumption route.

Let us take the case of an economy which was previously overstimulated by monetary inflation and is now headed into a severe recession or depression. Instead of allowing the market forces to readjust on their own through a painful but necessary transition period, the monetary authorities decide to intervene and prevent the economy from returning to a natural state of macro equilibrium, by increasing credits to business rather than to consumers, which, like government spending, would only make matters worse. There is no question that an increase in new credits can revive the capital markets, at least temporarily. But once a deflationary contraction takes hold, it takes much greater credit to get back to a normal (pre-recession) rate of profit. Companies are now in trouble, near bankruptcy, or insolvent. Business psychology is severely damaged. A certain amount of monetary expansion is necessary just to create sufficient demand to cover the excessive supply of capital goods in the production hierarchy. Consequently, assuming other things equal (tax rates, tariffs, foreign exchange rates, and so on), it will require a greater dose of new monetary inflation to reestablish the full employment of labor and resources. That is, the money supply will need to grow at a faster rate than the previous cycle. Additional money and credit will be necessary to make the economy grow at the previous boom rate. Thus, we can see that it is one thing to start a trend, and quite another to reverse it.

The expansion of new credits during a recession only postpones the inevitable. Certainly, if it was the fiat money inflation that caused the downturn in the first place, additional monetary expansion is not going to cure the malady. As Hayek states, "To combat the depression by a forced credit expansion is to attempt to cure the evil by the very means which brought it about; because we are suffering from a misdirection of production, we want to create further misdirection—a procedure which can only lead to a much more severe crisis as soon as the credit expansion comes to an end."[19] Furthermore, in his attack on Keynes in 1932, Hayek explains:

Indeed, it is the experience of all depressions and especially the present one, that the sales of consumption goods are maintained until long after the crisis; industries making consumption goods are the only ones which are prosperous and even able to absorb, and return profits on, new capital during the depression. The decrease in consumption comes only as a result of unemployment in the heavy industries, and since it was the increased demand for the products of the industries making goods for consumption which made the production of investment goods unprofitable, by driving up the prices of the factors of production, it is only by such a decline that equilibrium can be restored.

Any attempt to combat the crisis by credit expansion will, therefore, not only be merely the treatment of symptoms as causes, but may also prolong the depression by delaying the inevitable real adjustments.[20]

HAYEK'S RULE OF MONETARY ACCELERATION

Reinflation may buy some temporary relief, but it is destabilizing in the long run. The expansion of the higher-order capital markets is in constant jeopardy. Eventually the investment projects created by the new credit result in factor income, which ultimately fails to support the new level of capital investment. As Hayek states, the artificial inflationary boom is sustainable only "until the additional money becomes income. At that moment, the proportion of the capital creation must relapse to the level of voluntary savings activity, unless new credits are granted."[21] At that point, the aggregate demand vector moves in a different direction from the supply vector. Malinvestments become apparent in the higher orders of production.

New inflationary credits can ward off the inevitable contraction, but only by expanding the fiat money stock at a greater rate. Otherwise, the new money eventually becomes spendable income, and the income-receivers inevitably spend the money in the old pattern, curtailing the demand for capital goods.

That the central bank must expand the money supply at an ever-increasing rate in order to maintain a "no recession" policy is found in Hayek's writings and can reasonably be called, "Hayek's Rule of Monetary Acceleration." He states that an inflationary boom can only be sustained if the money supply is "kept artificially high by a progressively increasing rate of credit creation."[22] But such a short-run inflationary policy only leads to disaster in the long run. Mises says that it will lead to what he terms the "crack-up boom," a runaway inflation and a massive "flight into real goods."[23] Hence, if governments operating on a discretionary fiat money standard wish to avoid such a scenario, they must be willing to endure occasional recessions or depressions.

Continued stimulation of the producers' markets becomes less and less effective as the money supply is expanded at higher and higher rates. The distortions between the aggregate demand and supply vectors can only get worse, especially as people's inflationary expectations respond to the situation. Eventually, the authorities must come to recognize that a severe adjustment is necessary and inevitable in order to prevent a devastating runaway inflation.

TAX CUT DURING A RECESSION

Under the threat of a recession, Keynesian economists have frequently favored a policy of increased government spending combined with a tax cut as an effective two-pronged solution.

Such a policy will have both positive and negative effects on the economy. The tax cut will encourage savings and productivity by putting more money into the hands of consumers and investors instead of government bureaucrats. Tax reduction could therefore enhance output at virtually every stage of the intertemporal production process. Some stages may be more enhanced than others, however, depending on the type of tax reduction legislation passed. For example, a switch to a consumption tax and the elimination of capital-gains taxes on savings and investments would be highly favorable toward the earlier stages of production.

Increased government spending, however, coupled with higher deficits, could be highly detrimental in terms of the inefficiency of more government programs, the crowding out of capital projects on the private market, and creation of further malinvestments in the economy that eventually must be abandoned, especially if the Treasury debt is monetized by the central bank.

An accommodating monetary policy coupled with lower tax rates could bring about a substantial recovery in the economy and, in fact, the benefits of the tax cut could postpone the ill-effects of monetary disequilibrium for some time. The monetary expansion will create a boom/bust cycle, while the tax cut would stimulate a permanent change in consumption/savings patterns and encourage productivity. Figure 10.3 demonstrates how the increased savings can ameliorate the ill-effects of the boom-bust pattern in the capital goods markets as a result of the monetary inflation.

As the figure shows, the monetary inflation would eventually cause an imbalance in the capital goods market, but the genuine increase in savings counterbalances the eventual collapse in capital goods and prevents a worsening recession. How much countereffect would occur depends on the degree of change in the consumption/savings ratio as a result of the tax cut, as well as the magnitude of the monetary inflation.

Such a counterbalance can explain how an economy can postpone, sometimes for years, the ill-effects of monetary inflation. Two periods in recent economic history come to mind: First, the Kennedy tax cuts and expansionary monetary-fiscal policy in the early 1960s, followed by an economic boom which lasted until the late 1960s. Second, the Reagan tax cuts and expansionary monetary-fiscal policy which began in the early 1980s, followed by an economic

Figure 10.3. Effect of Monetary Disequilibrium and Increased Savings

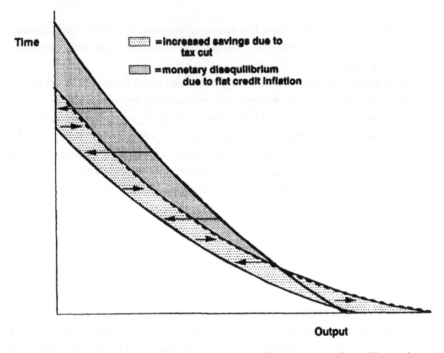

Dotted line = increased savings due to tax cut. Continuous line = monetary disequilibrium due to fiat credit inflation

boom which lasted until the late 1980s. In both cases, the recovery lasted longer than expected.

A PROGRAM FOR MONETARY STABILITY?

The above analysis suggests that government policy needs to be altered significantly. As it stands, central banks play a seriously destabilizing role in the economy. Central banks expand the money supply through the credit markets using such systems as open-market operations, lowering bank reserve requirements, setting the discount rate, and so forth. Such a monetary policy can only create disturbances in the economy leading to a boom-bust cycle.

There is another alternative, however, that some government officials and economists are considering, i.e., a form of direct consumption-oriented inflation. Hayek briefly discusses the idea (without endorsing it) when he refers to the difference in effects between fiat credit going to producers and fiat credit going to consumers,[24] and in evaluating Foster and Catchings's proposal for increasing the level of consumer purchases.[25] However, he does not elaborate on consumer-credit inflation because governments traditionally expand the money supply through business credit.

From the point-of-view of macroeconomic stability, consider the policy of abolishing the central bank and transferring monetary policy to the treasury department. In this way, the expansion of the money supply would no longer take place through the credit markets, but directly through transfer payments and other government payments. In short, since the central bank's open-market operations only create instability in the structure of the economy, there is no legitimate purpose in keeping it.

If, despite the problems inherent in inflation, the government is determined to maintain a fiat money standard, the adverse effects may be less severe if control of the money supply were turned over entirely to the treasury department. Federal deficits would be financed either through borrowing on the credit markets or by expanding the money supply by crediting its own account. Under the latter fiscal plan, the Treasury would not finance deficit spending by selling government bonds and other securities to banks, brokers, and individual investors. Instead, it would print new bills or credit its own account at commercial banks, and appropriate the funds to various military and social budgets. In a sense, this approach would be more forthright than the current covert method of pretending to have a product to sell (Treasury bonds). Meanwhile, the government's central bank could essentially be abolished, at least in terms of open-market operations.

Like any government plan, this one has its drawbacks. It means that the Federal government would no longer borrow money in the bond markets, but simply print the money it cannot cover by taxes. It also means that in order to increase the money supply steadily, the government would have to run a deficit each year equal to the monetary target. A balanced budget would mean no increase in the money supply at all, and a surplus budget suggests the possibility of deflation. This deliberate policy of regular deficit spending may be viewed as an unsound fiscal policy.

Under this new program, interest rates would undoubtedly move up, and would remain at a higher level as long as the increase in government spending remained intact. If government spending and federal deficits fluctuated significantly from year to year, the economy would fluctuate accordingly. But the expansion of the money supply need not create a volatile cycle if the government spent the new money directly on consumption and maintained a constant

level of spending. Figure 10.4 demonstrates the long-run effect of an inflationary consumer policy by government.

The outward shift in the production of consumer goods via government spending would mean a permanent change in the structure of production as long as
the government maintained deficit spending at the same level. The consumption/
savings ratio would shift in favor of consumption, by government edict. As a
result, the lower-order consumer goods industry would tend to expand more than
the higher-order industrial markets. No business cycle would develop because the
money would be spent at the end of the production process, not at the beginning.
Thus, the aggregate demand vector would be the independent variable, and the
aggregate supply vector would respond as the dependent variable.

There are four effects this policy would have on the structure of production,
as indicated in figure 10.4.

First, the expansion in the structure of production would occur primarily
at the consumption stage, not at the higher-order capital goods stage. Government spending, whether in the form of military or social programs, would be
considered primarily a form of consumer spending. Depending on the extent
of government intervention in the marketplace, the state might choose to allocate resources to the production of higher-order capital goods as well, but more

**Figure 10.4. Effects of Direct Government Spending through Monetary
Inflation**

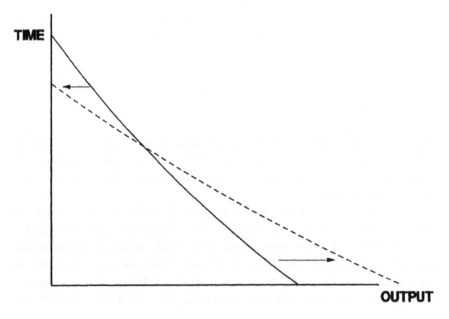

probably it would emphasize the purchase of final goods and services as well as welfare transfers, all of which should be regarded as "consumption."[26]

Second, the structure of production would be realigned away from the capital goods industry toward the consumer goods industry. The degree to which this change occurred would depend on the amount of monetary inflation. The slope of the structure of production (aggregate supply and demand vectors) would flatten as resources (land, labor, and capital) shifted toward the production of government consumer goods and services. In short, the economy would be less capitalistic, characterized by Hayek as "the capital-destroying effect of additions to consumers' credits."[27]

Third, interest rates would rise. Again, the degree to which interest rates rose would depend on the amount of inflation and the general inflationary psychology. Moreover, as long as the government pursued a consistent policy of direct inflationary consumption, interest rates would tend to reach a permanent, albeit higher, level based on their inflation premium.

It might be expected that an inflationary consumer policy involving an initial rise in interest rates and a period of capital consumption would appear as a typical slump. But the slump would probably come about gradually, as opposed to a rapidly developing crisis involving sharply rising interest rates.

Fourth, a policy of direct inflationary consumption would reduce the gyrations of the business cycle if—and this is a big if—government spending policies remained stable. This would be its greatest virtue over the present system. Following the initial adjustment period, relatively full employment could be maintained year after year. Since the inflation would be injected at the *end* of the economic production process rather than at the beginning, as is the case when inflation is created through the credit markets, false signals would not develop in the credit system and the capital-goods market.[28] The production process (the aggregate supply vector) will respond to the altered demand patterns (the aggregate demand vector) established by government policy. The only way a business cycle and monetary crisis could arise would be if the government's rate of monetary inflation fluctuated violently from year to year, or if the government inflated so greatly as to destabilize the public's confidence in the national currency.

Figure 10.5 compares supply-credit inflation to demand-credit inflation.

DEMAND-CREDIT INFLATION AS AN INCOME TAX

Government fiat inflation is often regarded as nothing more than a hidden tax. Although this is true, credit-induced inflation can be worse than a direct tax on

Figure 10.5. The Effect of Two Policies on the Economy: Supply-Side Inflation versus Demand-Side Inflation

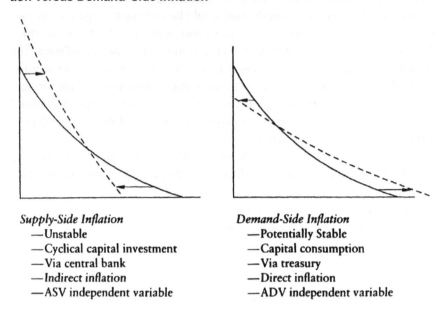

Supply-Side Inflation
 —Unstable
 —Cyclical capital investment
 —Via central bank
 —Indirect inflation
 —ASV independent variable

Demand-Side Inflation
 —Potentially Stable
 —Capital consumption
 —Via treasury
 —Direct inflation
 —ADV independent variable

income, sales, and so forth. We have seen that an inflationary policy carried out through the credit system causes a highly destabilizing economy. However, a policy of consumer-directed inflation is very similar in nature to an income tax. An income tax forces the redistribution of wealth, restrains economic incentives and the standard of living and, as long as the rates don't change, creates a stable non-cyclical environment.[29] The same can be said for direct monetary inflation. It redistributes wealth in favor of the government's interests, even while it creates a noncyclical, albeit less efficient, business environment. But it does so only in exchange for a lowering of economic incentives and the standard of living by curtailing the capitalistic structure of the economy.[30]

If the monetary authorities choose a policy of demand-credit inflation over supply-credit inflation, they should bear in mind that, while the economy will be relatively noncyclical, it will have its own set of serious challenges. Every form of government interventionism creates economy-wide problems; in this case, one set of problems is replaced with another set of problems. Supply-credit inflation is cyclical in nature, while demand-credit inflation need not be. Consumption-oriented inflation may not be cyclical, but it can cause stagnation. Consumer price inflation erodes the purchasing power of citizens, and high interest rates (above the natural rate under a voluntary consumption/savings pattern) retard business activity, just as high tax rates retard business activity. As John Stuart Mill commented, "The usual effect of the attempts of government to encourage consumption is merely to prevent saving; that is, to promote unproductive consumption at the expense of reproductive, and diminish the national wealth by the very means which were intended to increase it."[31] At least supply-credit inflation induces entrepreneurs to innovate, create new technologies, and alter the production process. Demand-credit inflation would tend to retard such entrepreneurial activity. Such a policy could be partially ameliorated by adopting a tax policy which encouraged savings, investing, and business activity. Many countries, such as Japan and West Germany, having adopted this type of tax program by imposing little or no tax on savings and capital gains. There is little doubt that such a favorable tax policy has contributed significantly to Germany's and Japan's spectacular growth rates since World War II.

THE THREAT OF RUNAWAY INFLATION

Another potentially serious problem is that instead of a quasi-independent central bank in charge of monetary inflation, the Treasury would ultimately have unlimited power to finance the government's expansionism. It could result in runaway inflation, as has been the case in many Latin American countries. Under a quasi-independent central bank, monetary authorities sometimes pressure the executive and legislative branches to reduce their spending demands. But no such limitation exists if the powers of money creation were solely in the hands of the Treasury. One solution would be to adopt a constitutional amendment severely limiting the inflation (to perhaps a monetarist rule), although it may be difficult to draft such an amendment without substantial loopholes. It may also be difficult to define "money supply." This could not be a balanced-budget amendment if the government wants the money supply to expand at a steady rate, because monetary expansion only comes about when the Treasury spends more than it takes in.

The point is this: if an automatic restriction cannot be placed on government spending, inflation could get out of hand as easily as, if not easier than, the current system.

Figure 10.6 illustrates the effect runaway inflation has on the economy. When the state prints money rapidly and spends it on consumption, the country gradually consumes its capital as businesses operate less productively and shift toward less risky, short-term investment projects. New construction slows down and older buildings are not maintained. The long-term bond market is wiped out,

Figure 10.6. Impact of Runaway Inflation

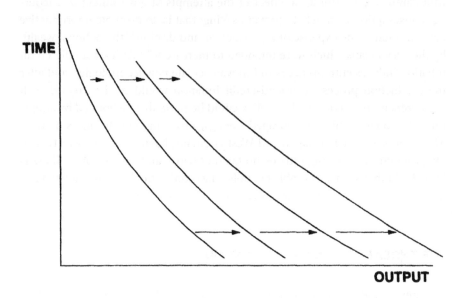

TIME

OUTPUT

and individuals seek refuge in short-term liquidity and inflation hedges. The hyperinflation leads to capital flight and foreign exchange controls. Eventually, the monetary system becomes so unreliable that the economy enters what Mises calls the "crack up" boom, where the local currency cannot be used at all.

It is worth noting that the aggregate supply and demand model used in the standard textbooks does not show the distorted effect runaway inflation has on the economic structure. Once full employment is reached, the aggregate supply curve becomes totally inelastic, so that any further increases in aggregate demand through new government spending programs (financed by inflation) simply cause prices to rise and have no negative effects on real output. But monetary inflation is not benign. Real output is seriously damaged by currency depreciation, a fact that demonstrates once again the inherent deficiency in the neoclassical macroeconomic model.

HAS THE U.S. ADOPTED A CONSUMPTION-ORIENTED INFLATION?

There is growing evidence that the United States has adopted a demand-credit inflationary policy since the 1970s. Hayek points out some of the characteristics of an inflationary consumptive society:

1. High wage level.
2. Expansion in capital expenditures occurring mainly in the service sector and other industries which directly serve the consumer (hotels, restaurants, entertainment, insurance, as well as doctors, lawyers, and so on).
3. High balance of trade deficit.
4. Underutilization of current capital and capacity.[32]

The United States has recently adopted a high consumer policy, but not necessarily because of its productive prowess. The monetary inflation during the 1980s, in particular, has gradually shifted toward consumer credit, not just business credit. Commercial banks have altered their advertising to the consumer in emphasizing credit cards, personal overdraft privileges, and home equity loans. The result has been an explosion in consumer spending. The Japanese and other foreigners have fulfilled the demands of U.S. consumers as the trade deficit has increased substantially since the 1970s. The rapid expansion of credit by the Federal Reserve in the 1980s also served the interest of producers as well as consumers. The credit portion going to business was still a source of macroeconomic disturbance, and will undoubtedly result in recessions in the future.

WHAT IS THE BEST MONETARY STANDARD?

Modern monetary theorists and federal bureaucrats have searched for years for an ideal monetary standard, one which would minimize the distortion and cyclical impact on the economy.

Clearly, the present-day system is the least adequate. Western governments, given the central banks are in control of the money supply, have created the worst of all monetary worlds. With no anchor, they create massive inflationary booms followed by devastating recessions/depressions and economic crises. The fractional reserve banking system makes the financial world even more fragile, as commercial banks and savings institutions become more illiquid.

No Money Growth?

There are other alternatives, however. Hayek favors the extreme case of prohibiting monetary inflation entirely, by adopting the drastic policy of prohibiting any increase in the money stock by the central bank as the only way to permanently stabilize the world's economies. In order to be "neutral" to industrial fluctuations, he writes, "the supply of money should be invariable."[33] Hayek's stringent policy would cause no distortions in the Aggregate Production Structure, and thus "constitute the only means of getting rid of cyclical fluctuations."[34] The central bank would become virtually impotent. At the same time, it would also cause strong deflationary pressure in a growth economy. Hayek dismisses the argument that deflation leads ipso facto to a depression. He refers to numerous economists, including Alfred Marshall and Arthur C. Pigou, to argue that "there is no harm in prices falling as productivity increases."[35] Hayek's views appear to be quite different from those he offered a few years earlier, when he suggested that an inelastic money supply would be obtained "at the price of curbing economic progress."[36] If price and wage rigidity continued to be a problem in the economy, this extreme monetary policy could have severe side effects. As Hayek observes, such a harsh policy can only be regarded as utopian.[37]

The Monetarist Rule

A more appealing method of controlling inflation is the monetarist rule, as advocated by Milton Friedman.[38] Under this device, the current monetary system would be preserved, but the growth of the fiat money supply would be limited to a constant annual growth rate equal to average economic growth (2 to 3 percent a year). The objective would be to maintain a stable price level while minimizing industrial fluctuations.

Imposing such a limitation on monetary growth after a lengthy period of inflation would, of course, precipitate a severe recession, if not a depression. To minimize the ill effects, Friedman advocates a gradual reduction in monetary growth until the monetary slow growth rate is reached.

Nevertheless, while the monetarist rule would provide for a more stable environment and would certainly be an improvement over the current haphazard approach, it would not eliminate the business cycle entirely. As Hayek points out, "But even if the money supply is increased just sufficiently to prevent a fall in prices, it must have basically the same effect on the structure of production as any other expansion in the quantity of money not 'justified' by an increase in output."[39] That is to say, monetary expansion, even at a low steady rate, will create macroeconomic imbalance in the APS, resulting in intermittent recessions. A steady increase in the money supply does not mean that the effect will be spread uniformly throughout the economy, because the monetary-induced below-market rate of interest will create systematic imbalance in the higher-order capital markets. Relative employment, prices, and output will be altered. In short, the monetarist rule would cause a movement away from intertemporal macroeconomic equilibrium.

Conceivably, the monetarists could attempt to spread the credit expansion over the entire intertemporal path of production, so as to minimize the macroeconomic distortions. Such a program could involve the extension of credit to both consumers and producers equally. This would only be possible if the investment and consumer markets were nearly equal in size. It is doubtful, however, that such a plan could be entirely effective, since consumers may not respond to the producers' plans in the expected way.

CONSUMER INFLATION POLICY

From a practical point of view, the idea of financing government deficits through direct monetary inflation may be appealing to government authorities. It would mean the abolition of the central bank's primary role, and perhaps the elimination of the central bank entirely. The banking interests could no longer profit from the violent fluctuations of the boom-bust economy. The treasury would reestablish itself as the primary tool of both monetary and fiscal policy. The two principal drawbacks to such a policy are that, first, the economy may stagnate into a capital consumption society, and second, the government is likely to expand its level of spending in the economy. Monetary inflation is an easy way to finance greater government involvement in the economy. Unlike the traditional avenue of increasing taxation overtly, monetary inflation is an *indirect* form of taxation, easily hidden from the voting public. Moreover, it can be potentially more destructive than taxation. Taxation of income is limited, but monetary inflation is not. It is only limited by the public's concern over higher consumer prices and the resulting loss of confidence. However, the consumer inflation approach might work if an institutional mechanism, such as a Constitutional amendment, could be devised to strictly limit the monetary inflation to a monetary rule of 2 to 3 percent. (As noted earlier, this is not a "balanced-budget" amendment.) Such an ironclad limitation on government is essential since the state is an "inherently inflationary institution."[40]

A MARKET APPROACH TO GOVERNMENT POLICY

While attempting to return to a market solution to macroeconomic instability, free-market economists urge the government to take a series of steps to spur recovery and permanent prosperity as quickly as possible.

First, free-market advocates have argued that the government should stop inflating, which is the source of trouble in the first place. In essence, while treating the symptoms, the cause must also be cured.

During the recession/depression phase, the government should be careful not to reinflate, however tempting it may be, because that would simply delay the inevitable adjustment process and create more malinvestments "which will have to be liquidated in some later depression."[41]

Lionel Robbins, in his classic work, *The Great Depression,* recommended a number of proposals that government should institute to bring about economic recovery. Governments should:

1. Encourage business to regain confidence to invest again, especially in long-term projects.
2. Establish stable foreign exchange rates.
3. Establish the international gold standard.
4. Emphasize greater prudence in foreign lending.
5. Remove trade barriers, such as quotas, exchange controls, and import duties and licenses. ("A removal of the grosser obstacles to trade would be a powerful stimulus to recovery."[42])
6. Encourage greater flexibility in prices and wage rates, and avoid wage-price controls, minimum wage, and so on.
7. Stop fostering monopolistic practices and economic protection.[43]

ENCOURAGING SAVINGS THROUGH TAX CUTS

Another free-market alternative is to consider stimulating savings during a recession, exactly opposite to the normal Keynesian recommendation. As stated earlier in this chapter, such a policy would encourage a renewal in the weak capital-goods industries. Savings could be encouraged by a combination of factors, such as the sharp reduction in or elimination of taxes on investment and savings income (interest, dividends, capital gains, and corporate income), elimination of interest deductions for consumer credit, and so forth. A national savings policy need not be compulsory, as in wartime, but it could be effected via tax policy. A tax cut would encourage higher savings by individuals and corporations, which in turn would lower interest rates and increase the demand for higher-order capital goods. The increased investment pool would prevent the capital-goods industry from declining further. This is why Rothbard comments, "In short, what can help a depression is not more consumption, but, on the contrary, less consumption and more savings (and, concomitantly, more investment). Falling prices encourage greater savings and decrease consumption by fostering an accounting illusion."[44] Furthermore, he adds, "The only way to hasten the curative process of the depression is for people to save and invest *more* and consume *less*, thereby finally justifying some of the malinvestments and mitigating the adjustments that have to be made."[45]

Rothbard also stresses that government should not make the fatal mistake of raising taxes, increasing tariffs, stimulating consumption, artificially maintaining prices and wages, or subsidizing unemployment during a recession/depression.[46]

WHAT ABOUT A COMMODITY STANDARD?

Lastly, many free-market economists favor a return to a bona fide gold standard as the ideal monetary system. While a return to a pure commodity standard may not be politically feasible at this point, it does have favorable arguments from an economic point of view.

First, a pure commodity (or gold) standard minimizes the chance of a serious business cycle and eliminates the need for a central bank to control the money supply. Under a genuine gold standard, there would be no false expansion of the higher-order capital-goods market through monetary inflation, followed by a crippling recession or depression. The government would not need to worry about how to handle a monetary or banking "crisis" under a pure gold standard, because such crises occur only when governments impose a pseudo gold exchange standard or establish a fiat money standard.

Second, a commodity or gold standard does respond to the "needs of business." It is not totally inelastic, as a credit-oriented fiat money standard would have to be in order to avoid a business cycle completely. As indicated in chapter 7, price deflation would stimulate new gold discoveries over the long term and would eventually cause an expansion in the gold-money supply without creating a boom-bust cycle. In terms of monetary inflation, a pure gold standard falls somewhere between Hayek's "no inflation" policy and Friedman's monetarist rule. Based on historical evidence, the money supply (the stock of gold) under a pure gold standard would expand between 1 to 5 percent. And, most importantly, there would be virtually no chance of a monetary deflation under 100 percent gold backing of the currency.

Third, establishing a gold standard would put a check on the temptation of government to expand its economic base. Since the state could no longer expand the money supply at little or no cost, its financing would be severely limited to either taxation or borrowing.

Consequently, a commodity-gold monetary standard offers a stable environment for consistent economic growth, a slightly declining price level, and a limitation of political power. Once a government adopted a pure commodity standard, the biggest problem would be to implement it without creating a prolonged depression based on the malinvestments built up over the decades of prior inflations. The move toward a gold standard would also involve a significant wealth transfer to the holders of gold. These two drawbacks make it highly unlikely that a gold standard will be reestablished any time soon.

NOTES

1. "The wisest choice is to advance on both fronts at once." Keynes, *The General Theory*, 375. W. H. Hutt says, "Very broadly, Keynesian policy seeks to restore coordination by making it possible for people to afford to buy." Hutt, *The Keynesian Episode*, 154.

2. "But the original Keynesian remedy for serious depression—the creation of consumer purchasing power that underlay the New Deal policy in the Thirties—has proved itself incapable of 'priming the pump' and of getting the economy going again. In fact, the Keynesians today have abandoned their master's remedy and now prescribe direct orders for capital goods in massive doses as the one therapy for a severe depression." Peter F. Drucker, *The New Society: The Anatomy of Industrial Order* (New York: Harper & Row, 1962 [1950]), 258–59.

3. Keynes, *The General Theory*, 119.

4. Durbin, *Purchasing Power and Trade Depression*, 162.

5. Tout and Hansen, "Annual Survey of Business Cycle Theory," 132.

6. Estey, *Business Cycles*, 242.

7. Keynes's statement that "Pyramid-building, earthquakes, even wars may serve to increase wealth" (*General Theory*, 129) is absurd, even if such events stimulate capital expenditures. If the public does not want or demand pyramids, earthquakes, or wars, how can they increase wealth? Regarding Keynes' pyramid scheme, L. Albert Hahn retorts, "But the building of pyramids is, in any circumstances, one of the most useless enterprises, since they serve as a residence not for the living but for the dead—and for very few dead at that." Hahn, *The Economics of Illusion*, 97.

8. Estey, *Business Cycle*, 243.

9. Keynes, *The General Theory*, 270. Also cf. Keynes, *Essays in Persuasion*, 148ff. In Hayek's words, Keynes wanted to create "direct inflation for consumption purposes," which would create a boom "quite as effective as would an excess of investment over saving." Hayek, "Reflections on the Pure Theory of Money of Mr. J. M. Keynes (continued)," 40–41.

10. Estey, *Business Cycles*, 242.

11. Robbins, *The Great Depression*, 71.

12. L. A. Hahn, *Common Sense Economics*, 139–40.

13. Traditionally, the solution to the depression was "to direct all possible effects toward a revival of activity in the capital goods industries," particularly by lowering wage rates to reduce losses. "Instead, all efforts were directed toward bolstering up consumption, and the maintenance of wage rates was one of the expedients adopted in order to attain that end." Phillips, McManus, and Nelson, *Banking and the Business Cycle*, 164.

14. Henry Ford, *My Life and Work* (Garden City, N.Y., 1922), 124.

15. Hughes, *The Vital Few*, 304.

16. Quoted in ibid., 305.

17. Mills, *Prices in Recession and Recovery*, 397–98. Italics added.

18. H. Parker Willis, "Inflation and Industry," in Willis and Chapman, *The Economics of Inflation*, 67. David McCord Wright states, "The businessman, then, who thinks only in terms of final sales to consumers, or the forecaster preoccupied with consumption, may alike find themselves caught in deep and disastrous errors." Wright, "What Is the Economic System?" 201.

19. Hayek, *Monetary Theory and the Trade Cycle*, 21–22.

20. Hayek, "Reflections on the Pure Theory of Money of Mr. J. M. Keynes (continued)," 43–44.

21. Hayek, *Monetary Theory and the Trade Cycle*, 215.

22. Ibid. See also Hayek, *Prices and Production*, 149–50.

23. Mises, *Human Action*, 427.

24. Hayek, *Prices and Production*, 11.

25. Ibid., 60–61.

26. "Resource-using expenditures by government are often considered 'investment,' and this classification forms an essential part of the Keynesian doctrine. We have argued that, on the contrary, all of this expenditure must be considered *consumption*. Investment occurs where producers' goods are bought by entrepreneurs, not at all for their own use or satisfaction, but merely to reshape and resell them to others—ultimately to the consumers. But government redirects the resources of society to *its* ends, chosen by it and backed by the use of force. Hence, these purchases must be considered consumption expenditures, whatever their intention or physical result." Rothbard, *Power and Market*, 128.

27. Hayek, *Prices and Production*, 154.

28. Austrian economists generally argue that monetary inflation inevitably leads to a business cycle. However, we see here that the traditional Austrian cycle theory does not fit a consumer-generated inflation, although Bellante and Garrison call it a "variation on the Austrian theme," (Bellante and Garrison, "Phillips Curves and Hayekian Triangles," 222). Several Austrian economists, including Mises and Hayek, refer to the possibility of consumer-oriented inflation (Mises calls it "simple inflation"), but the only Austrian economist I've found to recognize the different end results between a supply-side inflation and a demand-side inflation is Fritz Machlup, who wrote, "Credit granted only to producers will lead first to an expansion of the producers' goods industries (prosperity)

and later to a crisis and contraction (depression); credit granted only to consumers may lead directly to a painful contraction of the producers' goods industries." Machlup, *The Stock Market, Credit and Capital Formation*, 178. Cf. 192–93.

29. "Taxes are compatible with equilibrium. . . . The diffusion effect of inflation differs from that of taxation in two ways: (a) it *is not* compatible with a long-run equilibrium, and (b) the new money always benefits the first half of the money receivers and penalizes the last half. Taxation-diffusion has the same effect at first, but shifting alters incidence in the final reckoning." Rothbard, *Power and Market*, 65, 206n.S. Cf. Bellante and Garrison, "Phillips Curves and Hayekian Triangles," 222–23.

30. The idea of consumption-oriented inflation was the traditional approach prior to the creation of central banking, and was typically used to finance wars and revolutions. In fact, it was much the same as the ancient tradition in Rome and other city-states of clipping coins and debasing the currency. It did not cause a business cycle per se, but resulted in massive inflation, economic retardation, and the redistribution of wealth from the productive capitalists to the unproductive state and its constituents.

31. J. S. Mill, "Of the Influence of Consumption on Production," in *Essays on Some Unsettled Questions of Political Economy* (1844), quoted in *The Critics of Keynesian Economics*, ed. Henry Hazlitt, 2d ed. (New Rochelle, N.Y.: Arlington House, 1977), 25–26.

32. Hayek, "Capital Consumption," in *Money, Capital, and Fluctuations: Early Essays*, 142–53. Originally published in 1932.

33. Hayek, *Prices and Production*, 108.

34. Hayek, *Monetary Theory and the Trade Cycle*, 190.

35. Hayek, *Prices and Production*, 106n.

36. Hayek, *Monetary Theory and the Trade Cycle*, 190–91.

37. Ibid., 190.

38. See Milton Friedman, *A Program for Monetary Stability* (New York: Fordham University Press, 1960). In this book, Friedman recommends that the government expand the money supply at a constant 4 percent rate.

39. Hayek, *Money, Capital, and Fluctuations*, 94.

40. Rothbard, *America's Great Depression*, 29.

41. Ibid., 26.

42. Robbins, *The Great Depression*, 184.

43. Ibid., 125–59.

44. Rothbard, *America's Great Depression*, 24.

45. Rothbard, *Man, Economy and State*, 861. Elsewhere, I have argued that a major reason the U.S. and other western nations recovered from the 1930s depression was not due to an increase in government spending, but because of an unprecedented rise in savings rates. See my article, "Saving the Depression," 211–226.

46. Rothbard, *America's Great Depression*, 26.

ELEVEN

CONCLUSIONS: THE FUTURE OF ECONOMIC THEORY AND RESEARCH

If productivity and capital formation are its focal points, a micro-economic theory can also do what never before could be done in economics: to tie together microeconomics and macro-economics, if not make them into one.—Peter F. Drucker, *Toward the Next Economics*

WHAT HAS THIS WORK ACHIEVED SO FAR?

This treatise began with a critique of the current methodology used by economists to describe the economic behavior of the whole economy, the neoclassical orthodoxy, which, as reflected in the circular flow diagram, the aggregate supply and demand model, and the quantity theory of money, is an overly simplistic description of the economic forces at work and, therefore, is ultimately an incomplete and misleading account of economic affairs. The failure of macroeconomists to incorporate the time element in the economic process leads to several points of misunderstanding and inaccuracy. The neoclassical aggregation of investment into a single, timeless stage leads to the anti-growth, self-contradictory paradox of thrift. The orthodox schools have had difficulty in providing a satisfactory explanation of the boom-bust business cycle. Many have ignored the acute instability caused by monetary inflation, which cannot be reversed without enduring a serious readjustment process. Contemporary macroeconomists have been unable to foresee the financial chaos and instability in various sectors of the economy as a result of massive inflationary injections and other forms of institutional intervention by the government.

BENEFITS OF A STRUCTURAL APPROACH

But this book is not simply a criticism of modern economic theory. An inadequate theory will never be abandoned until a decent alternative is developed to replace it. This book has demonstrated the tremendous benefits that can be gained by using the alternative concept of the time structure of production. The Aggregate Production Structure is a reflection of the micro elements of macroeconomics. It can be extremely versatile, representing the past, present, and future of industrial output. It can pinpoint either equilibrium or disequilibrium. It can even integrate Keynesian themes, as in the discussion of the paradox of thrift. Consequently, the APS can apply to numerous macroeconomic problems.

This work has reached the following conclusions:

First, the Aggregate production structure is a complete general description of economic activity, taking into account aggregate demand at every level or stage of production. It also encompasses changes in aggregate supply—that is, technological change, productivity, capital deepening and widening, and new stages—all along the chain of economic transformation. It is worth noting, in this regard, that Keynes's attempt to develop a general theory to describe economic behavior was incomplete, based as it is, on final aggregate demand only. Keynes's theory of macroeconomics is not so general as it is specific. Aggregate demand must take into account demand at every level of output, not just final demand. It must look at the demand for raw products and unfinished goods, not just the demand for finished goods. Moreover, aggregate supply must also be considered at each stage. Therefore, Keynes's contribution should be viewed in a narrow sense: one that focuses on an aspect of macroeconomics that perhaps was ignored by classical economists. His study of final demand is indeed important. But it should not lead us away from the study of other and, in many ways, more important forms of analysis, i.e., intertemporal demand and supply for higher-order capital goods.

Second, Gross National Product is an incomplete and misleading measurement of economic activity, leaving out the production of all intermediate or unfinished goods during the year. As a result, GNP figures give the highly misleading impression that consumption expenditures (final goods) are by far the largest sector of the economy. The Aggregate Production Structure, as reflected in my alternative figure, Gross National Output, is a much better representation of the value of all work in the economy during the year. It shows that, in fact, the capital-goods producers are the most important sector in highly industrialized countries.

Third, the Knight-Clark concept of a stageless, timeless production function, especially in combination with the simple Keynesian model, has led to serious anti-savings and anti-growth conclusions. Using the APS apparatus, one can see that an atemporal capital structure, where capital goods are treated in a no-stage homogeneous manner, leads inevitably to the paradox of thrift, i.e., that increased savings reduces national income by taking money out of circulation. However, by adopting a more realistic intertemporal production process, with goods involved in numerous multiple stages of intermediate output, the paradox of thrift is proved to be fallacious in almost all cases. The dynamic changes possible in the APS indicate that an increase in autonomous savings will, *ceteris paribus,* lead to economic growth and the adoption of new technology by lowering interest rates, stimulating new stages of production, and encouraging more capitalistic techniques. Eventually, this shift increases real wages and final consumption, and even savings itself. In short, one comes to the opposite conclusion of the Keynesians: increased savings increases national income and the standard of living, and eventually increases savings itself. But it only does so gradually, in the future. Time is an essential element in making savings work.

Fourth, the APS offers a much better and more sophisticated view of the effects of monetary expansion, whether considering gold inflation under a pure commodity standard, an extension of business or consumer credits, or outright spending of the new money by the treasury. Based on the interrelationship of the Aggregate Supply Vector and the Aggregate Demand Vector, it is clear that the inflation models developed by the Keynesians and monetarists are highly inadequate. Keynes's view that the creation of government bank credit is "just as genuine as any other savings"[1] is as mythical as Hawtrey's argument that credits granted to producers will create increased demand for "all goods" in "an exactly equal extent."[2] It is clear from both of these positions that neither the Keynesians nor the monetarists have a time-structural basis to their macroeconomic theories. Nevertheless, whether they recognize the structure of production or not, changes in the APS as a result of monetary inflation can be extremely harmful, both in the short run or long run. The degree of damage caused by fiat inflation depends on how the new credit is injected into the system.

Fifth, the APS provides a lucid visual explanation of the phenomenon of inflationary recession, where national output declines while consumer prices continue to rise. The APS demonstrates that an inflationary recession is essentially a fiat credit phenomenon which occurs after the government has expanded the money supply far in excess of real economic growth rates. It is not simply a result of supply shocks, the standard Keynesian explanation for the recent inflationary recessions. Inflationary recessions are not just a reflection of a single consumer price index, but of prices all along the production axis—prices of raw commodities, producer products, and retail goods and services.

Sixth, the time structure of production resolves the debate over the validity of Say's law. We conclude that "supply creates its own demand" only when the production of specific goods meets the specific demands of consumers. We find that the universal conditions of equilibrium between aggregate supply and aggregate demand only exist in a primitive barter economy, or under a pure 100 percent commodity (gold) standard. Say's law falters when fiat money is introduced into the monetary system, causing a disturbance between aggregate supply and demand that take time and deregulation to mend. Goods and services will be produced for which there is not sufficient demand. Thus, Keynes was correct in criticizing the universality of Say's law, but it was not due to an insufficient aggregate demand, or the alleged disparity between the intentions of savers and investors. Rather, Say's law is sometimes invalidated because demand is of the "wrong" kind.

THE FUTURE OF ECONOMIC POLICY

Seventh, the application of the APS concept has been extremely valuable in assessing the impact of past government actions and future alternative policies.

A major economic objective of government leaders has been to increase a country's standard of living without creating sizeable macroeconomic imbalance and instability. In order to achieve this goal, governments need to find ways to stimulate savings and genuine capital formation. The best method is to remove barriers to capital accumulation. This plan should involve the reduction, or preferably the elimination of taxes on interest, dividends, and capital gains—not as a boon to wealthy passive investors, but as an encouragement to everyone, including wage and salary earners, to save and invest. As Morishima states, "In order to establish modern capitalism, in the sense of a progressive economic system where capital is accumulated and capitalistic production is carried out on a larger scale year by year, both capitalists and workers must be frugal by nature."[3]

In nations which already have an income tax, taxes on investment income and capital gains amount to a form of double taxation, and should be eliminated. Many European and Pacific Basin countries have adopted a plan of tax exemption on investments, which has been responsible in part for the dramatic growth in those regions over the past few decades. The dynamic model of the APS clearly shows the benefits of such a pro-investment program in terms of increased productivity, technological improvement, and higher wages. In fact, in many ways, I regard the principal purpose of this book is to provide a theoretical basis for reestablishing savings and capital formation as the primary goals of a national policy. The Keynesian prescription of high government spending, debt, and consumption has turned the world on its head, causing "undersaving on a massive scale," in the words of Peter F. Drucker.[4] It has made virtue a vice. Hopefully, my structure of production model will bring the world back to a sensible reality again.

I do not wish to imply from this "pro-savings" view that individuals should not establish their own time preference schedule. Individuals should be allowed to allocate present goods to present consumption and future expected consumption, as they see fit. If they wish to consume, and not save, that is their business. But if the choice is between taxation of present *and* future income, versus taxation of present income only, I would choose the latter. Better to exempt future income than to tax everything.

PROSPECTS OF A GOLD STANDARD

The only monetary policy that has no significant ill effects, and may in fact have some positive side benefits, is the expansion of the money stock under a pure gold standard. Of course, under a pure gold standard, the government would have a small, if inconsequential, role. The expansion of the money supply would come from private mining companies, not from the central bank, and would be based on the profitability of mining. In short, the government's monetary policy may be deemed laissez faire. Nevertheless, a passive role would be a significant improvement over the current activist policy. A 100 percent gold standard would never be deflationary. The stock of monetary metal would never decline. By the same token, the money supply would increase incrementally every year, sometimes 1 percent, sometimes 3 percent. But it would never get out of hand. According to historical experience, worldwide gold stocks would never grow by more than 5 percent in a year. Under 100 percent reserve requirements, commercial banks would not be subject to ruinous runs and a loss of confidence by the public. The only alleged drawback, from purely theoretical considerations, is that the money stock is unlikely to grow fast enough to maintain a stable price level. But such a characteristic may not be a drawback at all if wages and prices are not controlled artificially. In fact, under conditions of economic growth, with prices falling on average while wages remain stable, savings would be greatly encouraged, since prices could be expected to be lower in the future.

A gently falling price level may not have the ill effects that many monetarists claim and, in fact, would especially be beneficial to those on fixed incomes.

The greatest barrier to establishing a stable commodity standard is not economic in nature, but political. There is probably no way to return to a sound monetary system without hurting certain classes of people, or without causing a massive short-term adjustment process. This has been the principal stumbling block to the popularity of gold.

THE FIAT MONEY ALTERNATIVE

Under a fiat money standard, the only active inflationary policy that offers any possibility of noncyclical stability is a consumption-oriented inflation. Under this monetary policy, the government would create the new money and spend it directly on goods and services. After an initial adjustment period of capital consumption (probably in the form of an inflationary recession), the economy could achieve a new level of macro equilibrium. As long as the federal budget does not expand too rapidly, requiring a greater and greater inflation, the monetary expansion could be regarded as a hidden tax. In order to assure that government spending does not get out of hand, a constitutional limitation strictly limiting monetary growth would be necessary. Without it, a monetary policy in the hands of the treasury could be disastrous.

The current system of fractional reserve banking and monetary inflation through the capital markets is highly unstable. In addition, many industrial countries such as the United States impose high tax rates on capital formation and investment. All of these factors discourage economic growth. As this work has demonstrated, the effect of this fiat credit system is to cause a strong cyclical bias in the economy which is not inherent to capitalism (as the Marxists claim). The business cycle is highly injurious to long-term capital planning, and is likely to get worse. If the current fiscal and monetary instability is not completely revised voluntarily, it may soon be reorganized involuntarily by the force of chaotic economic events.

The monetarist rule of limiting fiat money creation to be approximately equal to real growth would be a definite improvement over the current system, especially if it included a move toward 100 percent banking reserves. Unfortunately, the malinvestments created in the past make it practically impossible to avoid a serious recession or depression in the future, if such a rule is instigated, even on a gradual basis. In fact, imposing a monetary rule may well undermine the public's confidence in the world's monetary system. If the world monetary system as we know it does not survive, the only reliable foundation the public can turn to is gold, the ultimate money, and it will no doubt play a significant role in a post-Keynesian world if we are to bring about permanent economic prosperity.

PROSPECTS FOR A NEW VIEW IN ECONOMIC THEORY

The time-oriented structure-of-production concept is an essential tool in analyzing macroeconomic events and government policies, and should be a central element of any macroeconomic study.

It is extremely unfortunate that this macroeconomic framework has been neglected for so long in the introductory and intermediate principles textbooks at colleges and universities. Mainstream textbook writers blundered by so readily adopting the Keynesian paradigm and the Knight-Clark capital concept after the Great Depression and the Second World War. This omission must be rectified, even though it will take some time, just as it took decades to eliminate the Bohm-Bawerkian time production concept from most of the textbooks under the Keynesian dominance. Admittedly the Keynesian macro version, as exemplified by the simple Keynesian cross between consumption and income, has been an easier concept for students to grasp than the complex structural approach. As Hutt notes, Keynesianism stresses "the notion of lack of purchasing power or lack of 'effective demand,' instead of the less easily grasped, but realistic, notion of defective coordination."[5] One of the reasons the flawed Keynesian model still dominates today's textbooks is that no sensible alternative has been found. Conceivably, however, once the time factor and a disaggregate approach are reenthroned in the macro textbooks, the more sophisticated Austrian triangles will replace the simplistic Keynesian cross, the AS-AD model, and the monetarist quadrangles, as the best analytical tool to describe macroeconomic events. At the very least, they should be considered side by side with the traditional neoclassical theories.

More and more economists from the entire economic spectrum are recognizing the need for a new macroeconomic paradigm which integrates the importance of time, the production process of goods and services, and the heterogeneous nature of capital goods. These economists include such wide-ranging theorists as John Hicks, Michio Morishima, Wassily Leontief, Kenneth Boulding, G. L. S. Shackle, and even Marxist economist Howard J. Sherman. They see the need to break down the macroeconomic models into their microeconomic components in order to analyze what is really happening in the material world.

Moreover, as was pointed out in the beginning of this book, many related disciplines also depend on a vertical time-integrated approach to economic analysis: distribution channels in marketing, related goods in input-output analysis, vertical integration in industrial organization, the transformation genealogy of manufactured products, and relative prices, employment, and production figures collected by data gatherers.

Figure 11.1 demonstrates the division between the conventional neoclassical synthesis and the time structure model developed in this work.

Figure 11.1. Methodology of Macroeconomic Theory

Conventional Neoclassical Model	Time-Structural Model
objective (cost of production)	subjective (utility)
horizontal	vertical
cross-sectional	longitudinal
homogeneous goods	heterogeneous goods
aggregative	disaggregative
macroscopic	microscopic
simple	complex
one dimensional	multi-dimensional
final aggregate demand	intermediate and final demand
circular flow	evenly rotating
continuous	discontinuous
stocks/flows	discrete
timeless	time structure
general prices	relative prices
general employment	relative employment
general unemployment	relative unemployment
general output	relative output
equilibrium	disequilibrium
cash balances	cash imbalances
static	dynamic
managerial	entrepreneurial

THE FUTURE OF ECONOMIC RESEARCH

Many other areas should be explored in detail in relation to the time structure of production. Here are some suggestions:

Length of Production Processes

First, research should be done on the time it takes to produce goods and services. Currently the period of production concept is a neglected area. How long on the average does it take for iron ore to become a part of a finished automobile or appliance? For a newly planted tree to become the outside of a house? For most agricultural products, the answer may be simply, one season. But for industrial goods, which involve numerous complex stages, the answer is not so obvious. The period of production must also include the waiting time between stages, that is, the inventory period. In fact, an unfinished product may lie idle in inventory longer than the actual time spent to produce it. The economics of inventories is a fruitful area which ought to be examined more fully. Ruth Mack's 1956 work for the National Bureau of Economic Research on the shoe-leather-hide industry is perhaps the only major study that includes some of the above points. Such studies need to be expanded.

Most businessmen and economists pay scant attention to the entire period of production because there are adequate inventories at practically every stage of output. The builder is not concerned with how long it takes for nails to be made, because nails are already in stock. Most tools and supplies are at his disposal without waiting. Only when there is a shortage of a particular input or when a specialized or high-cost item has to be made to order will customer or businessman ask, "How long will it take to get me this product?"

Although there would seem to be exceptions to the rule, the question of "How soon?" is surprisingly prevalent in today's economy. Frequently heard demands include: When will the book be finished? When can we move into the office building? When will the furniture be delivered? When will the new highway be completed? What year does the bond mature? How many years before she goes to college? When will he graduate from medical school? Thus, we see how time considerations are a constant factor in our economic lives.

The only study I know of regarding the average length of time it takes for an investment project to start producing is the research work done by Thomas Mayer in the 1950s. He surveyed several hundred firms, asking them to indicate how long it took them to complete specific projects, such as building a plant, machine, and so on. Although the time frame varied considerably between projects, the average time period between the design and actual completion of an investment project was 21 months.[6]

The Period of Consumption

The second question to be investigated is how long the period of consumption might be. Much research has already been completed on the durability of machines, producers' goods and consumers' goods, especially to determine accurately the depreciation schedules for tax and accounting purposes for machinery, equipment, and transportation. A thoroughgoing study of the age structure of durable capital and consumer goods would be extremely helpful in accurately describing the standard of living in a country.

MEASURING THE APS

A third subject for data gatherers to research is an accurate measure of the Aggregate Production Structure of the economy. As indicated in chapter 6, the Gross National Product is not an accurate reflection of economic activity in the country since it excludes all the intermediate inputs and includes only the final stages of consumption and the production of new capital goods. GNP is actually much more "net" than "gross." A better measurement of the gross output of all goods and services would be what I call the Gross National Output, or GNO.

The GNO could be measured for each country each year, as GNP is figured. Unfortunately, the critical figure in GNO data, the intermediate inputs of individual industries, are estimated for input-output models only, and are currently seven years behind in the United States. (The latest data is for 1982). The benchmark data for I-O models are compiled only every five years. This kind of national income statistic should be determined annually and in an up-to-date fashion as it is for GNP.

A much more difficult problem would be to construct the APS itself in graphic form. No longer dealing with a single number like GNP, the challenge is to decide where to place each industrial sector in the economy's vertical pyramid. Unlike GNP's horizontal output of final consumption, the APS's vertical axis measures the distance various stages are from final consumption. Undoubtedly there would be many roadblocks to measuring that distance. The period of production would have to be estimated, as noted above, with perhaps an estimate made for each stage of industrial output, based on general areas such as raw commodities, crude industrial products, wholesale manufactured goods and retail products. Such an approach is described in figure 5.16 on p. 171.

But even then there are other problems, such as circularity, raised in chapter 5. Constructing the APS will be a difficult task. The end result may be only a crude estimate. But once accomplished, such economy-wide triangles can be then used for comparing production from one year to the next, as well as for inter-country comparisons. It would be interesting to determine whether there is any connection between volume, time and stage development, and savings rates, interest rates, industrial growth, and government policy in terms of the macroeconomic time structure.

Roundaboutness and Economic Growth

Fourth, more research needs to be conducted on the degree of roundabout-ness in the production process and its relationship to economic growth. In what sense are new stages created by adopting lengthier techniques? To what degree does an increase in investment capital allow companies to modernize and adopt already-developed technologies, and to create innovations and new products? How does this expansion in the period of production and capital-intensity affect wage levels? These questions have been partially answered in relation to the automobile industry in the twentieth century, but more detailed research needs to be done in this field from a Böhm-Bawerkian framework. If more roundabout methods do indeed increase productivity, economic growth, and a country's standard of living, then Böhm-Bawerk's theory ought to be sub-jected to additional empirical studies.

Quantifying Malinvestments

Fifth, developing a way to measure the degree of malinvestments in an econ-omy caused by inflationary fiat credit might be another fruitful study by economists. Such studies might be able to pinpoint the level of macroeco-nomic imbalance in various countries, based on the changes in the money sup-ply. This may permit inter-country comparisons. Obviously, countries which inflate less would have a much lower index of macroeconomic instability than those which engaged in massive inflation of the money supply. Clearly some countries are more vulnerable than others to a recession or depression. The traditional method of detecting inflationary bias is by analyzing the strength or weakness of a country's currency in the foreign exchange markets. But per-haps estimating the degree and location of malinvestments could help predict the severity and duration of a recession or depression that would occur as the country returns to stability.

A More Realistic View of Inflation

Macroeconomists, especially monetarist, tend to make simple comparisons between the money supply and the price level. But economists need to take a more disaggregate or microeconomic approach by analyzing what is happening to prices at various stages of production. To determine future price inflation at the retail level, economists should took at current statistics such as the raw commodity price index, producers price index, and so on.

Application to Financial Markets

Sixth, a structural approach may be useful to individuals using economic data for investment analysis and portfolio management. Traditionally, financial economists and money managers have taken two approaches. The first one is macroscopic, i.e., looking at economy-wide data to make investment decisions. They decide whether the general economic climate is favorable toward the equity markets, and if so, they invest in a wide selection of stocks or in a widely-diversified mutual fund. Indicators may include interest rates, consumer price inflation, economic growth and industry-wide profits, and the money supply. On the other hand, if the economic indicators are negative, they may choose to be on the sidelines, or at least to reduce their exposure to the equity markets.

The second method is microscopic, focusing on individual industries and selecting stocks that appear to be favorably priced based on supply and demand factors on a company's fundamental data such as expected earnings. Currently, this method is eclectic in nature. Each sector of the market is analyzed independently, with little effort to relate one to another or to examine their distance from final consumption.

Both approaches could benefit from the intertemporal structural method developed in this work. For instance, we have noted that the consumer-goods industry is relatively more stable in terms of prices, employment, and output compared to capital-goods industries more distant from final use. Moreover, statistical work by Frederick Mills and others indicates that the most volatile area of the economy has traditionally been the raw commodities sector, the second most volatile has been the manufacturers' goods sector, and the least volatile the consumers' goods sector. Thus, the volatility of each market is intertemporally determined, as measured by the distance of each market from final use.

Such findings may be highly useful in constructing an investment portfolio if the prices of stocks can be related to their appropriate intertemporal stage. For example, in a typical inflation-induced stock market boom, the best stock performers may include such "early stage" industries as petroleum, offshore drilling, paper, electronics, aluminum, and gold mining. In a deflationary bear market, they may be the worst performers. Such volatility may also be evident in auto and homebuilding stocks, which are traditionally considered consumer markets. However, as we have indicated in chapter 6, the consumption of automobiles, homes, and other durable goods takes place over a long period of time, and therefore should be treated economically more as capital goods than consumer goods.

According to my own research, industries which tend to be less volatile generally include electric utilities, telephone companies, insurance companies, grocery store industries, drugstores, large chain restaurant businesses, household product industries, beverage markets, and large retail stores. All of these sectors are close to final consumption. Electric utilities, for example, may be generally less volatile because their earnings depend on a relatively steady customer base, which will probably use a more or less constant level of electricity from one year to the next. Demand is relatively inelastic.

Of course, not all consumer products are demand inelastic, and some consumer stocks may be highly volatile. Companies specializing in toys, leisure goods, recreation and gaming industries tend to be much more unstable. Luxury markets in general can be highly unstable according to economic conditions. Consumption should not be viewed homogeneously!

Conservative investors and money managers might limit their stock choices to securities in the more stable consumer area. In this manner, they would profit over the long run according to the level of economic growth, while avoiding the sharp corrections that affect other areas of the marketplace during bear markets. It is still necessary to investigate the strength of a particular company, however, since individual stocks sometimes move in opposite directions to the industry in general.

A more aggressive strategy is available to speculators and professional traders. During a bull market, they may seek higher profits by specializing in the most volatile category of stocks, those furthest removed from consumption, rather than in the stock market in general. They could invest in machine tools, offshore drilling, energy exploration, electronics, tires, mining, autos and housing, among others. Again, this method would not preclude a fundamental analysis of individual stocks, but it would seek to maximize profits by investing in the most volatile stock categories. However, timing would be critical, and speculators and traders would need to shift out of these rapidly moving stocks quickly, or even consider selling short, when the bull market is over.

Security analysts rely on *beta statistics,* but these do not necessarily describe the same relationship in the business cycle. *Beta* is defined as a measurement of the volatility of each stock in relation to the whole market or market sector. For example, the price of a stock over a period of time will be related to the New York Stock Exchange Composite Average.[7] If a stock has a beta of 1.50, it means that it is 50 percent more volatile than the general market, and thus, a higher risk stock.

However, the volatility of individual stocks in terms of their beta statistics does not necessarily correlate well with intertemporal stages, even if one looks at the betas for specific industries. One of the reasons is the lag time between stock movements and the business cycle. Sometimes certain industrial stock groups may move in the opposite direction to the general market, generating negative betas under certain time periods. Gold stocks have sometimes acted this way in the past. Moreover, beta statistics for individual industry and stocks are notoriously unstable and results depend entirely on the time period you use.[8]

Another difficulty is the fact that many large public companies are not exclusively devoted to a single stage of production. Major oil and tobacco companies, to use two examples, are often diversified into many areas unrelated to their basic market. As Bellante and Garrison state, "Some firms may operate within one stage, some in several sequential stages, and some in different stages of different production processes."[9]

Further research in this area should be highly rewarding. Investment textbooks on the market today show that there has been virtually no work done on the effects monetary inflation may have on various financial assets defined according to their intertemporal hierarchy. Inflation and deflation are discussed only in the simplest monetarist terms, using only the most general of indices (e.g., monetary inflation pushes stocks up, monetary deflation pushes stocks down, and so forth). Nowhere does any textbook writer comment how credit-induced inflation could favor securities in higher-order capital markets more than it does to consumer-goods stocks. Thus, new research in this area could be highly profitable, both academically and financially.

A THEORY OF OPTIMIZING PRODUCTIVITY

In an extremely perceptive essay published in 1981, Peter F. Drucker outlined the main tenets of what he hoped would become the "next economics." He dismisses the major schools of neoclassical orthodoxy as excessively macroeconomic in scope. The "house that Keynes built," which, according to Drucker, includes the monetarist pupils, has resulted in a "crisis in capital formation." To be successful, the next economics must "require a theory that aims at *optimizing* productivity." It will "have to be again micro-economic and centered on supply."[10] Certainly, the Far East and Pacific Basin countries, such as Japan, South Korea, Taiwan, Hong Kong, and Singapore, have adopted this "productivity" theory, fostering thrift, minimal tax on investments, reduced government intervention, relatively free trade, etc.—the antithesis of Keynesianism.

It is clear that the time-oriented structure of production, as embodied in the Aggregate Production Structure, is the key to linking microeconomics with macroeconomics. The APS is not entirely aggregative in nature, nor is it completely disaggregative. The golden mean is achieved by aggregating only those economic activities synchronized by their time distance from final consumption, and then leaving the intertemporal stages distinctly disaggregative. The result is the APS, an extremely useful and diversified tool able to analyze the "real economy of commodities and work and the symbol economy of money and credit."[11] This essential structure has undergone a long, time-consuming roundabout process. The foundation was built upon the great works of Menger, Böhm-Bawerk, Mises, and Hayek, among others. The Keynesian and monetarist diversions momentarily took our eyes off this magnificent structure and blurred our view of its fruits; but, clearly, this productivity microeconomic theory, which can be integrated into macroeconomics, is the "missing link" between micro and macro which has eluded economists from Alfred Marshall to the present.

It is time we returned to the foundations laid by Menger, Böhm-Bawerk, and Hayek and completed the unfinished macroeconomic structure, one that is only now beginning to show its full form and simple beauty.

To this end is this work dedicated.

NOTES

1. Keynes, *The General Theory*, 83.
2. Hawtrey, *Capital and Employment*, 250.
3. Morishima, *Why Has Japan 'Succeeded'?* 83.
4. Drucker, *Toward the Next Economics and Other Essays*, 11.
5. Hutt, *The Keynesian Episode*, 156.
6. Mayer, "Plant and Equipment Lead Times." Note that this time period does not include the amount of time it takes to produce the ingredients or raw materials needed for the plant or equipment, which are already in inventory. Mayer's work represents only a portion of the entire production process. With regard to inventory periods, Valerie A. Ramey indicates that total inventories held by durable-goods manufacturers represented almost five months of their GDP. See Ramey, "Inventories as Factors of Production and Economic Fluctuations," 340.
7. A comprehensive discussion of beta statistics can be found in Jerome B. Cohen, Edward D. Zinbarg, and Arthur Zeikel, *Investment Analysis and Portfolio Management,* 5th ed. (Homewood, Ill.: Irwin, 1987), 140–43, 159–62,194–98.
8. Ibid., 196–98.
9. Bellante and Garrison, "Phillips Curves and Hayekian Triangles," 215.
10. Drucker, *Toward the Next Economics,* 15, 13.
11. Ibid., 20.

REFERENCES

Abbott, Lawrence. 1967. *Economics and the Modern World.* 2d ed. New York: Harcourt, Brace and World.

Abramovitz, Moses. 1948. *The Role of Inventories in Business Cycles.* Occasional Paper 26 (May). New York: National Bureau of Economic Research.

Abrams, M. A. 1934. *Money.* London: Bodley Head.

Achinstein, Asher. 1950. *Introduction to Business Cycles.* New York: Thomas Y. Crowell.

Ackley, Gardner. 1978. *Macroeconomics: Theory and Policy.* New York: Macmillan.

Aftalion, Albert. 1913. *Les crises périodiques de surproduction.* 2 vols. Paris. Marcel Rivière.

———. 1927. "The Theory of Economic Cycles Based on the Capitalistic Techniques of Production." *Review of Economics and Statistics* (October):165–70.

Akerman, Gustaf. 1923–24. *Real Kapital und Kapitalzins.* 2 vols. Stockholm: Centraltryckeriet.

Åkerman, Johann H. 1932. *Economic Progress and Economic Crisis.* Translated by Elizabeth Sprigge and Claude Napier. London: Macmillan. Reprint. Philadelphia: Porcupine Press, 1979.

Alderfer, E. B., and H. E. Michl. 1957. *Economics of American Industry.* 3d ed. New York: McGraw-Hill.

Allen, Clark Lee, James M. Buchanan, and Marshall R. Colberg. 1954. *Prices, Income, and Public Policy.* New York: McGraw-Hill.

Anderson, B. M. 1922. *The Value of Money.* New York: Macmillan.

———. 1949. *Economics and the Public Welfare.* Princeton: D. Van Nostrand.

Anderson, Montgomery D. 1934. *Capital and Interest.* Chicago: Business Publications.

Appelbaum, E., and R. Harris. 1977. "Estimating Technology in an Intertemporal Framework: A Neo-Austrian Approach." *Review of Economics and Statistics* 59:161–77.

Atlantic Economic Journal. 1978. "Carl Menger and Austrian Economics" 6, no. 3, special issue (September).

Backhouse, Roger. 1985. *A History of Modern Economic Analysis.* Oxford: Basil Blackwell.

Bain, Joe S. 1953. *Pricing, Distribution and Employment.* New York: Holt, Rinehart and Winston.

Baranzini, Mauro, ed. 1982. *Advances in Economic Theory.* Oxford: Basil Blackwell.

Barry, Norman P. 1979. *Hayek's Social and Economic Philosophy.* London: Macmillan.

Bauer, P. T., and B. S. Yamey. 1957. *The Economics of Under-developed Countries.* Cambridge: Cambridge University Press.

Baumol, William J. 1970. *Economic Dynamics.* 3d ed. London: Macmillan.

———. 1977. *Economic Theory and Operations Analysis.* 4th ed. Englewood Cliffs, N.J.: Prentice-Hall.

Bell, Daniel, and Irving Kristol, eds. 1981. *The Crisis in Economic Theory.* New York: Basic Books.

Bell, John Fred. 1953. *A History of Economic Thought.* New York: Ronald Press.

Bell, Philip W., and Michael P. Todaro. 1969. *Economic Theory.* Nairobi: Oxford University Press.

Bellante, Don, and Roger W. Garrison. 1988. "Phillips Curves and Hayekian Triangles: Two Perspectives on Monetary Dynamics." *History of Political Economy* 20, no. 2 (Summer):207–34.

Bernholz, P. 1971. "Superiority of Roundabout Processes and Positive Rate of Interest: A Simple Model of Capital and Growth." *Kyklos* 24:687–721.

Bigman, David. 1979. "On Capital, Time and Neoclassical Parables." *Economic Inquiry* 17:359–69.

Bishop, George A. 1951. "A Note on the Overinvestment Theory of the Cycle and Its Relation to the Keynesian Theory of Income." *American Economic Review* 41 (March):149–60.

Black, John D. 1926. *Introduction to Production Economics.* New York: Henry Holt.

Blaug, Mark. 1975. *The Cambridge Revolution: Success or Failure?* 2d ed. London: Institute of Economic Affairs.

———. 1980. *The Methodology of Economics.* Cambridge: Cambridge University Press.

———. 1985. *Economic Theory in Retrospect.* 4th ed. Cambridge: Cambridge University Press.

Bliss, C. J. 1975. *Capital Theory and the Distribution of Income.* Amsterdam: North-Holland.

Blodgett, R. H. 1941. *Principles of Economics.* New York: Farrar and Rinehart.

Böhm-Bawerk, Eugen von. 1891. *The Positive Theory of Capital.* Translated by William Smart. New York: G. E. Stechart.

———. 1895–96. "The Positive Theory of Capital and Its Critics," *Quarterly Journal of Economics* (January 1895, April 1895, January 1896).

———. 1901. "The Function of Savings." *Annals of the American Academy of Political and Social Science* (May):58–70.

———. 1906. "Capital and Interest Once More." *Quarterly Journal of Economics* (November 1906, February 1907).

———. 1907. "The Nature of Capital: A Rejoinder." *Quarterly Journal of Economics* (November 1907).

———. 1959. *Capital and Interest.* 3 vols. Translated by George D. Huncke and Hans F. Sennholz. Spring Mills, Penn.: Libertarian Press.

Bordo, Michael David. 1975. "John E. Cairnes on the Effects of the Australian Gold Discoveries, 1851–73: An Early Application of the Methodology of Positive Economics." *History of Political Economy* 7, no. 3:337–59.

———. 1980. "The Effects of Monetary Change on Relative Commodity Prices and the Role of Long-term Contracts." *Journal of Political Economy* 88, no. 6:1088–1109.

Boucke, O. Fred. 1925. *Principles of Economics.* 2 vols. New York: Macmillan.

Boulding, Kenneth. 1934. "The Application of the Pure Theory of Population Change to the Theory of Capital." *Quarterly Journal of Economics* 48:645–66.

———. 1936. "Professor Knight's Capital Theory: A Note in Reply." *Quarterly Journal of Economics* (May):524–31.

———. 1941. *Economic Analysis.* New York: Harper and Brothers.

———. 1950. *A Reconstruction of Economics.* New York: John Wiley.

Bowley, Marian. 1973. *Studies in the History of Economic Theory Before 1870.* London: Macmillan.

Brainard, Harry G. 1959. *Economics in Action.* New York: Oxford University Press.

Bratt, Elmer Clark. 1961. *Business Cycles and Forecasting.* 5th ed. Homewood, Ill.: Richard D. Irwin.

Bray, Jeremy. 1982. *Production, Purpose and Structure.* London: Frances Pinter.

Breit, William, and R. L. Ransom. 1971. *The Academic Scribblers.* New York: Holt, Rinehart and Winston.

Bridel, Pascal. 1987. *Cambridge Monetary Thought.* London: Macmillan.

Brown, Arthur. 1987. "A Worm's Eye View of the Keynesian Revolution." In *J. M. Keynes in Retrospect,* edited by John Hillard. Upleadon, England: Edward Elgar.

Brown, H. G. 1936. *Economic Science and the Common Welfare.* 6th ed. Columbia, Mo.: Lucas Brothers.

Brown, J. Douglas. 1978. Foreword to *The Economic Axioms,* by Howard S. Piquet. New York: Vantage Press.

Brown, M., K. Stato, and P. Zarembka, eds. 1976. *Essays in Modern Capital Theory.* Amsterdam: North-Holland.

Buchanan, James, and Richard E. Wagner. 1977. *Democracy in Deficit: The Political Legacy of Lord Keynes.* New York: Academic Press.

Burmeister, Edwin. 1974. "Synthesizing the Neo-Austrian and Alternative Approaches to Capital Theory: A Survey." *Journal of Economic Literature* 12, no. 2 (June):413–56.

Burmeister, Edwin. 1980. *Capital Theory and Dynamics.* Cambridge: Cambridge University Press.

Burns, Arthur E., Alfred C. Neal, and D. S. Watson. 1948. *Modern Economics.* New York: Harcourt, Brace.

Butler, Eamonn. 1983. *Hayek: His Contribution to the Political and Economic Thought of Our Time.* New York: Universal Books.

———. 1985. *Milton Friedman: A Guide to His Economic Thought.* New York: Universal Books.

———. 1988. *Ludwig von Mises: Fountainhead of the Modern Microeconomics Revolution.* Aldershot, England: Gower.

Butos, William. 1965. "Hayek and General Equilibrium Analysis." *Southern Economic Journal* 52, no. 2 (October):332–43.

Bye, Raymond T. 1924. *Principles of Economics.* New York: F. S. Crofts.

Bye, Raymond T., and William H. Hewett. 1952. *The Economic Process.* New York: Appleton-Century-Crofts.

———. 1963. *The Economic Process.* 2d ed. New York: Appleton-Century-Crofts.

Cairnes, John E. 1873. *Essays in Political Economy.* London: Macmillan. Reprint. New York: Augustus M. Kelley, 1965.

Cannon, Edwin. 1917. *A History of the Theories of Production and Distribution from 1776 to 1848.* 3d ed. London: Percival. Reprint. New York: Augustus M. Kelley, 1967.

Canterbury, E. Ray. 1987. *The Making of Economics.* 3d ed. Belmont, Calif.: Wadsworth.

Carlson, Sune. 1956. *A Study in the Pure Theory of Production.* New York: Kelley and Millman.

Carter, Anne P. 1970. *Structural Change in the American Economy.* Cambridge: Harvard University Press.

Carver, T. N. 1901. "Clark's Distribution of Wealth." *Quarterly Journal of Economics* 15:578–602.

———. 1919. *Principles of Political Economy.* Boston: Ginn.

Cassel, Gustav. 1903. *The Nature and Necessity of Interest.* New York: Macmillan. Reprint. New York: Augustus M. Kelley, 1971.

———. 1932. *The Theory of Social Economy.* Translated by S. L. Barron. New York: Harcourt, Brace. Reprint. New York: Augustus M. Kelley, 1967.

Champernowne, D. G. 1945. "A Note on J. v. Neumann's Article." *Review of Economic Studies* 13 (33):10–18.

Chase, Richard X. 1979. "Production Theory." In *A Guide to Post-Keynesian Economics,* edited by Alfred S. Eichner. White Plains, N.Y.: M. E. Sharpe.

Chenery, Hollis B., and Paul G. Clark. 1959. *Interindustry Economics.* New York: John Wiley.

Clark, John Bates. 1893. "The Genesis of Capital." *Yale Review* 2 (November):302–15.

———. 1895a. "The Origin of Interest." *Quarterly Journal of Economics* (April 1895). 9:257–278.

———. 1895b. "Real Issues Concerning Interest." *Quarterly Journal of Economics* (October 1895). 10:98–102.

———. 1898. Introduction to *Overproduction and Crises,* by Johann Karl Rodbertus. London: Swan, Sonnenschein.

———. 1899. *The Distribution of Wealth.* New York: Macmillan. Reprint. New York: Augustus M. Kelley, 1965.

———. 1907. "Concerning the Nature of Capital: A Reply." *Quarterly Journal of Economics* (May 1907).

Clark, John M. 1935. *Strategic Factors in Business Cycles.* New York: National Bureau of Economic Research.

Clarkson, Kenneth W. 1977. *Intangible Capital and Rates of Return.* Washington, D.C.: American Enterprise Institute.

Cole, G. D. H., ed. 1933. *What Everybody Wants to Know About Money.* London: Victor Gollancz.

Conard, Joseph W. 1966. *An Introduction to the Theory of Interest.* Berkeley: University of California Press.

Cox, Reavis. 1965. *Distribution in a High-Level Economy.* Englewood Cliffs, N.J.: Prentice-Hall.

Curtis, Roy Emerson. 1928. *Economics.* Chicago: A. W. Shaw.

Desai, Meghnad. 1979. *Marxian Economics.* Totowa, N.J.: Littlefield, Adams.

———. 1982. "The Task of Monetary Theory: The Hayek-Sraffa Debate in a Modern Perspective." In *Advances in Economic Theory,* edited by Mauro Baranzini. Oxford: Basil Blackwell.

Dewey, Donald. 1965. *Modern Capital Theory.* New York: Columbia University Press.

Dolan, Edwin G., ed. 1976. *The Foundations of Modern Austrian Economics.* Kansas City, Kans.: Sheed and Ward.

Doll, John P., and Frank Orazem. 1984. *Production Economics.* 2d ed. New York: John Wiley.

Dorfman, Robert. 1959a. "A Graphical Exposition of Böhm-Bawerk's Interest Theory." *Review of Economic Studies* (February):153–58.

———. 1959b. "Waiting and the Period of Production." *Quarterly Journal of Economics* 73:351–67.

Dorp, E. C. van. 1937. *A Simple Theory of Capital, Wages, and Profit or Loss.* London: P. S. King.

Dow, Louis A. 1968. *Business Fluctuations in a Dynamic Economy.* Columbus, Ohio: Charles E. Merrill.

Dow, Sheila C. 1985. *Macroeconomic Thought.* Oxford: Basil Blackwell.

Drucker, Peter F. 1981. "Toward the Next Economics." In *The Crisis in Economic Theory,* edited by Daniel Bell and Irving Kristol. New York: Basic Books.

———. 1981. *Toward the Next Economics and Other Essays.* New York: Harper and Row.

Durbin, E. F. M. 1933a. *Purchasing Power and Trade Depression.* London: Jonathan Cape.

———. 1933b. "Money and Prices." In *What Everybody Wants to Know About Money,* edited by G. D. H. Cole. London: Victor Gollancz.

———. 1935. *The Problem of Credit Policy.* London: Chapman and Hall.

Eatwell, John, Murray Milgate, and Peter Newman, eds. 1987. *The New Palgrave: A Dictionary of Economics.* London: Macmillan.

Ekelund, Robert B., Jr., and Robert F. Hebert. 1975. *A History of Economic Theory and Method.* New York: McGraw-Hill.

Elliott-Jones, M. F. 1971. *Input-Output Analysis: A Nontechnical Description.* New York: Conference Board.

Ellis, Howard S. 1934. *German Monetary Theory, 1905–1933.* Cambridge: Harvard University Press.

Engels, Friedrich. [1894] 1981. Preface to *Capital,* by Karl Marx, vol. 3. Reprint. Harmondsworth, England: Penguin Books.

Estey, James A. 1950. *Business Cycles.* 2d ed. New York: Prentice-Hall.

Faber, Malte. 1979. *Introduction to Modern Austrian Capital Theory.* Berlin: Springer-Verlag.

———. 1981. "Modern Austrian Capital Theory and Orosel's Standard Neoclassical Analysis: A Reply." *Zeitschrift für Nationalökonomie* 41(1–2):157–76.

———, ed. 1986. *Studies in Austrian Capital Theory, Investment and Time.* Berlin: Springer-Verlag.

Fairchild, Fred R. 1962. *Understanding Our Free Economy.* 3d ed. Princeton: D. Van Nostrand.

Ferguson, C. E. 1971. *The Neoclassical Theory of Production.* Cambridge: Cambridge University Press.

Fetter, Frank A. 1910. *The Principles of Economics.* New York: Century.

———. 1927. "Clark's Reformation of the Capital Concept." In *Economic Essays Contributed in Honor of John Bates Clark,* edited by Jacob H. Hollander. American Economic Association. Reprint. New York: Books for Libraries Press, 1967.

———. 1977. *Capital, Interest, and Rent.* Compiled and edited by Murray N. Rothbard. Kansas City, Kans.: Sheed Andrews and McMeel.

Fink, Richard H. 1982. "Economic Growth and Market Processes." In *Supply-Side Economics: A Critical Appraisal*, edited by Richard H. Fink. Frederick, Md.: Aletheia Books.

Fisher, Allan G. B. 1933. "Capital and the Growth of Knowledge." *Economic Journal* 43 (September):379–89.

Fisher, H. F. 1933. *Great Britain and the Gold Standard: A Study of the Present World Depression*. London: Macmillan.

Fisher, Irving. 1896. "What Is Capital?" *Economic Journal* 6 (December):509–34.

———. 1906. *The Nature of Capital and Income*. New York: Macmillan.

———. 1907. *The Rate of Interest: Its Nature, Determination, and Relation to Economic Phenomenon*. New York: Macmillan.

———. 1922. [1911] *The Purchasing Power of Money*. 2d ed. New York: Macmillan Reprint. New York: Augustus M. Kelley, 1963.

———. 1930. *The Theory of Interest*. New York: Macmillan.

Fleming, J. M. 1935–36. "The Period of Production and Derived Concepts." *Review of Economic Studies* 3:1–17.

Fletcher, Gordon A. 1987. *The Keynesian Revolution and Its Critics*. New York: St. Martin's Press.

Foster, William Trufant, and Waddill Catchings. 1923. *Money*. 3d ed. Boston: Houghton Mifflin.

———. 1927. *Business Without a Buyer*. Boston: Houghton Mifflin.

Frank, Lawrence K. 1923. "A Theory of Business Cycles." *Quarterly Journal of Economics* (August):625–33.

Friedman, Milton. 1955. Comment in *Input-Output Analysis: An Appraisal*. Princeton: Princeton University Press.

———. 1968. *Dollars and Deficits*. Englewood Cliffs, N.J.: Prentice-Hall.

———. 1969. *The Optimum Quantity of Money and Other Essays*. Chicago: Aldine.

———. 1976. *Price Theory*. Chicago: Aldine.

Friedman, Milton, and Anna J. Schwartz. 1982. *Monetary Trends in the United States and the United Kingdom: Their Relation to Income, Prices, and Interest Rates, 1867–1975* Chicago: University of Chicago Press.

Frisch, Helmut, ed. 1981. *Schumpeterian Economics*. New York: Praeger.

Frisch, Ragnar. 1965. *Theory of Production*. Chicago: Rand McNally.

Gaitskell, H. T. N. 1933. "Four Monetary Heretics." In *What Everybody Wants to Know About Money*, edited by G. D. H. Cole. London: Victor Gollancz.

———. 1936. "Notes on the Period of Production." *Zeitschrift für Nationalökonomie* 7:577–88.

Galbraith, J. K. 1978. *The New Industrial State*. 3d ed. Boston: Houghton Mifflin.

Garrison, Roger B. 1978. "Austrian Macroeconomics: A Diagrammatical Exposition." In *New Directions in Austrian Economics*, edited by Louis M. Spadaro. Kansas City, Kans.: Sheed Andrews and McMeel.

———. 1979. "Comment: Waiting in Vienna." In *Time, Uncertainty, and Disequilibrium*, edited by Mario J. Rizzo. Lexington, Mass.: Lexington Books.

———. 1980. "Review of Faber (1979)." *Austrian Economics Newsletter* 2(2):5, 11.

———. 1981. "The Austrian-Neoclassical Relation: A Study in Monetary Dynamics." Ph.D. diss., University of Virginia.

————. 1983. "Gold: A Standard and an Institution." *Cato Journal* 3(1):233–38.

————. 1984. "Time and Money: The Universals of Macroeconomic Thinking." *Journal of Macroeconomics* 6, no. 2 (Spring):197–213.

————. 1985a. "A Subjective Theory of a Capital-using Economy." In *The Economics of Time and Ignorance,* edited by Gerald P. O'Driscoll, Jr., and Mario J. Rizzo. New York: Basil Blackwell.

————. 1985b. "Intertemporal Coordination and the Invisible Hand: An Austrian Perspective on the Keynesian Vision." *History of Political Economy* 17, no. 2 (Summer): 309–21.

————. 1986. "Hayekian Trade Cycle Theory: A Reappraisal." *The Cato Journal* (Fall):6:437–53.

————. 1987. "Full Employment and Intertemporal Coordination: A Rejoinder." *History of Political Economy* 19, no. 2 (Summer):335–41.

————. 1989. "The Austrian Theory of the Business Cycle in the Light of Modern Macroeconomics." *Review of Austrian Economics* 3:3–29.

Gay, David E. R. 1973. "Capital and the Production Process: A Critical Evaluation of the Böhm-Bawerk-Clark Debate and Its Relation to Current Capital Theory." Ph.D. diss., Texas A&M University.

Gemmill, Paul F., and Blodgett, Ralph H. 1948. *Economics: Principles and Problems.* 3d ed. New York: Harper and Brothers.

Gifford, C. H. P. 1933. "The Concept of the Length of the Period of Production." *Economic Journal* 43:611–18.

Gilbert, J. C. 1955. "Professor Hayek's Contribution to Trade Cycle Theory." In *Dundee Economic Essays,* edited by J. K. Eastham. Dundee: Dundee School of Economics.

————. 1982. *Keynes's Impact on Monetary Economics.* London: Butterworth.

Gordon, Leland J. 1950. *Elementary Economics.* New York: American Book.

Graham, Frank D. 1930. *Exchange, Prices, and Production in Hyper-Inflation: Germany, 1920–1923.* Princeton: Princeton University Press.

Grassl, Wolfgang, and Barry Smith, eds. 1986. *Austrian Economics.* London: Croom Helm.

Gunning, J. Patrick. 1985. "Causes of Unemployment: The Austrian Perspective." *History of Political Economy* 17(2):223–44.

Haavelmo, Trygve. 1960. *A Study in the Theory of Investment.* Chicago: University of Chicago Press.

Haberler, Gottfried. 1932. "Money and the Business Cycle." In *Gold and Monetary Stabilization,* edited by Quincy Wright. Chicago: University of Chicago Press. Reprinted in *The Austrian Theory of the Trade Cycle and Other Essays,* by Ludwig von Mises, et al., Auburn, Ala.: Ludwig von Mises Institute, 1983.

————. 1946. *Prosperity and Depression.* 3d ed. New York: United Nations.

————. 1986. "Reflections on Hayek's Business Cycle Theory." *Cato Journal* (Fall):421–35.

Hahn, F. H. 1966. "Equilibrium Dynamics with Heterogeneous Capital Goods." *Quarterly Journal of Economics* 80:633–46.

Hahn, F. H., and R. C. O. Matthews. 1964. "The Theory of Economic Growth—A Survey." *Economic Journal* 74 (December):779–902.

Hahn, L. Albert. 1949. *The Economics of Illusion.* New York: Squier.

————. 1956. *Common Sense Economics.* New York: Abelard-Schuman.

Hailstones, Thomas J., and Michael J. Brennan. 1970. *Economics*. Cincinnati: South-Western Publishing.

Hamberg, D. 1951. *Business Cycles*. New York: Macmillan.

Hansen, Alvin H. 1927. *Business-Cycle Theory*. Boston: Ginn. Reprint. Westport, Conn.: Hyperion Press, 1979.

———. 1951. *Business Cycles and National Income*. New York: W. W. Norton.

Harcourt, G. C. 1972. *Some Cambridge Controversies in the Theory of Capital*. Cambridge: Cambridge University Press.

———, ed. 1977. *The Microeconomic Foundations of Macroeconomics*. New York: Stockton Press.

———. 1986. *Controversies in Political Economy: Selected Essays*. Edited by O. F. Hamouda. New York: New York University Press.

Harwood, E. C. 1956. *Useful Economics*. Great Barrington, Mass.: American Institute for Economic Research.

Hausman, Daniel M. 1981. *Capital, Profits, and Prices*. New York: Columbia University Press.

Hawtrey, R. G. 1932. Review of Hayek's *Prices and Production*. *Economica* 12:119–25.

———. 1933. Review of Hayek's *Monetary Theory and the Trade Cycle*. *Economic Journal* (December):669–72.

———. 1937. *Capital and Employment*. London: Longmans, Green.

———. 1941. "Professor Hayek's Pure Theory of Capital." *Economic Journal* 51 (June–September):281–90.

Hayek, Friedrich A. 1931a. "Reflections on the Pure Theory of Money of Mr. J. M. Keynes." *Economica* 11:270–95.

———. 1931b. "A Rejoiner to Mr. Keynes." *Economica* 11:398–403.

———. 1932a. "Reflections on the Pure Theory of Money of Mr. J. M. Keynes (continued)." *Economica* 12:22–44.

———. 1932b. "Money and Capital: A Reply to Mr. Sraffa." *Economic Journal* (June).

———. 1932c. Review of Hawtrey's *Trade Depression and the Way Out*. *Economica* 12:126–27.

———. 1933. *Monetary Theory and the Trade Cycle*. Translated by N. Kaldor and H. M. Croome. London: Jonathan Cape.

———. 1934a. "Capital and Industrial Fluctuations." *Economica* (April).

———. 1934b. "On the Relationship Between Investment and Output." *Economic Journal* (June):207–31.

———. 1935a. *Prices and Production*. 2d ed. London: George Routledge. Reprint. New York: Augustus M. Kelley, 1967. First edition published in 1931.

———, ed. 1935b. *Collectivist Economic Planning*. London: George Routledge.

———. 1936. "The Mythology of Capital." *Quarterly Journal of Economics* (February 1936):199–228. Reprinted in *Readings in the Theory of Income Distribution*, ed. American Economic Association. Homewood, Ill.: Richard D. Irwin, 1951.

———. 1937a. *Monetary Nationalism and International Stability*. New York: Longmans, Green.

———. 1937b. "Investment That Raises the Demand for Capital." *Review of Economic Statistics* 19 (November):174–77.

———. 1939. *Profits, Interest and Investment*. London: Routledge. Reprint. New York: Augustus M. Kelley, 1969.

———. 1941. *The Pure Theory of Capital*. Chicago: University of Chicago Press.

———. 1942. "The Ricardo Effect." *Economica* 9, no. 34 (May):127–52. Reprint, in *Individualism and Economic Order*. Chicago: Henry Regnery, 1972 [1948].

———. 1944. "Price Expectations, Monetary Disturbances, and Maladjustments." In *Readings in Business Cycle Theory*, edited by Gottfried Haberler. New York: McGraw-Hill.

———. 1945. "The Use of Knowledge in Society." In *Individualism and Economic Order*, by Friedrich A. Hayek. Chicago: University of Chicago Press, 1948.

———. 1969. "Three Elucidations of the Ricardo Effect." *Journal of Political Economy* 77 (March–April):165–78. Reprinted in *New Studies in Philosophy, Politics, Economics and the History of Ideas*, by F. A. Hayek. London: Routledge and Kegan Paul, 1978.

———. 1972. *A Tiger by the Tail*. Compiled by Sudha R. Shenoy. London: Institute of Economic Affairs.

———. 1975. *Full Employment at Any Price?* Occasional Paper 45. London: Institute for Economic Affairs.

———. 1983. "The Keynes Centenary: The Austrian Critique." *Economist* 287, no. 7293 (June 11):45–48.

———. 1984. *Money, Capital, and Fluctuations: Early Essays*. Chicago: University of Chicago Press.

Henderson, James M., and Richard E. Quandt. 1958. *Microeconomic Theory*. New York: McGraw-Hill.

Hennings, K. H. 1972. "The Austrian Theory of Value and Capital. Studies in the Life and Work of Eugen von Böhm-Bawerk." Ph.D. diss., University of Oxford.

Hicks, John R., Albert Gailord Hart, and James W. Ford. 1955. *The Social Framework of the American Economy*. 2d ed. New York: Oxford University Press.

Hicks, John R. 1946. *Value and Capital*. 2d ed. Oxford: Oxford University Press.

———. [1932] 1963. *The Theory of Wages*. New York: St. Martin's Press. Contains both the first and second edition.

———. 1965. *Capital and Growth*. Oxford: Clarendon Press.

———. 1967. "The Hayek Story." In *Critical Essays in Monetary Economics*, J. R. Hicks. London: Oxford University Press.

———. 1971. *The Social Framework*. 4th ed. Oxford: Clarendon Press.

———. 1973a. "The Austrian Theory of Capital and Its Rebirth in Modern Economics." In *Carl Menger and the Austrian School of Economics*, edited by J. R. Hicks and W. Weber. Oxford: Oxford University Press.

———. 1973b. *Capital and Time*. Oxford: Oxford University Press.

———. 1974. "Capital Controversies: Ancient and Modern." *American Economic Review* 64, no. 2 (May):307–16.

———. 1977. *Economic Perspectives*. Oxford: Clarendon Press.

———. 1979. "Is Interest the Price of a Factor of Production?" In *Time, Uncertainty, and Disequilibrium*, edited by Mario J. Rizzo. Lexington, Mass.: Lexington Books.

———. 1980. "Equilibrium and the Trade Cycle." *Economic Inquiry* 18:523–34.

———. 1984. *The Economics of John Hicks*. Oxford: Basil Blackwell.

Hill, Martin. 1933. "The Period of Production and Industrial Fluctuations." *Economic Journal* 43 (December):599–610.

Hillard, John, ed. 1987. *J. M. Keynes in Retrospect.* Upleadon, England: Edward Elgar.

Hollander, Samuel. 1985. *The Economics of John Stuart Mill.* Toronto: University of Toronto Press. 1987. *Classical Economics.* Oxford: Basil Blackwell.

Holzman, Mathilda. 1953. "Problems of Classification and Aggregation." In *Studies in the Structure of the American Economy,* edited by Wassily Leontief, et al. New York: Oxford University Press.

Hudson, Michael. 1987. "Keynes, Hayek and the Monetary Economy," In *J. M. Keynes in Retrospect,* edited by John Hillard. Upleadon, England: Edward Elgar.

Hughes, Jonathan. 1986. *The Vital Few.* 2d ed. New York: Oxford University Press.

Humphrey, Thomas M. 1984. "On Nonneutral Relative Price Effects in Monetary Thought: Some Austrian Misconceptions." *Economic Review* (Federal Reserve Bank of Richmond) (May–June):13–19.

Hutchison, T. W. 1953. *A Review of Economic Doctrines, 1870–1929.* Oxford: Clarendon Press.

Hutt, W. H. [1939] 1977. *A Theory of Idle Resources.* Indianapolis: Liberty Press.

———. 1975. *A Rehabilitation of Say's Law.* Athens, Ohio: Ohio University Press.

———. 1979. *The Keynesian Episode.* Indianapolis: Liberty Press.

Jevons, W. Stanley. 1879. *The Theory of Political Economy.* 2d ed. London: Macmillan. Reprint. Harmondworth, England: Penguin, 1970. First edition published in 1871.

———. 1905. *The Principles of Economics.* London: Macmillan. Reprint. New York: Augustus M. Kelley, 1965.

Johansen, Leif. 1978. "On the Theory of Dynamic Input-Output Models with Different Time Profiles of Capital Construction and Finite Lifetime of Capital Equipment." *Journal of Economic Theory* 19, no. 2 (December):513–23. Reprinted in *Readings in Input-Output Analysis,* edited by Ira Sohn. New York: Oxford University Press, 1986.

Johansson, Alf. 1934. *Löneutvecklingen och Arbetslösheten.* Stockholm: Kgl. boktryckeriet, P. A. Norstedt och Söner.

Johnson, Harry G. 1973. *The Theory of Income Distribution.* London: Gray-Mills.

Kaldor, Nicholas. 1937. "Annual Survey of Economic Theory: The Recent Controversy on the Theory of Capital." *Econometrica* 5, no. 3 (July):201–33.

———. 1939. "Capital Intensity and the Trade Cycle." *Economica* 8 (February). Reprint, in Kaldor, *Essays on Economic Stability and Growth.*

———. 1942. "Professor Hayek and the Concertina-Effect." *Economica* (November). Reprint, in Kaldor, *Essays on Economic Stability and Growth.*

———. 1980. *Essays on Economic Stability and Growth.* 2d ed. London: Duchworth. First edition published in 1960.

Keirstead, B. S. 1959. *Capital, Interest and Profits.* New York: John Wiley.

Keynes, John Maynard. 1930. *A Treatise on Money.* 2 vols. London: Macmillan.

———. 1931. *Essays in Persuasion.* London: Macmillan. Reprint. New York: W. W. Norton, 1963.

———. 1931. "The Pure Theory of Money: A Reply to Dr. Hayek." *Economica* 11:387–97.

———. 1936. *The General Theory of Employment, Interest and Money.* New York: Macmillan. Reprint. New York: Macmillan, 1973.

Kirzner, Israel M. 1963. *Market Theory and the Price System.* Princeton: D. Van Nostrand.

———. 1966. *An Essay on Capital*. New York: Augustus M. Kelley.

———. 1976. "Ludwig von Mises and the Theory of Capital and Interest." In *The Economics of Ludwig von Mises*, edited by Lawrence S. Moss. Kansas City, Kans.: Sheed and Ward.

Kirzner, Israel M. 1986. *Subjectivism, Intelligibility and Economic Understanding*. New York: New York University Press.

Klausinger, Hansjörg von. 1986. "Hayek's *Prices and Production* Re-Analyzed: A Note." *Jahrbücher für Nationalökonomie and Statistik* 201(4):422–28.

Knight, Frank H. 1921. *Risk, Uncertainty and Profit*. New York: Harper and Row.

———. 1933. "Capitalistic Production, Time and the Rate of Return." In *Economic Essays in Honour of Gustav Cassel*. London: George Allen and Unwin.

———. 1934. "Capital, Time, and the Interest Rate." *Economica* New Series 3:(August):257–86.

———. 1935a. "Professor Hayek and the Theory of Investment." *Economic Journal* (March).

———. 1935b. "The Theory of Investment Once More: Mr. Boulding and the Austrians." *Quarterly Journal of Economics* 49:36–67.

———. 1935c. "Comment." *Journal of Political Economy* 43(5):625–27.

———. 1941. "Professor Mises and the Theory of Capital." *Economica* 8:409–27.

———. 1944. "Diminishing Returns from Investment." *Journal of Political Economy* 52:26–47.

———. 1946. "Capital and Interest." *Encyclopedia Britannica*. Vol. 4, 779–801. Reprinted in *Readings in the Theory of Income Distribution*. Edited by American Economic Association, 384–417. Homewood, Ill.: Richard D. Irwin.

———. 1950. Introduction to *Principles of Economics*, by Carl Menger. Glencoe, Ill.: Free Press.

Kregel, J. A. 1976. *Theory of Capital*. London: Macmillan.

Kuenne, Robert E. 1971. *Eugen von Böhm-Bawerk*. New York: Columbia University Press.

Kuznets, Simon. 1946. *National Income: A Summary of Findings*. New York: Arno Press.

———. 1953. "Relation Between Capital Goods and Finished Products in the Business Cycle." In *Economic Change*. New York: W. W. Norton.

Kydland, Finn E., and Edward C. Prescott. 1982. "Time to Build and Aggregate Fluctuations." *Econometrica* 50, no. 6 (November):1345–70.

Lachmann, Ludwig M. 1938. "Investment and Costs of Production," *American Economic Review* 28, no. 3 (September):469–81.

———. 1943. "The Role of Expectations in Economics as a Social Science." *Economica* 10 (February):12–23.

———. 1973. *Macro-economic Thinking and the Market Economy*. London: Institute of Economic Affairs.

———. 1974. "Comment: Austrian Economics Today." In *Time, Uncertainty and Disequilibrium*, edited by Mario J. Rizzo. Lexington, Mass.: Lexington Books.

———. 1976. "From Mises to Shackle: An Essay on Austrian Economics and the Kaleidic Society." *Journal of Economic Literature* 14:54–62.

———. 1977. *Capital, Expectations and the Market Process*. Kansas City, Kans.: Sheed Andrews and McMeel.

———. [1956] 1978. *Capital and Its Structure*. 2d ed. Reprint, Kansas City, Kans.: Sheed Andrews and McMeel.

———. 1986a. *The Market as an Economic Process.* Oxford: Basil Blackwell.

———. 1986b. "Austrian Economics Under Fire: The Hayek-Sraffa Duel in Retrospect." In *Austrian Economics,* edited by Wolfgang Grassl and Barry Smith. London: Croom Helm.

Laidlaw, David. 1982. *Monetarist Perspectives.* Cambridge: Harvard University Press.

Lange, Oskar. [1938] 1964. "On the Economic Theory of Socialism." Reprint, in *On the Economic Theory of Socialism,* edited by Benjamin E. Lippincott. New York: McGraw-Hill.

Lavoie, Don. 1983. "Economic Calculation and Monetary Stability." *Cato Journal* 3(1):163–70.

———. 1985a. *Rivalry and Central Planning: The Socialist Calculation Debate Reconsidered.* Cambridge: Cambridge University Press.

———. 1985b. *National Economic Planning: What Is Left?* Washington, D.C.: Cato Institute.

Leijonhufvud, Axel. 1968. *On Keynesian Economics and the Economics of Keynes.* New York: Oxford University Press.

———. 1977. "Costs and Consequences of Inflation." In *Microeconomic Foundations of Macroeconomics,* edited by G. C. Harcourt. New York: Stockton Press.

———. 1981. *Information and Coordination: Essays in Macroeconomic Theory.* New York: Oxford University Press.

———. 1986. "Real and Monetary Factors in Business Fluctuations." *Cato Journal* (Fall):409–20.

Leontief, Wassily. 1966. *Input-Output Economics.* New York: Oxford University Press.

Lerner, Abba P. 1949. "The Inflationary Process—Some Theoretical Aspects." *Review of Economics and Statistics* 31 (August): 193–200. Reprinted in *Essays in Economic Analysis.* London: Macmillan, 1953.

———. 1980. "A Keynesian on Hayek." *Challenge* (September–October):45–47.

Lewin, Peter. 1986. "Viewpoints on the 'New' Austrian Monetary Economics." *Austrian Economics Newsletter* (Spring):1–8.

Lindahl, Erik. 1939. *Studies in the Theory of Money and Capital.* New York: Farrar and Rinehart.

Littlechild, Stephen C. 1979. *The Fallacy of the Mixed Economy.* San Francisco: Cato Institute.

Longfield, Mountifort. 1971. *The Economic Writings of Mountifort Longfield.* Edited by R. D. Colliston Black. New York: Augustus M. Kelley.

Lundberg, Erik. 1937. *Studies in the Theory of Economic Expansion.* London: P. S. King. Reprint. New York: Augustus M Kelley, 1954.

Lusch, Robert F., and Virginia N. 1987. *Principles of Marketing.* Boston: Kent Publishing.

Lutz, Friedrich A. 1968. *The Theory of Interest.* Chicago: Aldine.

Lutz, F. A., and D. C. Hague, eds. 1965. *The Theory of Capital: Proceedings of a Conference Held by the International Economic Association.* London: Macmillan.

Lutz, Friedrich, and Vera Litz. 1951. *The Theory of Investment of the Firm.* New York: Greenwood Press.

Macfie, Alec L. 1934. *Theory of the Trade Cycle.* London: Macmillan.

Machlup, Fritz. 1935a. "Professor Knight and the 'Period of Production.'" *Journal of Political Economy* 43(5):577–624.

———. 1935b. "The Consumption of Capital in Austria." *Review of Economic Statistics* 17(1):13–19.

———. 1940. *The Stock Market, Credit and Capital Formation.* Translated by Vera C. Smith. London: William Hodge.

———. 1974. "Friedrich A. Hayek's Contribution to Economics." *Swedish Journal of Economics* 76(4):498–531.

———. 1976. *Essays on Hayek.* New York: New York University Press.

———. 1984. "Money, Credit, Capital and Cycles—Machlup on Hayek." In *Contemporary Economists in Perspective,* edited by William Breit and Kenneth A. Elzinga. Greenwich, Conn.: JAI Press.

Mack, Ruth P. 1956. *Consumption and Business Fluctuations: A Case Study of the Shoe, Leather, Hide Sequence.* New York: National Bureau of Economic Research.

Malanos, George. 1962. *Intermediate Economic Theory.* Chicago: J. B. Lippincott.

Marget, Arthur W. 1932. Review of Hayek's *Prices and Production. Journal of Political Economy* 40 (April):261–66.

———. 1932–33. "The Definition of the Concept of a 'Velocity of Circulation of Goods.'" Part 1. *Economica* 12:431–56; Part 2. *Economica* 13:275–300.

———. 1938–42. *The Theory of Prices.* 2 vols. New York: Prentice-Hall. Reprint. New York: Augustus M. Kelley, 1966.

Marshall, Alfred. [1920] 1961. *Principles of Economics.* 9th ed. Reprint. New York: Macmillan.

Marshall, L. C., et al. 1913. *Materials for the Study of Elementary Economics.* Chicago: University of Chicago Press.

Marx, Karl. [1867] 1976. *Capital.* Vol. 1. Translated by Ben Fowkes. Harmondsworth, England: Penguin Books.

———. [1885] 1978. *Capital.* vol. 2. Translated by David Fernbach. Harmondsworth, England: Penguin Books.

———. [1894] 1981. *Capital.* Vol. 3. Translated by David Fernbach. Harmondsworth, England: Penguin Books.

———. [1953] 1973. *Grundrisse.* Translated by Martin Nicolaus. Harmondsworth, England: Penguin Books.

Mayer, Thomas. 1960. "Plant and Equipment Lead Times." *Journal of Business* 33 (1960):127–32.

McCloughry, Roy. 1982. "Neutrality and Monetary Equilibrium: A Note on Desai." In *Advances in Economic Policy,* edited by Mauro Baranzini. Oxford: Basil Blackwell.

McConnell, Campbell R. 1987. *Economics.* 10th ed. New York: McGraw-Hill.

Means, Gardiner C. 1953. *Industrial Prices and Their Relative Inflexibility.* Washington, D.C.: U.S. Department of Agriculture.

Menger, Carl. [1871] 1976. *Principles of Economics.* Translated by James Dingwall and Bert F. Hoselitz. New York: New York University Press.

Mill, John Stuart. [1844] 1977. "Of the Influence of Consumption on Production." In *The Critics of Keynesian Economics,* edited by Henry Hazlitt. New Rochelle, N.Y.: Arlington House.

———. 1967. *Collected Works of John Stuart Mill.* Edited by J. M. Robson. Toronto: University of Toronto Press.

Milgate, Murray. 1979. "On the Origin of the Notion of 'Intertemporal Equilibrium.'" *Economica* 46:1–10.

———. 1982. *Capital and Employment*. London: Academic Press.

Miller, Ervin. 1978. *Macroeconomic Effects of Monetary Policy*. New York: St. Martin's Press.

Mills, Frederick C. 1936. *Prices in Recession and Recovery*. New York: National Bureau of Economic Research.

———. 1946. *Price-Quantity Interactions in Business Cycles*. New York: National Bureau of Economic Research.

———. 1948. *The Structure of Postwar Prices*. Occasional Paper 27 (July). New York: National Bureau of Economic Research.

Mises, Ludwig von. 1935. "Economic Calculation in the Socialist Commonwealth." In *Collectivist Economic Planning: Critical Studies on the Possibilities of Socialism,* edited by F. A. Hayek. Translated by S. Adler. London: Routledge.

———. 1934. *The Theory of Money and Credit*. Translated by H. E. Batson. London: Jonathan Cape. Reprint. Irvington-on-Hudson, N.Y.: Foundation for Economic Education, 1971.

———. 1943. "'Elastic Expectations' and the Austrian Theory of the Trade Cycle." *Economica* 10 (August):251–52.

———. 1949. *Human Action*. New Haven: Yale University Press.; 3d ed. Chicago: Henry Regnery, 1966.

———. 1976. "Inconvertible Capital." In *Epistemological Problems in Economics*. Translated by George Reisman. New York: New York University Press.

———. 1978. *On the Manipulation of Money and Credit*. Translated by Bettina B. Greaves, edited by Percy L. Greaves, Jr. Dobbs Ferry, N.Y.: Free Market Books.

———. 1980. *Planning for Freedom*. 4th ed. Spring Mills: Pa.: Libertarian Press.

———. 1981. *Socialism: An Economic and Sociological Analysis*. Translated by J. Kahane. Indianapolis: Liberty Press.

Mitchell, Wesley C. 1927. *Business Cycles: The Problem and Its Setting*. New York: National Bureau of Economic Research.

Mixter, C. W. 1897. "A Forerunner of Böhm-Bawerk (John Rae)." *Quarterly Journal of Economics* 11:161–90.

Modigliani, Franco. 1986. "Life Cycle, Individual Thrift, and the Wealth of Nations." *American Economic Review* 76(3):297–313.

———. 1987. "The Key to Saving Is Growth, Not Thrift." *Challenge* (May–June):24–29.

Moffat, James E., C. Lawrence Christenson, Mark C. Mills, William C. Cleveland, Samuel E. Braden, and Gerald J. Matchett. 1947. *Economics: Principles and Problems*. 4th ed. New York: Thomas Y. Crowell.

Moldofsky, N. 1982. "Review of Faber." *Economic Record* 58(162):295–97.

Moore, Geoffrey H. 1972. "The Cyclical Behavior of Prices." In *The Business Cycle Today,* edited by Victor Zarnowitz. New York: National Bureau of Economic Research.

Morgenstern, Oskar. 1979. *National Income Statistics: A Critique of Macroeconomic Aggregation*. San Francisco: Cato Institute. Reprinted from Morgenstern, *On the Accuracy of Economic Observations*. 2d ed. Princeton: Princeton University Press, 1963.

Morishima, Michio. 1976. *The Economic Theory of Modern Society*. Translated by D. W. Anthony. Cambridge: Cambridge University Press.

———. 1982. *Why Has Japan 'Succeeded'?* Cambridge: Cambridge University Press.

Moss, Laurence S. 1980. Review of Faber's *Introduction to Modern Austrian Capital Theory.* *Journal of Economic Literature* 18:1095–98.

Moss, Laurence S., and Karen I. Vaughn. 1986. "Hayek's Ricardo Effect: A Second Look." *History of Political Economy* 18(4):545–65.

Moulton, Harold G. 1935. *The Formation of Capital.* Washington, D.C.: Brookings Institute.

Myrdal, Gunnar. 1939. *Monetary Equilibrium.* Reprint. New York: Augustus M. Kelley, 1965.

Neisser, Hans. 1934. "Monetary Expansion and the Structure of Production." *Social Research* 1:434–57.

Neumann, J. von. 1945–46. "A Model of General Economic Equilibrium." *Review of Economic Studies* 13(33):1–9.

Niehans, Jurg. 1978. *The Theory of Money.* Baltimore: Johns Hopkins University Press.

Nurkse, R. 1935. "The Schematic Representation of the Structure of Production." *Review of Economic Studies* 2:232–44.

O'Brien, D. P. 1988. "Lionel Charles Robbins, 1898–1984." *Economic Journal* 98 (March): 104–25.

O'Brien, D. P., and John R. Presley, eds. 1981. *Pioneers in Modern Economics in Britain.* London: Macmillan.

O'Driscoll, Gerald P., Jr. 1977. *Economics as a Coordination Problem: The Contributions of Friedrich A. Hayek.* Kansas City, Kans.: Sheed Andrews and McMeel.

———. 1979. "Rational Expectations, Politics, and Stagflation." In *Time, Uncertainty, and Disequilibrium,* edited by Mario Rizzo. Lexington, Mass.: Lexington Books.

———. 1980. "Frank A. Fetter and 'Austrian' Business Cycle Theory." *History of Political Economy* 12(4):542–57.

O'Driscoll, Gerald P., Jr., and Mario J. Rizzo. 1985. *The Economics of Time and Ignorance.* Oxford: Basil Blackwell.

Orosel, Gerhard O. 1979. "A Reformulation of the Austrian Theory of Capital and Its Application to the Debate on Reswitching and Related Paradoxa." *Zeitschrift für Nationalökonomie* 39: 1–31.

———. 1981. "Faber's Modern Austrian Capital Theory: A Critical Survey." *Zeitschrift für Nationalökonomie* 41(1–2):141–55.

Pasinetti, Luigi L. 1977. *Lectures on the Theory of Production.* New York: Columbia University Press.

Patinkin, Don. 1965. *Money, Interest and Prices.* 2d ed. New York: Harper and Row.

Pellengahr, Ingo. 1986. "Austrians I Versus Austrians II: A Subjectivist View of Interest," and "Functionalist Versus Essentialist Theories of Interest." In *Studies in Austrian Capital Theory, Investment and Time,* edited by M. Faber. New York: Springer-Verlag.

Peterson, Shorey. 1949. *Economics.* New York: Henry Holt.

Phillips, C. A., T. F. McManus, and R. W. Nelson. 1937. *Banking and the Business Cycle.* New York: Macmillan. Reprint. New York: Arno Press, 1972.

Pick, H. J. 1977. "Materials, Resources and Production: An Engineer's View." In *Structure, System and Economic Policy,* edited by Wassily Leontief, 143–64. Cambridge: Cambridge University Press.

Pigou, A. C. 1935. "Inflation, Depression and Reflation." In *Economics in Practice.* London: Macmillan.

Piquet, Howard S. 1978. *The Economic Axioms.* New York: Vantage Press.

Preinreich, G. A. D. 1940. "The Economic Life of Industrial Equipment." *Econometrica* 8, no. 1 (January):12–44.

Presley, J. R. 1979. *Robertsonian Economics.* London: Macmillan.

Quesnay, François. 1972. *Tableau Economique. 3d ed.* Edited by Marguerite Kucznski and Ronald L. Meek. London: Macmillan. Originally published in 1758–59.

Rae, John. 1834. *Statement of Some New Principles on the Subject of Political Economy.* Boston: Hilliard, Gray. Reprint. New York: Augustus M. Kelley, 1964.

———. [1834] 1905. *The Sociological Theory of Capital.* Edited by Charles Whitney Mixter. New York: Macmillan. This is a reprint of *New Principles of Political Economy.*

Rae, John B. 1965. *The American Automobile.* Chicago: University of Chicago Press.

Ramey, Valerie A. 1989. "Inventories as Factors of Production and Economic Fluctuations." *American Economic Review* 79, no. 3 (June):338–54.

Ramsey, James B. 1980. *Economic Forecasting—Models or Markets?* San Francisco: Cato Institute.

Read, Leonard E. 1958. "I, Pencil, My Family Tree As Told To." *Freeman* 8, no. 12 (December 1958). Reprinted in *Free Market Economics: A Basic Reader,* compiled by Bettina B. Greaves. Irvington-on-Hudson, N.Y.: Foundation for Economic Education, 1975.

Reekie, W. Duncan. 1984. *Markets, Entrepreneurs and Liberty.* Brighton, England: Wheatsheaf Books.

Ricardo, David. [1821] 1951. *On the Principles of Political Economy and Taxation.* In *The Works and Correspondence of David Ricardo,* edited by Piero Sraffa. Vol. 1. Cambridge: Cambridge University Press.

Rizzo, Mario J. ed., 1979. *Time, Uncertainty, and Disequilibrium.* Lexington, Mass.: Lexington Books.

Robbins, Lionel. 1931. Foreward to *Prices and Production,* by F. A. Hayek. London: George Routledge.

Robbins, Lionel. 1932. "Consumption and the Trade Cycle." *Economica* 12 (November):413–30.

———. 1934a. "Production." In *Encyclopaedia of the Social Sciences.* New York: Macmillan.

———. 1934b. *The Great Depression.* London: Macmillan.

———. 1971. *Autobiography of an Economist.* London: Macmillan.

Robertson, Dennis H. 1915. *A Study of Industrial Fluctuations.* London: P. S. King.

———. 1926. *Banking Policy and the Price Level.* London: P. S. King.

———. 1934. "Industrial Fluctuation and the Nature Rate of Interest." *Economic Journal* 44 (December):650–56.

Robinson, Joan. 1953. "The Production Function and the Theory of Capital." *Review of Economic Studies* 21:81–106.

———. 1969. *The Accumulation of Capital.* 3d ed. London: Macmillan.

———. 1972. "The Second Crisis in Economic Theory." *American Economic Review* 62, no. 2 (May): 1–10.

Rodbertus, Johann Karl. 1898. *Overproduction and Crises.* Translated by Julia Franklin. London: Swan, Sonnenschein. Reprint. New York: Augustus M. Kelley, 1969.

Roll, Eric. 1934. *About Money.* London: Faber and Faber.

Rolph, Earl R. 1980. "On Austrian Capital Theory: A Comment." *Economic Inquiry* 18:501–3.

Röpke, Wilhelm. 1933. "Trends in German Business Cycle Policy." *Economic Journal* 43 (September):427–41.

———. 1936. *Crisis and Cycles.* Translated by Vera C. Smith. London: William Hodge.

———. 1963. *Economics of a Free Society.* Translated by Patrick M. Boarman. Chicago: Henry Regnery.

———. 1969. *Against the Tide.* Translated by Elizabeth Henderson. Chicago: Henry Regnery.

Rosenbloom, Bert. 1983. *Marketing Channels: A Management View.* 2d ed. Chicago: Dryden Press.

Rothbard, Murray N. 1962a. *Man, Economy and State.* Los Angeles: Nash.

———. 1962b. "The Case for a 100 Percent Gold Dollar." In *In Search of a Monetary Constitution,* edited by Leland B. Yeager. Cambridge: Harvard University Press, 1962. Reprint. Washington, D.C.: Libertarian Review Press, 1974.

———. 1970. *Power and Market.* Menlo Park, Calif.: Institute for Humane Studies.

———. 1975. *America's Great Depression.* 3d ed. Kansas City, Kans.: Sheed and Ward.

———. 1986. *The Brilliance of Turgot.* Auburn, Ala.: Ludwig von Mises Institute.

Rufener, L. A. *Principles of Economics.* Boston: Houghton Mifflin.

Salerno, Joseph T. 1989. "Comment on Tullock's 'Why Austrians Are Wrong About Depressions.'" *Review of Austrian Economics* 3:141–46.

Samuelson, Paul A. 1947. *Foundations of Economic Analysis.* Cambridge: Harvard University Press.

———. 1948. *Economics: An Introductory Analysis.* New York: McGraw-Hill.

———. 1961–62. "Parable and Realism in Capital Theory: The Surrogate Production Function." *Review of Economic Studies* 28:193–206.

———. 1964. "A. P. Lerner at Sixty." *Review of Economic Studies* 31:169–78.

———. 1966. "Paradoxes in Capital Theory: A Summing Up." *Quarterly Journal of Economics* 80:568–83.

Samuelson, Paul A., and William D. Nordhaus. 1989. *Economics.* 13th ed. New York: McGraw-Hill.

Samuelson, Paul A., and Robert M. Solow. 1956. "A Complete Capital Model Involving Heterogeneous Capital Goods." *Quarterly Journal of Economics* 70:537–62.

Say, Jean-Baptiste. [1821] 1880. *A Treatise on Political Economy.* Philadelphia: Claxton, Remsen and Haffelfinger. Reprint. New York: Augustus M. Kelley, 1971.

Scherer, F. M. 1970. *Industrial Market Structure and Economic Performance.* Chicago: Rand McNally.

Schumacher, E. F. 1935. "Inflation and the Structure of Production." In *The Economics of Inflation,* edited by H. P. Willis and J. M. Chapman. New York: Columbia University Press.

Schumpeter, Joseph A. 1939. *Business Cycles.* 2 vols. New York: McGraw-Hill.

———. 1934. *The Theory of Economic Development.* Translated by Redvers Opie. Cambridge: Harvard University Press.

———. 1951. *Ten Great Economists.* New York: Oxford University Press.

———. 1954. *History of Economic Analysis.* New York: Oxford University Press.

Scott, William A. 1933. *The Development of Economics.* New York: D. Appleton-Century.

Seligman, Ben B. 1962. *Main Currents in Modern Economics*. Glencoe, Ill.: Free Press.

Seligman, Edwin R. A. 1921. *Principles of Economics*. 9th ed. New York: Longmans, Green.

Sen, A. 1974. "On Some Debates in Capital Theory." *Economica* 41:328–35.

Shackle, G. L. S. 1933. "Some Notes on Monetary Theories of the Trade Cycle." *Review of Economic Studies* 1:27–28.

———. 1972. *Epistemics and Economics*. Cambridge: Cambridge University Press.

———. 1977. "New Tracts for Economic Theory, 1926–1939." In *Modern Economic Thought*, edited by Sidney Weintraub. Oxford: Basil Blackwell.

———. 1981. "F. A. Hayek." In *Pioneers of Modern Economics in Britain*, edited by D. P. O'Brien and John R. Presley. London: Macmillan.

Shand, Alexander H. 1984. *The Capitalist Alternative*. London: Harvester Press.

Sherman, Howard J. 1964. *Introduction to the Economics of Growth, Unemployment and Inflation*. New York: Appleton-Century-Crofts.

Sherman, Howard J., and Gary R. Evans. 1984. *Macroeconomics: Keynesian, Monetarist, and Marxist Views*. New York: Harper and Row.

Sherwood, Sidney. 1897. "The Function of the Undertaker." *Yale Review* (November):233–50.

Sickle, John V. Van, and Benjamin A. Rogge. 1954. *Introduction to Economics*. New York: D. Van Nostrand.

Skousen, Mark. 1987. "Saving the Depression: A New Look at World War II." *Review of Austrian Economics* 2:211–26.

Skousen, Mark. 1988. *The Economics of a Pure Gold Standard*. 2d ed. Auburn, Ala.: Praxeology Press.

———. 1989. "Why the American Economy Is Not Depression-Proof." *Review of Austrian Economics* 3:75–94.

Smith, Adam. [1776] 1976. *An Inquiry into the Nature and Causes of the Wealth of Nations*. Chicago: University of Chicago Press.

Smith, Barry. 1986. "Austrian Economics from Menger to Hayek." In *Austrian Economics*, edited by Wolfgang Grassl and Barry Smith. London: Croom Helm.

Smithies, Arthur. 1935. "The Austrian Theory of Capital." *Quarterly Journal of Economics* (November):117–50.

Sohn, Ira, ed. 1986. *Readings in Input-Output Analysis*. New York: Oxford University Press.

Solow, Robert M. 1965. *Capital Theory and the Rate of Return*. Chicago: Rand McNally.

———. 1974. Review of J. Hicks's *Capital and Time*. *Economic Journal* 84:189–92.

———. 1988. "Growth Theory and After." *American Economic Review* 78, no. 3 (June):307–17.

Spiethoff, Arthur. 1953. *Business Cycles*. New York: Macmillan.

Sraffa, Piero. 1932a. "Dr. Hayek on Money and Capital." *Economic Journal* 42 (March):42–53.

———. 1932b. "A Rejoinder." *Economic Journal* 42 (June):249–51.

———. 1960. *The Production of Commodities by Means of Commodities*. Cambridge: Cambridge University Press.

Stackelberg, Heinrich von. [1948] 1952. *The Theory of the Market Economy*. New York: Oxford University Press.

Stern, Louis W., and Adel I. El-Ansary. 1982. *Marketing Channels*. 2d ed. Englewood Cliffs, N.J.: Prentice-Hall.

Stigler, George J. 1941. *Production and Distribution Theories.* New York: Macmillan.

Stigler, George J., and James K. Kindahl. 1970. *The Behavior of Industrial Prices.* New York: Natonal Bureau of Economic Research.

Strachey, John. 1935. *The Nature of Capitalist Crisis.* New York: Covici-Friede.

Streissler, Erich. 1969. "Hayek on Growth: A Reconsideration of His Early Theoretical Work." In *Roads to Freedom: Essays in Honour of Friedrich A. von Hayek,* edited by E. Streissler. London: Routledge and Kegan Paul.

———. 1973. "To What Extent Was the Austrian School Marginalist?" In *The Marginal Revolution in Economics,* edited by R. D. Collison Black, et al. Durham, N.C.: Duke University Press.

———. 1977. "What Kind of Microeconomic Foundations of Macroeconomics Are Necessary?" In *The Microeconomic Foundations of Macroeconomics,* edited by G. C. Harcourt. New York: Stockton Press.

Strigl, Richard von. 1934. *Kapital and Produktion.* Vienna: Julius Springer.

———. 1988. "Capital and Production." Translated by Margaret Rudelich Hoppe and Hans-Hermann Hoppe. Manuscript.

Taussig, Frank W. 1896. *Wages and Capital.* New York: Macmillan. Reprint. New York: Augustus M. Kelley, 1968.

———. 1908. "Capital, Interest, and Dimishing Returns." *Quarterly Journal of Economics* 22 (May):333–63.

———. 1933. *Principles of Economics.* 3d rev. ed. New York: Macmillan.

Taylor, Fred M. 1921. *Principles of Economics.* 9th ed. New York: Ronald Press.

Thalenhorst, J., and A. Wenig. 1984. "F. A. Hayek's 'Prices and Production,' Re-Analyzed." *Jahrbücher für Nationalökonomie und Statistik* 199(3):213–36.

Tinbergen, J. 1935. "Annual Survey: Suggestions on Quantitative Business Cycle Theory." *Econometrica* 3:241–308.

Tintner, G. 1974. "Linear Economics and the Böhm-Bawerk Period of Production." *Quarterly Journal of Economics* 88:127–32.

Townshend, Hugh. 1940. Review of Hayek's *Profits, Interest and Investment. Economic Journal* (March):99–103.

Tout, Herbert, and Alvin H. Hansen. 1933. "Annual Survey of Business Cycle Theory: Investment and Saving." *Econometrica* 1:119–47.

Tullock, Gordon. 1987. "Why the Austrians Are Wrong About Depressions." *Review of Austrian Economics* 2:73–78.

———. 1989. "Reply to Comment by Joseph T. Salerno." *Review of Austrian Economics* 3:147–50.

Turgot, A. R. J. [1766] 1973. *Turgot on Progress, Sociology and Economics.* Edited and translated by Ronald L. Meek. Cambridge: Cambridge University Press.

———. [1766] 1976. "Reflections on the Formation and Distribution of Wealth." In *The Economics of A. R. J. Turgot,* edited by P. D. Groenewegen. The Hague: Martinus Nijhoff.

Uhr, Carl G. 1960. *Economic Doctrines of Knut Wicksell.* Berkeley: University of California Press.

———. 1966. *Economics in Brief.* New York: Random House.

———. 1985. "Wicksell and the Austrians." *Research in the History of Economic Thought and Methodology* 3:199–224.

Usher, Dan, ed. 1980. *The Measurement of Capital.* Chicago: University of Chicago Press and National Bureau of Economic Research.

Valentine, Lloyd M. 1987. *Business Cycles and Forecasting.* 7th ed. Cincinnati: South-Western Publishing.

Valentine, Lloyd M., and Carl A. Dauten. 1983. *Business Cycles and Forecasting.* 6th ed. Cincinnati: South-Western Publishing.

Valiente, Wilfredo Santiago. 1980. "Is Frank Knight the Victor in the Controversy Between the Two Cambridges?" *History of Political Economy* 12(1):41–64.

Wainhouse, Charles E. 1984a. "Hayek's Theory of the Trade Cycle: The Evidence from the Time Series." Ph.D. diss., New York University.

———. 1984b. "Empirical Evidence for Hayek's Theory of Economic Fluctuations." In *Money in Crisis,* edited by Barry N. Siegel. San Francisco: Pacific Institute for Public Policy Research.

Waugh, Albert E. 1947. *Principles of Economics.* New York: McGraw-Hill.

Weintraub, Sidney, ed. 1977. *Modern Economic Thought.* Oxford: Basil Blackwell.

Weizsacker, C. C. von. 1971. *Steady State Capital Theory.* Berlin: Springer-Verlag.

Whitehead, Geoffrey. 1986. *Economics Made Simple.* 13th ed. London: Heinemann.

Wicksell, Knut. 1934. *Lectures on Political Economy. 2* vols. Translated by E. Classen. London: Macmillan.

———. [1898] 1936. *Interest and Prices.* Translated by R. F. Kahn. London: Macmillan. Reprint. New York: Augustus M. Kelley, 1965.

———. 1958. *Selected Papers on Economic Theory,* edited by E. Lindahl. London: Allen and Unwin. Reprint. New York: Augustus M. Kelley, 1969.

Wien-Claudi, Franz. 1936. *Austrian Theories of Capital, Interest, and the Trade Cycle.* London: Stanley Nott.

Wieser, Friedrich von. 1927. *Social Economics.* Translated by A. Ford Hinrichs. Reprint. New York: Augustus M. Kelley, 1967.

Wiles, Peter, and Guy Routh, eds. 1984. *Economics in Disarray.* Oxford: Basil Blackwell.

Williamson, Oliver E. 1985. *The Economic Institutions of Capitalism.* New York: Free Press.

Willis, H. Parker, and John M. Chapman. 1935. *The Economics of Inflation.* New York: Columbia University Press.

Wiseman, J. 1985. "Lionel Robbins, the Austrian School and the LSE Tradition." *Research in the History of Economic Thought and Methodology* 3:147–59.

Wright, David McCord. 1947. *The Economics of Disturbance.* New York: Macmillan.

———. 1958. "What *Is* the Economic System?" *Quarterly Journal of Economics.* 72:198–210.

Yeager, Leland B. 1973. "The Keynesian Diversion." *Western Economic Journal* 11:150–63.

———. 1976. "Toward Understanding Some Paradoxes in Capital Theory," *Economic Inquiry* 14:313–46.

———. 1979. "Capital Paradoxes and the Concept of Waiting." In *Time, Uncertainty and Disequilibrium,* edited by Mario J. Rizzo. Lexington, Mass.: Lexington Books.

———. 1986. "The Significance of Monetary Disequilibrium." *Cato Journal* (Fall):369–99.

INDEX

Abbott, Lawrence, 94
Abramovitz, Moses, 166, 171n91
Abrams, M. A., 54, 180, 287
Abstinence, 28
Acceleration principle, 26, 53, 82, 295
Achinstein, Asher, 89, 116n51
ADV. *See* Aggregate Demand Vector
Aftalion, Albert, 26
Against the Tide (Röpke), 271
Aggregate consumption, 78n169
Aggregate demand: aggregate supply and,
  xv, 3, 8, 195; in APS, 350; consumer
  spending for, xxvi; in inflationary
  recession, 195; Keynesianism and, 85,
  236, 324, 330, 350; Keynes's law and,
  xxv–xxvi; for money, xv; saving and,
  xxvii, xxxiii, 225–26, *227*; underconsumptionist fallacy and, 53
Aggregate Demand Vector (ADV), *xxxviii*,
  xxxviii–xxxix, 4, 195–98, 244; APS and,
  192–95, *193, 194, 195*; ASV and, 284–
  86, *285*, 351; Hayek's Rule of Monetary
  Acceleration and, 332
Aggregate Effective Demand, xv
Aggregate production, *xlv*, 152–53
Aggregate Production Structure (APS),
  193, 194, 195, 228, 279, *281*; aggregate
  demand in, 350; analysis of, *187*, 187–88;
  capital goods and, 350–51; circular flow
  diagram and, 189–90; consumer goods
  in, *183*; decentralization and, 200–202;
  dual nature of, 188–89; ERE and, 184–
  85; GNP and, 178–83, *179, 182, 183*,

350, 358; Hayek and, 183; inflation and,
  341–42, 351; limitations of, 202–3, *203*;
  macroeconomics and, 199–200, 362;
  measurement of, 358; microeconomics and, 199–200, 362; Mills and, 311;
  neoclassical macroeconomics and, *198*,
  198–99, *239*; quantity theory of money
  and, 310–11; recession/depression and,
  351–52; Rothbard and, 179, *179*; saving
  and, 224–31, *225, 226, 227*, 251n48, 351;
  Say's law and, 190–92, *191*, 352; snapshot
  economy and, 188; technology and, 219–
  20, *220*; time and, 177–206
Aggregate spending, xx
Aggregate supply, xv, 3, 8, 195
Aggregate Supply Vector (ASV), *xxxviii*,
  xxxviii–xxxix, 4, 244; ADV and, 284–
  86, *285*, 351; APS and, 192–95, *193*,
  194, 195; Hayek's Rule of Monetary
  Acceleration and, 332
Åkerman, Gustav, 26, 79
Alderfer, E. B., 136–37, 250n33
America's Great Depression (Rothbard), 100
Anderson, Benjamin M., 3, 80, 190–91, 236
Anderson, Montgomery D., 169n59
Applied economics, 6
APS. *See* Aggregate Production Structure
Arrow-Debreu model, 107
Assembly line, 14, 132, 216
Asset bubbles, xxxvi–xxxviii
ASV. *See* Aggregate Supply Vector
"At Last, a Better Economic Measure"
  (Skousen), xii

Brennan, Michael J., 94
Bretton Woods Agreement, xviii
Brown, Arthur, 70n7
Brown, H. G., 90, 209–10
Buchanan, James, 318n76
Bureau of Economic Analysis (BEA), xi, xii, xv–xvi, xxix
Burns, Arthur E., 91
Bush tax cuts, xxvi
Business cycle, *305*; asset bubbles and, xxxvi–xxxviii; of Austrian economics, 312; Austrian economics and, 55; boom phase, 276–88; consumer spending in, xxxi–xxxii, 294–95; credit crunch phase, 288–89; fiat money and, 271–319; full employment and, 85–89; GO and, xiii, xiv, xx; gold standard and, 266–67; Hayek and, 89; Hicks and, 113; inflation in, 273–76; interest rate and, 113, 273–76; inventories in, 166; investment in, xxxi–xxxii; Mills and, 280; Mises and, 34; monetarist disequilibrium model of, xxv; natural rate of interest and, 34; NBER and, 280; overinvestment theory of, 61; price and, 300; production and, 55; recovery phase, 303–5, *304*; Ricardo effect in, 115n22; Say's law and, 312–13; Sherman and, 85; short run versus long run, 305–6; time and, *296–99*; Wicksell and, 25; Yeager and, 295. *See also* Boom-bust cycle; Recession/depression
Business Cycles & Forecasting (Valentine), 87–88
Business-to-business (B2B), xvi, *92*; consumer spending and, *xiv*; GDP and, xiv; GO and, xii, xiv; quarterly changes, 2007-2014, *xv*
Business-to-consumer (B2C), xxii
Business-to-government (B2G), xxii
Business Without a Buyer (Foster and Catchings), 58
Bye, Raymond T., 90, 93–94, 117n71, 155

Cairnes, John E., 265
Cambridge Switching Theorem, 110–12, *111*
Capital, 2–3, 16; Austrian economics and, 106–10; Böhm-Bawerk and, 20–22, 29, 167n12; Boulding and, 80; circulating, 14, 21, 26, 133; Clark, J. B., and, 29, 67; Clark-Knight theory of, 3, 66–67, 69, 80, 104, 129, 241, 242; classical economics and, 32–35; deepening of, 229; employment and, 283, *283*; fixed, 14, 132–33, 166, 167n10, 227, 274; Haavelmo and, 167n13; Hayek and, 68–69; income and, 33; Knight and, 67, 241; Lachmann and, 242; Lindahl and, 63; Menger and, 103–6; Mises and, 250n15; as permanent fund, 67; productivity and, xxxvi; Quesnay and, 13; Ricardo and, 35n7; saving and, xxxiii; Shackle and, 132; socialism and, 173; Solow and, 104–5; as stored labor, 152; for technology, 250n33; time and, 132; Uhr and, 170n75; Wicksell and, 25, 228; widening of, 228–29; working, 132–33, 274, 307
Capital (Marx), 17, 36n14
Capital and Growth (Hicks), 113
Capital and Interest (Böhm-Bawerk), 220
Capital and Its Structure (Lachmann), 97, 127
Capital and Production (*Kapital und Produktion*) (Strigl), 55, 75n87
Capital and Time (Hicks), liii, 120n144
Capital goods, 2; aggregate production of, 152–53; APS and, 177, 350–51; boom, 48, 277–91, 324; Clark, J. B., and, 29; in classical economics, 16; consumer goods and, 134, 155–56; demand for, 152, 289; as durable goods, 150–54; entrepreneur and, 249; in Germany, *95*; GNP and, 178; government spending and, 325; as higher-order goods, 153–54; income and, 282–84; inflation and, 277, *277*; as intermediate goods, 35, 150; labor and, 133–34, 282–83;

and, xvi; microeconomics and, 284; production from, xxv; productivity and, xxxvi; quarterly changes, 2007-2014, *xv*; saving and, xxxiii–xxxv, 238, 284; in U.S., xxv, xxvii; "use" economy and, xx, *xxi*

Consumption, 328, 330, 355; aggregate, 78n169; of commodities, 16; by entrepreneurs, 270n23; period of, 357; periods of production and, 154, *155*; production and, 166n5, 286; savings and, 326; underconsumptionists, 53, 57–61, 240; wage rates and, 44

Consumption-oriented inflation, 340–41, 348n30

Cost push inflation, 7

Cox, Reavis, 165, 204n14

CPI. *See* Consumer price index

Credit expansion, Wicksell and, 25

Credit markets, xli, 272, *274*, 274–75

Credit-Power and Democracy (Douglas), 58

Crises and Cycles (Röpke), 55

Les crises periodiques de surproduction (Aftalion), 26

The Crisis in Economic Theory (Bell and Kristol), 1

Crusoe model, 95

Dauten, Carl A., 288

Decentralization, 2, 200–202

Deflation, 238, 326; gold standard and, 262; profit and, 331; in recession/depression, 52–53, *301*, 302, 342

Demand: Aggregate Effective Demand, xv; for capital goods, 152, 289; for commodities, 38n59; for consumer goods, 26, 52; final demand effect, 244; final effective demand, 324; interest rate and, 195–98; Say's law and, 190; supply from, xxv, xxxi–xxxiii. *See also* Aggregate demand; Aggregate Demand Vector

Demand-credit inflation, 337–39, *338*

Demand-side economics, xvi, xxxi

Department of Commerce, xxix

Depression. *See* Great Depression; Recession/depression

Dewey, Donald, 107–8

The Distribution of Wealth (Clark, J. B.), 27, 29

Division of labor, 14, 157–58

Dolan, E. G., 181

Double counting, xix, xxvii, 181–82

Douglas, Clifford High, 57, 58–59

Dow, Sheila C., 85, 122n193

Dow Jones Industrial Average, xxii

Drucker, Peter F., xxv, 130, 230–31, 253n94, 349, 362

Durable goods, 15, 170n69, 203n1; capital goods as, 150–54; consumer goods as, 154–57, *156*; GNP and, 178; interest rate and, 26; period of consumption for, 357; production of, 150–57

Durbin, E. F. M., 57–61, 76n116, 249; production-consumption diagram of, *60*; recession/depression and, 325–26; underconsumptionists and, 240

Eastern Economic Journal, xii

Easy-money policy, xxxvii, xxxix

Econometrica, liii, 53, 58

Economic Analysis (Boulding), 80

The Economic Axioms (Piquet), 101–2

Economic Democracy (Douglas), 58

Economic growth: GO and, xiii; round-aboutness and, 32, 359; saving and, 207–54, *235*; technology and, 207–54

Economic Logic (Skousen), xi, xix, xx, xlvii

The Economic Process (Bye and Hewett), 93, 117n71

Economics (Gemmill and Blodgett), 91

Economics as a Coordination Problem (O'Driscoll), 101

Economics Made Simple (Whitehead), 96, 118n87

The Economics of Knut Wicksell (Uhr), liv

The Economics of Time and Ignorance
(O'Driscoll, Rizzo, and Garrison), 103
Economics on Trial (Skousen), xi, xlvi
Economics textbooks, 89–96
Economics Today, xii
Economic Theory in Retrospect (Blaug), 84,
122n192
Economist, xxvi, xl
Edison, Thomas, 230
Eichengreen, Barry, xl, xlixn5
Eisner, Robert, xxvii
Ekins, Paul, xxxiv, xlvi
Elementary Economics (Gordon), 94
Elements of Pure Economics (Walras), 24
Elliott-Jones, M. F., 204n10
Ellis, Howard S., 26, 41
Employment: APS and, 180; capital and,
283, *283*; consumer goods and, 203n6;
full, 85–89, 238, 337; inflation and, xxx-
viii; producer goods and, 203n6; saving
and, xxvii, 235. *See also* Unemployment
Engels, Friedrich, 17, 36n16
Entrepreneurs: bank credit for, 288; cap-
ital goods and, 249; consumption by,
270n23; investment and, 347n26; production and, 128–29; profit and, 308
Epstein, Gene, xii
ERE. *See* Evenly rotating economy
An Essay on Capital (Kirzner), 99
Estey, James A., 86–87, 292; business cycle
and, 280; deflation and, 326; on price,
300; purchasing power doctrine and,
328; quantity theory of money and, 310;
on recession/depression recovery, 304;
saving and, 248
Evans, Gary R., 84–85
Evenly rotating economy (ERE), xxxix; APS
and, 184–85; interest rate and, 185–87,
204n23

Faber, Malte, 108, 150–51
Fairchild, Fred R., 94

Fallacy of aggregation, 241
Fallacy of composition, 237
Fetter, Frank A., *33*, 33–34, 221, 229
Fiat money, 257, 355; business cycle and,
271–319; Hayek's Rule of Monetary
Acceleration and, 332; hidden costs of,
313–14; inflation and, 266, 331; interest
rate and, 273–76; Keynesianism and,
326; Say's law and, 312–13
Final demand effect, 244
Final effective demand, 324
Final goods and services: APS and, 188;
GDP and, xii, xiii, xxvii; GNP and, 178;
matrix of, 135–36, *136*; production and,
130–31; Taussig and, 167n6; time pref-
erence for, 286; "use" economy for, xx
Fisher, Irving, 33, 39n97, 306, 314n2
Fixed capital, 14, 132–33, 166, 167n10, 227,
274
Flynn, Sean, xvii
Forbes, xii
Forbes, Steve, xii
Ford, Henry, 216, 220, 328–29
Ford, James W., 92
Form utility, 168n16
Foster, William T., 57–58, 190, 253n86
Four-stage general model of economy,
xxviii, *xxviii*
France, xxvi, xxx
Frank, Lawrence, 292
Friedman, Milton, xxxix, xli–xlii; on
Eichengreen, xlixn5; gold standard and,
257; inflation and, 311; Keynesianism
and, 8n9, 253n94; malinvestments and,
xliv; monetarists and, 342; money sup-
ply and, 330–31; saving and, 233
Frisch, Ragnar, 169n54
Full employment, 85–89, 238, 337
Fundists, 123n203

Gaitskell, H. T. N., 58–59
Galbraith, J. K., 216

Gross National Product (GNP) *(Continued)* 294; national income and, 183; production and, 181; Rothbard and, 180–81; value added approach to, 178, 181, *182*

Gross Output (GO), xi–xlviii; as aggregate demand for money, xv; for aggregate spending, xx; B2B and, xii, xiv; BEA on, xv–xvi; benefits of, xiii–xv; in business cycle, xiii, xiv, xx; consumer spending in, xxix; controversies with, xix–xx; economic growth theory and, xiii; GDP and, xi–xii, xiii, xvii, xxix, xlixn3; I-O and, xviii; "make" economy in, xvii; total spending and, xxix–xxx. *See also* Gross National Output

"Gross Output by Industry" (BEA), xi

Gross value, of output, 163, *164*

Grundsätze der Volkswirtschaftslehre (*Principles of Economics*) (Menger), 17, 36n17, 37n24, 109

Haavelmo, Trygve, 104, 167n13, 210

Haberler, Gottfried, 52–53

Hahn, F. H., 3

Hahn, L. Albert, liv, 2; APS and, 190; on bank credit, 80–81; common sense economics of, 80–82, 127; fixed capital and, 227; Keynes and, 346n7; purchasing power doctrine and, 328; saving and, 231, 234; on saving and inflation, 316n29; Say's law and, 205n28

Hailstones, Thomas J., 94

Hamberg, D., 86, 292

Hanke, Steve, xii, xvi

Hansen, Alvin H., 53–54, 86, 113, 236, 292, 326

Harcourt, G. C., lv

Hart, Albert Gailord, 92

Hausman, Daniel M., 107, 121n162

Hawtrey, R. G., 52, 68, 73n46; consumer spending and, 294–95; inflation and, 286; money supply and, 330–31;

production and, 170n68; quantity theory of money and, 310

Hayek, Friedrich von, xxxvi, xxxix, liii, liv, 26, 70n5, 335, 362; APS and, 183, 188; Bellante on, 150, 314n10; business cycle and, 89; consumer goods and, 150, 225, 226; deflation and, 342; Durbin and, 57–61; Evans and, 84–85; Garrison on, 150, 314n10; gold standard and, 267; on Hawtrey, 294–95; Hicks and, 113; inflation and, 341–42; Kaldor and, 67–69; Keynes and, xvi–xvii, lvi–lvii, 41, 70n7, 331–31; macroeconomics and, 41–78; money supply and, xlii, xliii, 250n42, 273; no-money-growth policy of, 53; O'Driscoll and, 101; on profit, 44; on recession/depression, 291, 303; Ricardo effect and, 115n22, 288–89; saving and, 86, 232, 243; Seligman and, 83–84; Shackle and, 148; Sherman and, 84–85; socialism and, 172; Swedish economics and, 62–64; Thalenhorst and Wenig and, 109–10; theoretical framework of, 42–45; trade cycle theory of, 53, 75n83; triangles of, lv, 43, *43*, 47, 73, 83–84, 99, 101, 150; underconsumptionists and, 57–61; unemployment and, 278

Hayek's Rule of Monetary Acceleration, 332

Hewett, William H., 93–94, 117n71, 155

Hicks, John R., liii, lvii, 70n7, 79, 91, 92, 108, 120n144, 355; Dow and, 122n193; on fundists and materialists, 123n203; on Hayek, 42; roundaboutness and, 113–14; saving and, 231

Higher-order goods, 37n20; APS and, 228; capital goods as, 153–54; consumer spending on, xxxiii; easy-money policy and, xxxvii; inflation and, xli; interest rate and, 84, 198, 288; Keynesianism and, 241; land as, 157; malinvestment in, 332; Menger and, 173; profit from, 287; Schumpeter on, 170n66;

unemployment and, 293; value of, 205n34; wage rates and, 44
Hill, Martin, 167n12
History of Economic Analysis (Schumpeter), 13, 70n2
Hoarding, 245–48
Hobson, J. A., 57, 234
Holzman, Matilda, 161–63
Homogeneous capital stock, 107
Homogeneous goods, 18
Homogeneous jelly, 3
Hoover, Herbert, 328, 329
Hoppe, Hans-Hermann, 75n87
Hoppe, Margaret Rudelich, 75n87
Horizontal division of labor, 157
Horizontal economy, 127
Hughes, Jonathan, 329
Human Action (Mises), 34, 35
Humphrey, Thomas M., 39n97
Hutt, W. H., 248, 355

Imputation of value, 18–19, 36n8
Income: capital and, 33; capital goods and, 282–84; Dewey and, 107; interest rate and, 276; national, 78n169, 183, 294; saving and, xxvii, 240. *See also* Wage rates
Index of leading Economic Indicators, xxx, 295
Inflation, xxxviii, 53, 286, 287–88, 315n23, 346n9; Abrams and, 287; APS and, 341–42, 351; Austrian economics and, xl–xli, 71n17, 347n28; in boom-bust cycle, xl; boom-bust cycle and, 276–77, 303–4; in business cycle, 273–76; capital goods and, 277, *277*; cash balance approach to, 272; central banks and, 308; consumer spending and, xxxviii, 272; consumption-oriented, 340–41, 348n30; cost push, 7; demand-credit, 337–39, *338*; fiat money and, 266, 331; full employment and, 337; gold standard

and, 261, 263, *264*, *265*; Hayek's Rule of Monetary Acceleration and, 332; higher-order goods and, xli; interest rate and, 122n191, 273–76; malinvestment and, xli, 359; monetarists and, 309, *309*, 311, 342–43; monetary policy for, 334–37; money supply and, 271–76, 308, 331; natural rate of interest hypothesis and, xxxvii; natural rate of unemployment and, xli; in 1970s, 280; output and, 287; production and, 279–80, *280*; rational expectation theory and, 306–8; realistic view of, 359; in recession/depression, 100, 300–303, *301*, *302*, *303*; relative costs and, xliv; relative price and, xliv; Ricardo effect and, 316n41; runaway, 339–40, *340*; saving and, 286–87, 316n29; supply-credit, 337–39, *338*; transmission mechanism for, xl–xliv; unemployment and, 277–78
Inflationary recession, 100–103
Input-output tables (I-O), xviii, xxix, xlvii, 4–5, 149, 358
Interest and interest rate: ADV and, 195–98; ASV and, xxxviii, 244; bank credit and, 26; business cycle and, 113, 273–76; of central banks, xliv; Clark, J. B., and, 29; demand and, 195–98; durable goods and, 26; ERE and, 185–87, 204n23; fiat money and, 273–76; Hausman and, 121n162; higher-order goods and, 84, 288; income and, 276; inflation and, 122n191, 273–76; investment and, 315n11; Keynes and, 245; Keynesianism and, 245; long-term, 288; Mises and, 314n1; period of production and, 276; Piquet and, 205n40; price and, 25, 38n59; production and, xxxii–xxxiii; productivity theory of, 21, 29; relative price and, 318n71; roundaboutness and, 106, 111; saving and, 223–24, *224*, 234–35, 275; Seligman and, 84; short-term,

inflation and, 271–76, 308, 331; Keynesianism and, 3; price and, 359; quantity theory of money and, 308–9

Moore, Geoffrey, 56

Morishima, Michio, lv, lvii, 2, 5–6, 106, 134, 168n18, 355

Moss, Laurence S., 288

Moulton, Harold, 169n46, 231

Mr. Keynes and the 'Classics' (Hicks), liii

Multiplier principle, 82, 326

Myrdal, Gunnar, 63, 227, 278

National Bureau of Economic Research (NBER), xliii, 55–57, 280, 357

National income, 78n169, 183, 294

Natural rate of interest, *xxxvii*, xxxvii–xxxix; business cycle and, 34; capital goods and, 63; ERE and, 185

Natural rate of unemployment, xli

Natural saving rate, xxxvi

The Nature and Necessity of Interest (Cassel), 25

The Nature of Capital and Income (Fisher), 33

NBER. *See* National Bureau of Economic Research

Neal, Alfred C., 91

Necessities, production of, 15

Nelson, R. W., 55

Neoclassical macroeconomics: APS and, *198*, 198–99, *239*; investment and, 349; I-O and, 5; methodology of, *356*; production function of, 2; recession/depression and, 301; saving and, 241, *242*

Net exports, xiii, xxv

Neumann, J. von, 121n165

A New Architecture for the U.S. National Accounts (Landefeld, Jorgenson, and Nordhaus), xi, xvii

New Classical economists, xliii

Newmarch, William, 266

New York Times, xxv

Niehans, Jurg, 262

No-money-growth policy, 53

Nondurable goods, 15

Nordhaus, William D., xi, xvii

North, Gary, lv, 268n2

O'Driscoll, Gerald P., Jr., 42, 101, 103, 197

Orders of industry, 20

Orosel, Gerhard O., 108–9

Output: APS and, 177; gross value of, 163, *164*; inflation and, 287; price and, 7; of production, 161–63, *164*; quantity theory of money and, 308–9, 310; saving and, xxvi, 240; Shackle and, 287; volatility in, 280–82. *See also* Gross National Output; Gross Output

Overinvestment theory, 61

Paradox of thrift, liii, 234–42, 237–38, *238*, 351

Pareto, 113

Pascal, Bridel, 61

Patinkin, Don, 9n10

Period of consumption, 357

Period of production, 20, 63, 68; average, 21–23, 38n48, 114; of Böhm-Bawerk, 99; consumption and, 154, *155*; interest rate and, 276; length of, 143–46, *144*; measurement of, 164–65; Shackle and, 230

Permanent fund, 3, 28, 29, 67, 99

Peterson, Shorey, 92–93, 165–66, 222

Phillips, C. A., 55

Pick, H. J., 163

Pigou, Arthur C., 342

Piquet, Howard S., 101–3, *102*, 149; APS and, 190; durable goods and, 170n69; interest rate and, 205n40; marginal productivity theory of distribution and, 204n27; production and, 167n14

Planning for Freedom (Mises), 255

Point input, point output model, xlvii

Polak, N. J., 168n19

Portfolio management, xliv

The Positive Theory of Capital (Böhm-Bawerk), 21, 24, 27

The Power of Economic Thinking (Skousen), xlvi–xlvii

Price: ADV and, 4; ASV and, 4; business cycle and, 300; inflexibility of, 300; interest rate and, 25, 38n59; Mills and, 55–57; monetarists and, 318n76; money supply and, 359; output and, 7; production and, 9n20; quantity theory of money and, 308–9; of raw materials, 56–57, 279, 300, 360; socialism and, 173; volatility in, 280–82; wage rates and, 97; Wicksell and, 25. *See also* Relative price

Prices and Production (Hayek), 41–70, 70n5, 84, 101, 109, 150

Prices in Recession and Recovery (Mills), liv, 56–57

Principal orders of industry, 158

Principles of Economics (*Grundsätze der Volkswirtschaftslehre*) (Menger), 17, 36n17, 37n24, 109

Principles of Economics (Jevons), 20

Principles of Economics (Marshall), 89–90

Principles of Economics (Taussig), 32–33

The Principles of Economics (Fetter), 33–34

The Problem of Credit Policy (Durbin), 60–61

Producer goods: in APS, *183*; Bye and Hewett and, 155; from capital goods, 133; complementary nature of, 138–42; employment and, 203n6; from raw materials, 133; Wicksell and, 24–25, *25*

Production: assembly line and, 132; Böhm-Bawerk and, 20–22, 208–15; building simple model of, *137*, 137–38; business cycle and, 55; businessman's approach to, 128–29; central planning for, 172–74; circularity of, 147–50; Clark, J. B., and, *27*, 27–28; classical economics and,

16–17; of commodities, 147; complexity of, 159–61, *161*, *162*; from consumer spending, xxv; consumption and, 166n5, 286; of durable goods, 150–57; entrepreneur and, 128–29; final goods and services and, 130–31; gestation period for, 94; GNP and, 181; GO and, xv; gold standard and, 263–66; Hahn, L., and, 80–82, *81*; Hansen and, 292; Hawtrey and, 170n68; inflation and, 279–80, *280*; interest rate and, xxxii–xxxiii; inventories and, 165–66, 171n91; Jevons and, 19–20; Johansson and, 63–64; joint, 138–42, *141*, *143*; labor for, 157–58; land for, 157–58; Longfield and, 15; of luxuries, 15; macroeconomics and, 5–6; "make" economy and, xx, *xxi*; marketing channels and, *131*, 131–32; Marx and, 16–17; Menger and, 18; Morishima and, 106, 168n18; of necessities, 15; one-stage of, 35n6; output of, 161–63, *164*; Piquet and, 167n14; practical examples of, 136–37; price and, 9n20; process and order of, 133–35, *134*, *135*; Rae and, 15; in recession/depression, 53; services for, 158–59, *159*; single-stage, 240; Smith and, 14; socialism and, 172–74; stages of, 292, *293*; structure of, 127–75; synchronization of, 27, 31–32, 135–36, *136*; Taussig and, *31*, 31–32; technical structure of, 9n10; temporal structure of, 9n10; time and, 18, 35, *62*, 62–63, 79–123, 129–30; uncertainty in, 18; wage rates and, 329; Wicksell and, 24–25, *25*; Wieser and, 20–22. *See also* Aggregate production; Aggregate Production Structure; Period of production

Production Economics (Black), 209

Production of Commodities by Means of Commodities (Sraffa), 109

Productive capital, 16

Productive labor, 14, 35n5

Productivity: Böhm-Bawerk and, 231; capital and, xxxvi; consumer spending and, xxxvi; microeconomics and, 206n47; optimization of, 362–63; roundaboutness and, 94; wage rates and, xxxvi

Productivity theory of interest, 21, 29

Profit: in capital goods, 25; deflation and, 331; entrepreneurs and, 308; Hayek on, 44; from higher-order goods, 287; from lower-order goods, 287; Marx and, 16; saving and, xxxiii; wage rates and, 48, 55, 121n162, 329

Profits, Interest and Investment (Hayek), 67

Prosperity and Depression (Hawtrey), 52

Public Choice school, 318n76

Purchasing Power and Trade Depression (Durbin), 58

Purchasing power doctrine, 327–29

The Pure Theory of Capital (Hayek), 68–69

Puritan ethic, 45

Quantity theory of money, 3–4, 308–12, *309*

Quesnay, François, 13

Rae, John, 15, 36n11, 215

Ramey, A., 363n6

Rational expectation theory, 306–8

Raw materials, 117n71; APS and, 188; in inventories, 165–66; Mills and, 360; price of, 56–57, 279, 300, 360; producer goods from, 133

Read, Leonard, 160

Real cash balance effect, xli, 3–4

Real Kapital and Kapitalzins (Åkerman), 26

Recession/depression: APS and, 351–52; capital goods and, 289–91, 347n13; consumer spending in, xxvi, xxxii; CPI and, 351–52; deflation in, 52–53, *301*, 302, 342; Durbin and, 325–26; GDP in, xiv; Hayek on, 291, 303; inflationary

recession, 100–103; inflation in, 100, 300–303, *301*, *302*, *303*; Keynesianism in, 323–25, *324*, 346n2; neoclassical macroeconomics and, 301; production in, 53; quantity theory of money and, 310; recovery from, 303–5, *304*; saving in, 58, 238; tax cuts in, 333–34, *334*; unemployment in, 292–93. *See also* Great Depression

Recovery phase, of business cycle, 303–5, *304*

"Reflections on the Formation and Distribution of Wealth" (Turgot), 13–14

Relative costs, xliv

Relative price, xxii; aggregates and, 4; APS and, 279; inflation and, xliv; interest rate and, 318n71; Mills and, 56; quantity theory of money and, 310; saving and, 316n33

Ricardo, David, 15, 16, 35n7, 36n17

Ricardo effect, 67–68, 84, 115n22, 288–89, 316n41

Ricardo-Mill theory of distribution, 22

Rizzo, Mario J., 103

Robbins, Lionel, 41, 51, 55, 70n5, 74n59, 275, 276, 287, 288; inflation and, 315n23; purchasing power doctrine and, 328

Robertson, Dennis H., 61

Robinson, Joan, 51, 74n62, 110

Rogge, Benjamin a., liv, 95–96, 291

Rolph, Earl, 144–45, 147–48

Röpke, Wilhelm, 55, 157, 180, 225–26, 271

Rosenbloom, Bert, 131, *131*

Rothbard, Murray N., liv, 99–100; APS and, 179, *179*, 190; Böhm-Bawerk and, 210; durable goods and, 151, 203n1; ERE and, 185; GNP and, 180–81; gold standard and, 267, 270n19; money and, 205n39; production and, 133–34; on recession/depression recovery, 304; saving and, 222, 231–32, 243, 277; on services, 158–59

Solow, permanent fund and, 3
Solow, Robert M., xlvii, 3, 104–5, 120n144
Spiethoff, Arthur, 87–88
Sraffa, Piero, 109, 110, 147
Stackelberg, Heinrich von, 94–95
Stigler, George J., 56, 75n93, 83, 144
Stored labor, 152
Streissler, Erich, 23, 37n21, 37n24, 38n50, 71n15
Strigl, Richard, 55, 75n87
The Structure of Postwar Prices (Mills), 57
A Study of Industrial Fluctuation (Robertson), 61
Supply: aggregate, xv, 3, 8, 195; from demand, xxv, xxxi–xxxiii; interest rate and, 195–98; Say's law and, 190. *See also* Aggregate Supply Vector; Money supply
Supply-credit inflation, 337–39, *338*
Supply-side economics, xvi, xvi–xvii, xxv, xxxi–xxxiii
Suzuki, Yoshio, xxxix
Swedish economics, 24–26, 62–64
Synchronization: of Clark, J. B., 99, 136; of production, 27, 31–32, 135–36, *136*

*T*ableau Economique (Quesnay), 13
Taussig, Frank W., *31*, 31–32; APS and, 188–89; final goods and services and, 167n6; period of production and, 144; on production complexity, 159–60; snapshot economy and, 130; technology and, 209
Tax cuts, xxvi, 333–35, *334*
Taylor, Fred M., 90, 172
Taylor, John, xlvi
Technology: APS and, 219–20, *220*; for automobile, 215–17; capital for, 250n33; economic growth and, 207–54; impact of, 208–10; interest rate and, 220–21; saving and, 207–54; theoretical representation of, 211–14, *212, 213, 214*
Ten Great Economists (Schumpeter), 34

Textbooks, 89–96
Thalenhorst, J., 109–10
The Theory of Economic Development (Schumpeter), 34
The Theory of Idle Resources (Hutt), 248
Theory of Money and Credit (Mises), liv, 34
The Theory of Political Economy (Jevons), 19
The Theory of the Market Economy (Stackelberg), 94–95
Theory of Wages (Hicks), 113
Time: APS and, 177–206; business cycle and, *296–99*; capital and, 132; money and, 205n46; production and, 18, 35, *62*, 62–63, 79–123, 129–30. *See also* Period of production
Time preference: for final goods and services, 286; interest and, 21, 33; interest rate and, 220–21; saving and, *225*
Tinbergen, J., 74n78
"Total Output," in United Kingdom, xi
Total spending, xxix–xxx
Tout, Herbert, 53–54, 326
Toward the Next Economics (Drucker), 349
Trade cycle theory, 53, 75n83, 116n51
Trade Depression and the Way Out (Hawtrey), 295
Treatise on Money (Keynes), 234
Triangles, of Hayek, lv, 43, *43*, 47, 73, 83–84, 99, 101, 150
Triangulation, I-O and, 5
Triple counting, xix, xxvii
Tucker, Rufus S., 259
Tugan-Baranovsky, Michel, 87–88
Turgot, A. R. J., 13–14

*U*hr, Carl G., liv, 9n20, 151–52, 170n75; Austrian economics and, 79; technology and, 214–15; on Wicksell, 25
Underconsumptionists, 53, 57–61, 240
Unemployment, xxii, 277–78, 292–93; natural rate of, xli
Unfinished goods, 133, 135–36, *136*

United Kingdom, xi, xxvii, xxx

United States (U.S.): Bush tax cuts in, xxvi; consumer spending in, xxv, xxvii; consumption-oriented inflation in, 340–41; gold standard in, 282; Index of Leading Economic Indicators for, xxx; price and output volatility in, 280–82

Universal four-stage model of economy, *xviii*, xviii–xix

Unproductive labor, 14

U.S. *See* United States

"Use" economy, xii, xx, *xxi*

Valentine, Lloyd M., 87–89, 288

Value: genealogy of, *33*, 33–34; gross, 163, *164*; of higher-order goods, 205n34; imputation of, 18–19, 36n8; labor theory of, 15

Value added approach, xlvi, *xlvi*, 178, 181, *182*

Value Added Tax (VAT), xxix, 7

Value and Capital (Hicks), 113–14

Van Sickle, John V., liv, 95–96, 291

VAT. *See* Value Added Tax

Vaughn, Karen I., 288

Veblen, Thorstein, 57

Vertical division of labor, 157

Vertical genealogy, 2

Vertical integration, 6

Wage rates: consumption and, 44; higher-order goods and, 44; investment and, 236; price and, 97; productivity and, xxxvi; profit and, 48, 55, 121n162; purchasing power doctrine and, 328–29; saving and, 58

Wages and Capital (Taussig), 32

Wainhouse, Charles, 103

Wall Street Journal, xii, xiii

Walras, Léon, 2, 17, 24, 113; Clark-Walrasian "horizontal" method, 1, 5, 14, 25

Warburton, Clark, 314n2

Wasshausen, David, xv–xvi

Watson, D. S., 91

Waugh, Albert E., 91

The Wealth of Nations (Smith, A.), xlviin1, 14–16

Wenig, A., 109–10

White, Horace, 208–9

Whitehead, Geoffrey, 96, 118n87, 158–59

Wicksell, Knut, 24–26, 36n17, 38n59; Cambridge Switching Theorem and, 110; capital and, 228; durable goods and, 151–52; natural rate of interest and, 185; production and, 24–25, *25*

Wien-Claudi, Franz, 54–55, 231

Wieser, Friedrich von, 20–22, 41, 208

Williamson, Oliver E., 6

Willis, H. Parker, 330

Working capital, 132–33, 274, 307

World War II, 68, 87, 91, 272

Wright, David McCord, 169n45

Yamey, B. S., 250n34, 253n97

Yeager, Leland, 112, 122n189, 295

Yield curve, xxii, 185–87, *186*, 288, 289, *289*

ABOUT THE AUTHOR

MARK SKOUSEN is Presidential Fellow at Chapman University in California. He earned his PhD in Economics at George Washington University (1977). In 2004–5, he taught Economics and Finance at Columbia Business School and Columbia University. He has also taught Economics, Finance, and Business at Barnard, Mercy and Rollins Colleges, and Chapman University. Since 1980, Skousen has been editor in chief of *Forecasts & Strategies*, a popular award-winning investment newsletter. He has been an economic analyst for the Central Intelligence Agency, a columnist to *Forbes* magazine, chairman of Investment U, and past president of the Foundation for Economic Education (FEE) in New York. He has written for the *Wall Street Journal, Forbes,* the *Christian Science Monitor,* and the *Journal of Economic Perspectives.* His economics works include *The Making of Modern Economics, Economic Logic,* and *EconoPower.* His investment books include *Investing in One Lesson,* and *The Maxims of Wall Street.* In 2006, he compiled and edited *The Compleated Autobiography by Benjamin Franklin.* His latest book is *A Viennese Waltz Down Wall Street: Austrian Economics for Investors.* In honor of his work in Economics, Finance and Management, Grantham University renamed its business school the Mark Skousen School of Business.

Printed and bound by CPI Group (UK) Ltd, Croydon, CR0 4YY

16/04/2025

14658443-0004